KANT'S SYSTEM OF NATURE

C000093187

# Kant's System of Nature and Freedom

*Selected Essays*

PAUL GUYER

CLARENDON PRESS · OXFORD

# OXFORD
## UNIVERSITY PRESS

Great Clarendon Street, Oxford OX2 6DP

Oxford University Press is a department of the University of Oxford.
It furthers the University's objective of excellence in research, scholarship,
and education by publishing worldwide in

Oxford New York

Auckland Cape Town Dar es Salaam Hong Kong Karachi
Kuala Lumpur Madrid Melbourne Mexico City Nairobi
New Delhi Shanghai Taipei Toronto

With offices in

Argentina Austria Brazil Chile Czech Republic France Greece
Guatemala Hungary Italy Japan Poland Portugal Singapore
South Korea Switzerland Thailand Turkey Ukraine Vietnam

Oxford is a registered trade mark of Oxford University Press
in the UK and in certain other countries

Published in the United States
by Oxford University Press Inc., New York

© Paul Guyer 2005

The moral rights of the authors have been asserted
Database right Oxford University Press (maker)

First published 2005

All rights reserved. No part of this publication may be reproduced,
stored in a retrieval system, or transmitted, in any form or by any means,
without the prior permission in writing of Oxford University Press,
or as expressly permitted by law, or under terms agreed with the appropriate
reprographics rights organization. Enquiries concerning reproduction
outside the scope of the above should be sent to the Rights Department,
Oxford University Press, at the address above

You must not circulate this book in any other binding or cover
and you must impose the same condition on any acquirer

British Library Cataloguing in Publication Data

Data available

Library of Congress Cataloging in Publication Data

Data available

Typeset by Kolam Information Services Pvt. Ltd, Pondicherry, India
Printed in Great Britain
on acid-free paper by
Biddles Ltd, King's Lynn, Norfolk

ISBN 0-19-927346-4   9780199273461
ISBN 0-19-927347-2 (Pbk.)   9780199273478

1 3 5 7 9 10 8 6 4 2

# CONTENTS

# ABBREVIATIONS

| | |
|---|---|
| *APV* | *Anthropology from a Pragmatic Point of View* |
| Col. | *Moral Philosophy from the Lectures of Professor Kant, Winter Semester 1784–85*, ed. Georg Ludwig Collins |
| *CPJ* | *Critique of the Power of Judgment* |
| *CPracR* | *Critique of Practical Reason* |
| *CPuR* | *Critique of Pure Reason* |
| FI | First Introduction to the *Critique of Judgment* |
| Friedländer | Lectures on Anthropology from the Winter Semester 1775–6, according to the manuscript Friedländer |
| *G* | *Groundwork for the Metaphysics of Morals* |
| *MM*, DR | Metaphysics of Morals, '*Doctrine of Right*' |
| *MM*, DV | Metaphysics of Morals, '*Doctrine of Virtue*' |
| Mrong. | *Morality According to Professor Kant: Lectures on Baumgarten's Practical Philosophy*, 3 January 1785, ed. C. C. Mrongovius |
| *Notes* | *Notes on the Observations on the Feeling of the Beautiful and Sublime* |
| *OP* | *Opus postumum* |
| R | 'Reflections' from *Kant's Handschriftliche Nachlass* |
| *Rel.* | *Religion within the Boundaries of Mere Reason* |
| Rischmüller | *Notes on the Observations on the Feeling of the Beautiful and the Sublime*, ed. Marie Rischmüller (Kant Forschungen, vol. iii) |
| TP | 'On the Common Saying: That May Be Correct in Theory, but it is of No Use in Practice' |
| Vig. | *Notes on the Lectures of Mr Kant on the Metaphysics of Morals*, begun 14 October 1793, ed. Johann Friedrich Vigilantius |

# Introduction

Was Immanuel Kant a systematic philosopher? This is not an easy question to answer. Although he certainly borrowed many aspects of the outward organization of his critical philosophy from his great predecessor Christian Wolff, Kant was not a systematic philosopher by the standards of Wolff, who covered all of the topics of philosophy in detail first in nine German volumes and then in twenty-five Latin volumes, and never claimed that his own three *Critiques* constituted more than the preliminaries to a genuine system of philosophy in the Wolffian sense. And he was not regarded as a systematic philosopher by such illustrious successors as Karl Leonhard Reinhold, Johann Gottlieb Fichte, or Georg Wilhelm Friedrich Hegel, all of whom held that a genuinely systematic philosophy must be derived from a single principle, the possibility of which Kant strenuously denied. Contrary to his successors, Kant insisted that human thought is inexorably riven by fundamental dualities—the distinction between sensibility and understanding, the distinction between phenomena and noumena, or appearance and reality, and above all the distinction between theoretical and practical reason. It can often look as if Kant thinks that theoretical reasoning and practical reason constitute two separate domains of human thought that cannot possibly be joined in a single system: in theoretical reasoning we use the pure forms of sensibility and understanding, that is our pure intuitions of the structure of space and time on the one hand and the fundamental logical structures of discursive thought on the other, to define the basic laws of a realm of nature that cannot be influenced by our moral conceptions of how things ought to be, while we appeal to pure practical reason to determine how truly free beings ought to relate to themselves and one another regardless of what they actually do. Thus it can seem as if in Kant's view the realms of nature and freedom, while each possesses its own kind of systematic laws and organization, can never be joined in a single system.

But although Kant did not think that the scientific laws of nature and the moral laws of freedom could ever be *derived* from a single principle, neither did he think that they could be left to define merely parallel but unconnected realms of human thought. On the contrary, after establishing the fundamental laws of nature in his first *Critique* and the fundamental principle of morality in his second, Kant wrote a third *Critique* precisely in order to show how the laws of nature and the laws of freedom could be *joined* in a single and coherent view of the place of human beings as moral agents in the natural world. In the words of its Introduction, the aim of the *Critique of the Power of Judgment* is nothing less than to show that

Although there is an incalculable gulf fixed between the domain of the concept of nature, as the sensible, and the domain of the concept of freedom, as the supersensible, so that from the former to the latter (thus by means of the theoretical use of reason) no transition is possible, just as if there were so many different worlds, the first of which can have no influence on the second: yet the latter **should** have an influence on the former, namely the concept of freedom should make the end that is imposed by its laws real in the sensible world, and nature must consequently also be able to be conceived in such a way that the lawfulness of its form is at least in agreement with the possibility of the ends that are to be realized in it in accordance with the laws of freedom.—Thus there must still be a ground of the **unity** of the supersensible that grounds nature with that which the concept of freedom contains practically, the concept of which, even if it does not suffice for cognition of it theoretically or practically, and thus has no domain of its own, nevertheless makes possible the transition from the manner of thinking in accordance with the principles of the one to that in accordance with the principles of the other. (*CPJ*, Introduction II, 5:175–6)

Kant emphasizes in this passage that the moral law must be realizable in the domain of nature even though the moral law cannot be either derived from or limited by mere nature. In the words of his first sketch of his moral philosophy in the 'Canon of Pure Reason' in the first *Critique*, we must believe that we can transform the natural world *into* a 'moral world' (A 808–9/B 836–7), not merely imagine a moral world parallel to or beyond or in some other way independent of the natural world. He also emphasizes in this passage that our conception of the realizability of the demands of morality in the realm of nature will not amount to knowledge in the ordinary sense, the kind of knowledge of facts and laws within the realm of nature that we can have in everyday life and science; this is a point that Kant made in the first two *Critiques* through his doctrine of the 'postulates' of pure practical reason, and that he makes in the third *Critique* by rewriting this doctrine in terms of his new conception of 'reflecting' rather than 'determining' judgment (*CPJ*, Introduction IV, 5:179), which yields 'regulative' rather than 'constitutive' principles. At the same time, Kant's suggestion that the laws of the realm of nature have no influence at all on the laws of the realm of freedom is a bit misleading: in fact, his considered view is that we must use the very same capacity for reasoning that allows us to systematize our knowledge of nature in order to figure out how we could systematize the conduct of free agents in a moral world, or what he calls in the *Groundwork for the Metaphysics of Morals* a 'realm of ends', a 'whole of all ends in systematic connection (a whole both of rational beings as ends in themselves and of the ends of his own that each may set himself)' (G, 4:433). Kant's basic idea is that to think rationally is to think systematically: to think about nature rationally is to think about it systematically: to think about our own conduct rationally is to think about it systematically; and ultimately we must think about how mankind could collectively achieve a systematic union of ends within the system of nature.

The essays collected in this volume attempt to elucidate Kant's vision of the unification of the system of nature and the system of freedom in a single system of nature and freedom which cannot be derived from and therefore guaranteed by any single principle but which must instead be held out as the final end of human thought and conduct. The essays in Part I, 'The System of Nature', explore Kant's view that we must be able to conceive of the laws of nature as comprising a system of laws, and also look at a threat to the unifiability of the laws of nature in a single system that worried him, namely the possibility of insuperable differences between organic nature and the rest of nature. The essays in Part II, 'The System of Freedom', explore Kant's general view that the moral law is a law for achieving systematic coherence in the conduct of free agents, and then examine the application of that general conception of moral law to the concrete circumstances of human life, which gives rise to both a system of collectively enforceable property rights and a system of ethical duties that can be enforced only by individual respect for the moral law. Finally, the essays in Part III, 'The System of Nature and Freedom', examine Kant's attempt to unify the system of nature and the system of freedom in his revival but drastic revision of the traditional conception of teleology, primarily in the second half of the third *Critique* but in other texts from the earliest part of his career to its very last stage as well.

The essays presented here were written over a period of fifteen years for a variety of occasions and audiences, so there are both similarities and differences but I hope no great inconsistencies among them. It might be helpful if I offer a little orientation here without unduly delaying the reader from turning to the essays themselves.

The first three essays in Part I concern the role of the ideal of systematicity in Kant's conception of empirical scientific knowledge of nature. Chapters 1 and 2 were among the first of the papers in this collection to be written. Chapter 1, 'Reason and Reflective Judgment: Kant on the Significance of Systematicity', argues that Kant's conception of the role of systematicity in theoretical cognition underwent a major change between the *Critique of Pure Reason* and the *Critique of the Power of Judgment*: while in the first work Kant treats the goal of systematicity primarily as a desire of the faculty of reason to organize particular concepts and laws that have already and independently been established by the application of the rules of understanding to the data furnished by sensibility, in the later work Kant emphasizes that the truth of empirical laws of nature cannot be established in the first place except in so far as they are part of a system of laws. Kant does not draw attention to this change in his views, but he marks it by reassigning the search for systematicity from the faculty of reason to the newly introduced faculty of reflecting judgment, which is in the business of searching for the empirical concepts by means of which the most general concepts of nature, namely the categories supplied by the understanding, can be applied to the empirical data of sensibility. Chapter 2, 'Kant's Conception of Empirical Law', focuses on the implication of this change of view for Kant's conception of our knowledge of empirical laws, particular causal laws, which Kant had recognized in the first *Critique* is not simply given to us *a priori* along with our *a priori* knowledge of the general principle that every event has some cause, but which he only subsequently recognized requires more than just the application of that general principle to empirical data: it requires that such laws be found as part of a system of laws. This is not just because looking for particular laws as part of a larger system is heuristically helpful, but also because particular laws can derive their *necessity* only from their position within a system. This essay also explores the implications of this recognition for Kant's epistemology as a whole, namely that if particular causal laws can be known only as part of a system which is itself never completely given but is only a regulative ideal, then our knowledge of the empirical world and even the unity of our own consciousness which depends on that knowledge are also regulative ideals that are never completely given. Chapter 3, 'Kant on the Systematicity of Nature: Two Puzzles', returned to the issues of the first two chapters after an interval of a dozen years. The two puzzles it explores are why Kant thinks we must make the 'transcendental' presupposition that nature itself and thus its laws are systematic rather than just adopt systematicity as a heuristic principle for our investigation of nature, and why Kant suggests that our discovery of systematicity in nature must be accompanied by a feeling of pleasure yet one that is not very noticeable. I propose that Kant thinks that it is only by presupposing that nature itself is systematic that we can lend an appearance of necessity to particular laws of nature even before we have discovered the whole system of them, which in any case we shall never completely do, and that his ambivalent attitude towards the association of a feeling of pleasure with the discovery of systematicity among the laws of nature reflects the complexity of our thought about systematicity, where we must both presuppose their systematicity to ground the necessity of particular laws of nature and yet at a deeper level recognize that the existence of that systematicity among the concrete laws is really contingent, and thus as it were a pleasant surprise.

The remaining two chapters in Part I explore more particular issues in Kant's conception of a systematic natural science. Chapter 4, 'Kant's Ether Deduction and the Possibility of Experience', investigates a problem that obsessed Kant in his final, uncompleted attempt to write a 'Transition from the Metaphysical Foundations of Natural Science to Physics,' which is recorded in the collection of late papers known as the *Opus postumum*. The point of this paper, which was written in the same period as Chapters 1 and 2, is to illustrate in the case of a particular concept that Kant thought to be necessary in order to give a naturalistic explanation of both motion and our perception of it how the line between *a priori* and empirical knowledge ultimately becomes fuzzy rather than hard-and-fast, just as Kant's recognition that the goal of a system of empirical knowledge is only a regulative rather than constitutive principle suggests it should. Chapter 5, 'Organisms and the Unity of Science', discusses what Kant thought to be the major challenge to the ideal of a unitary system of empirical knowledge of nature, namely those features of organisms that do not seem to be explicable by means of mechanical causal laws. In the 'Critique of Teleological Judgment,' Kant seemed to be committed to the view that defining characteristics of the organic such as growth, self-repair, and reproduction could never be explained mechanically, although he gave varying accounts of the reason for this conviction. But Kant clearly did not regard this issue as resolved and returned to it in the *Opus postumum*, where he made many attempts to unify the principles of organic and inorganic causation under some single, higher-order force. This essay touches upon these attempts, although not in the detail they deserve, and suggests that it was ultimately the fact that we comprehend organic processes on the model of our own free conduct that led Kant to think there is some fundamental divide between the organic and the inorganic. This essay thus points the way to the question about the unifiability of the natural and the moral worlds that is the focus of the essays in Part III.

The essays in Part II, 'The System of Freedom', examine Kant's view that our central task in practical reasoning is to discover and fulfil the conditions for the systematic union of ourselves as free agents who are ends in themselves and of the particular ends that we set for ourselves in the exercise of our freedom—the ability that for Kant defines our very humanity. In the first of these, Chapter 6, 'Kant on the Theory and Practice of Autonomy,' I argue that the key idea of Kant's practical philosophy is that we can achieve individual autonomy, negatively conceived as freedom from domination by both our own inclinations and the inclinations of others, only by conducting ourselves in accordance with universal laws which allow action only on those of our inclinations that can be joined in a systematic union with our other actions and the similarly constrained actions of others. I also argue that this conception of the conditions for genuine freedom of action can be separated from Kant's metaphysical theory of the freedom of the will, although he himself did not recognize this. In the next two chapters I explore in detail Kant's conception of the realm of ends as a systematic union of both ends in themselves and the particular ends that they set for themselves. Chapter 7, 'The Form and Matter of the Categorical Imperative', argues that Kant's multiple formulations of the categorical imperative, culminating in his two different versions of a third formulation, one of which calls for a union of all of our *maxims* in a collective legislation and the other of which calls for a union of all of our *ends* in a realm of ends, reflects his underlying idea that we must all treat ourselves and each other as ends in themselves who get to choose their own maxims and also as end-setters who must all be both allowed and indeed help each other in pursuing our individual ends as long as that can be coherently done. Chapter 8, 'Ends of Reason and Ends of Nature: The Place of Teleology in Kant's Ethics', explores in more detail the model of human action that underlies Kant's moral theory and shows why the realization of a systematic union of ends would under ideal conditions produce the collective happiness that Kant calls the highest good, the ultimate goal of morality that we must believe to be realizable in nature. Here I also distinguish Kant's moral teleology from the assumption that morality must answer to goals that nature sets *for us*, the more traditional conception of the place of teleology in Kant's ethics that H. J. Paton defended half a century ago.

Chapters 9 and 10 examine the implications of Kant's general conception of the goal of morality as systematicity in both our recognition of our equal standing and our pursuit of particular ends for his 'Doctrine of Right', that is, his legal and political philosophy, and his 'Doctrine of Virtue', that is, his account of ethical duties as contrasted to those duties that can be legally enforced through the collective authority and power of a political entity. Since Kant expounds his doctrine of right before his doctrine of virtue, even though he treats duties of right as merely the subset of moral duties generally that happens to be both physically and morally suitable for coercive enforcement, I follow him in placing Chapter 9, 'Kant's Deductions of the Principles of Right', before Chapter 10, which treats 'Kant's System of Duties' more generally but gives special attention to the duties of virtue. In Chapter 9 I consider Kant's view that individual claims to property can be made in a way consistent with the general demands of morality only if they are made as part of a system of property rights that is acceptable to all affected by it, and also argue that for Kant such rights could be coercively enforced only if such enforcement could itself be shown to be consistent with and even demanded by morality. In Chapter 10 (which appears here for the first time) I expound in more detail than elsewhere the theoretical conception of systematicity that Kant brings to bear in his practical philosophy, use it to bring out one aspect of Kant's theory of property that is not touched upon in the previous chapter, namely that individual property rights can ultimately be justly claimed only in a system of global justice, and then discuss in detail how Kant's characteristic division of all moral duties into perfect and imperfect duties to self and others can be understood as a scheme for the systematic preservation and promotion of the freedom of every human being to set and pursue his or her own ends.

In Part III, I turn to Kant's attempt to unify the legislations of nature and freedom in a single system of nature and freedom. Chapter 11, 'The Unity of Nature and Freedom: Kant's Conception of the System of Philosophy', examines Kant's argument that we must be able to conceive of the goal of the highest good as realizable within the realm of nature from the *Critique of Pure Reason* to the *Opus postumum*. Kant's return to this issue in the 'Doctrine of Method' of the 'Critique of Teleological Judgment' in the *Critique of the Power of Judgment* after he had already extensively treated it in the *Critique of Practical Reason* suggests that he felt that his characterization of the presupposition of the realizability of the highest good in nature as a postulate of pure practical reason had not made his departure from traditional metaphysics sufficiently clear, and that he could make his position clearer in the form of a revision of traditional teleology into a regulative ideal of reflecting judgment. The record of his thinking in his final years in the *Opus postumum* makes it evident that he felt compelled to return to this issue yet again under the pressure of the revival of Spinozism in the 1790s and the emergence of absolute idealism in such authors as Friedrich Schelling. But he felt no temptation to turn from his transcendental idealism to the new form of idealism; rather, he tried to clarify his earlier ideas by arguing that both the system of moral laws (personified in the image of a divine lawgiver) and the system of laws of nature must be regarded as projections of the human mind, and therefore as necessarily unifiable. Chapter 12, 'From Nature to Morality: Kant's New Argument in the "Critique of Teleological Judgment" ', examines Kant's method for the unification of the realms of nature and freedom in the third *Critique* in more detail. Here I argue that Kant thought not only that we must be able to believe that the moral goal of the highest good can be realized in nature, but also that our task of systematizing our conception of nature itself requires the idea that nature itself have a point, an 'ultimate end', the only possible candidate for which is the 'final end' of morality, namely the perfection of our own virtue as well as the realization of our freely and rationally chosen ends that constitutes our happiness. Thus Kant argues that both the task that is set for us by morality and the task of comprehending nature as such point to the same conclusion. Finally, Chapter 13, 'Purpose in Nature? What is Living and What is Dead in Kant's Teleology?', (which appears here for the first time in English and in its entirety) reviews and evaluates this complex, culminating argument of Kant's entire philosophy. Here I argue that even though Kant's conception of a teleological natural science survives only in the scientific goals of a unified theory of physical forces and of a physical explanation of biological phenomena, towards at least the latter of which such great steps have been taken in the last half-century, the implications of Kant's view that we must think of our moral goals as systematically realizable in a systematic nature remain of great importance: Kant's teleology can remind us that we must always consider the implications of our actions for the entire system of nature within which we live and on which we depend—to the extent, always limited of course, to which we can actually do so—and moreover that we must realize that we have the right to exploit the rest of nature only for our morally acceptable ends, not for every whim and wish of our mere inclinations.

I first studied the *Critique of Pure Reason* in a brilliant course given by Robert Nozick. During that course, Bob became deeply interested in Kant's theory of regulative ideas. I am sorry he did not live to see this book, and I dedicate it to his memory.

# PART I

The System of Nature

# Reason and Reflective Judgment: Kant on the Significance of Systematicity

In the *Critique of Pure Reason*, Kant assigns the origin as well as the employment of the regulative ideal of systematicity in empirical knowledge to the faculty of pure theoretical reason, although, to be sure, to reason in its "hypothetical" rather than "apodeictic" employment (A 646–7/B 674–5).[1] In the *Critique of Judgment*, however, published only three years after the revised second edition of the *Critique of Pure Reason*, the regulative ideal of systematicity is reassigned to the newly introduced faculty of reflective judgment. Kant offers some explanation of what he means by reflective judgment; but he does not mention that the assignment of the regulative ideal of systematicity to this new faculty represents a revision of his previous view—indeed, he does not even mention that he had a previous view about systematicity. Commentators have generally followed Kant in passing over this revision in silence: even those with a special interest in the topic of systematicity indiscriminately speak of it as a product of either reason or reflective judgment.[2] Yet surely Kant must have had some reason for making this change. What could it have been?

Assuming that one knows what Kant means by "reason," a natural place to begin consideration of this question is with his conception of "reflective judgment." Kant describes "judgment in general" as "the faculty of

This chapter originally appeared in *Nous*, 24 (1990), 17–43, and is reprinted here with permission of the editors.

[1] Citations from the *Critique of Pure Reason* are located in the usual fashion by their pagination in the first (A) and/or second (B) edition. Citations to *CPJ* and FI are located by volume and page number of the Akademie edition: *Kant's gesammelte Schriften*, vol. 5 (*CPJ*) and vol. 20 (FI), herausgegeben von der Preussischen Akademie der Wissenschaften (Berlin: Walter de Gruyter, 1900). Translations are my own. I use boldface type rather than italics to indicate emphasis in Kant's texts, since the original printed versions of Kant's main books indicated emphasis by the use of *Fettdruck* (larger, fatter type) rather than the *Sperrdruck* (spaced type) of later German publications or the italics of English publications.

[2] e.g. G. Buchdahl, "The Relation between 'Understanding' and 'Reason' in the Architectonic of Kant's Philosophy," *Proceedings of the Aristotelian Society* 67 (1966–7), 210; and id., "The Conception of Lawlikeness in Kant's Philosophy of Science," *Synthese* 23 (1971), 32–3.

thinking the particular as contained under the universal" (*CPJ*, Introduction IV, 5:179) or the "faculty for **subsumption of the particular under the universal**" (FI, II, 20:21). Any particular task of subsumption, he then suggests, may take one of two forms: "the universal (the rule, the principle, the law)" may be given, in which case it is the task of judgment to find a particular that can be subsumed under the universal; conversely, a particular may be given, "for which the universal is to be found." In the first case, judgment is to be called "determining" or "determinant" (*bestimmend*); in the second, it is called "reflecting" or "reflective" (*reflectirend*) (*CPJ*, Introduction IV, 5:179). This contrast suggests that determinant and reflective judgment are mutually exclusive, that is, that in any single case of the subsumption of a particular under a universal either the particular or universal must be given, but not both, and thus that either determinant or reflective judgment must be employed to connect the universal and particular, but not both. So, it would seem, if a universal concept or law is given under which particulars must be subsumed, for example a category such as causality or a principle of empirical thought such as the law that every event has a cause, only determinant judgment can be employed to seek out the instances of the concept or rule. Conversely, when reflective judgment must be employed, then, since the universal is not given but is to be found, it could not be one which is given, such as a category, but only some universal which is not antecedently given. Determinant and reflective judgment would not seem capable of joint involvement in the subsumption of a single particular under a single universal concept or law.

Such an inference, however, is unwarranted. Perhaps when judgment is either given or must find a universal which is directly applicable to a particular, i.e. applicable to an empirical intuition without the mediation of any further concept (as the universals *white* and *paper* are applicable to this sheet), and thus, so to speak, only two terms are involved, then judgment must be either determinant or reflective but not both. But when subsumption is not so simple, when more than two terms are involved, when, for instance, an abstract universal such as causation can only be applied to a sensible particular through an intermediate causal concept, such as a concept of a particular kind of chemical or mechanical causation, then perhaps reflective and determinant judgment may both be required to accomplish the single task of applying the given universal to the given particular. Determinant judgment may be set the task of applying the abstract concept to sensible particulars, but if intermediate concepts have to be discovered in order to do that then reflective judgment may be needed to find those concepts and thus complete the task assigned to determinant judgment.

Such a possibility of cooperation rather than opposition between determinant and reflective judgment provides the key for an answer to my opening question. In the *Critique of Pure Reason* Kant basically treats the systematicity of empirical knowledge as a cognitive desideratum which is independent of any demand of the understanding and instead more closely allied to pure reason's own demand for unconditional completeness in knowledge. In the *Critique of Judgment*, however, Kant works toward a recognition of the way, indeed several ways, in which systematicity functions in the task of applying the pure categories of the understanding and the transcendental laws of experience which they ground to the actually given sensible particulars of empirical experience. He thus has reason to associate the ideal of systematicity with judgment rather than reason, with the task of subsumption rather than with an independent objective of completeness; but since systematicity works in the application of the categories to particulars precisely by guiding a search for intermediate universals, empirical concepts or laws which are necessary to apply the categories but which are not given by the categories, it is most appropriately assigned to reflective rather than determinant judgment.

The role of the ideal of systematicity in the application of the categories to empirical objects can explain why Kant reassigns this ideal from reason to reflective judgment. The merely regulative status of this ideal, however, creates an obvious problem: if the concept of systematicity is needed to complete the application of the categories to empirical intuition and thereby constitute the unity of experience, yet remains more an open-ended task than a condition which can ever be completely satisfied in intuition, then must not the unity of experience itself also become a regulative ideal rather than a constitutive concept? Kant was not eager to draw this implication; indeed, perhaps his difficulty with it explains why he did not draw attention to his reassignment of the ideal of systematicity from reason to reflective judgment. But a fundamental revision in his concept of the *a priori* certainty of the unity of experience may nevertheless be the inevitable outcome of Kant's recognition of the role of the regulative ideal of systematicity in applying the categories to experience.

I

Before we can examine Kant's conception of the function and status of the regulative ideal of systematicity in the *Critique of Pure Reason* we must note that systematicity is not the only regulative ideal which Kant recognizes in that work. In fact, Kant recognizes at least two other kinds of regulative ideal, each of which could be incorporated into a system of empirical knowledge as Kant understands such a goal but each of which could also function as an independent objective of reason. Neither of these other two kinds of regulative ideal is reassigned from reason to reflective judgment in the third *Critique*, so it is important to distinguish them from the ideal of systematicity before investigating the reassignment of that ideal.

(i) The first of the three kinds of regulative ideal in the first *Critique* is the "regulative principle of pure reason" (A 508/B 536) that Kant introduces in order to solve the "Antinomy of Pure Reason." This is essentially a *quantitative* ideal of the indefinite extendability of any empirical synthesis. Kant suggests the quantitative nature of this form of ideal in his opening statement of Section 8 of the "Antinomy," where the term "regulative principle" is first used: "Since no maximum of the series of conditions in a sensible world is **given**, as to a thing in itself, through the cosmological principle of totality, [it] can only be **set as a task**." He then formulates a rule for the conduct of this task:

The principle of reason is therefore really only a **rule** that prescribes a regress in the series of the conditions of given appearances, which is never allowed to come to rest at something absolutely unconditioned. It is therefore not a principle of the possibility of experience and of the empirical cognition of the objects of the senses, thus a principle of the understanding, for every experience is confined in its limits (in accord with the given intuition); it is therefore also not a **constitutive principle** of reason to extend the concept of the sensible world beyond all possible experience; it is rather a principle of the greatest possible continuation and extension of experience, according to which no empirical limit can count as an absolute limit, therefore a principle of reason which postulates **as a rule** what should be done by us in the **regress**, and does not anticipate what is given **in the object** prior to all regress.[3] (A 508–9/B 536–7)

The postulate of reason is that because nothing presented in intuition can count as an absolute or unconditioned limit, we should always attempt to extend our empirical syntheses beyond whatever empirical limit may have been reached at any time. Such extension will take different forms, of course, depending upon whether the empirical synthesis in question is a "mathematical" one, adding or dividing objects occupying determinate regions of space and/or time, or a "dynamical" one, adding additional

---

[3] Kant uses the three different terms "*Princip*," "*Principium*," and "*Grundsatz*" in this passage. I have translated them all as "principle" because I can discern no intended difference of meaning among them.

antecedent causes to the explanation of an event or additional contingencies to such an explanation; but in any of these cases the extension of the series is still quantitative in nature: additional members, whether themselves quantities or not, are to be added to the series.

In all of these cases it is presumably the form of *intuition* which determines that additional members always *can* be added to the series; *reason* is involved because the rule says not just that the series always *can* but that it always *should* be extended. This norm seems to flow from the nature of reason itself, or from a "logical precept, to advance toward completeness in the ascent to even higher conditions and by that means to bring the greatest possible unity of reason to our knowledge" (A 309/B 365). Intuition presents no absolute limits, and thus allows for the indefinite extension of any synthesis; reason requires the indefinite extension of syntheses under the guise of its own interest in maximization, perhaps as an asymptotic substitute for the unconditioned. Understanding, finally, would seem to have to carry out the bidding of reason by applying the categories (or intermediate empirical concepts) to the ever new regions of space and time which intuition affords to reason, but has no clearly defined interest of its own in the extension of knowledge beyond any set bounds. In the case of the purely quantitative regulative ideal of maximizing the extension of knowledge, pure reason's interest in maximization dictates that the understanding be set to work to exploit the opportunities which our form of intuition affords reason.

The "Appendix to the Transcendental Dialectic" (A 642/B 670 ff.) takes up the contrast between the "constitutive" and "regulative employment" of the "ideas of pure reason" or "transcendental ideas." Kant's initial characterization of this regulative employment of ideas of pure reason clearly suggests that understanding can accomplish its assigned work on its own without any assistance from reason, but that reason has an independent interest in discovering "a certain collective unity" among the products of understanding. It is less clear about exactly what constitutes such collective unity:

Reason therefore really has only the understanding and its purposive ordering as its object; and as understanding unifies the manifold in the object through concepts, so reason for its part unifies the manifold of concepts through ideas, insofar as it sets a certain collective unity as the goal of the actions of the understanding, which would otherwise be occupied only with distributive unity. (A 643–4/B 671–2)

The contrast between "collective" and "distributive" unity might remind one of Kant's earlier contrast between "synthetic" and "analytic" unity

(B 133–4 n.), and thus suggest that something is being contrasted to that simple form of unity which obtains when a number of particulars are straightforwardly subsumed under a universal, such as a number of sheets of paper under the universals *white* and *paper*. But Kant has not actually defined the present contrast. He next says that what reason seeks to add to the products of the understanding is "the **systematic** in cognition": "If we take an overview of the cognition of understanding in its entire circumference, we find that that which reason quite uniquely orders and seeks to bring about is the **systematic** in cognition, that is, its connection according to a principle" (A 645/B 673). What this involves still remains unclear. Several remarks, however, suggest that the purely quantitative ideal of indefinite extension is at least prominently included in this goal. Thus Kant says that the regulative use of the ideas of pure reason is intended to give the concepts of the understanding "the greatest unity along with the greatest extension" (A 664/B 672), and then stresses the aspect of extension: "we want to [extend] the understanding beyond every given experience (part of the whole possible experience), thus also to fit it to the greatest possible and most extreme extension" (A 645/B 673). So, as in the solution of the "Antinomy," it looks as if Kant's first thought is just that reason prescribes that understanding always seek to extend the reach of its own concepts to ever further empirical intuitions. Thus, reason seeks to extend the domain for the application of the concepts of the understanding, but does not otherwise add to or organize the concepts employed by the understanding.

(ii) Kant's initial remarks about the unity of reason seem to add a second regulative ideal to that of maximum extension, that of *pure* or *idealized* fundamental explanatory concepts—an ideal of an explanatory minimum rather than quantitative maximum. Kant characterizes "the **systematic** in cognition" as a "unity of reason" which "always presupposes an idea of reason, namely that of the form of a whole of cognition, which precedes the determinate knowledge of the parts and contains the conditions for determining *a priori* the position of each part and its relation to the others" (A 645/B 673), and then goes on to suggest that what accomplishes this are explanatory concepts of pure, fundamental substances, e.g. "**pure earth, pure water, pure air,** etc." Such concepts are necessary, he says, "in order precisely to determine the share that each of these natural causes has in the appearance" (A 645/B 674). Several pages later, Kant again suggests that what reason requires is explanation in terms of a pure principle, indeed not several but just one such principle:

The idea of a **fundamental force,** although logic does not tell us whether such a thing exists, is at least the problem for a systematic representation of the manifold of force. The logical principle of reason requires that this unity be brought about as far as possible, and the more the appearances of one and another force are found identical among themselves, the more probable does it become that they are nothing but different expressions of one and the same force, which can be called (comparatively) their **fundamental force.** . . . The comparatively fundamental forces must in turn be compared with each other in order thereby . . . to come closer to discovering a single radical, that is, absolute fundamental force. This unity of reason is however, merely hypothetical. (A 649/B 677)

The idea seems to be that although the requirements of the understanding are satisfied as long as every appearance is subsumable under some causal law or other, regardless of the existence of any relations among these causal laws, the unity of reason requires that understanding's causal laws be seen as expressions of the operation of some small number, ultimately one, explanatory force or agency. Understanding, it would appear, is responsible for the idea of force itself, that is, for the requirement that phenomena be given causal explanations; reason adds its own constraint to the understanding's positing of forces. Reason requires the minimization of pure forces, thus that different empirical forces be seen as resulting from different admixtures of pure forces or from some sort of different expressions of one pure force in empirically different contexts. Such a fundamental force or forces would be both pure and ideal or hypothetical, that is, something never found without variation due to empirical circumstances and only posited rather than demonstrated; but it or they would nevertheless remain a necessary ideal of reason guiding the employment of the understanding in some way not required for the accomplishment of understanding's own task of grounding the transcendental unity of apperception.

   (iii) Positing a fundamental force or forces would obviously impose a certain form of systematicity on a system of explanatory empirical concepts: all such concepts would be conceived of as expressions, perhaps even ordered in certain determinate ways, of the one or several underlying pure forces. However, Kant also introduces a more general characterization of systematicity in logical rather than explanatory terms. This conception of systematicity might be at least partially satisfied by the posit of fundamental forces, but might not require the posit of such forces for its satisfaction, and should therefore be understood as a third and more general conception of the regulative ideal of reason.

The introduction of this more general ideal of systematicity might be marked by Kant's reference to "a school-rule or logical principle, without which no employment of reason takes place" (A 652/B 680); for he had earlier denied that the ideal of a fundamental force was something about which logic informed us. Under the guise of a "logical principle," Kant now tells us, reason in fact introduces three desiderata over and above that unity of concepts required by the understanding. The ideal of systematicity is defined by the "logical law of genera" or "homogeneity" (A 653–4/B 681–2), the principle of "**species**, which calls for manifold-ness and diversity in things" (A 654/B 682), and finally a law of the "**affinity** of all concepts";[4]

Reason therefore prepares the field for the understanding: 1. through a principle of the **homogeneity** of the manifold under higher genera; 2. through a principle of the **variety** of that which is homogeneous under lower species; and in order to complete the systematic unity, it further adds 3. a law of the **affinity** of all concepts, which demands a continuous transition from each species to every other through step-by-step increase of the difference. We can name these the principles of the **homogeneity, specification**, and **continuity** of forms. The latter arises through the unification of the first two, in that the one completes system-atic connection in the idea by ascending to higher genera as well as by descending to lower species, for then all varieties are related to one another, since they all derive from all the degrees of the extended determination of a single, highest genus. (A 657–8/B 685–6)

Kant starts off by saying that the first two laws of homogeneity and specification give rise to the third law of affinity, but ends by suggesting that, on the contrary, homogeneity and specification are both conse-quences of an underlying ideal of affinity. The latter impression is strengthened a few pages later when he speaks of a single "logical law of the *continui specierum* (*formarum logicarum*)," or a law of the con-tinuum of species or logical forms, and suggests that the whole idea of systematicity is a consequence of the supposition that we are always given a *continuum formarum* rather than a *vacuum formarum* (A 659–60/B 687–8). The idea seems to be that if we suppose that there is an infinite and continuous variation among natural forms, or forms of natural objects, then we will see both that any species we have

---

[4] This concept of affinity must be distinguished from the concept of *transcendental* affinity introduced in the transcendental deduction (A 121–2) as that necessary connection among the manifold of intuitions which is necessary for the transcendental unity of apperception; the issue suggested by *CPJ* is precisely whether affinity in the present sense is a condition of the unity of experience and thus transcendental affinity, or not. This will be discussed further in the sequel.

distinguished can nevertheless be subsumed under some higher genus reflecting some property that they share, but also that under any species we have distinguished we can subsume subspecies reflecting differences among objects sharing the essential characteristics of the higher species. In fact, neither homogeneity nor specification implies continuity of forms: discontinuous species might nevertheless be subsumable under ever higher classifications, and under any species there might be an infinite variety of discontinuous forms; but a true continuity of forms does imply that any particular classification of them might be simplified upwards or refined downwards.

Kant links this notion of an ideal of systematicity in classification of natural forms based on their continuity with the two types of regulative ideal previously mentioned; but it is clear that the connection is not tight, especially between this ideal of systematicity and the purely quantitative ideal introduced in the "Antinomy," and thus that the continuum of forms should be seen as an independent ideal. First, the quantitative ideal of the indefinite extension of knowledge which is supposed to solve the problems of the "Antinomy" requires positing ever further regions of space and time, and perhaps even ever further filled regions of space and time, but does not require that the occupants of those regions be qualitatively and not just numerically distinct from all that is already known, nor that those items be similar to what is already known in any way other than their pure spatio-temporal form. Thus, the quantitative ideal of the maximal extension of knowledge does not imply either maximal unity or maximal diversity in Kant's senses of "homogeneity" and "specification." Second, the *classificatory* homogeneity and variety of species or types of natural objects which Kant seems to have in mind do not obviously imply the regulative ideal of fundamental *explanatory* power or powers which Kant has described, although a hierarchy of explanatory laws would certainly be one instance of homogeneous variation and would imply a hierarchical classification of the objects exemplifying those laws insofar as their causal powers are concerned. Perhaps Kant, like Locke, even believed that the classifiable properties of natural objects *are* all powers, so that a systematic organization of powers would imply a systematic classification of the objects themselves. But even then, the regulative ideal of fundamental powers would not imply the *continuity* of those powers, or the requirement of infinitely gradual variation; and that would remain an independent regulative ideal even if applied to the case of fundamental explanatory powers.

Kant makes it plain that the idea of the continuum of forms can only be seen as a regulative ideal for two reasons: we actually encounter discrete forms in nature, and in any case the task of searching for intermediate forms is open-ended and not completable in any empirical synthesis:

One easily sees that this continuity of forms is a mere idea, no object congruent to which is exhibited in experience: **not only** because objects in nature are really divided and must thus constitute in themselves a *quantum discretum* ... **but also** because we cannot make determinate empirical use of this law, in that through it not the least criterion of affinity is indicated, according to which and how far we are to seek the degree of their difference, but nothing more than a general indication that we have to seek it. (A 661/B 689)

At the same time, however, it must also be clear that Kant supposes that we must impute amenability to systematic conceptualization to nature itself. That is, although Kant conceives of the ideal of systematicity as prescribing a certain form of organization among our classificatory *concepts* of objects, he does not think of it as a purely internal feature of our conceptual schemes which can be constructed in them regardless of the character of the objects of experience which we are given in empirical intuition. On the contrary, he thinks it can be rational to attempt to satisfy the goal of a systematic organization of knowledge only if we are in a position to suppose that the objects of our inquiry are amenable to such a classification, that is, that a continuum of specific variations and similarities lies in them waiting to be discovered and is not simply an artifact of our conceptual scheme itself. Kant reiterates this claim a number of times, suggesting both that the independent existence of system in nature must be presupposed in order to encourage us in the search for it but also, perhaps even more importantly, that it must be assumed so that we can be sure that we will not be frustrated by failure when we do search for it. Thus Kant writes about the ideal of specification, or of positing ever-increasing diversity of species:

This manner of thought is evidently grounded in a logical principle, which intends the systematic completeness of all cognition, [namely, the law that,] beginning with the genus, I should descend to the manifold that may be contained under it, and in such a way seek to create extension for the system, in the same way ... in which I seek to create unity by ascending to the genus. ... But one easily sees that this logical law would be without sense and application if it were not grounded in a **transcendental law of specification**, which, to be sure, does not require a real **infinity** in regard to differences of the things which can be given as objects to our senses, since for that the logical law, which merely asserts the **indeterminateness** of the logical sphere in regard to its possible division, does not give occasion; but which obliges the understanding to seek subspecies under every species which is given to us and smaller differences under every difference. (A 655–6/B 683–4)

In the first place this transcendental law can be understood as encouraging us to seek for the satisfaction of the ideal of systematicity:

This law of specification cannot be derived from experience; for this cannot yield such wide-ranging disclosures. Empirical specification would soon come to a stop in the differentiation of the manifold, if it were not guided by the already antecedent transcendental law of specification as a principle of reason to seek it and always to suspect it even when it is not immediately revealed to the senses. That absorbent earths are of different kinds (chalk and muriatic earths) required for its discovery an antecedent rule of reason which made seeking the difference a task for the understanding by presupposing that nature is so rich [in such differences]. (A 657/B 685)

The presupposition that nature is infinitely rich in differentiations encourages understanding to the ever-increasing diversification of its classifications. Further, Kant suggests that even if we regard ourselves as already engaged in the *task* of searching for systematicity without any additional need for encouragement, the supposition of the actual existence of the continuum of homogeneous variation in nature is required if understanding is not to be frustrated in its attempt to fulfill the regulative ideal of systematicity. So he writes, now in the case of continuity rather than specification, "This logical law of the *continuum specierum (formarum logicarum)* presupposes a transcendental law (*lex continui in natura*), without which the use of the understanding would only be led astray by that prescription, in that it would perhaps take a course exactly opposed to nature" (A 660/B 688). Systematicity cannot be viewed solely as a feature of our conceptual scheme, which can be imposed on nature, understood precisely as that which is given to us, no matter what; the empirical data which nature offers must themselves be amenable to systematization if systematicity is to be attained. The systematizability of nature must be presupposed if we are rationally to adopt the regulative ideal of systematicity; it is not a product of adopting the regulative ideal. Thus, the regulative ideal can be characterized in purely logical terms as a structural feature of our knowledge, but satisfaction of the ideal commits us to a claim about the objects of experience themselves. Such a principle must be transcendental in that it concerns objects of experience yet is not merely empirical. But, of course, the characterization of a principle as transcendental can also connote that it is a necessary principle of the possibility of experience (B 40), and thus necessarily true if the possibility of experience is granted. What must now be considered is whether Kant really means to sustain such a claim, and if so, how.

In one sense, systematicity is only a regulative ideal because no particular degree of conformity with it can be specified *a priori*—indeed, we can even determine *a priori* that no particular degree of conformity to it is the maximum. The principles of systematicity are ideas which reason can follow "only asympotically," and they thus have only "objective, but indeterminate validity" (A 663/B 691). But in the same place he says this Kant also says that they are "synthetic *a priori* propositions" which "serve as rule[s] for possible experience"; and the final sentence of the last extract also suggests that systematicity is a condition of the possibility of the unity of experience itself and thus a transcendental principle as secure as the categories and principles of judgment themselves. In this case, it might have no less secure standing than the dynamical principles of the possibility of experience themselves, such as the principle of causation—which Kant also characterizes as regulative rather than constitutive precisely because the particular form in which experience will satisfy them cannot be determined *a priori* (A 179/B 222). This is also suggested in another, frequently cited passage. If we were to suppose, Kant argues, that the powers of nature were not homogeneous and that "the systematic unity of their derivation were not in accord with nature," then "an idea would be set as a goal which is entirely opposed to the constitution of nature." But this "unity according to principles" cannot be "accidental,"

For the law of reason, to seek it, is necessary, since without it we would not even have reason, without this however no coherent use of the understanding, and in the absence of this no adequate criterion of empirical truth, and in regard to the latter we must presuppose the systematic unity of nature as objectively valid and necessary throughout. (A651/B 679)

Kant's statement is resounding. Unfortunately, he does not explain how or why systematicity is required in order to have an empirical criterion of truth. On the contrary, most of what he says in the first *Critique* suggests that the understanding can succeed in subsuming empirical intuitions under empirical concepts without reference to any constraint of systematicity, and that the discovery of systematicity satisfies only an additional interest of reason rather than the fundamental interest of the understanding in the unity of experience itself. If this is so, then the law of reason which not only prescribes the search for systematicity but also postulates its existence in nature, although transcendental in some sense, would not be a necessary condition of the possibility of the unity of experience itself.

Another passage, arguing that a transcendental law must ground the logical law of unity or homogeneity as well as the logical law of specification to which I have already referred, also makes the strong claim that without the assumption of (this component of) systematicity the use of the understanding and thus the possibility of experience itself will be undermined:

> If among the appearances which offer themselves to us there were such a great diversity, I will not say of form (for in that regard they might be similar to one another), but in content, i.e. regarding the multiplicity of existing beings, that even the most acute human understanding could not discover the least similarity through the comparison of them (a case which can easily be thought), then the logical law of genera would simply not hold; and there would not even be any concept of genus or indeed any general concept, indeed any understanding, which has to do solely with such concepts. The logical principle of genera therefore presupposes a transcendental one if it is to be applied to nature (by which I here understand only objects that are given to us). According to this principle necessary uniformity is presupposed in the manifold of a experience (although of course we cannot determine its degree *a priori*), because without this no empirical concepts, therefore no understanding would be possible. (A 653–4/ B 681–2)

Here at least Kant's argument is obvious: if the diversity of natural forms were so great that even in spite of their common spatio-temporal form no two could ever be recognized as similar and thus classified together, the understanding would not be able to apply any empirical concepts whatsoever to empirical intuitions, and would thus be incapable of securing the possibility of experience, which requires at least that some empirical concept be applicable to any empirical intuition. Unfortunately, it is not apparent that empirical *concepts* themselves must be subsumable under higher-order but still empirical genera for this degree of homogeneity in the manifold of empirical *objects* themselves to obtain.[5] Without going to the lengths of a Strawsonian thought-experiment, it would seem that a universe of recurring but non-systematic shapes, colors, or tones—e.g. perhaps just one shape, color, and tone occuring in different combinations—would suffice for the application of a set of empirical, general concepts without yielding any hierarchical *system* of classifications.

Indeed, Kant's present claim that systematicity is a condition for the possibility of understanding itself appears incompatible with his earlier introduction of the notion of "affinity of all appearances" into the

---

[5] Of course, any empirical concepts must be subsumable under the categories themselves—but then the categories should be understood as *forms* for empirical concepts rather than higher-order empirical concepts.

transcendental deduction of the categories. In the first-edition deduction
Kant had argued that the "subjective and **empirical** ground of reproduction [of appearances] according to rules [in] **association**," which is a
psychological capacity required for the actual deployment of empirical
concepts, presupposed an "objective ground which makes it impossible
that appearances should be apprehended otherwise than under the condition of a possible synthetic unity of this apprehension"; he named this
objective ground of reproduction in empirical imagination or of "all
association of appearances" "affinity" and implied that it was entailed
by the principle of the conformity of all appearances to the "unity of
apperception" itself (A 121–2; see also Kant's discussion of the "synthesis
of reproduction in imagination" at A 100–2). This form of affinity is, as it
were, the objective correlative of the unity of apperception: it is precisely
whatever lawlikeness is required in the manifold of intuition in order to
ensure that one can make a unified experience out of it, which is to say
whatever lawlikeness of experience is required to ensure that some
empirical concept or other can be applied to any given intuition. This
transcendental concept of affinity itself implies no particular connection
*among* empirical concepts, such as is connoted by the regulative ideal of
affinity as a continuum of forms. And in the transcendental deduction
Kant appeared to leave no room for the idea that anything other than the
categories of understanding which are imposed on appearances *a priori*
and the rules of judgment which they imply—i.e. the axioms of intuition,
analogies of experience, and so on—could be necessary to constitute or
ground this transcendental affinity. The condition for the possibility of
experience which is now supposed to be supplied only by the transcendental law of systematicity, it seems, should already have been supplied
in the form of transcendental affinity; if not, then the categories and
principles of the understanding do not in fact supply the complete
necessary conditions of the unity of experience.

One might interpret Kant's assertion that systematicity is needed to
ensure the possibility of the understanding itself as a tacit retraction of
his earlier claim that the unity of apperception *grounds* objective affinity
rather than *depending* on it, and thus of his theory that the understanding
can *impose* order on nature through the *a priori* rules derivable from the
categories alone.[6] Although Kant may come close to such a retraction in
the *Critique of Judgment* in 1790, however, that is not what happens in

---

[6] I have certainly argued that he is not entitled to the first-edition deduction's doctrine
of affinity; see P. Guyer, "Kant on Apperception and *A Priori* Synthesis," *American
Philosophical Quarterly* 17 (1980), 205–12; and id., *Kant and the Claims of Knowledge*
(Cambridge: Cambridge University Press, 1987), 142–9.

the treatment of regulative ideals in the *Critique of Pure Reason*; instead, it seems more reasonable to interpret Kant as predominately advocating an alternative account of the status of the ideal of systematicity precisely in order to avoid such a retraction of the doctrine of objective affinity and the whole metaphysical model of the imposition of order on nature for which it stands. This alternative is simply the theory that systematicity satisfies reason's interest in unconditional completeness, and that reason searches for systematicity in the output of the understanding for interests of its own; precisely because it is in its own interest rather than that of understanding that reason postulates nature's amenability to system-atization does Kant insist that no transcendental deduction of this regu-lative ideal or its satisfaction is possible, though of course the objective affinity of all appearances was the culmination of the (first-edition) transcendental deduction.

Thus, Kant concludes his discussion of the regulative ideal of systema-ticity by asserting that this ideal is sought in the name of reason's interest in completeness, that it is sought among the products of the understand-ing and therefore applied indirectly to the objects of the understanding, but that precisely because it is sought in the name of reason rather than understanding it cannot be demonstrated to hold necessarily of the objects of the understanding even though there is also no antecedent reason to think that these objects will frustrate it. These suppositions are illustrated in the following claims:

Understanding is an object for reason, just as sensibility is an object for the understanding. Making systematic the unity of all possible empirical acts of the understanding is an occupation for reason, just as the understanding connects the manifold of appearances through concepts and brings it under empirical laws.... Now since every principle which establishes *a priori* for the understanding thorough-going unity of its employment also holds, although only indirectly, of the object of the understanding: so the principles of pure reason also have objective reality in regard to the latter; only not in order to **determine** something in them, but only to indicate the method according to which the empirical and determinate use of the understanding in experience can be made thoroughly harmonious with itself... I entitle all subjective principles which are derived, not from the constitution of the object, but from the interest of reason in a certain possible perfection of the cognition of this object, **maxims** of reason. There are therefore maxims of speculative reason, which rest merely on its speculative interest, although it may to be sure seem that they are objective principles. (A 665–6/B 693–4)

Here Kant suggests that it is reason's interest in completeness which, applied to the understanding itself rather than, say, to the forms of

intuition (as in the first and second Antinomies), gives rise to systematicity, and that there is no function indispensable for the understanding's
successful accomplishment of its own tasks which cannot be performed
without the postulation of systematicity. Understanding itself does not
require that its own employment be in some sense harmonious; reason
does. Of course, if the concepts of understanding are organized systematically then there must be some sense in which the objects to which those
concepts applied are also systematically ordered, but this does not render
the idea of systematicity objective in the full sense of a *necessary* condition for the use of the understanding: "the application of the concepts of
the understanding to the schema of reason," the "idea of the **maximum** of
division and unification of the cognition of the understanding," "is not a
cognition of the object itself (as in the case of the application of the
categories to their sensible schemata), but only a rule or principle of the
systematic unity of all use of the understanding" (A 665/B 693). The ideal
of systematicity may be objective in form but not in transcendental
status.

Kant exploits his thesis that systematicity is sought in the interest of
reason rather than understanding with one argument suggesting that this
is necessary in order to avoid an antinomy on the score of systematicity
itself. For one thinker, he asserts, "**extent** (of universality)" or "**unity**
(according to the principle of aggregation)" may have greater interest,
for another "**content** (of determinateness)" or "**multiplicity** (according to
the principle of specification)" (A 654/B 682, A 666/B 694). A naturalist
may always be searching for ever finer differences among specimens, a
physicist for ever more encompassing laws or explanations. If these
competing interests were driven by constitutive principles of the understanding, Kant argues, that is, principles necessary for the possibility of
knowledge of objects at all, contradiction, or at least irresolvable tension,
could arise; but as long as it is recognized that these principles of
systematicity express only interests of reason, indeed different aspects
of reason's single interest in systematicity, there is no need to fear that any
tension between them will undermine the work of the understanding
itself:

If either of these merely regulative principles [were] treated as constitutive, they
could be contradictory as objective principles; but if one considers them merely
as **maxims**, then it is no real contradiction, but only a different interest of reason,
which causes the separation of ways of thinking. In fact reason has only a single
interest, and the conflict of its maxims is only a difference and mutual limitation
of the methods for satisfying this interest.... neither of these two principles rests
on objective grounds, but only on the interest of reason... (A 666–7/B 694–5)

Exactly *what* contradiction Kant has in mind is less than clear; the difficulties in simultaneously pursuing both variety and unity seem more practical than logical or theoretical, more a question of limits on time and resources than anything else. But the plausibility of Kant's argument does not matter for the present point: Kant obviously thinks that if the principles of homogeneity and variety were principles of the understanding itself, then they could never be balanced off against one another, but, as manifestations of an independent interest of reason which are not actually necessary for understanding itself, then, since they can never be fully satisfied and must always be limited in their practical application, there is no reason why they cannot be balanced off against one another. Satisfaction of these concerns is in any case optional as far as the basic work of the understanding in constituting the unity of experience itself is concerned.

That systematicity is an interest of reason but not necessary for any coherent use of the understanding itself is also implied by Kant's remarks on the possibility of a transcendental deduction of the regulative ideals. In the first half of the Appendix to the Transcendental Dialectic, to which our attention has been confined thus far, Kant simply denies that there can be any such deduction of the rules for systematicity:

they seem to be transcendental, and although they contain mere ideas for the guidance of the empirical use of reason, which the latter can follow only as it were asymptotically, that is, merely approximately, nevertheless as synthetic *a priori* propositions they have objective but indeterminate validity and serve as a rule for possible experience, and can really be used in its elaboration as heuristic principles with good success, yet without one being able to accomplish a transcendental deduction of them...which is always impossible with respect to ideas. (A 663–4/B 691–2)

Only a few pages later in the second half of the Appendix, on "The Final Purpose of the Natural Dialectic of Human Reason," however, Kant claims that it must be possible to give some form of deduction of ideas of reason, no matter how different from that given for the categories, if they are to have even "the least, even if only indeterminate, objective validity" (A 669–70/B 697–8). Any problem about reconciling these two claims, however, is forestalled by the character of the deduction which Kant goes on to give. He says that it will be a sufficient proof that "it is a necessary **maxim** of reason to proceed according to such ideas" if it can be shown that they "always expand empirical cognition without ever being able to be opposed to it" (A 671/B 699); but all that is necessary to prove that is the reminder that even in postulating ultimate explanatory entities[7] "we do not really [intend to] expand our knowledge beyond the possible objects of experience but only expand the empirical unity of the latter through the systematic unity which the idea of the schema [of reason] gives us, which thus does not hold as a constitutive but merely as a regulative principle" (A 674/B 702). That is, what makes this weak form of deduction so easy to accomplish is precisely the fact that systematicity is not a factor which enters into understanding's constitution of empirical knowledge itself, but only an additional desideratum which reason seeks to find or construct in the empirical knowledge produced by understanding. It is again suggested that considerations of systematicity may play a *heuristic* role in the actual expansion of empirical knowledge, to which the nature of empirical knowledge can offer no sort of principled opposition; but this role is no more than heuristic. Again there is no hint that systematicity is a necessary condition for any successful use of understanding at all.

In spite of a few suggestions to the contrary, then, Kant's position in the *Critique of Pure Reason* is clearly that the regulative ideal of systematicity, like other regulative ideals, is a product of reason's intrinsic interest in unconditioned completeness. It can be applied to the empirical concepts which are the output of the understanding but there is no ground for supposing it to be a necessary condition for understanding's successful discovery and deployment of such concepts. Let us now see whether Kant's reassignment of the ideal of systematicity is not linked to a reassessment of this position.


II


Kant deals with the systematicity of natural kinds and empirical laws considered collectively in the two introductions to the *Critique of Judgment*, although not in the body of the work, which considers the formal and material purposiveness of individual natural objects in the critiques of aesthetic and teleological judgment respectively.[8] The ideal of systematicity is now treated as lying in the domain of the faculty of judgment at least in part for the simple reason that a system of concepts subsumes some concepts under others, lower species under higher

---

[7] Here Kant actually collapses the distinction between the types (ii) and (iii) of regulative ideals which I earlier distinguished.

[8] Of course, the *Critique of Aesthetic Judgment* does not confine itself to the formal purposiveness of individual natural forms alone, but rather treats those as paradigmatic and then the beauty of works of art as derivative from the paradigmatic case.

genera; so that even if it were in the interest of reason in which systematicity was sought it would still fall to the faculty of judgment to actually
discover and display it: judgment "is obliged to bring particular laws
under higher although still always empirical laws, even concerning that
which differentiates them under these same universal laws of nature" (FI,
IV, 20:209). Further, this work clearly involves reflective as well as
determinant judgment because these various empirical universals must
be sought and are not simply given through or with the pure concepts of
the understanding or the categories: judgment "is not merely a faculty for
subsuming the particular under the universal (whose concept is given),
but also, conversely, a faculty for finding the universal for the particular.
Understanding, however, abstracts from all multiplicity of possible empirical laws in its transcendental **legislation**" (FI, IV, 20:209–10). So any
laws or concepts intervening between empirical intuitions and the pure
categories of the understanding have to be found and applied by judgment, regardless of for what reason or in what interest they are sought.
But Kant now has a deeper reason as well for assigning systematicity to
judgment instead of reason: he is now more clearly drawn to the view
that some sort of systematic harmony of natural forms, even though it
can only be "presupposed" rather than deduced to obtain in nature, is a
condition of the application of the categories to any empirical manifold
and not just an additional desideratum which is not itself necessary for
the basic application of the categories to objects of experience.

In the so-called first introduction to the *Critique of Judgment*, at least,
Kant does not assert such a thesis unequivocally; but he does at least
suggest a reason why it should be so which goes beyond anything clearly
stated in the *Critique of Pure Reason*. This is a new recognition that
although understanding alone can supply the highest laws of experience,
or even better the general *form* for laws of experience, understanding
itself is not in a position to ensure that the data we are actually given in
empirical intuition will be sufficiently well-organized to allow us to
discover in them or apply to them empirical concepts and laws of the
sort required by understanding. For that matter, the faculty of judgment
cannot *ensure* that we are actually given appropriate data either, but it is
its task to attempt to apply the pure concepts of the understanding to
empirical intuition through intermediate empirical concepts which represent a systematization of our experience, and it must at least presuppose that what we are given is sufficiently systematizable for it to pursue
such an objective rationally. In other words, Kant moves toward a
retraction of the first *Critique*'s doctrine of objective affinity and instead
suggests that the presupposition that the understanding's requirements

for the possibility of experience are satisfied is itself only a matter for judgment.

Such an insight does not clearly emerge in the first of the two sections of the first introduction which Kant devotes to the topic of systematicity, Section IV, "Of Experience as a System for the Power of Judgment." Kant does draw a contrast here between formal laws of thought due to the understanding alone and more concrete laws of nature, which cannot be ascribed to that source:

> that nature directs itself according to our understanding in its merely formal laws (by means of which it is an object of experience in general) is easily seen, but in respect of particular laws, of their multiplicity and their heterogeneity, nature is free of all the limitations of our legislative faculty of cognition, and it is a mere presupposition of the power of judgment, in behalf of its own use in ascending from the empirically particular to more general yet empirical...laws, which grounds that principle [that experience is a system]. (FI, IV, 20:210–11)

Thus Kant clearly expresses the idea that nature itself is not actually governed by the purely formal laws of the faculty of understanding, and that the use of the faculty of judgment requires some independent presupposition about the lawfulness of nature. But that which judgment seeks and presupposes in nature still seems to be described as a form of organization among empirical laws which are discoverable in some way independent of it, and not the very possibility of discovering empirical laws at all.

So Kant still writes as if the systematicity of empirical laws were a supervenient property on those laws themselves:

> In the *Critique of Pure Reason* we have seen that the whole of nature as the sum of all objects of experience constitutes a system according to transcendental laws, namely those which the understanding itself gives *a priori* (for appearances, namely, **in so far** as they, connected in one consciousness, are to constitute experience). Just so, experience also, in both universal as well as particular laws...must constitute a system of possible empirical laws. For that is demanded by the unity of nature ... So far now is experience in general regarded according to transcendental laws of the understanding as a system and not a mere aggregate. (FI, IV, 20:208–9)

The systematicity of empirical laws, it seems, supervenes on the systematicity of objects according to transcendental laws; that is, what judgment must presuppose is not that objects in nature are themselves sufficiently systematic for empirical laws or classifications for them to be discovered, but rather that those laws or classifications are hierarchically organized. Thus Kant continues:

But from this it does not follow that nature is also a system **comprehensible** to the human faculty of cognition according to **empirical laws**, and that the thoroughgoing systematic connection of its appearances in one experience, thus this itself as a system, is possible for humans. For the multiplicity and heterogeneity of empirical laws could be so great that it would to be sure be partially possible for us to connect perceptions in one experience according to occasionally discovered laws, but never possible for these empirical laws themselves to be brought to unity of relation under a common principle, if namely, as is yet possible (as far as the understanding can determine *a priori*), the multiplicity and heterogeneity of these laws, along with the natural forms corresponding to them, were infinitely great and presented us with a raw chaotic aggregate and not the least trace of a system, although we must presuppose such a thing according to transcendental laws. (FI, IV, 20:209)

Kant seems to be hedging his bets—so such unusual qualifications as "partially" (*theilweise*) and "occasionally" (*gelegentlich*) suggest—but the basic idea still seems to be that it is at least in principle possible for one level of empirical law sufficient to satisfy the most general demands of the understanding to be discovered apart from any considerations of systematicity, and that it is an additional question, gratuitous as far as the most basic concerns of the understanding are concerned, whether these laws themselves form a system. Kant appears to be contrasting a chaotic aggregate and orderly system of what are in either case empirical laws. While an additional principle of judgment may need to be presupposed in order to postulate that empirical laws are systematic, no such principle appears to be a necessary condition for the discovery of empirical laws themselves.

In the next section of the first introduction, however, entitled simply "Of Reflective Judgment," Kant suggests a different picture: while it may be logically possible for empirical uniformities to exist without systematic or hierarchical connection among themselves, it is not reasonable to expect finite creatures like ourselves to be able to *discover* uniformities among all empirical objects sufficient to ground empirical laws or concepts about those objects unless those uniformities are themselves organized in some systematic fashion. Here Kant's idea seems to be that while the "universal concepts of nature" furnished by the categories are always applicable to empirical intuitions, this fact alone does not ensure that an empirical concept can be found for every empirical intuition; to be assured of the latter we must also presuppose that there is a manageable number of uniformities in nature, and that these uniformities are so organized that already known empirical concepts will provide us with access to other concepts suitable for application to any given empirical intuitions through shared features. The presupposition of systematicity, in other words, is tied up with the possibility of discovering empirical concepts themselves:

The principle of reflection about given objects of nature is: that for all things in nature empirical determinate **concepts** can be found, which is as much to say as that in the products [of nature] one can always presuppose a form which is possible according to universal laws cognizable by us. For if we could not presuppose this and did not base our treatment of empirical representations on this principle, then all reflection would be undertaken at random and blindly, thus without a grounded expectation of its agreement with nature. (FI, V, 20: 211–12)

Thus, the principle of judgment is a presupposition of the possibility of the universal applicability of empirical concepts themselves. The assumption of systematicity is required specifically in order to ensure that the diversity of natural forms does not exceed our capacity to discover empirical uniformities. "In regard to the universal concepts of nature," he writes, "under which a concept of experience (without particular empirical determination) is first possible, reflection already has its guide in the concept of a nature in general, that is, the understanding"; but more than the guidance of the understanding alone is required to ensure that for all empirical intuitions determinate empirical concepts can always be discovered. That can only be ensured by the further presupposition that nature has confined its uniformities to a system manageable by the likes of us:

But for those concepts, which are first to be found for given empirical intuitions, and which presuppose a particular law of nature, according to which alone **particular** experience is possible, the power of judgment requires a special, equally transcendental principle of its reflection... For the question is, how could one hope to arrive through comparison of perceptions at empirical concepts of that which is common to the different natural forms if in these (as it is yet possible to think) nature, on account of the great diversity of its empirical laws, had created such great heterogeneity that all or at least most comparison was useless for bringing forth a unity and hierarchy of species and genera under them. All comparison of empirical representations in order to cognize empirical laws and in accordance with these **specific** but in their comparison with others also **generically harmonious** forms in natural things presupposes: that also in regard to its empirical laws nature has observed a certain economy appropriate to our power of judgment and a uniformity comprehensible by us, and, as an *a priori* principle of the power of judgment, this presupposition must precede all comparison. (FI, V, 20:213)

This is Kant's central, novel claim about systematicity in the first introduction to the *Critique of Judgment*. It does not come right out and say that the unity of apperception itself requires the discoverability of specific empirical concepts; on the contrary, Kant still seems to suppose that there is some way in which the categories, as the most general concepts of nature, can apply to empirical intuitions without the satisfaction of further conditions for the application of empirical concepts. But here Kant does claim that the presupposition of the systematicity of nature is required not just to ensure that we can systematize our empirical concepts, which are themselves discoverable without reference to such systematicity, but in order to ensure that for any empirical intuition we can find at least some empirical concept. A restricted number of uniformities in nature is necessary for that purpose, Kant argues. He also seems to assume that such a restricted number of uniformities will be hierarchical, leading to classifiability of lower species under even smaller numbers of higher ones. Strictly speaking, that does not follow. But one can easily imagine Kant extending his argument to suggest that empirical concepts will always be discoverable for any natural form only if that form has at least some similarities with other classifiable natural forms, which would in turn require that the concepts of the several species be subsumable under one or more higher genera. That, at least is where Kant seems to point: "This principle now can be none other than that of suitability to the faculty of judgment itself, [i.e. that] sufficient relation is to be found in the immeasurable multiplicity of things according to possible empirical laws in order to bring them under empirical concepts (classes) and these under more universal laws (higher genera) and so to arrive at an empirical system of nature" (FI, V, 20:215).

Kant claims that judgment must presuppose the systematicity of nature in order to be assured of always being able to find empirical concepts for our intuitions, and even that this presupposition is "equally transcendental" as the laws of understanding itself. Yet he also draws back from explicitly asserting that the discoverability of empirical concepts is actually a condition of the possibility of the unity of apperception, and thus from asserting that the presupposition of systematicity is as secure as the postulation of the categories, or, conversely, that the unity of experience depends on the presupposition of systematicity and is itself only a regulative ideal:

Thus the power of judgment makes the **technic** of nature the principle of its reflection *a priori*, yet without being able to explain this or determine it more precisely, or to have for that an objective ground for the determination of the universal concept of nature (from a knowledge of things in themselves), but rather only in order to be able to reflect according to its own subjective laws, according to its need, yet at the same time in accord with laws of nature in general. (FI, V, 20:214)

In the first introduction to the third *Critique*, then, by gliding over the necessity of empirical concepts for experience in general, Kant avoids the explicit implication that the presupposition of systematicity is a condition of the possibility of experience itself; he thus avoids demoting the unity of experience to a regulative ideal. Does he come any closer to this fundamental revision of his critical philosophy in the introduction which he subsequently published with the whole work?

## III

As in the unpublished first introduction, the published introduction to the *Critique of Judgment* treats the presupposition of the systematicity of nature in only two sections (again Sections IV and V). Part of Kant's treatment here reiterates the argument of Section V of the first introduction that the uniformities of nature must be presupposed to be manageable in number and systematic in organization if we are to be assured, not of their existence, but of their discoverability:

For it can easily be thought: that regardless of all the uniformity of natural things according to the universal laws, without which the form of an empirical cognition in general would not even be possible, the specific diversity of the empirical laws of nature together with their effects could nevertheless be so great, that it would be impossible for our understanding to discover a comprehensive order in them . . . and to make a connected experience out of such confused (really only infinitely manifold, for our power of comprehension ill-suited) stuff. (*CPJ*, 5:185)

Again the suggestion is that we must presuppose a degree of organization among the uniformities of nature in order to have a reasonable expectation of discovering them.

However, Kant also advances a new and quite distinct argument linking systematicity even more closely to the conditions of the possibility of experience. In this argument he suggests that, contrary to some suggestions of the *Critique of Pure Reason*, not only the universal law of causation but individual laws of nature must be seen as necessary truths in order to serve their function in the unification of experience; that we can gain no insight into the necessity of individual laws of nature from the necessity of the most general laws of nature (the principles of empirical knowledge); but that we can approximate such necessity by seeing individual laws of nature as parts of a system of empirical laws—such a system as would be imposed on nature, Kant imagines, not by an intelligence like ours which is capable of imposing only the most general form on its experience, but by an intelligence capable of ordering nature in every detail. Kant obviously thinks this argument is important, for he reiterates it twice. First, in Section IV:

Only there are such manifold forms of nature, as it were so many modifications of the universal transcendental concepts of nature, which are left undetermined by those laws which the pure understanding gives *a priori*, since these concern only the possibility of a nature (as object of the senses in general), that there must therefore also be laws for this, which as empirical may, to be sure, be contingent according to **our** understanding, but which, if they are to be called laws (as the concept of nature also demands), must be seen as necessary from a principle, even if unknown to us, of the unity of the manifold. (*CPJ*, 5:179–80)

This principle, he continues, can only be that "particular empirical laws, in regard to that which is left undetermined in them through [the general laws of nature], can only be considered according to such a unity as they would have if an understanding (even if not ours) had given them in behalf of our faculty of cognition in order to make possible a system of experience according to particular laws of nature" (*CPJ*, 5:180).

This argument, such as it is, turns on the requirement that empirical laws be necessary if they are to be called laws. In his next, and slightly more detailed, exposition of the idea, Kant links the requirement of necessity to the analysis of causality itself. This passage must be quoted especially because here Kant explicitly refers to the "possibility of experience," and thus makes as plain as he ever does that systematicity is not simply an independent interest of reason but a prerequisite for the employment of the faculty of understanding itself:

We find among the grounds of the possibility of an experience first, to be sure, something necessary, without which nature in general (as the object of the senses) could not be thought; and this rests on the categories, applied to the formal conditions of all intuitions possible for us...But now the objects of empirical cognition are determined in so many ways besides that of the formal time-condition, or, so far as one can judge *a priori*, are determinable, so that specifically differentiated natures, beside what they have in common as belonging to nature in general, are still capable of being causes in infinitely many ways: and each of these ways must (according to the concept of a cause in general) have its rule, thus import necessity: although because of the constitution and the limits of our faculty of cognition we may not understand this necessity.... so judgment must assume *a priori* as a principle for its own use that that which is contingent in the particular (empirical) laws of nature nevertheless has to be sure for us not groundable yet still thinkable lawful unity in the connection of its manifold in a content of experience which is possible in itself. (*CPJ*, 5:183–4)

Here Kant suggests that particular causal laws must be necessary (not just particular conjunctions of events seen as necessary relative to particular causal laws which are themselves contingent); that we have no *a priori* insight into such necessity on the basis of the objective validity of the categories, even including that of causation; but that we can in some way satisfy this demand for necessity by seeing individual causal laws as part of a "system according to empirical laws."

Kant does not pause to spell out how such a system would satisfy this demand; presumably he takes it as obvious that in such a system lower laws would be entailed by higher laws, perhaps also higher laws by lower laws, and that these relations of entailment would to some degree satisfy our demand for necessity even though we might still be able to imagine that the system as a whole could be replaced by some other, though equally systematic set of empirical laws. He at least suggests such a conception a page later, when he states that if we have a subordination of species and genera "such that each approaches another through a common principle" then "a transition from one to another and thereby to a higher principle will be possible" (*CPJ*, 5:185). But he does not provide us with more detail on this point. What is more important, however, is that, in spite of having so clearly linked the satisfaction for this demand for necessity by means of the postulation of systematicity with the possibility of experience itself, Kant nevertheless makes it plain that while such systematicity may be "presupposed *a priori* ... by the faculty of judgment in behalf to its reflection," it is nevertheless "recognized as objectively contingent by the understanding" (*CPJ*, 5:185). He argues that we cannot give a psychological, i.e. empirical deduction of the postulation of systematicity—we are dealing with an *ought*, not an *is* (*CPJ*, 5:182)—so we must be prepared to give what is in some sense a transcendental deduction; yet we must also recognize that even if it is required for the task of fleshing out our conception and judgments of causation we still must acknowledge that the principle of systematicity is not objective, but "represents only the unique way in which we must proceed in reflection on objects in nature in aiming at a thoroughgoingly connected experience." Nature's satisfaction of such a principle even seems like a lucky accident to us, and for that reason brings an appreciable sense of pleasure with it (*CPJ*, 5:184).

On the one hand, then, Kant argues that the principle of systematicity is a "transcendental principle of cognition," but on the other hand that we are not capable of proving it (*CPJ*, 5:184). It is necessary because without it we can neither be sure that we can discover laws of nature nor recognize them as laws—that is, necessities—if we do recognize them; but we cannot prove it because we really cannot imagine that we are capable of imposing systematic organization on the objects of nature regardless of how they present themselves to us. We must presuppose that they are systematic, but we also recognize that it is a lucky accident that they are. Kant does not explicitly retract the first *Critique*'s doctrine of transcendental affinity and the entire metaphysical picture it implies, the picture on which we unfailingly impose complete order on the utterly plastic material furnished to us by remarkably cooperative things in themselves. But once he has linked the ideal of systematicity so closely to such fundamental requisites of the possibility of experience itself, an admission like this comes pretty close to the surrender of such a meta-physical model of our relation to reality:

Judgment also has an *a priori* principle for the possibility of nature in itself, but only in a subjective respect, by means of which it prescribes a law, not to nature (as autonomy) but to itself (as heautonomy) for reflection on [nature] ... (*CPJ*, 5:185–6)

This is as much of a concession as we can expect from Kant that we can determine *a priori* the conditions of the possibility of experience but not ourselves guarantee that nature will always satisfy them, and that talk of autonomy and self-legislation will have to be reserved for the practical rather than theoretical realm.

# 2

# Kant's Conception of Empirical Law

Kant characterizes experience in terms of the ancient distinction between matter and form. Experience, he says, 'contains two very heterogenous elements, namely a **material** for cognition from the senses and a certain **form** for ordering it, from the inner source of pure intuition and thought' (A 86/B 118).[1] It is natural to think that Kant's accommodation between rationalism and empiricism takes place in terms of these two fundamental components of experience: he pays homage to rationalism with his theory that we have synthetic *a priori* knowledge of the spatial and temporal form of empirical objects (from pure intuition) and of the categorial form of the judgments we make about them and thus of the concepts which we formulate of them (from pure thought or understanding); but he firmly insists on empiricism when it comes to particular judgments about empirical objects. We may know *a priori* that any empirical object must bear some determinate spatial and causal relation, for instance, to any other; but to know what location some particular object actually has and what causal powers it possesses is an entirely empirical matter, determined solely by the contents of the particular perceptions or empirical intuitions which we have of it. Or so it may seem in the *Critique of Pure Reason*. In the *Critique of Judgment*,

This chapter was originally presented at the 1990 Joint Session of the Mind and Aristotelian Societies, and appeared in *Proceedings of the Aristotelian Society*, suppl. vol. 64 (1990), 221–42. It is reprinted here by courtesy of the Editor of the Aristotelian Society.

[1] Citations to the *Critique of Pure Reason* are located by the pagination of the first (A) and second (B) editions of 1781 and 1787 respectively. The translations are my own, based on the text edited by Raymund Schmidt (Hamburg: Felix Meiner Verlag, 1930). Citations to the *Critique of Judgment* (*CPJ*) will be located by section number and volume and page number as in volume 5 of the so-called Akademie edition, *Kant's gesammelte Schriften*, edited by the Königlichen Preussischen Akademie der Wissenschaften (Berlin: Walter de Gruyter & Co. and predecessors, 1990– ). The text of the *Kritik der Urtheilskraft* was edited by Wilhelm Windelband. Citations to the so-called first introduction to the *Critique of Judgment* (FI) will be located by volume (20) and page number from the Akademie edition; this text was edited by Gerhard Lehmann. Citations to the *Opus postumum* (OP) will be given by volume (21 or 22) and page number of their appearance in *Kants gesammelte Schriften*; those volumes were also edited by Gerhard Lehmann. Translations from *CPJ*, FI, and OP are also my own.

however, Kant attempted to develop a more detailed conception of the relation between *a priori* and empirical elements in the formulation and acceptance of particular empirical laws. He no longer thought that we simply have *a priori* knowledge of the forms of experience and purely empirical knowledge of individual laws of nature, but saw that individual laws of nature are always an amalgam of empirical input and non-empirical assumption. In particular, he saw that an *a priori* conception of a systematic unity of empirical law has to be added to the forms of pure intuition and thought in order to make empirical intuitions yield empirical laws. But he also recognized that this conception of systematicity is never more than a regulative ideal. Thus Kant suggests that fully determinate knowledge of empirical laws can never be more than a regulative ideal for creatures with our cognitive constitution.

## I. EMPIRICAL LAWS IN THE *CRITIQUE OF PURE REASON*

In the second edition of the first *Critique*'s transcendental deduction of the categories, Kant claims that the categories themselves do not yield *a priori* knowledge of particular empirical laws. He suggests that all possible empirical perceptions must be connected by an empirical synthesis, which presumably employs empirical laws to connect them, and that such synthesis must 'stand under' the categories, but that particular laws of nature cannot actually be derived from the categories:

all appearances of nature, as far as their connection is concerned, must stand under the categories, on which nature (considered merely as nature in general) depends, as the original ground of its necessary lawfulness (as *natura formaliter spectata*). However, the pure faculty of understanding, through mere categories, does not suffice to prescribe any *a priori* laws to appearances other than those on which **a nature in general**, as lawfulness of experience in space and time, depends. Particular laws, since they concern empirically determined appearances, can **not be completely derived** from those, although they all stand under them. Experience must come in for [particular laws] to become known; but about experience in general, and about that which can be cognized as an object thereof, these *a priori* laws alone can give us instruction. (B 165)

Obviously, the category of causation or the general principle that every event has a cause does not itself imply that penicillin eliminates bacterial infections; astute empirical observations were needed to discover such a specific empirical law of nature. That's common sense. But what may be less clear is that Kant's position implies not only that empirical data must always be added to the categories of the understanding in order to arrive at empirical laws, but also that nothing else needs to be. As he puts it, 'these *a priori* laws alone can give us instruction' about empirical objects. No additional *a priori* assumptions of a substantive or methodological nature seem to be required in order to make empirical intuitions yield empirical laws.

Such an interpretation of Kant's intent is needed, at any rate, in order to reconcile this passage with his remarks bearing on knowledge of empirical laws in the first edition of the transcendental deduction. For here Kant claims that although empirical laws cannot be deductively derived from the categories alone, they must yet be treated as 'particular determinations' or special cases of those highest concepts of the understanding. He says that 'Although we learn many laws through experience, yet these are only particular determinations of yet higher laws, among which the highest (under which all others stand) themselves come from the understanding *a priori*' (A 126), and reiterates the point at length:

However exaggerated, however nonsensical it may sound to say: the understanding is itself the source of the laws of nature, and thus of the formal unity of nature, nevertheless such an assertion is correct and appropriate to its object, namely experience. To be sure empirical laws, as such, can by no means derive their origin from pure understanding, just as little as the immeasurable multiplicity of appearances can be entirely comprehended from the pure form of sensible intuition. But all empirical laws are only particular determinations of the pure laws of the understanding, under which and according to whose norm they are all first possible... (A 127–8)

The highest laws of the understanding, the *a priori* categories or principles of judgment, do not logically imply any empirical laws of nature because empirical intuitions are always needed to give them empirical content, just as empirical intuitions must be added to the pure forms of intuition to represent any objects as located at any determinate region of space or time. But once those empirical intuitions are given, nothing else is needed for the discovery of empirical laws. No other 'norm' is needed, and the empirical laws determined by empirical intuitions are to be regarded as 'particular determinations' of the categories. Kant's idea must be that the categories (in their schematized form) instruct us to look for particular patterns among empirical intuitions, such as, for instance, constant conjunction of spatially contiguous and temporally successive appearances in the case of causation, and that when under the instruction of the categories we do discover such patterns among the empirical intuitions then nothing more will be needed to discover empirical laws.

The categories themselves, it seems, furnish both a *guarantee* that we can discover empirical laws applying to any empirical intuitions and all the *method* that we need to discover these laws.

Kant appears to complicate this simple picture in the Appendix on the 'Regulative Employment of the Ideas of Pure Reason' attached to the Transcendental Dialectic of the first *Critique*. This appendix has the ostensible purpose of showing that although the three traditional metaphysical conceptions of a substantial soul, complete world-whole, and absolutely necessary being cannot have the constitutive role previously claimed for them but revealed in the Transcendental Dialectic to rest on logical fallacies, they do have a legitimate role, sometimes described as heuristic (see A 663/B691), as regulative ideals for the use of reason. Most of Kant's effort, however, is devoted not to these three conceptions but to another concept, the idea of a systematic unity among empirical laws of nature about properties of objects such as their forces. Such a systematic unity obtains when a classification of objects and their properties displays homogeneity, variety, and continuity: that is, when objects are so conceived that (i) any given classifications of them may be subsumed under some higher classification (homogeneity), (ii) when under any single classification further more detailed classifications may be subsumed (variety or specification), and (iii) when the transition between forms at different levels is continuous, so further levels of classification might always be introduced (affinity or continuity) (see A 657–60/B 685–8). Kant points out that such a form of organization cannot be considered just a property of our system of concepts or laws, but must also be thought of as a collective property of the objects represented by those concepts or laws: reason cannot coherently systematize its concepts of e.g. forces yet also consider it 'possible that all forces are heterogeneous and the systematic unity of their derivation not in accord with nature' (A 651/B 679). Kant then suggests that the postulation of systematic unity among such empirical concepts is some sort of necessary condition, obviously additional to the categories themselves, for the discovery of empirical truth and thus for the establishment of empirical laws of nature:

The law of reason to seek [such systematicity] is necessary, since without it we would have no reason, but without this no coherent employment of the understanding, and in the absence of this no sufficient criterion [*Merkmal*] of empirical truth, and in regard to the latter we must presuppose the systematic unity of nature as throughout objectively valid and necessary. (A 651/B 679)

The use of the term 'criterion' or 'mark' suggests that the idea of systematic unity will play some sort of methodological role in arriving at

empirical truth or knowledge of empirical laws, that the goal of systematic unity in our concepts is a 'norm' to be applied to empirical intuitions
in addition to the categories after all. But Kant does not spell out what
this methodological use would be.

He does, however, suggest that an assumption of systematic unity
among natural forms may be necessary to guarantee the possibility of
discovering empirical truths, for only such an assumption will ensure
that the number of empirical regularities which we have to discover will
be sufficiently small for a finite intellect such as ours:

> If among the appearances which offer themselves to us there were so great a
> variety... that even the most acute human understanding could not discover the
> least similarity by comparison of one with another (a case which may easily be
> thought), then the logical law of genera would have no place, and there would be
> no place for any concept of genus, or any general concept, indeed even no place
> for understanding, which has entirely to do with such concepts. The logical
> principle of genera therefore presupposes a transcendental one... According to
> this principle necessary homogeneity is presupposed in the manifold of a possible
> experience (although we cannot of course determine its degree *a priori*), since
> without this no empirical concepts, thus no experience would be possible.
> (A 653–4/B 681–2)

The *a priori* objective validity of the categories, Kant can be taken to
suggest, implies that for every empirical intuition some regularity exists
which connects it to some others, and through them eventually to all
others; but the categories alone do not suffice to guarantee that the
number of such regularities is sufficiently small to be grasped by us,
and thus do not guarantee that we can actually find an empirical law
for any given empirical intuition. In order to be assured that we can
always find such a law, we need to make the additional assumption that
the forms of natural objects are systematically organized.

Kant's argument seems to omit a step, for one would think that we
could also reasonably be ensured of discovering empirical laws as long as
their number were sufficiently small, even if there were no particular sort
of organization among them. Systematicity would seem to be a sufficient
but not a necessary condition for the discovery of empirical laws. Perhaps
what Kant thought, however, was that in view of the infinite number of
particular objects in nature it would be absurd to postulate a *numerical*
limit on the number of the forms or types to be found among them, and
that some sort of systematic organization among a potentially infinite
number of forms would then be our best guarantee of being able to find a
concept for any given object: even if the number of forms was very large,
as long as we could reach any particular empirical form by following out

the branches of some relatively short tree of concepts we would still have a reasonable guarantee of being able to find an empirical concept for any empirical intuition.

So Kant seems to assert that systematicity is methodologically necessary to discover empirical laws, and to provide at least a sketch of an argument that an assumption of systematicity is necessary to guarantee the discoverability of empirical laws. Thus he seems to modify his initial suggestion that no *a priori* 'instruction' beyond the categories is necessary to guarantee that an empirical law can be found for any empirical intuition or to find it. No sooner does he do this, however, then he apparently takes it back by arguing that systematic unity among concepts is not in fact necessary for the understanding to accomplish its task of empirical synthesis of empirical intuitions by empirical concepts but is instead only a supplemental goal of the faculty of reason, an interest in logical completeness which is independent of our fundamental need to synthesize empirical manifolds.

Thus, shortly after the passages just cited, Kant says that reason's idea of the 'complete systematic unity of all concepts of the understanding' is 'only a rule or principle for the systematic unity of all employment of the understanding', not a condition for the use of the understanding as such (A 665/B 693). He then says that although reason's rule of systematic unity holds 'indirectly' of objects of the understanding, it does not '**determine**' anything in such objects,

but rather only indicates the procedure, according to which the empirical and determinate use of the understanding [in] experience can be made thoroughgoingly harmonious with itself, by bringing it in connection with the principle of thoroughgoing unity **so far as possible,** and deriving it therefrom. (A 665–6/B 693–4)

Kant then goes on to make it clear that the principle of systematicity, which is merely regulative and subjective, does not contribute to the actual constitution of empirical knowledge—thus, presumably, to the discovery of particular empirical laws—but serves only an independent interest of reason:

I call all subjective principles which are not derived from the constitution of the object but rather from the interest of reason in a certain possible completeness of the cognition of this object **maxims** of reason. Thus there are maxims of speculative reason, which rest merely on its speculative interest, although it may well seem as if they are objective principles. (A 666/B 694)

Kant illustrates his point by arguing that different thinkers may be more interested in one of the components of systematicity than in another, and that this is possible precisely because the idea of systematicity is merely a maxim of reason rather than any necessary condition for the use of the understanding (A 666–7/B 694–5). Thus the suggestion that the idea of systematic unity is actually a necessary condition for the discovery of empirical laws seems to be dropped.[2]

## II. EMPIRICAL LAWS IN THE *CRITIQUE OF JUDGMENT*

Kant does not draw back from the connection between systematicity and empirical law in the *Critique of Judgment*, however. Here he unequivocally argues that our knowledge of empirical laws is dependent on a 'transcendental principle' that nature is systematically organized which we must presuppose as a principle for the use of our power of judgment but which we cannot actually prescribe to nature itself (e.g. *CPJ*, Introduction V, 5:181; FI, V, 20:209). He reiterates that the goal of systematicity is indeterminate and can only be approximated or, as he says in his *Opus postumum*,[3] approached 'asymptotically' (e.g. *OP*, 21:53, 79, 90, 93, 99, 176; 22:8). Given the indispensable role as a 'transcendental principle' which is now assigned to systematicity as a condition of the possibility of experience, this implies that determinate knowledge of empirical laws is itself only a regulative ideal.

It may seem surprising to have a general theory of knowledge of empirical law ascribed to the *Critique of Judgment*. On first glance, the book reads as an uneasy conjunction of Kant's theory of judgments of taste and his theory of teleological judgments about natural organisms.

---

[2] In fact, Kant's wavering on the issue of systematicity is not yet over at this point in the *Critique of Pure Reason*. In the second half of the Appendix to the Transcendental Dialectic, which is primarily concerned with the heuristic value of natural theology, he once again suggests the strong view of the role of systematicity implied at A 651/B 679 ff. Here he says that 'the systematic connection which reason can give to the empirical use of the understanding not only advances its extension but also confirms the correctness of it' (A 680/B 708). Again, however, he fails to explain how the idea of systematicity is actually put to such a use.

[3] This phrase does not refer to all of Kant's posthumously published writing, but rather to a specific set of manuscripts for a work on the 'transition' from 'metaphysical principles of natural science' to actual physics on which he worked, without bringing it to completion, from 1796 until a year before his death in 1804. It is these manuscripts which are published in volumes 21 and 22 of *Kants gesammelte Schriften*. They are extraordinarily repetitive, but contain interesting evidence of Kant's last thoughts about the concept of experience and its role in transcendental philosophy as well as his specific efforts to add *a priori* knowledge of matter to physics beyond those *a priori* principles of motion derived in his *Metaphysical Foundations of Natural Science* of 1786.

Both of these are loosely related as forms of 'reflective judgment,' a special form of judgment which seeks to discover universals for given particulars, that Kant contrasts to the type of judgment apparently employed in ordinary empirical knowledge, now called 'determinant judgment,' which seeks to discover particulars to which already given universals may be applied (see *CPJ*, Introduction IV, 5:179, and FI, V, 20:211). As a theory of such 'reflective judgment', it might seem as if the *Critique of Judgment* would be irrelevant to the theory of empirical knowledge of the *Critique of Pure Reason*. However, the assumptions that aesthetic and teleological judgment are the only forms of reflective judgment and that reflective and determinant judgment are always employed independently of each other, on which such a restrictive reading of the third *Critique* depends, are both false. Rather, since, as Kant now emphasizes, the categories are merely formal concepts which do not directly yield empirical concepts and which cannot be directly applied to empirical objects without empirical concepts, and since intermediate universals must be found which are not just given by the categories, reflective as well as determinant judgment must be employed in the discovery of any empirical knowledge.[4] The *Critique of Judgment* thus has fundamental implications for Kant's general theory of empirical knowledge as well as for the special subjects of aesthetics and teleology because there are really three rather than two forms of reflective judgment: reflective judgment about the forms of natural objects considered individually (aesthetic judgment), reflective judgment about relations of purposiveness among particular systems of natural objects (teleological judgments), and reflective judgment about the systematicity of our concepts of natural objects in general.[5] It is in his consideration of this third form of reflective judgment that Kant revises his earlier conception of our knowledge of empirical laws.

[4] I have examined the role of reflective judgment in ordinary empirical knowledge at greater length in 'Reason and Reflective Judgment: Kant on the Significance of Systematicity', *Nous*, 24 (1990): 17–43; Chapter 1 in this volume.

[5] The second and third forms of reflective judgment are clearly distinguished at FI, VI (20:217): 'That nature in its empirical laws so specifies itself, as is required for a possible experience, as a **system** of empirical knowledge, this form of nature contains a logical purposiveness, namely that of its harmony with the subjective conditions of the power of judgment in regard to the possible connection of empirical concepts in the whole of an experience. But this yields no implication of its aptness for generating a real purposiveness in its products, i.e. individual things in the form of systems: for these could always, as far as intuition is concerned, be mere aggregates and yet be possible according to empirical laws which are connected with others in a system of **logical division** ... ' Systematic unity of the *concepts* of objects does not imply that the objects concerned constitute a system serving any particular purpose.

Two related ideas underlie Kant's argument that reflective judgment about the regulative ideal of the systematicity of empirical laws is necessary to acquire knowledge of such laws at all. Neither of these thoughts is foreign to the *Critique of Pure Reason*, but they are more clearly stated in the *Critique of Judgment* and their implications more clearly recognized. The first of these, stressed in the introduction to the *Critique of Judgment* (which exists in two versions),[6] is that the categories of the faculty of understanding are merely 'universal concepts of nature' that lack all 'particular empirical determination' (FI, V, 20:212), or 'universal transcendental concepts of nature' that define the 'possibility of a nature (as an object of the senses) in general' but leave 'particular empirical laws' undetermined (*CPJ*, Introduction IV, 5:179–80). By these phrases Kant suggests, perhaps more clearly than in the first *Critique*, that the categories define only the general *concept* of law-governed objects of nature, but imply nothing about the determinate content of any particular laws of nature. 'The universal laws of nature', Kant states, 'certainly yield [a thoroughgoing] connection [of empirical cognition] among things generically, [i.e.] as things of nature in general, but not specifically, as such particular beings of nature (*Naturwesen*)' (*CPJ*, Introduction V, 5:183).

Kant's second assumption is employed throughout the introductions to the *Critique of Judgment*, but made explicit only halfway through its second part, the 'Critique of Teleological Judgment'. This is the claim that for a discursive intellect of the sort possessed by humans, where knowledge of existence is never furnished by concepts but always depends on the addition of intuitions to concepts, propositions about particulars can never be known to be other than contingently true. Claims that formal structures like those of pure intuition or the categories must be manifest in any objects that can be known by us can be treated as necessarily true, since they concern the only conditions under which representations can present objects at all;[7] but empirical laws,

[6] The first draft of the introduction, which Kant rejected on the stated ground that it was too long, was turned over to J. S. Beck for his *Erläuternder Auzug aus den kritischen Schriften des Herrn Prof. Kant* (3 vols., Riga, 1793–6). Beck published a condensed version. Subsequent nineteenth-century editions of Kant's works included those passages under the title *Über Philosophie überhaupt*. It was not published in its entirety until volume 5 of the Cassirer edition of Kant's works appeared in 1922; it is since always referred to as the 'First Introduction' to the *Critique of Judgment*. The version published with the text was written subsequently, perhaps after the completion of the text itself. It is usually referred to as the 'published introduction.'

[7] Even in this case considerable care is needed to characterize the type of necessity which Kant is actually entitled to assert; but we cannot enter into that issue here. For some discussion, see my *Kant and the Claims of Knowledge* (Cambridge: Cambridge University Press, 1987), chapter 16.

since they concern the properties and behavior of particular populations of objects in nature, cannot be more than contingently true.

Kant presents this premise in several steps. First, he associates the distinction between concepts and intuitions with that between possibility and actuality: he says that concepts 'go merely to the possibility of an object', and that actuality, that is, 'the positing of a thing in itself (outside [our] concept)', can be given only by sensible intuitions (*CPJ*, §76, 5:402). Concepts describe merely possible forms for particular objects; what forms actually exist can be evidenced only by sensible intuitions and can never be derived from concepts alone. But then this also means that assertions that particular forms exist in nature are contingent: if possibility is a feature only of claims about abstract or formal concepts, then so is necessity; and if such general conceptions do not determine what particular forms of objects exist, then there can be no assertions of necessary truth about the latter which go beyond the bare conditions of the possibility of experience. Thus: 'The particular as such contains something contingent in regard to the universal' (*CPJ*, §76, 5:404).

Kant makes it clear that this reasoning is to apply to our conception of particular *laws* of nature:

This contingency appears quite naturally in the **particular**, which the power of judgment is to bring under the **universal** of the concepts of understanding; for through the universal **of our** (human) understanding the particular is not determined; and it is contingent in how many different ways different things which yet agree in a general characteristic can be presented to our perception. Our understanding is a faculty of concepts, i.e. a discursive understanding, for which it must be contingent what and how different the particular that is given to it in nature and which can be brought under its concepts may be ... this contingency of the agreement of nature in its products according to **particular** laws ... makes it so difficult for our understanding to bring the manifold thereof to the unity of cognition; a business which [an understanding like] ours can only bring off through the harmony of natural characteristics with our own faculty of concepts, which is very contingent ... (*CPJ*, §77, 5:406)

The existence of any one set of empirical uniformities rather than another is, on a rigorous view of the limits of our cognitive capacities, ineluctably contingent. The abstract concepts of the understanding can only be brought down to the level of particularity by intuition, but intuition brings contingency along with it. This remains true even if we ascribe the task of finding empirical uniformities intermediate between the formal conditions of the possibility of experience and individual objects to the cognitive faculty of reflective judgment: the intermediate concepts delivered by this faculty, although of course universals rather than particulars at, so to speak, a merely grammatical level, still describe features of actual existence rather than conditions of the possibility of experience.

These premises constitute the background for Kant's argument about the role of systematicity in knowledge of empirical laws. Yet Kant also insists that this point of view on empirical uniformities must be reconciled with another, on which no empirical uniformity can be considered an empirical *law* unless we are in a position to ascribe *some* form of necessity, or something playing the role of necessity, to it. This point was not made in the first *Critique*. But it is not the only problem about empirical laws which Kant now raises.

Kant considers the reflective judgment of empirical laws in general, as opposed to reflective judgments in aesthetics and teleology, in sections IV and V of both introductions to the *Critique of Judgment*. Here he more clearly states the problems he is proposing to solve than the solutions he is proposing. Even so, he fails to mark the difference between several distinct problems. In fact, Kant seems to have had at least four different ideas in mind. First, and most closely related to his final view in the first *Critique*, he sometimes seems simply to assume that the systematic organization of empirical laws is an intrinsically desirable form of unity in experience, although distinct from and not presupposed by the unity of particular empirical intuitions in empirical synthesis. Second, Kant emphasizes that the proof that the categories are the necessary conditions of the possibility of experience does not itself guarantee that particular empirical laws instantiating the general concepts of nature can actually be found for any given empirical intuitions. Or he argues as if the categories might guarantee that there are objective uniformities in nature, but not that they are necessarily discoverable by us: there might be so many of them and they might be so infrequently manifested in our limited range of empirical intuition that we are not sufficiently often exposed to any to discover them. This would be a major revision of his doctrine in the Transcendental Deduction, where he seemed to assume that the unity of apperception ensures that laws of the appropriate specificity can be found for the empirical synthesis of any perceptions and does not itself require an independent guarantee that such laws can be found (see especially A 108). Third, Kant seems to recognize that not only a guarantee that empirical laws can be found but also a method for finding them in the face of the potentially enormous diversity of empirical intuitions must be added to the general concept of nature furnished by the categories. This revokes the first *Critique*'s position that even though empirical laws are not deducible from the categories, no other 'instruction' or 'norm' is needed to reach them. Now Kant's position is that the ideal of systematicity adds an *a priori* structure intermediate between the categories and empirical intuitions which must be employed if empirical laws are to be discovered. Finally, Kant makes the new point that, in spite of the logical contingency of particular uniformities among particular existences, if empirically observed uniformities are also to be regarded as *laws of nature* then something must be found which lends them at least an approximation of necessity. Here his idea seems to be that in conceiving of the objects of our experience as nature we cannot get by with the two types of necessity which are fairly clearly established in the *Critique of Pure Reason*, namely the necessity of the most general intuitional and conceptual forms of experience and the necessity of particular (objective) successions of states of affairs relative to some (in fact particular) laws of nature; the laws of nature themselves must, Kant supposes, also possess some kind of necessity, even though they are not deducible from the categories and therefore cannot be known *a priori* on the basis of the categories.

Although Kant does not make the distinctions among these problems explicit, they can all be recognized in his texts. In the first introduction, Kant emphasizes the need for a guarantee for the discoverability of empirical laws and hints at the need for a method for their discovery, but does not raise the problem of the quasi-necessity of particular empirical laws:

The principle of reflection on given objects of nature is: that for all things in nature empirically determinate **concepts** can be found, which is to say as much as that one can always presuppose in nature's products a form which is possible according to universal laws cognizable by us. For if we could not presuppose this and did not lay this principle at the base of our treatment of empirical representations, then all reflection would be undertaken haphazardly and blindly, thus without a grounded expectation of its agreement with nature.

In regard to the universal concepts of nature, under which in general a concept of experience (without particular empirical determination) is first possible, reflection already has its direction in the concept of nature in general, i.e. in the understanding, and the power of judgment requires no special principle of reflection ... But for those concepts, which are first to be found for given empirical intuitions, and which presuppose a particular law of nature, by which alone all **particular** experience is possible, the power of judgment requires a special, equally transcendental principle for its reflection ... For it must be asked how one could hope to attain to empirical concepts of that which is common to different natural forms through comparison of perceptions if (as it is yet possible to think), on account of the great diversity of their empirical laws, such a hetereogenity were found that all, or at least most comparison were useless for bringing forth uniformity and a hierarchical order of kinds and genera under them. All comparison of empirical representations, in order to discover empirical laws and **specific** forms in natural things which are to be cognized through their accord with these but also with other, **generically agreeing** laws, presupposes that in regard to its empirical laws nature has observed a certain economy appropriate to our power of judgment and a uniformity which is comprehensible by us, and this presupposition, as an *a priori* principle of the power of judgment, must precede all comparison. (FI, V, 20:212–13; for a similar statement see also FI, IV, 20:208–9)

Here Kant emphasizes that even if the pure laws of the understanding ensure the lawfulness of nature in general, it is an additional assumption that the number of empirical laws actually to be found in nature is sufficiently 'economical' to allow the likes of us actually to discover them. When he says at the outset that without such an assumption our reflection would be 'haphazard and blind', he also seems to hint that the entirely general concepts (categories) furnished by the understanding leave us without a method for discovery.

In the published introduction, Kant begins by stressing that the entirely general categories leave open an indeterminate variety of alternative systems of empirical laws, and then asks how the necessity of particular empirical laws may be established in the face of this variety. But Kant really compresses two questions into one: first, how may a *unique* set of empirical laws be selected from the alternatives; and second, on what basis (and in what sense) may this unique set be seen as *necessarily true*? Kant states his problems three times (*CPJ*, Introduction IV, 5:179–80; V, 5:182–3 and 184–5); here is the second of those statements:

In the grounds of the possibility of experience we find first, of course, something necessary, namely the universal laws, without which nature in general (as object of the senses) cannot be thought; and these rest on the categories, applied to the formal conditions of all intuition which is possible for us . . . E.g. understanding says: All alteration has its cause (universal law of nature) . . . But now in addition to this formal time-determination the objects of empirical cognition are determined in so many ways, or, so far as one can judge *a priori*, are determinable in so many ways, that specifically-distinct natures . . . can be causes in infinitely many ways; and each of these ways must (according to the concept of a cause in general) have its rule, which is a law, thus carries necessity with it: even though on account of the constitution and limits of our cognitive faculty we cannot have insight into this necessity. (*CPJ*, Introduction V, 5:182–3)

In his final statement, Kant says that it is the concept of nature rather than that of causation which creates the need for necessity:

These rules, without which there would be no progress from the general analogy of a possible experience to a particular condition, [understanding] must think as laws (i.e. as necessary), since they would otherwise not constitute an order of nature, although it does not cognize their necessity or ever have insight into it. So although it can determine nothing *a priori* in regard to these (objects), it must yet, in order to pursue these empirical so-called laws, have an *a priori* principle, that, namely, according to them a cognizable order of nature is possible ... (*CPJ*, Introduction V, 5:184–5)

Kant's wonderful phrase 'empirical so-called laws' (*empirischen sogen-annten Gesetzen*) can be taken to symbolize the complexity of the conception of empirical law he is trying to develop. No particular natural uniformities are themselves conditions of the possibility of experience, and thus necessarily true of objects in the sense in which the latter are; yet it is a necessary condition of the possibility of experience that we find *some* particular set of determinate empirical laws for the perceptions we actually encounter. Further, to do justice to the idea that these are *laws* we must also find a way of seeing them as necessities which determine the course of nature and not just accidental patterns emerging from nature.

Although unduly condensed, Kant's statements of the problems in knowledge of empirical laws are clear and uncomplicated. His suggestions about the solution to these problems are neither. Kant suggests that they can all be resolved by the single 'subjectively necessary transcendental *presupposition*' that 'this worrisome boundless diversity of empirical laws and heterogeneity of natural forms does not pertain to nature, rather that it, through the affinity of particular laws under more general ones, qualifies as an experience as an empirical system' (FI, IV, 20:209). But behind this general claim Kant seems to have at least three different ideas. First, although a 'subjectively necessary transcendental presupposition' that, even though it affords a boundless field of empirical intuition which can never be numerically exhausted,[8] nature is amenable to a set of empirical laws which is manageable by subjects with intellectual limits like ours is not, in the end, a guarantee that we can impose such a limit on it in the same way in which we can impose conformity to the more general categories or forms of intuitions, still it is a reasonable assumption for us to make on behalf of the use of our power of judgment. We must thus suppose that the order of nature is sufficiently economical for us to grasp if it is to be reasonable for us to continue our efforts at investigating it. Further, in order to preserve the idea that order is always

---

[8] This of course we know from the infinite extension of space and time as forms of intuition.

a product of intellectual activity, we can think of this as if an intellect more powerful than our own, thus not confined to producing only abstract rules as ours is, imposed a determinate order on nature for our convenience (see *CPJ*, Introduction IV, 5:180).

Second, attempting to discover empirical laws not yet known by procedures exploiting the possibilities of ascent and descent from ones that are known which are afforded by a hierarchical system of classification is a reasonable method for searching for laws in the diversity of empirical intuition. The use of the logical hierarchy of species and genus in the pursuit of empirical laws may not furnish us with a decision-procedure for confirming or rejecting empirical hypotheses, but it is better than blindly groping about, attempting to perform Baconian induction without any means of antecedently generating reasonable hypotheses. Filling in the structure of a system will give us a reasonable way of formulating empirical hypotheses.

Third, the inclusion of an empirical hypothesis at a determinate position in a hierarchical system of concepts or laws cannot make it deducible directly from the categories, and thus cognizable strictly *a priori* and genuinely necessary, but it has some explanatory value and can lend the hypothesis at least an approximation of necessity. Of course inclusion in a system cannot make any particular uniformity absolutely necessary because the system as a whole may be only contingently true relative to possible alternative systems; but a uniformity which is part of a system will not appear completely accidental either.

The first introduction, which stressed the problem of underdetermination to the exclusion of the problem of the quasi-necessity of empirical laws, correspondingly stresses the issue of economy in its solution:

All comparison of empirical representations in order to cognize empirical laws and **specific** natural forms which accord with these . . . yet presupposes that in regard to its empirical laws nature has observed a certain economy appropriate to our power of judgment and a uniformity which is comprehensible by us, and this presupposition, as a principle of the power of judgment, must precede all comparison. (FI, V, 20:213; see also IV, 20:209)

This text makes only a passing suggestion that the ideal of systematicity offers some methodology for the discovery of empirical laws as well: without the presupposition of systematicity, Kant writes, 'we could not hope to find our way about in a labyrinth of the multiplicity of possible particular laws' (FI, V, 20:214).

Kant's statement of his solution in the published introduction touches on more issues. Here Kant suggests, although certainly not with adequate detail, that we must presuppose that nature is systematic in order to have a reasonable expectation of finding empirical laws, in order to have anything thing like a method for finding them, and in order to create any semblance that particular laws of nature are necessarily true. All of these points are hinted at in the continuation of the last passage cited from the published introduction:

in order to pursue these empirical so-called laws, [the understanding] must lay an *a priori* principle at the base of its reflection, namely that a cognizable order of nature is possible according to them, a principle of the sort which is expressed by the following propositions: that there is in [nature] a subordination of genera and species which is comprehensible by us; that each of these approaches the others according to a common principle, so that a transition from one to another and thereby to a higher genus is possible; that, although it initially seems unavoidable for our understanding to assume that there are as many different kinds of causality as there are specific differences of natural effects, these may nevertheless stand under a smaller number of principles, with the discovery of which we have to occupy ourselves, and so on. This agreement of nature with our faculty of cognition is presupposed *a priori* by the power of judgment in behalf of its reflection on nature according to empirical laws, while the understanding simultaneously acknowledges it as contingent... since if we did not presuppose it we would not have any order of nature according to empirical laws, thus no clue for an experience to be ordered in these in all of their manifoldness and for the investigation of them.

For it may easily be thought, that in spite of all the uniformity of natural things according to the universal laws, without which the form of experiential cognition could not even take place, the specific difference of the empirical laws of nature and their effects could nevertheless be so great, that it would be impossible for our understanding to discover a comprehensible order in them, to divide [them] into genera and species, and to use the principles of the explanation and comprehension of one for the explanation and conception of another as well...
(*CPJ*, Introduction V, 5:185)

In the course of this passage, Kant emphasizes that in spite of the acknowledged contingency of empirical laws we must presuppose that their variety is not in fact too great for us to grasp, and that we must presuppose that we will find systematic organization among these laws in order both to find a 'clue' for their discovery and also to construct explanatory relationships among them. These explanatory relationships, in turn, seem to be what is intended to give us some sense of the necessary truth of particular empirical laws at least relative to the system to which they belong. Having its position determined by its logical relationship to laws at other levels of a system of empirical laws, by which Kant evidently means a system in which causal or explanatory laws are subsumed under one another as well as classificatory concepts being ordered into genera and species,[9] is as close as an empirical law can come to necessity.

If the postulation of systematicity is indispensable for the status as well as discovery of empirical laws, however, then our knowledge of such laws is subject to major constraints—precisely those associated with the idea of a regulative principle. Kant suggests two such constraints in the introductions to the third *Critique*. The first is the constraint of indeterminacy. By this I do not mean underdetermination, i.e. that a choice between alternative systems is always obviously available. This is in fact a logical possibility, but if it were always to be thought of as a real epistemic possibility than no headway would have been made on the issue of the infinite multiplicity of empirical laws at all; Kant must be assuming that at any time only one systematization of empirical laws is likely to present itself very forcefully. Rather, the point is that there can be nothing which counts as a *complete* systematization of laws: a system can always be carried further, and there is no telling how far it may have to be carried to find the empirical law for some particular observation. As Kant puts it, judgment posits systematicity as the 'technic of nature' 'without being able to explain it nor determine it more precisely' (FI, V, 20:214). The ideal of systematicity is quantitatively indeterminate, as indeed follows from the requirement of continuity and as Kant had already stated in the first *Critique* (see especially A 663/B 691 and A 668/B 696).

Second, the idea of systematicity must be brought to our actual perceptions rather than simply discovered in them, and is in that sense *a priori*. But it cannot simply be imposed on them regardless of their empirical content; we are dependent upon nature itself to satisfy our search for systematicity. Kant's position on this is delicate. On the one hand, he clearly states that the principle of the systematicity of nature is a transcendental principle in the sense that compliance with it is in fact a necessary condition of the possibility of the experience of external objects under empirical law. As he says, 'A transcendental principle is one through which the universal condition under which alone things can become objects of our cognition in general is represented *a priori* ... the principle of the finality of nature (in the multiplicity of its empirical laws) is a transcendental principle' (*CPJ*, Introduction V, 5:181). On the other hand, however, Kant does recognize that although we must approach the observation of nature with intellectual norms and expectations add-

---

[9] This was in fact already evident in the *Critique of Pure Reason*, where Kant spoke of *powers* before he even introduced his characterization of a hierarchical system of (classificatory) *concepts*.

itional to the categories we cannot really guarantee that nature will satisfy our search for empirical laws by these means: the idea of systematicity must be brought to nature *a priori* but cannot be imposed upon it. The principle of reflective judgment, Kant says, cannot be 'borrowed' from experience because it must 'ground' the 'systematic subordination' of empirical laws. He then continues:

The reflective power of judgment must give such a transcendental principle as a law only to itself, and must not derive it from elsewhere (for then it would be determinant judgment) nor prescribe it to nature; since reflection on the laws of nature must be directed by nature and not nature by the conditions according to which we attempt to acquire this entirely contingent concept of it. (*CPJ*, Introduction V, 5:180)

The adjudication between rationalism and empiricism, then, must not take place simply at the level of the general distinction between form and matter in experience, and systematicity is not just an extra ornament that reason hopes to find in empirical laws which are just handed to it by the understanding. Rather, Kant recognizes that all knowledge of particular empirical law depends on both an *a priori* but indeterminate and regulative conception of systematicity and actual empirical input. Knowledge of empirical law is not simply a matter of filling in the schemata provided by the categories with the details offered by empirical intuition, but of projecting[10] the idea of systematicity upon such data and attempting thereby to move from known to new laws—an open-ended process which can never lead to completely determinate results, but without which we have neither a method for coping with the boundless multiplicity of empirical observation nor any basis for even a qualified satisfaction of the demand for necessity in empirical laws.

---

[10] This term is borrowed from Philip Kitcher's 'Projecting the Order of Nature', in Robert Butts, editor, *Kant's Philosophy of Physical Science* (Dordrecht and Boston: D. Reidel Publishing Co., 1986), pp. 210–35. I found this the most useful study of Kant's conception of the methodology of empirical systematicity, although I do not think that Kitcher appreciates the difference between Kant's supposition that systematicity is just an independent goal of reason in the first *Critique* and his several grounds for suggesting that it is an indispensable condition of knowledge of empirical law itself in the third.

# 3

# Kant on the Systematicity of Nature: Two Puzzles

In the two introductions to the *Critique of the Power of Judgment*,[1] Kant treats the establishment of a system of logical hierarchy among our concepts of objects in and laws of nature as the first goal of the reflecting use of the power of judgment. A number of scholars have looked to Kant's treatment of systematicity in the third *Critique* as his answer to Hume's problem about the rationality of induction, which does not seem to be addressed in Kant's treatment of causation in the second "Analogy of Experience" in the first *Critique*.[2] Others have argued that the conception of reflecting judgment introduced in the discussion of systematicity is the key to Kant's subsequent treatments of both aesthetic and teleological judgment and their interconnection, thus the key to the unity of the third *Critique*.[3] More generally, Kant's theory of the regulative principles of reflecting judgment might seem to offer a model for the

This chapter originally appeared in the *History of Philosophy Quarterly*, 20 (2003), 277–95, and is reprinted here with the permission of North American Philosophical Publications, Inc.

[1] All citations to the *Critique of the Power of Judgment* will be to Immanuel Kant, *Critique of the Power of Judgment*, edited by Paul Guyer, translated by Paul Guyer and Eric Matthews (Cambridge: Cambridge University Press, 2000). This edition contains both versions of the introduction, and explains the relation between the two introductions at pp. xlii–xliii. Citations will be located with the abbreviations FI (First Introduction) or *CPJ* (the published text), section number, and volume and page numbers from the so-called Akademie edition of Kant's works, *Kant's gesammelte Schriften*, edited by the Royal Prussian (later German and Berlin–Brandenburg) Academy of Sciences (Berlin: Georg Reimer, subsequently Walter de Gruyter & Co., 1900– ). The pagination of this edition is reproduced in the margins of the Cambridge edition.

[2] For example, Philip Kitcher, "Projecting the Order of Nature," in *Kant's Philosophy of Physical Science*, ed. Robert E. Butts (Dordrecht: Reidel, 1986), pp. 201–35, reprinted in *Kant's Critique of Pure Reason: Critical Essays*, ed. Patricia Kitcher (Lanham, Md.: Rowman & Littlefield, 1998), pp. 219–38; and Juliet Floyd, "Heautonomy: Kant on Reflective Judgment and Systematicity," in *Kants Ästhetik—Kant's Aesthetics—L'Esthétique de Kant*, ed. Herman Parret (Berlin and New York: Walter de Gruyter, 1998), pp. 192–218.

[3] Most recently, Henry Allison, *Kant's Theory of Taste: A Reading of the Critique of Aesthetic Judgment* (Cambridge: Cambridge University Press, 2001), chaps. 1 and 2.

treatment of such theoretical desiderata as simplicity, parsimony, and systematicity that has troubled modern philosophy of science for decades.[4] But Kant's treatment of systematicity is both brief and obscure, and it is far from clear how it bears on issues of continuing interest such as the problem of induction and the structure of scientific theories as well as how it is connected to Kant's own theory of aesthetic judgment. Here are two particular puzzles about Kant's theory of systematicity.

First, although Kant is insistent that the principle of scientific systematicity is only regulative rather than constitutive, unlike the universal principle of causation to which all objects of experience are necessarily subject—thereby threatening the idea that systematicity could contain the answer to a problem about the induction of causal laws—he also insists that this principle is not merely a logical principle, that is, a principle prescribing the search for a certain sort of organization among our concepts, but also a transcendental principle, that is, a principle that has the semantic form of an assertion about the objects of nature themselves, although presumably an assertion that must be weaker in epistemic force than some other such assertions. In his first characterization of a possible principle for the faculty of judgment in the "First Introduction," he writes:

Yet the power of judgment is such a special faculty of cognition, not at all self-sufficient, that it provides neither concepts, like the understanding, nor ideas, like reason, of any objects at all, since it is a faculty merely for subsuming under concepts given from elsewhere. Thus if there is to be a concept or a rule which arises originally from the power of judgment, it would have to be a concept of **things in nature insofar as nature conforms to our power of judgment,** and thus a concept of a property of nature such that one cannot form any concept of it except that its arrangement conforms to our faculty for subsuming the particular given laws of nature under more general ones even though these are not given; in other words, it would have to be the concept of a purposiveness of nature. (FI, II, 20:202)

And a few sections later, after he has made the distinction between "determining" judgment, which seeks to determine an underlying concept by means of a given empirical representation, and "reflecting" judgment, which, given such an empirical representation, seeks to make a concept for it possible, he states that "The principle of reflection on given objects of nature is that for all things in nature empirically

---

[4] For example, see Margaret Morrison, *Unifying Scientific Theories: Physical Concepts and Mathematical Structures* (Cambridge: Cambridge University Press, 2000), at pp. 12–16.

determinate **concepts** can be found" (FI, V, 20:211). He then argues that although "On first glance, this principle does not look at all like a synthetic and transcendental proposition, but rather seems to be tauto-logical and to belong to mere logic," nevertheless

the (reflecting) power of judgment, which also seeks concepts for empirical representations, as such, must further assume for this purpose that nature in its boundless multiplicity has hit upon a division of itself into genera and species that makes it possible for our power of judgment to find consensus in the comparison of natural forms and to arrive at empirical concepts,

and that this means that "the power of judgment presupposes a system of nature which is also in accordance with empirical laws...*a priori*, consequently by means of a transcendental principle" (FI, V, 20:211–12 n.). These remarks suggest that Kant intends the principle of systema-ticity to be understood as more than merely heuristic, more than some-thing that guides the conduct of our own inquiry without really asserting anything about its objects. But they also naturally raise the question, why must the search for the logical goal of systematic organization among our concepts presuppose the transcendental principle that nature itself is actually systematic? If this goal is sufficiently important for us, would we need some sort of promise that it can be attained in order to make our pursuit of it rational? Wouldn't our pursuit of this goal be rational as long as we possessed and believed that we could possess *no* compelling evidence that the realization of it is *impossible*?[5]

The second puzzle about Kant's treatment of systematicity concerns the connection between systematicity and pleasure that presumably ought to obtain given the centrality of pleasure in Kant's theory of aesthetic judgment. Kant begins both versions of the introduction to the third *Critique* by suggesting that there may be a special connection between the faculty of judgment, as one of the three higher faculties of cognition, and the faculty for the feeling of pleasure and displeasure, as one of the three more general faculties of the human mind, alongside the faculties of cognition and desire; in particular, he suggests that the faculty of judgment may provide the *a priori* principle for the faculty of pleasure and displeasure (FI, III, 20:207–8; *CPJ*, Introduction III, 5:177). Yet at least in the First Introduction, he also suggests that it is only *aesthetic*

---

[5]  Most writers on Kant's conception of systematicity take for granted his assumption that it is rational to pursue logical systematicity only if we have assurance that nature itself is systematic. See, for example, Margaret Morrison, "Methodological Rules in Kant's Philosophy of Science," *Kant-Studien*, 80 (1989), pp. 155–72, at pp. 157 and 159; and Fred L. Rush, Jr., "Reason and Regulation in Kant," *Review of Metaphysics*, 53 (2000), pp. 837–62, at p. 842.

judgment, particularly the judgment of beauty, that reveals a special connection between the faculty of judgment and the faculty for feeling pleasure and displeasure (see FI, XI, 20:244), and he says nothing about any connection between the discovery of systematicity among our empirical concepts of nature and the feeling of pleasure and displeasure. Moreover, there would seem to be an obvious conflict between the presupposition of the systematicity of nature itself and Kant's explanation of our pleasure in beauty: for while the former seems to postulate the *necessity* of our success in the pursuit of systematicity, it seems to be central to Kant's explanation of our pleasure in a beautiful object that it strike us as *contingent*. Kant stresses that beauty must strike us as *unintended*; indeed, in his initial exposition of his explanation of the experience of beauty in the published Introduction, Kant suggests that both the search for beauty and the existence of beauty are unintentional. The "apprehension of forms in the imagination can never take place without the reflecting power of judgment, even if unintentionally, comparing them to its faculty for relating intuitions to concepts," and it is only "if in this comparison the imagination . . . is unintentionally brought into accord with the understanding . . . through a given representation and a feeling of pleasure is thereby aroused [that] the object must be regarded as purposive for the reflecting power of judgment" (*CPJ*, Introduction VII, 5:190). Indeed, even in the case of beautiful products of fine art, which are incontrovertibly products of human intention, Kant stresses that their beauty must still *seem* unintentional: "In a product of art one must be aware that it is art, and not nature, yet the purposiveness of its form must still seem to be as free from all constraint by arbitrary rules as if it were a mere product of nature" (*CPJ*, 45, 5:306). But then what connection could there be between a general principle of reflecting judgment that seems to guarantee success in our exercise of judgment and an explanation of a paradigmatic case of reflecting judgment, namely aesthetic judgment, which stresses that beauty must strike us as unintended, unexpected, in a word, contingent?

I have previously raised both of these questions about Kant's treatment of systematicity and his connection of judgments of systematicity and aesthetic judgments as two forms of reflecting judgment.[6] I now want to argue that careful attention to the *published* Introduction to the third *Critique*, the very last piece of the text that Kant wrote as his publisher was rushing to complete the production of the book, shows that Kant

---

[6] See *Kant and the Claims of Taste* (second edition, Cambridge: Cambridge University Press, 1997), pp. 43–4 and pp. 73–4.

must have been sensitive to these problems too, for there he offers solutions to both of them. First, he offers a new account of the role of the presupposition of systematicity in the acquisition of empirical concepts, holding not that the assumption that nature itself is systematic plays just a motivational or heuristic role in the search for a system of concepts, which would be rational in the mere absence of evidence for the non-systematicity of nature, but that it is essential for our conception of the *necessity* of empirical laws; and since we possess particular empirical laws prior to possessing a complete system of them, the only way we can ground our sense of the necessity of those laws is by positing that they reflect the existence of systematicity in nature itself. If the necessity of laws of nature implies their truth at all times,[7] then this new conception of the role of the assumption of systematicity might be indeed be a step toward a solution of the problem of induction. At the same time, Kant also makes it clear that although this postulation of the systematicity of nature has the transcendental form of a proposition about nature itself, we also at least tacitly recognize that its epistemic status is regulative rather than constitutive, thus that nature's compliance with it is ultimately contingent, and therefore that we are indeed pleased to discover in actual systematicity nature's unintended compliance with our own cognitive needs. There is thus in the end no conflict between the transcendental principle of reflective judgment and the explanation of our experience of beauty, because our pleasure is an index of our recognition of contingency in both cases. This result, however, casts doubt on the assumption that Kant's treatment of systematicity can provide a conclusive answer to Hume's doubts about induction: if our pleasure in beauty is an index of our recognition that nature contingently favors us with beauty but is not compelled to provide it, then our pleasure in the discovery of systematicity among our concepts of nature may also express our recognition that nature favors us with such regularity but cannot be regarded as compelled to provide it.

## I. THE NECESSITY OF SYSTEMATICITY?

In the *Critique of Pure Reason*, Kant characterizes reason as the faculty that searches for completeness in various sorts of chains of things conditioned and their conditions, and subjects its pretension to find such completeness with its own resources alone to coruscating criticism. But

---

[7] See *Critique of Pure Reason*, A 145/B 184.

then Kant allows a chastened faculty of reason two legitimate roles: in the Appendix to the Transcendental Dialectic, once the futility of its attempts to operate on its own have been diagnosed, reason is allowed to add the ideal of systematicity to the theoretical cognition produced by the understanding, while in the "Canon of Pure Reason" of the Doctrine of Method Kant launches his campaign to show that pure *practical* reason is by itself the source of the fundamental principle of morality and the ideal of a "moral world" (A 809/B 837). Since the argument of the Transcendental Dialectic has been that reason goes astray when it attempts to operate without the materials furnished by sensibility and beyond the boundaries of that faculty, it is only natural that in the Appendix Kant should present the legitimate theoretical use of reason as occurring only in the application of the ideal of systematicity to empirical concepts grounded in the senses and organized by the understanding. Thus, while there are two passages that suggest without explanation that reason and its ideal of systematicity are somehow directly involved in the generation of empirical concepts and cognition (A 651/B 679 and A 654/B 682), Kant's overwhelming tendency in the Appendix is to present the goal of hierarchical systematicity, defined in terms of the homogeneity, specificity, and affinity of empirical concepts or forms (A 657–8/B 685–6) as a desideratum of the faculty of reason itself, something that this faculty seeks to impose on the empirical concepts generated by the understanding from the raw material of sensibility for its own behalf. This passage can stand for many:

Reason never relates directly to an object, but solely to the understanding and by means of it to reason's own empirical use, hence it does not **create** any concepts (of objects) but only **orders** them and gives them that unity which they can have in their greatest possible extension, i.e., in relation to the totality of series.... Thus reason really has as object only the understanding and its purposive application. (A 643–4/B 671–2)

Kant apparently means that the understanding needs to find concepts that can apply across extensions of objects, and is capable of doing so on its own, and that it is only the faculty of reason that is interested in uniting the concepts found by the understanding into a logical system that seeks to minimize the number of higher-order explanatory and classificatory concepts (homogeneity), to maximize the number of lower-order explanatory and classificatory concepts (specificity), and to find a maximally (although never completely) dense series of concepts between the highest- and the lowest-order concepts that we find (affinity).

While Kant treats the ideal of systematicity as an interest of the faculty of reason that is apparently not necessary for understanding to find a mere aggregate of empirical concepts suitable for its own purposes,[8] and thus as a regulative ideal rather than a constitutive principle of theoretical cognition (A 647/B 675), and while he suggests that on that account we might initially be tempted to suppose that the ideal of the "systematic unity or the unity of reason of the understanding's cognition is a **logical** principle" but not "a **transcendental** principle of reason" (A 648/B 676), he quickly corrects any such impression. "In fact it cannot even be seen how there could be a logical principle of rational unity among rules unless a transcendental principle is presupposed, through which such a systematic unity, as pertaining to the object itself, is assumed *a priori* as necessary" (A 650–1/B 679–80). That is, he supposes, in order rationally to seek for systematicity among our concepts of nature, we have to assume that nature itself is systematic, for if we did not suppose this, he argues, "then reason would proceed directly contrary to its vocation, since it would set as its goal an idea that entirely contradicts the arrangement of nature" (A 651/B 679). Kant then argues in the second half of the Appendix that as a transcendental even if only regulative principle, the principle of the systematicity of nature requires a transcendental deduction, although this cannot not have the same form as the transcendental deduction of constitutive principles such as (those derived from) the pure concepts of the understanding (A 669–70/B 697–8). I will not pause to worry about the persuasiveness of such a proposed deducation, but will comment only that in the first *Critique* Kant had already formulated the idea that the principle of systematicity could be transcendental rather than merely logical, that is, have the semantic form of being about nature itself rather than merely about our concepts of nature, while at the same time being merely regulative rather than constitutive in epistemic force.

In the *Critique of the Power of Judgment*, Kant reassigns the search for systematicity from the faculty of reason to the newly introduced

---

[8] Henry Allison argues that any empirical concept, such as the concept of gold, is necessarily part of a system of concepts, because it subsumes a multiplicity of instances beneath it, for example "different types of gold," and because its constituent predicates, such as being yellow, a metal, malleable, and so on, are themselves more general than gold; see *Kant's Theory of Taste*, pp. 33–4. But it does not follow from this that the instances that the concept subsumes are themselves necessarily divisible into intermediate species of any kind, as Kant requires, nor is it immediately obvious that any group of classificatory concepts must comprise a system of genera and species of kinds of substances, as Kant also requires. And it is hardly obvious that even if any class-concept must be part of *some* system of genera- and species-concepts, then *all* of our class-concepts are part of *one* hierarchical system.

reflecting use of the faculty of judgment. Kant holds that it is reflecting judgment that searches for concepts which are not immediately given for empirical intuitions that are—we already encountered Kant's definition of reflecting judgment in the first draft of the Introduction, and in the published version he writes "If, however, only the particular is given, for which the universal is to be found, then the power of judgment is merely **reflecting**" (*CPJ*, Introduction IV, 5:179). He now maintains that the categories and the most general laws of nature associated with them, such as the category of causation and the general principle that every event has a cause, are, to be sure, immediately given, but cannot themselves be directly applied to empirical intuitions: they give the necessary forms for empirical concepts, but do not by themselves yield empirical concepts, even when given the data of empirical intuition by sensibility. As Kant puts it,

The understanding is of course in possession *a priori* of universal laws of nature, without which nature could not be an object of experience at all; but still it requires in addition a certain order of nature in its particular rules, which can only be known to it empirically... without which there would be no progress from the general analogy of a possible experience in general to the particular. (*CPJ*, Introduction V, 5:184)

Thus, if the ideal of systematicity is the ideal of the reflecting use of judgment, and reflecting judgment is necessary to discover the empirical concepts that are the medium through which alone the merely "universal laws of nature" furnished by the understanding and its categories can be applied to empirical intuition, then the use of the principle of systematicity will be necessary not merely to satisfy reason's own interest in systematicity or "collective unity," but even to accomplish understanding's goal of discovering any concepts at all for empirical intuitions, or "distributive unity."

The reassignment of the principle of systematicity from reason to reflecting judgment thus represents a major revision in Kant's theory of empirical knowledge, which may have ramifications for some of his most fundamental claims.[9] Here I will only raise two questions: Why is the ideal of systematic unity among our empirical concepts necessary for the discovery of any empirical concepts at all, and why should the ideal of

---

[9] I have touched upon some of the larger issues involved in two earlier papers, "Reason and Reflective Judgment: Kant on the Significance of Systematicity," *Nous*, 24 (1990), pp. 17–43, especially p. 43; and "Kant's Conception of Empirical Law," *Proceedings of the Aristotelian Society*, suppl. vol. 64 (1990), pp. 221–42, especially 241–2; reprinted as Chapters 1 and 2 of this volume.

systematicity be conceived of as a transcendental and not merely a logical principle?

Although Kant is as insistent in the first draft of the Introduction to the third *Critique* as he was in the first *Critique* that the principle of systematicity is transcendental and not merely logical (see FI, V, 20:214), the account of the role of this principle in the discovery of empirical concepts that he offers there does not make it clear why we must posit a transcendental principle of systematicity. Basically, Kant makes two points. First, he suggests that the necessary accordance of "experience in general" with the "transcendental laws of the understanding," which is enough to assure us that some concept and law or other must in principle exist for any empirical intuition we encounter, is not itself enough to assure us that we can actually *find* a law for any empirical intuition: the number of these laws might be so great, and instances of them so infrequent, that we could not actually discover the laws for many phenomena even given a general assurance that they exist. To counter this unpleasant possibility, it seems, we must posit that there is in fact a system of laws (FI, IV, 20:209). Second, Kant seems to think that the assumption that particular laws of nature are part of a system of laws will give us a heuristic or research strategy for the discovery of laws, preventing "all reflection" from becoming "arbitrary and blind" (FI, V, 20:212). The assumption of systematicity allows us to proceed "artistically," or suggests a method to "find our way in a labyrinth of the multiplicity of possible empirical particular laws" (FI, V, 20:214). Kant offers no illustration of what he has in mind, so we can only conjecture that he thinks that the project of organizing our empirical laws of nature into a system will give us a way to proceed in formulating and testing hypotheses: when attempting to find laws for some new set of data, we should first try one that fits best into the system of laws that we already know; if that doesn't seem to work, formulate and test another one that might fit into our system with only a little tinkering, and so on.

There are, however, problems with each of these suggestions. First, if our problem is just that the sheer number of possible laws of nature may be overwhelming, it would seem that we could maintain our motivation in searching for laws simply by assuming that the number of laws of nature is *small* enough for us to manage; why should we have to assume that they are internally *organized* in any systematic way? Second, even if the assumption that the laws of nature are internally organized in a particular way has heuristic value, giving us a procedure to follow in the formulation and testing of hypotheses, why should we have to assume the transcendental principle that nature itself *is* systematic in order to adopt the logical principle of systematicity as a heuristic? Given the value of the heuristic, it would seem rational to employ it as far as we can as long as we have no conclusive evidence that nature is *not* systematic. (And it is in any case hard to imagine what could count as such evidence.) So even when the first Introduction does suggest why we should not merely assume that the laws of nature are manageable in number but also seek for systematicity among them, it does not seem to explain why we need the transcendental principle that nature itself is systematic, that "nature in its boundless multiplicity has hit upon a division of itself into genera and species that makes it possible for our power of judgment to find consensus in the comparison of natural forms" (FI, 20:212 n).

In the published Introduction, however, Kant provides a different account of the necessity of positing systematicity, which does suggest why the principle of systematicity must be transcendental and not merely logical. Here Kant suggests that the problem concerning empirical laws of nature is not merely that the general laws of nature furnished by the categories are compatible with an indeterminate number of empirical instantiations, but rather that in this circumstance no particular empirical generalization by itself can appear to us as truly *lawlike* or *necessarily true*.[10] Yet an empirical generalization must in some sense appear to be necessary in order to count as a law of nature. Thus Kant writes in section IV:

But there is such a manifold of forms in nature, as it were so many modifications of the universal transcendental concepts of nature that are left undetermined by those laws that the pure understanding gives *a priori*, since these pertain only to the possibility of a nature (as object of the senses) in general, that there must nevertheless also be laws for it which, as empirical, may seem to be contingent in accordance with the insight of **our** understanding, but which, if they are to be called laws (as is also required by the concept of a nature), must be regarded as necessary on a principle of the unity of the manifold, even if that principle is unknown to us. (*CPJ*, Introduction IV, 5:179–80)

And in the next section Kant makes similar remarks (see *CPJ*, Introduction V, 5:183–4). He does not explain why we must be able to regard individual causal laws as in any sense necessarily true; he only hints that

---

[10] Rush ("Reason and Regulation," p. 845) suggests that this idea is already present in the *first* Introduction, at 20:203 and 208–11. However, I think that a careful reading of those pages shows that Kant is there concerned only with the "lawlike interconnection" of empirical generalizations, or with the necessity *of a system* of them (20:203). He does not yet suggest that a system of empirical laws is necessary precisely in order to confer necessity upon the *individual* laws that comprise such a system.

we need particular laws that can be regarded as necessary in order to pass from "the general analogy of a possible experience" to a "particular" one (5:183). But if we take this to be an allusion to the second "Analogy of Experience" in the first *Critique*, then a certain picture suggests itself. In the second Analogy, causal laws are held to be necessary in order to distinguish representations of objective successions of events from merely subjective successions of representations (e.g., A 189/B 234, A 193/B 238). Kant's idea seems to be that while a succession of representations alone does not prove that there is any change going on in the objective world, the derivation of a series of events from relevant causal laws and of the succession of representations from the succession of events so derived would.[11] Now Kant's position in the second Analogy has sometimes been understood only to attribute to individual objective sequences of events the necessity of the consequent, that is, the necessity of such a sequence occurring relative to some generalization which is not itself regarded as necessarily true, while treating particular causal laws as empirical and contingent.[12] But at least in the third *Critique* Kant's position seems to be that if particular causal laws themselves are to play the role assigned to them in the "Analogies of Experience" and more generally in the "Postulates of Empirical Thinking in General" in the *Critique of Pure Reason*—that of grounding assertions of the objectivity of successions of events beyond our own representations (second Analogy) and more generally of grounding the empirical application of the modal concept of necessity (third Postulate)[13]—then they must themselves be able to be regarded as necessarily true. But how can they be so regarded? They cannot be deduced directly from the transcendental and universal law of causation, because multiple but apparently alternative causal laws are compatible with the general form of that principle. And presumably, although Kant does not explicitly assert this, for any finite number of empirical observations we could also formulate some number

---

[11] For this interpretation, see my *Kant and the Claims of Knowledge* (Cambridge: Cambridge University Press, 1987), chapter 10, or my "Kant's Second Analogy: Objects, Events and Causal Laws," in *Kant's Critique of Pure Reason: Critical Essays*, ed. Patricia Kitcher, pp. 117–43.

[12] See, for example, H. J. Paton, *Kant's Metaphysic of Experience* (London: George Allen & Unwin, 1936), vol. 2, p. 275. For further references to this traditional interpretation, see Rush, "Reason and Regulation," p. 846 n. 21. Rush endorses the traditional interpretation.

[13] For a discussion of Kant's empirical interpretation of the concept of necessity in terms of causal connection in the third Postulate, see my article "The Postulates of Empirical Thinking in General and the Refutation of Idealism," in *Immanuel Kant: Kritik der reinen Vernunft*, ed. Georg Mohr and Marcus Willaschek (Berlin: Akademie Verlag, 1998), pp. 297–324.

of alternative causal generalizations, so our empirical data will not force one particular causal law on us any more than the universal law of causation will. In these circumstances, then, when a particular causal law will not appear to be *necessitated* either by the universal law of causation or by our empirical data, what can make it appear necessary?

Kant's answer to this question is that particular causal laws will appear to be necessary only if embedded in a system of such laws. Thus he writes:

Thus we must think of there being in nature, with regard to its merely empirical laws, a possibility of infinitely manifold empirical laws, which as far as our insight goes are nevertheless contingent (cannot be cognized *a priori*); and with regard to them we judge the unity of nature in accordance with empirical laws and the possibility of the unity of experience (as a system in accordance with empirical laws) as contingent. But since such a unity must still necessarily be presupposed and assumed, for otherwise no thoroughgoing interconnection of empirical cognitions into a whole of experience would take place, because the universal laws of nature yield such an interconnection among things with respect to their genera, as things of nature in general, but not specifically, as such and such particular beings in nature, the power of judgment must thus assume it as an *a priori* principle for its own use that what is contingent for human insight in the particular (empirical) laws nevertheless contains a lawful unity, not fathomable by us but still thinkable, in the combination of its manifold into one experience possible in itself. (*CPJ*, Introduction V, 5:183–4)

Kant's idea is that particular empirical generalizations will only seem lawlike or necessarily true if they are represented as part of a system of such generalizations. (He also supposes that since necessity is always the product of a mind's imposition of order on a manifold of data, then such a system of necessary laws must also be conceived of as a product of a mind, even if not of our own mind (*CPJ*, Introduction IV, 5:180). But I leave that point aside here.) Presumably Kant's thought is that an individual empirical generalization, which will seem contingent when considered in isolation, will appear to be necessary when it is embedded in a system of such generalizations, particularly a system structured by the logical relations of homogeneity and specificity, where generalizations at any level will appear to be entailed by the more general laws above them and confirmed by the more detailed laws beneath them.[14]

---

[14] For a similar account of what Kant might have had in mind, see Rush, "Reason and Regulation," pp. 846–7.

If this is indeed what Kant has in mind, then one further premise would explain why he treats the principle of systematicity as a transcendental and not just a logical principle, that is, a proposition about nature itself rather than merely an ideal for our concepts of nature, although of course a proposition about nature that can only be asserted with regulative rather than constitutive force. This assumption would be the natural one that there will be many circumstances in which we may need to regard some particular empirical generalization as necessary even though we do not yet possess the whole system of generalizations that would entail and confirm it, indeed perhaps that this will always be our condition. If this is so, then we cannot count on being able to see the particular generalization in question as being necessitated by our current system of concepts. So if we are nevertheless to be able to see it as necessary, we must instead be able to regard it as necessitated by a system of regularities beyond our concepts, that is, by a system of regularities existing in nature itself. Only the postulation of such systematicity in nature will lend the appearance of necessity to individual laws of nature in our condition of no doubt often and perhaps always fragmentary knowledge of nature. Thus the principle of the systematicity of nature must be transcendental and not just logical.

This explanation of the transcendental principle of systematicity employs premises that Kant does not explicitly assert, but makes sense of what otherwise seems to be a wildly ungrounded assertion. In the absence of evidence for an alternative explanation, we can at least regard this as a reconstruction of an argument that could have lead Kant to the position that he adopts.

## II. THE PLEASURE OF SYSTEMATICITY?

While insisting that the principle of systematicity must have the semantic form of a transcendental rather than merely logical principle, however, Kant continues to maintain that it is regulative rather than constitutive. Kant also expresses this point with his contrast between "heautonomy" and genuine "autonomy":[15]

---

[15] The significance of Kant's term "heautonomy" has been stressed by Juliet Floyd in "Heautonomy: Kant on Reflective Judgment and Systematicity," in *Kants Ästhetik— Kant's Aesthetics—L'Esthétique de Kant*, ed. Herman Parret, pp. 192–218; and, following Floyd, Allison, in *Kant's Aesthetic Theory*, pp. 41–2. I am not convinced that the concept of heautonomy (which is used only in the introductions, one time in each, and nowhere in the body of the third *Critique*) adds any clarification to Kant's more general contrast between constitutive and regulative principles.

The power of judgment thus also has in itself an *a priori* principle for the possibility of nature, though only in a subjective respect, by means of which it prescribes a law, not to nature (as autonomy), but to itself (as heautonomy) for reflection on nature, which one could call the **law of the specification of nature** with regard to its empirical laws, which it does not cognize in nature *a priori* but rather assumes in behalf of an order of nature cognizable for our understanding in the division that it makes of its universal laws when it would subordinate a manifold of particular laws to these. Thus if one says that nature specifies its universal laws in accordance with the principle of purposiveness for our faculty of cognition, i.e., into suitability for human understanding in its necessary business of finding the universal for the particular that is offered to it by perception ... then one is thereby neither prescribing a law to nature nor learning one from it by means of observation (although that principle can be confirmed by the latter). For it is not a principle of the determining but rather merely of the reflecting power of judgment. (*CPJ*, Introduction V, 5:186)

Although we must conceive of systematicity as if it exists in nature itself in order to lend a sense of necessity to the particular empirical laws that we claim to know in advance of the actual possession of a complete system of such laws, we also recognize that this conception of nature cannot be conclusively demonstrated in the same way that, supposedly, a general principle of nature such as the universal law of causation can be. So this principle is transcendental in content, but merely regulative in force.

And this fact provides the basis for Kant's answer to the second puzzle raised at the outset of this paper. That puzzle, it will be remembered, is that Kant draws no connection between pleasure and the principle of systematicity at all in the first Introduction, and indeed that his accounts of the judgment of systematicity and of aesthetic judgment seem to pull in opposite directions: what we need in the case of the pursuit of systematicity among empirical laws of nature seems to be something like a guarantee that such systematicity can be found, while the explanation of our pleasure in beauty seems to depend precisely upon the fact that the beauty of an object appears contingent, at least relative to any concept under which we can subsume the object.[16] In the published version of the

---

[16] Or at least, the beauty of an object appears relative to any concept other than the concept of beauty itself. But of course our predication of beauty of an object depends upon our experience of its beauty, and cannot be the ground for the latter. This point could perhaps be more clearly made in Malcolm Budd's otherwise useful interpretation of aesthetic judgment as a species of reflective judgment, "The Pure Judgment of Taste as an Aesthetic Reflective Judgment," *British Journal of Aesthetics*, 41 (2001), pp. 247–60, at pp. 259–60. Anthony Savile has stressed the importance of the experience of beauty in an actual judgment of taste, as opposed to the judgment of beauty which is merely the content of an actual judgment of taste, in "Taste, Perception, and Experience," in his *Kantian Aesthetics Pursued* (Edinburgh: Edinburgh University Press, 1993), pp. 1–16.

Introduction, Kant addresses precisely this problem by making it clear that we understand that the principle of systematicity as a principle of reflective judgment is regulative rather than constitutive, heautonomous rather than autonomous, and thus that at some level we recognize that nature's compliance with this principle is contingent rather than necessary. For that reason, we are do not merely take it for granted that we will discover systematicity in nature, and are in fact noticeably pleased when we do discover it:

Now this transcendental concept of a purposiveness of nature is neither a concept of nature nor a concept of freedom, since it attributes nothing at all to the object (of nature), but rather only represents the unique way in which we must proceed in reflection on the objects of nature with the aim of a thoroughly interconnected experience, consequently it is a subjective principle (maxim) of the power of judgment; hence we are also delighted (strictly speaking, relieved of a need) when we encounter such a systematic unity among merely empirical laws, just as if it were a happy accident which happened to favor our aim, even though we necessarily had to assume that there is such a unity, yet without having been able to gain insight into it and to prove it. (*CPJ*, Introduction V, 5:184)

The key to Kant's position here, as is so often the case, is the recognition that we can think at two levels at once, or conceive of the same matter from different points of view: we can conceive of nature as a system and thus of particular empirical laws as necessary while still retaining our deep sense of the contingency of nature's satisfaction of our own cognitive requirements. To the extent that we retain the latter recognition, we are pleased when nature does in fact satisfy our own cognitive purposes, just as we are when we find that it contingently does so in the beautiful form of an individual object.

Indeed, Kant wrote a separate section of the published Introduction, which has no parallel in the first draft, in order to emphasize this point and to try to describe more fully the complex state of mind in which our delight in the systematicity of nature is embedded. Section VI emphasizes precisely that although the conception of nature itself as systematic is required for us to conceive of particular laws of nature as necessary, at the very same time we also recognize that nature's satisfaction of our own cognitive needs is ultimately contingent and, when we do in fact discover it, a ground for pleasure. Kant begins the section by reminding us that

This correspondence of nature in the multiplicity of its particular laws with our need to find universality of principles for it must be judged, as far as our insight goes, as contingent but nevertheless indispensable for the needs of our understanding, and hence as a purposiveness through which nature agrees with our aim, but only as directed to cognition. (*CPJ*, Introduction VI, 5:186)

Kant next observes that "The attainment of every aim is combined with the feeling of pleasure," although he then tacitly reformulates this generalization as the premise that the attainment of every aim where that attainment cannot be taken for granted as entailed by the very constitution of our own cognitive faculties is combined with the feeling of pleasure. This is what he actually assumes when he states that the compliance of nature with the categories alone is not the ground of any appreciable pleasure, because that is entailed by the very constitution of our own cognitive faculties, but the discovery of systematicity among the laws of nature is the ground of such a pleasure, because it is not entailed by the character of our cognitive faculties alone:

In fact, although in the concurrence of perceptions with laws in accordance with universal concepts of nature (the categories) we do not encounter the least effect on the feeling of pleasure in us nor can encounter it, because here the understanding proceeds unintentionally, in accordance with its nature, by contrast the discovered unifiability of two or more empirically heterogeneous laws of nature under a principle that comprehends them both is the ground of a very noticeable pleasure, often indeed of admiration, even of one which does not cease though one is already sufficiently familiar with its object. (*CPJ*, Introduction VI, 5:187)

However, as if working through the complexity of his thought as he writes,[17] Kant immediately modifies the final claim just made:

To be sure, we no longer detect any noticeable pleasure in the comprehensibility of nature and the unity of its division into genera and species, by means of which alone empirical concepts are possible through which we cognize it in its particular laws; but it must certainly have been there in its time, and only because the most common experience would not be possible without it has it gradually become mixed up with mere cognition and is no longer specially noticed.—It thus requires study to make us attentive to the purposiveness of nature for our understanding in our judging of it ... so that if we succeed in this accord of such laws for our faculty of cognition, which we regard as merely contingent, pleasure will be felt. (*CPJ*, Introduction VI, 5:187–8)

In other words, we can lose our sense of pleasure in the systematicity of nature if we associate it too closely with nature's necessary subjection to the categories, but we can also make ourselves attentive to the purposiveness of nature and recover that sense of pleasure. Perhaps this complex

[17] As mentioned earlier, the published Introduction was written in great haste in March 1790, as the publisher was finishing the typesetting of the body of the work; see *CPJ*, Editor's Introduction, pp. xl–xli.

phenomenology of pleasure in the purposiveness of nature, modeled in a chronological pattern of forgetting and then recovering, is an expression of the complex philosophical attitude toward the systematicity of nature that we adopt, regarding it both as a transcendental principle which grounds the necessity of particular empirical laws but at the same time as a regulative rather than constitutive principle, compliance with which we cannot literally impose upon nature but must be grateful to find in nature.

Kant's remark that "the most common experience would not be possible" without the unity of the division of nature into genera and species would certainly bear discussion, for that could be taken to be further evidence of Kant's recognition that the categories cannot actually be applied to empirical intuitions except through empirical concepts. Further, as I already suggested, Kant's suggestion that our pleasure in the discovery of systematicity in nature is an expression of our underlying recognition of the contingency of the existence of such systematicity may undercut the idea that we can find a conclusive resolution of Hume's doubts about the rationality of induction in the third *Critique*: we may take pleasure in the recognition of the lawlikeness of laws of nature as grounded in their membership in a system of laws precisely because we recognize that there is ultimately no guarantee for the existence of such lawlikeness. Unfortunately, there is no room here to explore this issue further. Rather, I will conclude simply by saying that Kant's claim that we must be able to take pleasure in nature's ultimately contingent satisfaction of our demand for systematicity, even if we sometimes lose sight of this pleasure, is clearly meant to prepare the way for his initial statement of his account of aesthetic judgment in the ensuing section VII, where he ascribes our pleasure in a beautiful object precisely to its unintentional satisfaction of our own basic conditions for cognition.[18] The difference between the two cases, of course, is that there is no danger of the experience of beauty becoming "mixed up with the most common experience," so there is no danger that we will forget our pleasure in a beautiful object and have to recover it by an exercise of attention. Our pleasure in beauty is the paradigmatic example of the "transcendental

---

[18] Of course, in a beautiful work of art as opposed to a beautiful product of nature, its satisfaction of our general conditions for cognition is not *unintended*; (Kant assumes that) the artist wants to produce a beautiful work and strives to do so. But it is the point of his theory of genius that there is still a sense in which the beauty of a beautiful work of art is *unintentional*: the rules by which the artist guides her work are not in fact sufficient to produce a beautiful object, and the difference between what the artist can intend and the beautiful outcome of her work must be made up by the gift of nature.

explanation" (FI, VIII, 20:230) of pleasure as a state of mind that "has a causality in itself, namely that of **maintaining** the state of the represen- tation of the mind and the occupation of the cognitive powers without a further aim," so that "We **linger** over the consideration of the beautiful because this consideration strengthens and reproduces itself" (*CPJ*, 12, 5:222).[19] But before that difference could be made clear, Kant first had to show in what way the judgment of systematicity and the judgment of taste are alike as instances of pleasurable reflecting judgment, and that is the task I have argued he finally discharged in the published Introduction to the third *Critique*.

[19] Thus I disagree with the approach of Jay M. Bernstein, who has built an interpret- ation of Kant's conception of *aesthetic* pleasure as something we forget or even repress and must recover on a claim which I take Kant to intend to apply only to our pleasure in the discovery of systematicity in nature; see Jay M. Bernstein, *The Fate of Art* (University Park: Pennsylvania State University Press, 1990), pp. 17–65.

# 4

# Kant's Ether Deduction and the Possibility of Experience

Beginning with the *Critique of Judgment* of 1790, Kant attempted to push the technique of transcendental deduction beyond its original austere limitation to such abstract generalities as the pure concepts of understanding of the *Critique of Pure Reason* and the mutual implication between the moral law and freedom deduced in the *Critique of Practical Reason*. Nowhere did Kant take this tendency further than in his attempt to provide a transcendental deduction of a material or "ether" pervading all of space and time, which is recorded at many places in the *Opus postumum* but especially prominently in the "Übergang 1–14," apparently written in the middle trimester of 1799. Here Kant repeatedly tried to prove that the existence of an ether, that is, a continuous matter which is "**all-extended, all-pervasive**, uniformly **agitating** itself throughout all parts of the space which it **occupies** (*occupat*) or also fills by repulsion (*replet*) and infinitely **enduring** in this motion" (21:593.12–15),[1] is nothing less than a condition of the possibility of experience. As he puts it, "There must be matter filling space [and] unremittingly moving itself through agitating forces (through attraction and repulsion) before the position of any particle in space can be determined. This is the basis of all matter as the object of possible experience. For this first makes experience possible" (21:550.27–551.1).[2]

*Prima facie*, the claim that there is an ether seems too empirical plausibly to be the kind of condition of the possibility of experience

This chapter originally appeared in the *Akten des Siebenten Internationalen Kant-Kongresses*, ed. Gerhard Funke (Bonn: Bouvier Verlag, 1991), vol. ii, pt. 1, pp. 119–32, and is reprinted here with permission of the publisher.

[1] Citations from the *Opus postumum* are taken from the edition by Gerhard Lehmann in *Kant's gesammelte Schriften*, edited by the Prussian and later German Academy of Sciences (Berlin: Walter de Gruyter & Co. and predecessors, 190– ), vols. 21 and 22 (1936–8). Citations are located by volume, page, and line numbers as in the present case. Translations are my own.

[2] See also 21:225.12–19, 21:547.22–548.4 and 21:572.16–24 among numerous other passages.

which is supposed to be demonstrated by a transcendental deduction. Such deductions are supposed to deliver synthetic *a priori* conclusions, free of any empirical content. And not only Kant's conclusion but also the several considerations which he offers as premises for his deduction of the existence of such an ether seem to be or include empirical assumptions which would be incompatible with our conception of the *a priori* even if synthetic premises which are required for any transcendental deduction. Such a conclusion, however, would be too hasty. On the one hand, the concept of the ether and its properties, while not as abstract as the concepts of the categories, is not exactly an empirical concept either, but something more like a constraint on the concepts and propositions of any acceptable physical theory; that is why it is a part, not of physics, but of what Kant calls the "transition from the metaphysical first principles of natural science to physics." As Kant says, the ether is not immediately detectable by the senses nor is its existence merely an empirical hypothesis, but rather it is a postulate necessary for conducting physical inquiry. Kant says that "the ether is not a hypothetical material but the proof of its reality is a hypothetical proof" (21:545.17–18); its proof "is not a direct proof from experience, because such a thing would never yield [it] *a priori*, but an indirect proof from the principle of the possibility of an experience valid for all matter taken together" (21:544.17–19). He expands:

The assumption of the existence of an all-encompassing all-penetrating and all-moving matter which fills the worldspace is an hypothesis which to be sure cannot be confirmed by experience but which if it has an *a priori* ground must come forth as an idea from reason... One easily sees that the existence of such a material is not an object of experience and **derived** from thence, i.e. empirically provable, but must rather be postulated as the object of possible experience which can also take place conditionally indirectly *a priori*... (21:576.2–13)[3]

However exactly its status should be described, the concept of the ether is not an ordinary empirical concept. On the other hand, the general claims about the character of experience on which the arguments for it depend do seem more specific than the extremely abstract characterizations of experience which figure in the transcendental deduction of the first *Critique*, which are at least in principle limited to the claims that experience must always be ascribable to a continuing self, be successive, and

---

[3] For some of Kant's many similar statements on this theme, see 21:229.23–230.6, 21:230.26–231.7, 21:236.20–237.3, 21:536.17–19, 21:540.13–23, 21:542.26–543.11, and 21:548.14–549.13.

allow its subject to make a distinction between subjective and objective.[4] But while the premises of Kant's ether deduction certainly go beyond the pure concept of experience, it would be equally misleading to think of them as mere empirical hypotheses. If anything, the premises of Kant's ether deduction may suggest that there is no completely hard-and-fast line between pure and empirical characterizations of experience. Such a conclusion would cast doubt on the purity of transcendental deductions, but might also explain why transcendental deductions at least sometimes really seem to deliver synthetic and not quite empirical even if not entirely *a priori* results. The proper conclusion to draw, then, might be that Kant's arguments for the ether are really transcendental deductions but that transcendental deductions must always straddle the border between completely pure and empirical assumptions about the nature of human experience.[5]

Kant suggests at least four different arguments for the existence of an ether:

1. All of space and time constitute a unified object of experience, which is possible only if there is a single subject of forces pervading all of space and time and linking the contents of all of their various places and times into a single dynamical system.

2. No empty regions of space and time can be perceived, and all of space and time must therefore be filled with some sort of matter.

3. Nothing in space and time can be perceived except by transmission of some force from the object to the subject of perception, and since objects may be perceived at any point in space and time there must be some medium for the transmission of such force throughout all of space and time.

4. There can be no external agency for the origination of motion in a physical system occupying all of space and time, so there must be some original force of motion within the system, which can be nothing less than a self-moving and all-pervasive ether.[6]

---

[4] For present purposes it is hardly necessary to specify the premises of the original transcendental deduction more precisely. For my own view of the range of premises which Kant actually attempts to employ, see my *Kant and the Claims of Knowledge* (Cambridge: Cambridge University Press, 1987), ch. 3, pp. 73–90.

[5] Of course, Kant might not have quite intended such a conclusion—he sometimes seems to shy away from by insisting that the proposition that the ether exists is not synthetic at all but rather "analytic (merely logically explicative) and depending solely on the principle of identity" (21:559.13–14).

[6] Eckart Förster, in his article "Kant's Notion of Philosophy," *Monist* 72 (1989): 285–304, lists three different reasons for the existence of the ether: "(1)...perception must be thought of as the effect of moving forces on my subject...(2) The formation of

Each of these seems problematic as a transcendental deduction. (1) and
(2) seem to exploit specific as well as controversial claims about the
nature of space and time rather than any pure concept of experience.
(3) seems to concern empirical conditions for the occurrence of perceptions of a sort that are typically excluded from *a priori* theories of
knowledge. (4), finally, seems to be precisely the sort of metaphysical
claim about first causes that Kant had argued, in the "Transcendental
Dialectic" of the first *Critique*, leads to nothing but illusion. However,
although the details of Kant's ether deductions are certainly obscure and
questionable, these threats to their status as transcendental arguments
are less serious than first appears. Contrary to first appearance, (1), (2),
and (3) do not go radically beyond the terrain of Kant's original transcendental theory of experience, although they make it clear that
this is far from a mere analysis of the concept of experience. And point
(4), far from being intended to add an illusory metaphysical element
to the foundations of natural science, is exactly the opposite: it
expresses Kant's insistence that questions about the origin of motion be
treated physically rather than metaphysically, internally rather than
externally.

Some illustrations of Kant's own exposition of these points will prepare us for their more detailed consideration. We may consider first a
passage which asserts points (1), (2), and (3):

The **transition** from the metaph. first prin. of nat. sci. to physics … starts from
the subjective principle of the connection of the manifold of moving forces of
matter in one experience …

The **empty** space between two wholes of matter and the empty time between
two moments as boundaries are not objects of possible experience for non-being
cannot be perceived, thus arise herefrom the following propositions: There is
external experience as a collective whole of all perceptions, i.e. as **one** all-
encompassing possible experience. There exists an object of sense outside of us
for the **perception** of which external moving forces of matter are required, the
empirical representation of which connected in one subject is the **basis** of all
appearances which together constitute the unity of experience.

---

material bodies is not possible by the fundamental forces of attraction and repulsion
alone; it requires furthermore the agitations of the ether. (3) Empirical space, in order to
be sensible, has to be thought of as being filled with a continuum of forces which 'as it
were … hypostasizes' it" (pp. 297–8). Förster's (1) corresponds to my point (3), and his (2)
is, I think, intended by Kant to be a more specific consequence of my more general point
(4); Förster's (2) comprehends both my (1) and (2), but, even though both may ultimately
depend on the same assumption, it is worth distinguishing them because Kant frequently
expounds them separately and because even if my (2) might imply (1) the converse is not
true, and they are not therefore equivalent propositions.

Now the agitation of the senses of the subject through some matter is that which alone makes possible outer perceptions and these moving forces must be thought of *a priori* as connected in one experience without gaps (that is without any **empty** [place] being mixed in because that would not be an object of possible perception) in one absolute whole which yet, as such, is also no object of possible experience. (21:582.6–583.9)[7]

This passage holds that the existence of a unique although not directly experienced matter which is the subject of all forces follows from the impossibility of perceiving empty spaces or times (2), from the unity of all physical objects in space and time (1), and from the need for an all-pervasive medium for the transmission of the agitation on which perception physically depends (3).[8] Another passage makes points (2), (3), and (4):

There can be no experience of empty space, therefore no inference to the object thereof. In order to be instructed of the existence of a matter I need the influence of a matter on my senses. The proposition that there are empty spaces can therefore be neither a mediate nor an immediate empirical proposition...
—The proposition that there are empirical bodies presupposes the proposition that there is matter whose moving forces and motion precedes the generation of a body in time...—This formation however, which is to proceed from matter itself, must have a first beginning, the possibility of which is to be sure incomprehensible but which, as self-activity, is not to be doubted. There must therefore be a matter which as internally penetrating...all bodies and at the same time perpetually moving them (as *potentia*) constitutes a whole subsisting for itself and, internally self-moving, serves as the basis for all other movable matter...(21:216.12–217.2)

This passage asserts that an all-pervasive ether must exist because there can be no experience of empty space (2), because all perception requires transmission of physical force (3), and because there must be some intrinsically moving rather than externally moved agency in any complete physical system (4).

Let us now consider Kant's claims in more detail, starting with claim (l) that the complete unity of all objects of experience in a single space and time requires the existence of an ether penetrating every region of space and moment of time. Kant repeatedly asserts that there must be an absolute unity of experience which can only be grounded in material connections among the objects of experience: for example,

---

[7] For a very similar conjunction of points, see also 21:576.20–577.15.
[8] It will also be noticed that this passage suggests that point (1) is entailed by point (2); we will return to that issue shortly.

Now the absolute unity of possible experience is at the same time the unity of the collective material [of experience] thus also of the forces of matter which move the senses. Thus there already lies in the concept of the *a priori* unity of experience (before everything empirical as an aggregate of perceptions) the concept of a system of agitating forces of matter as necessarily belonging in experience. (21:595.19–596.4)[9]

Sometimes, however, Kant explicitly grounds this claim about the unity of *experience* in a prior claim about the unity of *space*: "Subjectively considered there is only one outer experience for there is only one space" (22:610.16–17). At greater length,

There is only one space and only one time and only one material in which all motion will be found. The real and objective principle of experience which makes a single whole according to form allows no unfilled space outside itself and in itself...

The basis of the whole of the unification of all moving forces of matter is the ether (as it were the hypostasized space itself in which everything moves)...

Ether is perceptible space denuded of all its other qualities at least in thought as the principle of the unity of experience in all dimensions... (21:224.3–16)

Here Kant moves directly from the premises that all spatial objects must comprise parts of a single space and that some matter is needed to make space perceptible to the conclusion that such matter must fill every region of this single all-encompassing space.

Such an argument would seem to be open to two sorts of objections. First, that all objects which are spatial at all must constitute regions of a single space and more generally that all objects of experience must constitute parts of a single experience obviously go beyond what can be inferred from any mere *concept* of experience. The first of these claims, to be sure, has already been made in Kant's "Transcendental Aesthetic," and so should be synthetic *a priori* and thus available for use without damaging a transcendental deduction; the second, however, goes beyond any ordinary concept of the experience of a single self and seems to introduce a stronger conception of experience than previously encountered. More problematic, however, is Kant's apparently untroubled inference from the claim that all objects must be uniquely ordered, which is to say positioned, in a single all-encompassing space to the conclusion that an all-pervasive system of matter is required to do this. This is troubling because the third "Analogy of Experience" of the first *Critique*

---

[9] Other passages asserting the same point are too numerous to list; for a few examples, see also 21:545.2–20 and 21:572.25–573.22.

argues that any two objects may be assigned determinate spatial position relative to each other as long as there are dynamic relations of interaction between them, but does not specify that there must be a continuous bridge of matter between them. In other words, an all-pervasive ether would seem to be a precondition of an all-encompassing spatial order only if the possibility of action at a distance were precluded.

Kant addresses the issue of action at a distance only in passing, and we will not consider it here;[10] instead, his basic strategy is to ground the proposition (1) that the unity of all spatial objects depends upon an ether on the claim (2) that since no empty regions of space can be perceived there can in fact be no empty regions of space: "Now the concept of the whole of external experience presupposes [that] all moving forces of matter [are connected in a collective unity and indeed in full space (for empty [space] whether it be inside or outside of bodies is no object of possible experience)]" (21:572.25–573.1). This attempt to ground the unity of space in the impossibility of empty space depends upon the assumption that the only thing which could separate non-unified spaces would be regions of empty space, which may be controversial. But it is clear that Kant is prepared to give great weight to the principle that because empty space cannot be perceived there can be no empty space, and in many passages he rests the proof of the ether directly on this principle.

Kant bluntly asserts that empty space or time cannot be perceived: "Empty space and so also empty time are no object[s] of possible experience;—the non-being of an object of perception cannot be perceived" (21:549.17–19). He does not worry about the legitimacy of the inference from the *imperceivability* of empty space to the *non-existence* of empty space precisely because the entire deduction of the ether is supposed to be confined within the limits of possible experience.[11] It looks, then, as if Kant is willing to rest his argument for the ether on the simple syllogism that no point in space can be perceived unless filled with some matter, any point in space may be perceived, and therefore there is no point in space that is not filled with matter (*mutatis mutandis* for time).

So Kant's whole argument for the ether thus far comes down to the simple claim that empty space or time cannot be perceived. Is this merely an empirical assertion about the perception of space and time? Or is its status more complex than that? In fact, Kant does have more to say in behalf of this principle. He does not just assert that empty space cannot

---

[10] See, for example, 21:604.12–32.
[11] See, for instance, 21:547.7–16.

be perceived but derives this conclusion from his even more basic assumption that space and time are infinitely divisible, thus that there can be no absolute boundary between empty and filled regions of space; and since at least some regions of space must be filled, otherwise there would be no experience at all, it is absolutely empty regions which are precluded—there is nothing which could absolutely bound an empty region from a filled one:

An empty space is thinkable but not detectable, i.e. no object of possible experience. For which reason atomism, a theory of the composition of the manifold of matter which occupies space by means of full [spaces] and empty [ones] mixed between them...is a groundless system. For no part of matter is indivisible, the empty can simply not be an object of possible experience...From these two putative elements, the perceptible and the imperceptible...a world cannot be cobbled together. (21:235.28–236.7)[12]

Thus, Kant's arguments about the unity and non-emptiness of all regions of space ultimately turn on one of the basic results of the "Transcendental Aesthetic," although not one that was directly employed in the original transcendental deduction of the categories: the continuity or infinite divisibility of space and time. Because all regions of space and time are merely ideal parts of a single space and time, which are also continuous so that there can be no determinate boundaries between such regions, there can be nothing to introduce any absolute boundaries between regions of space and time. So if any regions of space and time are filled with matter and force, as must clearly be the case, then all regions of space and time must be. Such an argument is hardly immune from criticism; one could argue that Kant begs many questions in simply assuming that the formal properties of the pure intuitions of space and time necessarily apply to physical objects within space and time. But my concern for the present is only with the character of Kant's argument: and here it is clear that he is not attempting to deduce the existence of the ether from anything he regards as simply an empirical observation about our perception of space, nor from a pure concept of experience, but from a synthetic *a priori* premise about the nature of space. In this regard the deduction of the ether should count as a transcendental deduction with a premise that is neither simply empirical nor purely conceptual.

We may now turn to (3), Kant's claim that there must be an ether to ensure the possibility of transmission of perceptions to the subject from any region of space. Here Kant's argument starts with the premise that the perception of any object always requires the transmission of motion

---

[12] See also 21:218.19–27 and 21:542.12–18.

from that object to the sensory organs of the perceiving subject: "External *perceptions* however for possible experience ... are themselves nothing other than the effect [*Wirkung*] of agitating forces of matter on the perceiving *subject*" (21:577.6–9).[13] Kant then apparently argues that since I can perceive an external object at any point in space there must be a medium capable of transmitting the effect of agitating forces at any such point to me; this can only be an ether which is present at every point in space. This is his fullest exposition of this argument:

There must be a matter which constitutes a whole in worldspace and originally fills all spaces through moving forces for emptiness hinders connection and *Continuität*.

In every place in space and time there must be an object of possible experience, consequently also moving forces which are suppressed and made ineffective by no other object of the senses [i.e.] ether.

For if from the object in space to me no sensation as the effect of the moving force could be effected from the point [in space] to my sense[s] then I would not even be informed of its presence. (21:537.21–31)

This argument obviously makes strong assumptions. First, it assumes that the causation of perception must be understood in the same terms as are available for any other causal connections. Second, it must assume either that perception of an object at any point in space is possible, and thus that a cause of perception is located at every point in space, or else that even if not every point in space *contains* a perceivable object that there is no point in space *from* which some object cannot be perceived, thus that there must be a medium for the transmission of perception to and through every point in space; this in turn seems to presuppose the impossibility of physical action at a distance without some physical medium.

The latter of these assumptions seems open to a variety of problems; more generally, the very idea of attempting to derive physical consequences from causal conditions of the possibility of empirical perception may seem out of place in transcendental philosophy, part of the physiology rather than epistemology of perception. In fact, however, the present argument just works out consequences of the first *Critique*'s "Refutation of Idealism." In that argument, Kant demonstrated that we could make determinate judgments about the order of even subjective

---

[13] For several of Kant's many other similar statements, see 21:552.7–9 and 21:587.27–30. In the latter passage, Kant says that "All outer experience depends upon the subject being externally affected by agitating forces of matter (for the synthetic unity of perception is that which is called experience), whose outer existence is however proved through this its effect."

representational states only if we viewed them as lawfully caused by the effect of outer objects on us.[14] Thus he argued that temporally determinate experience is possible only if mental states of the subject are viewed as part of a single causal order including external objects as well; now he is simply characterizing the causal mechanism of this single realm by means of the physical concept of agitating forces. Particular assumptions about non-empty space and action at a distance aside, his argument simply depends on the assumption, already implicit in the "Refutation of Idealism," that any empirical theory of perception must in principle involve causal connections capable of linking two objects in physical space.[15] As Kant puts it:

Now these perceptions **subjectively considered** are effects of the moving forces of matter (namely as empirical representations) and belong as such to the total unity of **possible** experience. The total unity of moving forces, however, is objectively the effect of the absolute whole of the elementary matter. (21:601.23–602.6)

It might seem as if Kant is simply offering an empirical argument for the existence of an ether as the explanation of perception. But he is perhaps better understood as arguing more abstractly that an empirical theory of perception must be possible, and then appealing to the theory of the ether for further constraints on a possible theory of perception. In this way the boundary between empirical and transcendental theory is softened without Kant's argument simply becoming an empirical hypothesis: the more general theory of experience requires an empirical theory of perception and places some constraints on it, even if additional physical assumptions are necessary to make the concepts so arrived at completely concrete. The possibility of an empirical theory of perception is at least required on transcendental grounds.

We may now turn to Kant's final ground for the postulation of an ether, the idea that a complete physical theory requires some self-moving matter. Here the possibility of a transcendental argument seems even more unlikely, for Kant appears to be making the kind of inference to a first cause which, according to the "Transcendental Dialectic," is

---

[14] For defense of this interpretation, see my "Kant's Intentions in the Refutation of Idealism," *Philosophical Review* 92 (1983): 329–83, or *Kant and the Claims of Knowledge*, part IV, pp. 279–329.

[15] A similar connection between Kant's ether argument and the "Refutation of Idealism" is suggested by Eckart Förster in "Kant's Notion of Philosophy" (see note 6 supra) and "Kant's Selbstsetzungslehre," in Förster, ed., *Kant's Transcendental Deductions: The Three Critiques and 'Opus postumum'* (Stanford: Stanford University Press, 1989), pp. 217–38, especially p. 230.

rendered inevitable by reason's interest in the unconditioned but which can never be confirmed within the limits of possible experience, where neither a first moment of time nor the modality of necessity can ever be rendered intuitable. In fact, however, Kant's point appears to be that an original source of motion must be posited *within* an adequate physical theory precisely in order to avoid the temptation of a dialectical inference to a source of motion—a first mover—*outside* the confines of the physical system of motion. In other words, Kant's claim that a complete physical theory must postulate an all-pervasive self-moving matter, even if that seems mysterious, can be seen as a constraint necessary in order to avoid the characteristic defect of purely mechanical world-systems, namely that they can adequately account for the *transmission* of motions but must postulate an extra-mundane first mover in order to account for the *origination* of motion.

Several passages give clear evidence of Kant's intention. This passage makes the point in logical terms, threatening merely mechanical physics with an infinite regress:

The moveable insofar as it is only moving through the motion of something else is mechanical: insofar however as it is originally [*uranfänglich*] moving through its own force, it is moved dynamically.

Mechanically-effected motion is not original and moved matter requires another moving matter in order to bring it into [motion]. . . . but to derive a motion from a preceding one presupposes an infinite regress of causes, [thus] the dynamical principle of motion cannot be effected other than as a postulate of an infinitely and beginninglessly moved and moving matter in space and time which, infinitely divided, preserves all matter in motion. (21:227.10–22)

Later Kant suggests that his "postulate" of dynamical motion internal to any physical system is designed to avoid the *deus ex machina* which necessarily infects any merely mechanical system of physics: "Some motion must be **original** i.e. matter must somewhere simply begin to be moved, the possibility of which is incomprehensible according to a purely mechanical principle but is not permitted to be derived from an immaterial cause (from God) in the transition to natural science from the metaph. first princ. of nat. sci. because such a transition would thereby become self-contradictory" (21:560.23–561.2). In other words, in order to avoid the danger of exceeding the limits of possible experience any physical theory must be placed under the constraint of postulating an internal source of motion. Again we do not simply have an appeal to empirical hypothesis, but rather an *a priori* argument for the necessity of a certain kind of empirical theory.

There are obviously many questionable steps in Kant's arguments for the existence of the ether, and there would be many difficulties in reconciling these arguments with current physical theory. This paper has not been intended to render Kant's arguments plausible. My intent has only been to show that Kant did indeed comply with his own aim of avoiding merely empirical hypotheses for the explanation of particular empirical observations, and that he was instead engaged in a more general enterprise of deriving general constraints on the form of acceptable physical theory from general claims about the conditions of the possibility of experience. As we have seen, the premises to which he really appeals in his several arguments for the ether include his own principles of (i) the ideality and infinite divisibility of spatial and temporal boundaries, (ii) the need to include the causation of perceptions in a single system of physical causation, and (iii) the need to avoid appeal to transcendent agencies when constructing theories within the bounds of experience. None of these premises can be regarded as either a mere concept of experience or a merely empirical hypothesis—they mix the empirical and the transcendental in a more complicated way than that. Obviously no examination of such a special subject as Kant's ether deduction can suffice by itself to establish a general thesis about transcendental deductions, but if the present paper even suggests that perhaps transcendental deductions work, to the extent that they do, precisely by straddling the ordinary boundary between the merely empirical and the purely conceptual, then my aim will have been achieved.

# 5

# Organisms and the Unity of Science

## 1. ORGANISMS AND THE THREAT TO THE UNITY OF SCIENCE

In the appendix to the Transcendental Dialectic in the *Critique of Pure Reason*, Kant outlines his vision of the unity of our science of nature as a goal imposed upon us by the character of our own reason. "If we survey the cognitions of our understanding in their entire range," he says, "then we find that what reason quite uniquely prescribes and seeks to bring about concerning it is the **systematic** in cognition, i.e., its interconnection based on one principle" (A 645/B 673).[1] Kant illustrates the kind of unifying principle he has in mind with the concept of a "power," or the "causality of a substance" (A 648/B 677), and thus suggests that a systematic science of nature must ultimately be based on a single kind of causation, or a "fundamental power," presumably exerted by a single kind of substance, underlying what would initially seem to be the many kinds of causation and many kinds of substances we encounter in our experience of nature. To be sure, Kant stresses that the idea of such a power "is at least the problem set by a systematic representation of the manifoldness of [the] powers" of nature (A 645/B 573),[2] and a few pages later he stresses again that

This chapter was originally presented at a conference on Kant and the sciences at Virginia Polytechnic Institute and State University, and first appeared in Eric Watkins (ed.), *Kant and the Sciences* (Oxford: Oxford University Press, 2001), pp. 259–81.

[1] Translations from the *Critique of Pure Reason* are from Immanuel Kant, *Critique of Pure Reason*, tr. and ed. Paul Guyer and Allen W. Wood (Cambridge: Cambridge University Press, 1998). Translations from the *Opus postumum* are from Immanuel Kant, *Opus postumum*, ed. Eckart Förster, trans. Eckart Förster and Michael Rosen (Cambridge: Cambridge University Press, 1993). Translations from Kant's pre-Critical writings are from Immanuel Kant, *Theoretical Philosophy, 1755–1770*, ed. and trans. David E. Walford (Cambridge: Cambridge University Press, 1992). Translations from Kant's metaphysics lectures are from Immanuel Kant, *Lectures on Metaphysics*, ed. and trans. Karl Ameriks and Steve Naragon (Cambridge: Cambridge University Press, 1997). Translations from the *Critique of Judgment* are mine.

[2] Actually, in his first illustration of the application of the idea of a fundamental power, Kant is talking about the idea of a fundamental power underlying various *mental* capacities in human psychology, and the word "the" which I have interpolated in this citation

Systematic unity (as mere idea) is only a **projected** unity, which one must regard not as given in itself, but only as a problem; this unity, however, helps to find a principle for the manifold and particular uses of the understanding, thereby guiding it even in those cases that are not given and making it coherently connected. (A 647/B 675)

Because no specific and determinate conception of the unifying principle for all knowledge of nature in the form of a single kind of causation or power is actually given by reason's mere idea of it, Kant calls it a "regulative" rather than "constitutive" principle for our conduct of scientific inquiry.

This designation suggests that this goal of a single principle explaining everything in nature may never be fully realized, but at the same time seems to assume that we will never encounter anything in our experience which could conclusively prove that this goal *cannot* be reached:

What is strange about these principles ... is this ... even though they contain mere ideas to be followed in the empirical use of reason, which reason can follow only asymptotically, as it were, i.e., merely by approximation, without ever reaching them, yet these principles, as synthetic propositions *a priori*, nevertheless have objective but indeterminate validity, and serve as a rule of possible experience, and can even be used with good success, as heuristic principles, in actually elaborating it. (A 663/B 691)

The idea of a single type of matter, operating ultimately by means of a single type of causation or power, Kant seems to suppose, is one that we can never reasonably expect to be fully exemplified in our empirical science of nature, but yet at the same time one that we can know *a priori* will never be conclusively falsified by it.

In the "Critique of Teleological Judgment," however, the second half of the *Critique of Judgment* published nine years after the *Critique of Pure Reason*, Kant appears to argue precisely what the first *Critique* had supposed never could be shown, namely that we have good reason to suppose that we can never succeed in bringing all of nature under a single principle attributing a single fundamental power to a single kind of substance. The third *Critique* appears to argue that we can never explain fundamental and indispensable properties of what Kant calls "organized beings" and "physical ends," that is, what we now call organisms, by means of the same mechanical laws of causation by which we can at least potentially fully explain the behavior of inanimate matter in all of its myriad forms. Organisms, Kant argues, depend on "a causality that

replaces the pronoun "its," which refers to the mind as the seat of the powers being unified.

cannot be combined with the mere concept of a nature without ascribing an end to nature" (*CPJ*, §64, 5:371).[3] Kant argues that it is only our experience of organisms that forces us to explain anything in nature by means of final causes, thus teleologically rather than mechanically, so he is not mounting an *a priori* argument that reason's idea of ultimately explaining everything in nature by means of a single fundamental power is doomed. But his position in the first *Critique* seemed to express an *a priori* assurance that the possibility of approaching ever closer to such an explanatory ideal could not be confuted by experience, thus even an empirical reason for assuming the necessity of teleological explanation would conflict with that position. So the question naturally arises, does Kant's account of our teleological judgment of organisms in the third *Critique* undermine his assurance in the first that we can always asymptotically approach the ideal of a single fundamental power and principle for all of our knowledge of nature?

In the "Critique of Teleological Judgment," Kant further argues that once we have been forced to introduce teleological judgment in order to accommodate our experience of some objects in nature, namely organisms, it is natural for us to see whether the whole of nature, even including the vast array of inorganic materials and objects that would not of themselves force teleological judgment upon us, may not also be judged teleologically, as part of a single system in which the organic and inorganic are all related as means to some ultimate end. Thus Kant says:

> It is thus only matter, insofar as it is organized, which necessarily carries with it the concept of it as an end of nature, since its specific form is at the same time a product of nature. But this concept necessarily leads to the idea of the whole of nature as a system in accordance with the rule of ends, to which idea all mechanism of nature must be subordinated in accordance with principles of reason (at least to investigate the appearance of nature thereby). (*CPJ*, §67, 5:378–9)

And indeed, Kant continues, once our experience of organisms has led us to consider whether all of nature may not be looked at as a system of means to some final end, it also becomes inevitable for us to consider whether there may not be a teleological explanation for the existence of natural beauty as well, although this is a question that Kant had explicitly abjured in the "Critique of Aesthetic Judgment" (see *CPJ*, §31, 5:279–80):

---

[3] Citations to the *Critique of Judgment* include the section number, along with the volume and page numbers of the Akademie edition.

Also beauty of nature, i.e., its concordance with the free play of our cognitive faculties in the apprehension and the judging of its appearance, can be considered in this manner as an objective purposiveness of nature in its entirety, of which the human being is a member: when, that is, the teleological judging of it by means of natural ends, which has been provided to us by organized beings, has justified us in the idea of a great system of the ends of nature. (*CPJ*, §67, 5:380)

Thus Kant argues that our experience of organisms leads us to consider all of nature from a teleological point of view, and thus presumably to explain everything in it by reference to final as well as mechanical causation. And then our question about the first *Critique*'s ideal of a systematic science unified by its single ultimate principle of explanation becomes even more pressing. Does Kant end up asserting not just that some objects in nature must be explained by one fundamental principle while others can only be explained by another, but rather that every object in nature must be susceptible of two radically different kinds of explanation?

If so, perhaps this would solve rather than exacerbate the conflict between Kant's account of organisms and his ideal of the unity of natural science, and do so in a manner continuous with one of Kant's earliest ideas. Early in his career, Kant had argued that it is not any contingency relative to the laws of nature, for example, miracles, that furnishes the basis for conceiving of an intelligent and purposive author of nature, but the very regularity of those laws, which can be conceived as the means through which the author of nature achieves his ends. This is the vision that Kant called "the revised method of physico-theology" (2:123) in *The Only Possible Basis for a Demonstration of the Existence of God* of 1763. Here Kant wrote that

The spirit of true philosophy is most powerfully manifest in the following method of judging the perfect provisions of nature.... Above all, it allows neither nature's aiming at interest, nor all its harmoniousness, to hinder it from trying to discover their foundations in necessary and universal laws. And in the attempt to discover these grounds, it always pays careful attention to the preservation of unity, displaying a rational aversion to multiplying the number of natural causes in order to explain the benefits and harmony of nature. If, in addition to this, the physico-theological mode of judging also concentrates its attention on the universal rules which are capable of explaining the ground of the necessary connection, which holds between, on the one hand, that which occurs naturally without special provision, and, on the other hand, the rules relating to the advantage and convenience of rational beings, and if one then proceeds to ascend to the Divine Being—if all these conditions are satisfied, then this mode of judging will fulfill its obligations in a fitting fashion. (2:136-7)

Kant's idea is that it is precisely a systematic explanation of all the phenomena of nature by some single, coherent sets of laws, presumably one conforming to the regulative ideal for a systematic cognition of nature subsequently outlined in the *Critique of Pure Reason*, that is the only basis for a successful inference from features of nature to the existence of God, who demonstrates both his wisdom and his power precisely by being able to accomplish all of his rational ends *through* the uniform and unified laws he has legislated for nature. Such a view would then suggest a model for the resolution between the regulative ideal of the unity of science on the one hand and the teleological view of the world as a whole to which we are led by our experience of organisms on the other: We could see a systematic cognition of nature ultimately aimed at the recognition of a single fundamental principle, as the only natural goal of our *theoretical* use of reason, while at the same time allowing that from a standpoint other than that of theoretical reason alone it might be natural for us to see this very systematic unity of natural laws as the means by which some higher purpose—of God or, as it may turn out, ourselves—is realized.

I believe that the *Critique of Judgment* was meant to be Kant's mature statement of such a vision, and that his basic reason for discussing organisms at all was precisely that these are the objects *within* our experience that can prompt us to take this twofold view of nature. But the special case of organisms also threatened the grand vision by threatening the assumption that there could be a single mode of explanation for all of nature within the theoretical point of view: the "Critique of Teleological Judgment" offers specific reasons why we cannot comprehend organisms by a mechanical model of causation and thus cannot use a single mode of explanation for all objects *in* nature. The material that has come down to us under the name of the *Opus postumum* indicates that Kant continued to struggle with this problem for the rest of his life. So we need to examine Kant's arguments about the exceptional status of organisms in both the third *Critique* and the *Opus postumum*. In doing so, we shall find the following. In the "Critique of Teleological Judgment," Kant provides three different arguments for the necessity of judging organisms teleologically. First, we cannot comprehend the reciprocal causality demonstrated in various organic processes by means of our ordinary conception of causation, but can comprehend it only by conceiving of it as if it were the expression of purposive design. Second, our conception of life itself is inconsistent with the application of our ordinary conception of causation, in the form of the law of inertia, to all matter, so we have to view life as having a source outside of matter.

Third, we cannot explain the complete determinacy of living organisms by means of the always merely general laws of nature that our ordinary science provides us. Each of these arguments is in fact problematic. The third argument proves too much, for it applies to all particular objects, not just organisms, and thus would not show that there is any fundamental difference between the laws that we can formulate for organisms and those we can formulate for the rest of nature. Kant does not explicitly acknowledge this objection, but he also does not seem to have repeated this argument after the third *Critique*, so perhaps he silently let it drop. By contrast, Kant himself rejects the second argument in the *Opus postumum*, by arguing that the law of inertia would render *all* motion inexplicable in a self-contained universe unless that universe includes an internal source of motion, to be found in an all-pervasive and self-moving ether which can also be considered as a *vis vivifica*, a life-force that is apparently sufficient to explain the phenomenon of organic life. Finally, in the *Opus postumum* Kant tries to refine rather than reject the initial argument of the "Critique of Teleological Judgment": that we can only understand the reciprocal causality we observe in organisms by seeing it as if it were the product of purposive design. However, Kant's most explicit refinement of this argument, that the *unity* of the design of an organism implies an indivisible and hence immaterial substance as its cause, is a clear case of a paralogism of pure reason. This leaves standing what is perhaps only the passing suggestion that we must conceive of the purposiveness of organisms as an exception to the ordinary laws of nature because we can only conceive of purposiveness itself on the model of our own *free* purposiveness. But since our only reason for conceiving of our own purposiveness as free is our recognition of our obligation under the moral law, and Kant always argues that our own freedom as moral agents must be fully compatible with the complete determination of our behavior as natural beings by natural laws, he at least *should* conclude that organisms too, just like ourselves, can at least in principle be understood by viewing them from the two different standpoints of theoretical and practical reason, rather than by seeing two different kinds of law at work *within* nature. Thus Kant should have reached the position that although the distinction between the organic and the inorganic may be the most fundamental distinction to be drawn in the complete classification of matter, and our experience of organisms may play a special heuristic role in suggesting a teleological view of the whole of nature to us, it is only our awareness of the freedom of our own purposiveness that leads us to conceive of the purposiveness of organisms as necessitating a fundamental split between the teleological and mechanical views of nature—in which case, however, we should also conceive of the teleological view even of organisms as thoroughly compatible with the ideal of a complete mechanical explanation of their behavior. But there is no adequate evidence that Kant ever did reach such a settled view of what we learn from the case of organisms.


## 2. THE ARGUMENTS OF THE "CRITIQUE OF TELEOLOGICAL JUDGMENT"

### 2.1

The first argument of the "Critique of Teleological Judgment," and the one to which Kant devotes the most space, is that paradigmatic organic processes cannot be understood by our ordinary, mechanical conception of causation. Kant does not define this ordinary conception, but seems to assume that it is both logically and temporally unidirectional: that is, the character of a composite whole is always explained by the character of its parts, which are in turn both logically independent of and temporally antecedent to the whole. His argument is then that we are incapable of explaining organic processes such as reproduction, growth, and self-preservation simply as processes of combining antecedently extant, fully formed parts into a subsequent whole or of adding such parts to an already existing whole and thereby changing its character, processes in which the (combination or addition of) antecedent parts would always be the cause and the subsequent whole or its modified state would always be the effect. Instead, on Kant's account, we can only conceive of an organism as "cause and effect of itself" (*CPJ*, §64, 5:370). In the case of reproduction—the most opaque of Kant's examples—the idea seems to be that instead of one or two antecedent combinations of parts (the parents) producing a subsequent new combination of parts (the offspring)—a process that could be explained mechanically—reproduction actually involves a whole, namely a species, producing one of its own parts, namely a member of the species (*CPJ*, §64, 5:371).[4] In the case of growth, the idea is that instead of simply adding pre-existing parts to itself, a growing organism "first processes the matter that it adds to itself

---

[4] Kant actually uses the word *Gattung*, which in taxonomic contexts is ordinarily translated as "genus" in contrast to *Art*, translated as "species"; but since his example here does not depend on any contrast between levels of classification, his point may best be seen by taking *Gattung* to mean "species" in the ordinary contemporary sense of a population any of whose members are capable of combining to produce fertile offspring.

into a specifically-distinct quality, which the mechanism of nature outside of it cannot provide, and develops itself further by means of a material which, in its composition, is its own product" (*CPJ*, §64, 5:371). For example, a growing plant, instead of just adding bits of soil and water to itself, transforms the material that it takes in into its own characteristic form of cellulose; this is to be understood as the whole plant modifying what are to become its parts, rather than the converse. Finally, in the case of organic self-preservation or self-maintenance, parts are seen as having a reciprocal dependence on each other as well as upon the whole: In a deciduous tree, for instance, the continued life of the whole tree depends upon the proper functioning of such parts as its roots and leaves, but then again the emergence of a new set of leaves each spring depends upon the continued health of the whole tree; and while the growth of the roots each season depends upon the sugar produced by the leaves, at the same time the leaves can only function if they are supplied with water by the roots: In Kant's words, "the preservation of the one part" of the tree "is reciprocally dependent on the preservation of the other" (*CPJ*, §64, 5:371). These various forms of reciprocal dependence—the dependence of a whole on its parts but at the same time of the parts on the whole, and the reciprocal dependence of parts on each other—Kant thinks of as cases of reciprocal causation: The whole is both effect and yet cause of its parts, and the parts are both cause and effect of each other. And this, Kant claims, cannot be understood by our ordinary model of causation, because "insofar as the causal combination is thought merely through the understanding, it is a connection that constitutes a series (of causes and effects) which always goes in one direction [*immer abwärts geht*]" (*CPJ*, §65, 5:372).

To cope with this, Kant supposes, we need to conceive of the production and functioning of organisms by means of a conception of final (*nexus finalis*) rather than merely mechanical or efficient causation (*nexus effectivus*) (*CPJ*, §65, 5:372), where final causes are understood on the model of our own intentional production of artifacts. "In the sphere of the practical," Kant says, "(namely of art), we readily find such a connection, as where, e.g., the house is, to be sure, the cause of the moneys that are taken in as rent, but yet, conversely, the representation of this possible income was the cause of the erection of the house" (*CPJ*, §65, 5:372). That is, in a case of final causation such as our own intentional production of an artifact, the whole can be both cause and effect of itself without violating our unidirectional conception of efficient causation in this way: Our *representation* of the whole (and of its potential value) is the cause (a final cause) of our acquisition and/or fabrication of the necessary parts (as material cause), the ensuing combination of which in accordance with a plan (a formal cause) derived from that antecedent representation of the whole is the (efficient) cause of the subsequent actual existence of the intended whole. Thus, Kant proposes that we can reconcile the reciprocal causation that we observe in organisms with the only form of causation we actually understand, progressive or unidirectional causation, by thinking of organisms as if their complex organization is the product of an antecedent design for them which is part of an intelligible unidirectional causal sequence. And if this is so, then we must also think of there being some purpose that organisms serve, for an intelligent agent does not create a design (a formal cause) without some purpose (a final cause) in mind: In Kant's words, the "causality" behind organisms "must be assumed as if it were possible only through reason; but this is then the faculty for acting in accordance with ends (a will); and the object, which is represented as possible only through this, will be represented as possible only as an end" (CPJ, §64, 5: 370).[5]

Of course, the analogy between the human production of artifacts and the natural functioning of organisms is only partial. In particular, while we conceive of there being a variety of reciprocal relations among the parts of an artifact, such as the parts of a complex watch, that can only be explained by reference to an antecedent design, we do not conceive of a watch as being able to replace its own parts as needed—"one wheel is not the efficient cause of the production of another" (CPJ, §65, 5:374)—nor do we conceive of our artifacts as being able to reproduce themselves.[6] In other words, though we appeal to our own artifacts to understand organisms, in the case of artifacts our exercise of causation is external to the functioning of the object once we have produced it, while in the case of an organism "its parts themselves combine into the unity of a whole by being reciprocally cause and effect of its form" (CPJ, §65, 5:373). More generally, the intricacy of organisms exceeds our own capacity for design. So, Kant says, "we say far too little about nature and its capacity in organized products when we call this an **analogue of art**" (CPJ, §65, 5:374), or at least of our art. Thus, although we must conceive of the agency behind the design of organisms in analogy with our own voluntary production of artifacts, we must also conceive this agency as possessing intellect and powers greater than our own. Only

[5] See also CPJ, §84, 5:434.
[6] Well, we didn't in Kant's time: watches and Jacquard looms could not produce more of themselves. Perhaps computer-driven machine tools can or shortly will be able to make more computer-driven machine tools.

thus can our conception of the causality behind organisms be that "of a being that possesses a causality according to concepts adequate for such a product" (*CPJ*, §65, 5:373). And since we have neither empirical evidence nor theoretical proof of the existence of such an author of nature—though later Kant will remind us that we have good grounds in practical reason for postulating such a thing—we can only use the notion of an organism as the product of design as a regulative principle for heuristic purposes. In Kant's words,

The concept of a thing, as an end of nature in itself, is thus not a constitutive concept of understanding or of reason, but it can still be a regulative concept for the reflective power of judgment, in accordance with a remote analogy with our causality in accordance with ends, for guiding the investigation of objects of this sort and reflecting on their supreme ground. (*CPJ*, §65, 5:375)

Kant's idea is that we can use the analogy between organisms and our own designed artifacts to posit ends for particular parts of the organisms, which will in turn guide us in our investigation of the mechanical causation manifested in those organs.

In spite of the limits that must restrict any analogy between ourselves and the causality behind the existence of organic nature, in Kant's view this analogy suffices to introduce a conception of not only internal but also external purposiveness for organic nature: That is, we must not just represent the parts and the whole of organisms as reciprocally related, but must also be able to conceive of some purpose for their very existence. Moreover, once we have conceived of an intelligent and purposive author of organic nature, it is inevitable for us to conceive of such a being as the author of all of nature, and as having a purpose in the creation of nature as a whole: "This concept necessarily leads to the idea of the whole of nature as a system in accordance with the rule of ends, to which idea all mechanism in nature must be subordinated in accordance with principles of reason (at least to investigate the appearance of nature thereby)" (*CPJ*, §67, 5:379).[7] This feature of the analogy leads to the larger argument that is the chief point of the "Critique of Teleological Judgment": Though we are driven to raise the question of the purpose of nature by (the limits of) our theoretical comprehension, only practical reason can furnish a candidate for this end, namely our own existence as

---

[7] The suggestion that if it is inevitable for us to look at organisms as if they were products of design then it also becomes natural for us to look at all of nature as if it were in the service of an overarching end—at least for heuristic purposes—is repeatedly expounded; for other passages see *CPJ*, §67, 5:380; §72, 5:391; §75, 5:398; §78, 5:414; and §82, 5:427.

moral agents. Thus reflection on nature leads us to the goal of our own morality, while at the same time, by means of the argument from the idea of the highest good that Kant restates in the final sections of the third *Critique*, morality itself also requires us to think of nature as a realm in which the ends that we set for ourselves as moral agents may be realized, and thus leads to the same postulate of the intelligent author-ship of nature to which we are driven by the peculiarities of comprehend-ing organisms. But a detailed discussion of this argument must be omitted here.[8]

## 2.2

Kant's second argument against a unified treatment of inorganic and organic matter comes in the course of the Dialectic of Teleological Judgment. In order to resolve an apparent antinomy between the maxims that everything in nature can be explained mechanically and some things in nature can only be explained by final causes (*CPJ*, §70, 5:387), Kant considers different possible accounts of what might explain the appear-ance of purposiveness in nature. We might consider these to be alterna-tive accounts of the ontological rather than the epistemological status of purposiveness in nature, since they are alternative accounts of what such purposiveness might be rather than accounts of how we might come to know it exists. The proposed accounts fall into two groups, each of which has two members. On one side is what Kant calls the "idealism" of natural ends, which would maintain that purposiveness in nature is "unintentional" and merely apparent and can be explained away by a proper understanding of the laws of nature; on the other side is the "realism" of natural ends, which maintains that purposiveness in nature is "intentional" and cannot be explained away—at least not by us, for we must remember that the epistemological status of this claim is regulative and heuristic (*CPJ*, §72, 5:391). The two species of the ideal-ism of natural ends are those of "casuality" (*Casualität*) or "accidental-ity," on the one hand, and "fatality" on the other. Casuality is the view of Democritus or Lucretius that all complexity in nature, *a fortiori* the appearance of purposiveness, is due to the utterly random collision of particles; fatality is the view of Spinoza that everything in nature can be explained as due to the inexorable laws of an original being but is not due to any intelligence in such a being (*CPJ*, §72, 5:391). The two species of

---

[8] I have further explored this "master argument" of the "Critique of Teleological Judgment" in Chs. 11 and 12 below.

the realism of natural ends are the "physical" and the "hyperphysical": The first, or "hylozoism," is the view that life, and purposiveness, is "in matter, or, through an animating inner principle, in a world-soul"; the second, or "theism," is the view that the principle of organic life is not within the organisms themselves but is "a primordial ground of the world-all, as an intelligent being producing it with intention" (*CPJ*, §72, 5:392). Kant then argues that the Lucretian view does not even explain the appearance of design in nature, while the Spinozist view explains too much, by leaving no room even for the appearance of contingency in nature (*CPJ*, §73, 5:393). Then—and this is the argument we are interested in—he claims that "hylozoism" or physical realism with regard to natural ends must fail, because the idea that matter could contain in itself an originating life-force, let alone a principle of action in accordance with purposes, is incompatible with the law of inertia. As Kant puts it, "the possibility of a living matter" is contradictory because "lifelessness, **inertia**, constitutes the essential character of matter" (*CPJ*, §73, 5:394); presumably the law of inertia implies that matter can never originate any change at all unless acted upon by an agent external to it.

Kant had stated this argument in his metaphysics lectures (*Metaphysik L1*) as early as the mid-1770s:

Animals are not mere machines or matter, rather they have souls; for everything in the whole of nature is either inanimate or animate. All matter as matter (matter as such) is inanimate. From what do we know that? The concept we have of matter is this: Matter is an extended, impenetrable, inert thing. When, e.g., we perceive a mote on a paper, then we look to see whether it moves. If it does not move of itself, then we hold it to be inanimate matter, which is inert, and which would remain lying for all eternity if it were not moved by something else. But as soon as a matter moves, then we look to see whether it moved itself voluntarily. If we perceive that in the mote, then we see that it is **animate**, it is **an animal**. An animal is thus an animated matter, for life is the faculty for determining oneself from an inner principle according to the power of choice. But matter, as matter, has no inner principle of self-activity, no spontaneity to move itself, rather all matter that is animate has an inner principle which is separated from the object of outer sense, and is an object of inner sense.... Thus: All matter which lives is alive not as matter but rather has a principle of life and is animated. But to the extent matter is animated, to that extent it is **ensouled**. (28:275)

Presumably Kant would have had to refine this argument to take care of the case of plants as well as animals: Plants would appear to have the power to generate motion from some internal principle, but not from the power of choice, and thus would not seem to be ensouled (even from a merely regulative point of view). So perhaps the noninertial principle of motion in plants could thus not be represented as an immaterial substance conjoined to lifeless matter like an animal's soul, but might instead have to be represented as the product of a soul-like substance that is not literally joined to its matter. But this would only mean that plants would draw us even more directly to the idea of an intelligent author of their design than animated organisms do.

In the Dialectic of Teleological Judgment, Kant does not expound the argument in such detail, let alone distinguish between its application to plants and to animals. But he does complete his discussion of the systems of purposiveness by arguing that although we can have no direct evidence for the truth of theism, that is, for the actual existence of a purposive and intelligent author of nature, at least this hypothesis is internally coherent, free of an outright contradiction like hylozoism, and can thus be adopted as a principle for reflective if not for determinant judgment (*CPJ*, §73, 5:394). This conclusion, of course, paves the way for the larger objectives of the third *Critique*.

## 2.3

In the next part of the Dialectic, Kant gives an extended exposition of his third argument for the special status of natural ends. This is the argument that because of the discursive character of our understanding, that is, its restriction to the use of general concepts, there must always be much in the form of any particular entity in nature that cannot be regarded as determined by our general concepts for it: In cognition by means of our understanding "the particular is not determined by it through the general, and the former cannot therefore be derived from the latter alone" (*CPJ*, §77, 5:406). Kant then interprets this to entail that much in the particular forms of nature remains contingent (*zufällig*) relative to all the general concepts of nature that we do or can ever possess. And this in turn he takes to mean that the *agreement* or *harmony* (*Zusammenstimmung*) of particular forms in nature with our general concepts must seem contingent to us. But this, he supposes, is incompatible with the very "possibility of an agreement of the things in nature with the power of judgment," and to make even this possibility intelligible to ourselves we must therefore "think of another understanding, in relation to which, and especially to the end that is ascribed to it, we can represent that agreement of natural laws with our power of judgment . . . as **necessary**" (*CPJ*, §77, 5:407). That is, in order to explain even the possibility of our comprehension of particular things in nature, we have to postulate an intelligent author of nature whose concepts make necessary what appears merely contingent to us.

I am expounding this as a separate argument in Kant's thought about the distinctive character of organisms because it turns on neither the alleged reciprocal causality of organisms nor the supposedly self-contradictory concept of living matter. Kant himself does not draw a clear boundary between this argument and his original argument that the reciprocal causality characteristic of organisms is incompatible with our ordinary conception of causality. In fact, he intertwines these two arguments in his very first exposition of the argument about the special causality of organisms, taking that argument to imply the "**contingency** of the form [of an organism] in relation to reason given all the empirical laws of nature," and then arguing that because reason must nevertheless be able to "cognize the necessity in every form of a product of nature," it must therefore introduce at least the idea of a causality of nature, that is, a designer of it, for whom what appears contingent to us can be necessary (*CPJ*, §64, 5:370). Yet there is at least one key difference between the arguments of §64 and §77: In the argument of *CPJ*, §64, particular features of the forms of organisms will appear contingent relative to the *causal* concepts of our understanding because those concepts are incapable of representing reciprocal causality; in the argument of §77 the forms of organisms appear to be contingent relative to *any* concepts of our understanding just because those concepts are always general and therefore necessarily leave something in their particular objects indeterminate. So it seems worth considering the argument of §77 as a separate argument in the larger project of showing that our experience of organisms requires us to introduce a teleological conception of nature into the principles of reflective judgment.

## 3. THE FATE OF THESE ARGUMENTS

I now turn to the problems with these arguments and to Kant's further attempts to clarify the special status of organisms in the *Opus postumum*. I will consider the fate of these arguments in an order inverse to that in which I have just expounded them.

### 3.1

I begin with the argument from the contingency of natural forms to the need for a special principle of intelligent design to explain them (2.3) because of the obvious problem with this argument. By the obvious problem with this argument I do not mean to refer to the question it might well suggest: Why do we need to postulate an author of nature with concepts of its particular forms that make everything in them necessary in order to explain even the *possibility* of our successfully applying general concepts to them? This is indeed a question that can be raised about all of Kant's arguments for postulates, whether of reflective judgment or practical reason, but it is a difficult question that I will not pursue here.[9] Rather, the obvious problem is simply that the argument from contingency as separately stated in §77 has nothing special to do with *organisms*: It is a general argument that can be made about all particulars in nature, organic or inorganic, because any general concept leaves something undetermined about any particular object that falls under it. Any general concept of a kind of mineral, for example, will leave many things undetermined about any particular mineral sample that is subsumed under it, for example, its size or weight, perhaps its color or smell, perhaps even the number of neutrons in the atoms of its different isotopes. And if we are looking for a guarantee that our power of judgment will always be able to come up with even a general concept for any particular object we encounter, as Kant's argument about the conditions for even the possibility of harmony between our power of judgment and nature suggests, we will need that guarantee just as much for all the variegated minerals we encounter as well as for the immense diversity of organisms we experience.

Kant does not appear to make this objection to his own argument explicitly. But in the published introduction to the *Critique of Judgment*—the very last part of it to be written, as we know, extracted out of Kant by the publisher's constant pleading as the typesetting of the rest of the text approached completion—Kant deploys an argument of the same form in a way that presupposes its utter generality. This is his argument that because the categories of pure understanding that we are always able to impose upon our experience of nature in virtue of the constitution of our own minds furnish only the most general laws of nature, such as the general principles of causality or conservation, our confidence that we can succeed in discovering a system of particular laws

---

[9] For some discussion of this general issue, see my "In praktischer Absicht: Kants Begriff eines Postulats der reinen praktischen Vernunft," *Philosophisches Jahrbuch* 104 (1997): 1–18, translated as "From a Practical Point of View: Kant's Conception of a Postulate of Pure Practical Reason," in my *Kant on Freedom, Law, and Happiness* (Cambridge: Cambridge University Press, 2000), 333–71.

of nature can only be based on the idea, valid of course for the reflective use of judgment only, that the particular laws of nature are also due to an understanding, but an understanding more powerful than our own. In Kant's words:

There are such manifold forms of nature, as it were so many modifications of the general transcendental concepts of nature that are left undetermined by those laws that the pure understanding gives *a priori*, because these only pertain to the possibility of a nature (as an object of the senses), that there must also be laws, which, although they may certainly be contingent as empirical according to the insight of **our** understanding, must nevertheless, if they are to be called laws (as is also demanded by the concept of a nature), be regarded as necessary on the basis of a principle of the unity of the manifold, even if it is unknown to us....Now this principle can be nothing other than that...the particular empirical laws, with regard to that which is left undetermined in them by [our general concepts of understanding], must be considered in accordance with such a unity as would be given to them by an understanding (even if not ours) for the sake of our faculty of cognition, in order to make possible a system of experience in accord with particular laws of nature. (*CPJ*, Introduction IV, 5:179–80)

At this point in the Introduction Kant has said nothing about the special status of organisms—that is not mentioned until section VIII of the Introduction, and then only barely. Instead, at this point he seems to assume that all of the particular laws of nature that we can discover can be unified into a single system, regardless of what particular objects in nature they deal with, and to be arguing that in order to overcome the appearance of contingency that appears to threaten our confidence in *that* possibility we must postulate the idea of a guiding intelligence behind the laws of nature. This argument would appear to apply to laws of geology and mineralogy just as well as to laws of biology and psychology and to imply that we could be led to the idea of an intelligent principle for nature by reflecting on the necessary conditions for the determinacy of any of these laws as well as on the condition of the possibility of unifying all such laws in a single system.

This argument in the Introduction is of the same form as the argument of §77, arguing that we can only ascribe necessity to something left contingent by the generality of our own concepts by postulating an understanding which does not suffer from this defect of our own. This at least implies that the argument of §77 has nothing to do with organisms in particular. Kant does not state this explicitly, but neither does he use this argument again in any of his discussions of the status of organisms after the *Critique of Judgment*.

3.2

I now turn to Kant's argument that organisms require a special mode of judgment because the law of inertia requires that matter be conceived as lifeless (2.2). Kant seems to undermine the premise of this argument in the *Opus postumum* by arguing that we cannot conceive of nature in general as a purely inertial system merely transmitting from one region or object to another the effects of some initial external impetus. Instead, he argues throughout this work, any conception of nature requires the postulation of an internal principle of motion that we can construe as the origin of all motion in nature. So at least insofar as the organic is that which contains its own internal principle of motion, the organic is not by that fact alone distinguished from inorganic matter. Kant's intentions in the mass of notes that have come down to us as the *Opus postumum* are notoriously obscure. Nevertheless, it seems reasonably clear that he wanted to make a transition from pure philosophy to an empirically applicable physics by constructing a system *of forces* that could ultimately be seen as deriving from some single elementary force, and that he wanted also to make a division of the fundamental types of *matter*. In the latter division, the distinction between organic and inorganic matter is always primary, and Kant often presents the purposiveness evident in the former but not the latter as the basis of this distinction. At the same time, it seems as if Kant also wanted to argue that both organic and inorganic matter can be joined in a single system of forces, because even inorganic matter cannot, contrary to the assumption underlying Kant's rejection of hylozoism in the *Critique of Judgment*, be understood as utterly lifeless, but is instead connected to a force that is also adequate to explain the mobility of living things.

This is, to be sure, not evident in everything that Kant writes in the *Opus postumum*. In an early passage, for instance, he writes that "**living** force (by impact) (*vis viva*) is different from the **vivifying** force (*vis vivifica*). The latter, in a separate world-system (and its generation) is perhaps the cause of **plants** and **animals**" (*OP*, 22:210). This seems to suggest that there is a difference between the *vis viva* of inorganic matter and the *vis vivifica* of organic matter, and that the difference between these two forces is enough to entail that the organic and the inorganic constitute two separate world-systems.

Subsequently, however, Kant devotes many pages to arguing that motion in a system of even inorganic bodies cannot be understood as due to impact operating through the law of inertia alone, but that an internal and perpetual source of motion must be posited within nature itself, as the fundamental force of a fundamental matter that is never directly observed but is not a mere postulate (like God or the immortal soul) either—

a matter, distributed in the whole universe as a continuum, uniformly penetrating all bodies, and filling [all space].... Be it called ether, or caloric, or whatever, it is no **hypothetical material**... rather it can be recognized, and postulated *a priori*, as an element necessarily belonging to the transition from the metaphysical foundations of natural science to physics. (*OP*, 21:218)

Kant gives a variety of reasons for this "*a priori* postulate," but it is important to note that none of them is restricted to any one kind of matter. Some of his arguments have to do with the conditions of the possibility of our perception of objects at a distance; others have to do with the very possibility of the existence of bodies, independent of the fact that we perceive them. One early passage argues for the ether for two reasons: first, to have a force even more fundamental than the opposed forces of attraction and repulsion which are necessary to explain how matter can coalesce, being neither infinitely dispersed nor infinitely condensed into a single point; second, to explain why motion does not cease in the universe.

All matter must have repulsive forces, since otherwise it would fill no space; but attractive force must also be attributed to it, since otherwise it would disperse itself into the infinity of space—in both cases space would be empty. Consequently, one can think of such alternating impacts and counterimpacts [as existing] from the beginning of the world, as a trembling (oscillating, vibrating) motion of the matter which fills the entire universe, includes within itself all bodies, and is both elastic and at the same time attractive in itself. These pulsations constitute a living force....

An elastic fluid in the state of internal vibration necessarily occupies a greater space than in the state of rest. Thus is brought about, as the effect of a living force, the extension of matters in cosmic space....

The reason to assume such a hypothesis is that, in the absence of such a principle of the continual excitation of the world-material, a state of lifeless stasis would come about from the exhaustion of the elastic forces in the unceasing universal attraction, and a complete cessation in the moving forces of matter would occur. (*OP*, 21:310)

The vibration of an all-pervasive ether, Kant believes, can be understood as a single form of motion with both attractive and repulsive properties, and thus as the most fundamental force in a system of forces; and only the perpetuity of this motion can explain the continued extension as well as motion of the more obvious, visible bodies in the universe.

The details of such arguments as this for the ether are, of course, obscure, but we need not worry about them for my present point. This point is just this; In spite of Kant's distinction between *vis viva* and *vis vivifica*, the theory of force alone need not imply an essential contrast between organic and inorganic matter for the simple reason that even the motion of mere inorganic matter cannot be explained by the impact forces of *vis viva* alone. The very existence of inorganic matter alone is enough to entail the existence of an internal, noninertial source of motion in the physical world and thus undermines the argument of the *Critique of Judgment* that living matter is self-contradictory because the motion of matter is governed by inertia alone. And accordingly, Kant appears to drop this argument too from his search for the differentia between organic and inorganic matter in the *Opus postumum*.

### 3.3

This is not to say, however, that Kant eliminates all distinction between organic and inorganic matter in the *Opus postumum*. On the contrary, as I mentioned, he repeatedly presents the distinction between organic and inorganic as the most fundamental distinction in the system of matter —though at the same time he generally does portray this distinction, in contrast to the one passage cited above (*OP*, 22:210), as a distinction *within* a single system of matter rather than between two separate world-systems. Moreover, Kant also continues to portray the major ground for the distinction between the organic and the inorganic in the same terms he uses in his primary argument in the "Critique of Teleological Judgment." Thus Kant writes:

The definition of an organic body is that it is a body, every part of which is there **for the sake of the other** (reciprocally as end and, at the same time, means). ... An organic (articulated) body is one in which each part, with its moving force, necessarily relates to the whole (to each part in its composition). (*OP*, 21:210–11)

At the same time, Kant clearly devotes much effort to trying to make more precise both why the reciprocal causality that defines the distinction between the organic and the inorganic should lead to the connection of the organic to an immaterial principle, and then how that immaterial principle is to be conceived as related to the matter of organisms as well as to the material world in general. Why are these still issues for him? What could he see as missing from the argument of the third *Critique*?

The argument of the third *Critique* is unstable. Kant starts by arguing that it is our experience of organisms that initially leads us to the thought of an intelligible purposiveness in nature because of particular organic processes which are resistant to any mechanical explanation given the resources of our own understanding (*CPJ*, §65, 5:375–6). We then attempt to extend the idea of purposiveness to nature as a whole (*CPJ*, §67, 5:379–80); Kant does not in fact say why we inevitably do this, but we can conjecture that the desire for universality that is the essence of reason makes such an attempt inevitable. Once we try this, however, a tension between mechanical and final explanation inevitably suggests itself, which is ultimately resolved by the suggestion that we conceive of these two forms of explanation as applying at two different levels, namely, the sensible and the supersensible, and that we further conceive of the supersensible purposiveness of nature as being fulfilled through the mechanical laws of sensible nature: "The principle which is to make possible the compatibility of the two [kinds of explanation] in judging nature in accordance with them must lie in that which lies outside of both (hence also outside the possible empirical representation of nature), but which contains the ground of these, i.e., in the supersensible" (*CPJ*, §78, 5:412). But once this move is made, mechanical and teleological explanation are compatible everywhere in nature, and it is not clear whether there is any special reason why organisms need remain resistant to complete mechanical explanation at the level of sensible appearance; rather, the unique experience of organisms seems to be a ladder that can be thrown aside once we have ascended to the transcendental idealist reconciliation of mechanism and teleology. And indeed, Kant seems to shift from his original insistence that it is the specific structure of our understanding that sets an *a priori* limit to our possible success in explaining organic processes to a much vaguer suggestion that there is nothing particular in organic processes that necessarily defeats our ability to use mechanical explanation, though some general limit inherent in our understanding, perhaps its mere finitude, will prevent us from explaining everything about organisms. Thus, Kant begins his solution to the antinomy of teleological judgment by asserting that "[w]e can by no means prove the impossibility of the generation of organized products of nature through the mere mechanism of nature" (*CPJ*, §71, 5:388), and that we must therefore use the idea of the purposiveness of organic nature "only as a guide for reflection, which always remains open for all mechanical grounds of explanation" (5:389). And he concludes his entire discussion of the antinomy by emphasizing even more forcefully that we can set no *a priori* limit on how far we can progress in understanding everything in nature by means of mechanical principles alone:

Now since it is entirely indeterminate and always indeterminable for our reason, how much the mechanism of nature can do as means to its final end; and since it must always be assumed to be possible, on account of the above-mentioned intelligible principle of the possibility of a nature in general, that nature can be thoroughly explained in accordance with both generally harmonizing laws (the physical law and that of final causes): We therefore do not know how far the mechanical kind of explanation that is possible for us may go.... 

On this is grounded the authority... and even the duty to explain all products and occurrences in nature, even the most purposive, mechanically, as far as stands within our power (whose limits within this kind of investigation we cannot state). (*CPJ*, §78, 5:414–15)

But if, as this last remark suggests, there is in fact no particular *a priori* limit to our power to explain even organisms mechanically, what becomes of the special status of organisms that was supposed to force a teleological view of nature upon us in the first place? Is it just an empirical fact, a matter of empirical psychology rather than of transcendental psychology, that organisms suggest the idea of purposiveness to us? Is this enough to support the whole weight of Kant's teleology, in which he clearly wants to argue that science leads us to the same twofold conception of nature that morality also requires us to conceive?

As is typical of him, Kant never explicitly acknowledges that the argument of the "Critique of Teleological Judgment" might be in danger of collapsing in this way. But in the *Opus postumum* he does seem to be searching for a way in which to allow for unlimited mechanical explanation of organisms while still showing that they necessarily introduce the thought of an immaterial principle. What he now tries to argue is that organisms are genuinely material, and for that reason comprise a single system with inorganic matter, but that organisms, unlike other matter, *must* be linked to an immaterial cause, and for this reason do necessitate the thought of an immaterial ground for nature as more than a matter of empirical psychology. But since he can no longer use the argument from inertia for this end, he looks for a new reason to argue that the special complexity of organisms does not just test the extent of our cognitive powers, but specifically proves the necessity of an immaterial ground for themselves and then for nature as a whole.

One argument that Kant repeatedly tries is this: The thought of an antecedent design for the reciprocal causality of organisms does not force the thought of an immaterial cause of them on us just because of the temporal antecedence of the thought of design, but because the very thought of a design itself must have a kind of *unity* or *simplicity* that nothing material ever has; that is, it is not the temporal location of the idea of an organism that is a problem for mechanical explanation, but the very fact that such an idea is a *thought* at all. In one of its simplest versions, this argument is stated thus:

An organic body presupposes an organizing principle, whether inner or outer. The latter must be simple, for otherwise it would itself require an organization. As simple, it cannot be a part of matter (for each part of matter is always itself composite). So the organizing principle of the organic body must be outside space in general. It can, however, be internally active in one respect, while being external in another: that is, in another substance, the world-spirit. (*OP*, 22:295)

In another passage, that might be thought to bring in a complicating factor by emphasizing that the organizing thought for an organized body is an intention, Kant writes thus:

An organic natural body is thus thought of as a **machine** (a body arranged **intentionally** as to its form). Under no circumstances can it be a property of matter to have an **intention** (since it is the absolute unity of a subject which **connects** the manifold of representation in one consciousness); for all matter (and every part of it) is composite. (*OP*, 22:548)[10]

But the key claim is still that the reason why the design of an organism necessarily introduces the idea of an immaterial cause of it is the absolute incompatibility between the indivisible unity of a thought and the infinitely composite and divisible nature of matter. Thus Kant argues that while organisms are material machines, they must be designed and animated by something immaterial—not because matter is ruled by inertia, but because it is never a true unity.

This is certainly a new argument in the *Opus postumum*. Unfortunately, it is not an argument that the critical Kant of the previous decade would have tolerated, for it succumbs to the very error that Kant diagnosed in the first *Critique* in the Paralogism of Pure Reason: It confuses the *logical* unity or simplicity of a thought with the ontological indivisibility of the substance in which that thought inheres. As Kant said in the Paralogism, "The proposition 'A thought can only be the effect of the absolute unity of a thinking being' cannot be treated as analytic" (A 353). This is because "Through the [representation] I, I always think an absolute but logical unity of the subject (simplicity), but I do not cognize the real simplicity of my subject" (A 356–7). The argument of the Paralogism

---

[10] See also *OP*, 22:547.

is just that one can never make a valid inference from the formal or logical properties of a thought to the structure of the substance that has that thought. Presumably the same would hold of the thought of a design: In whatever sense such a thought must be thought to be a unity, we just cannot automatically assume that the subject that thinks that thought must also be simple. Thus even conceding the unity of the thought of a design and a purpose for an organism does not seem to force us to posit an immaterial substance as its subject.

This new argument for the special nature of organisms in the *Opus postumum* clearly fails by the standards of the *Critique of Pure Reason*. However, although the last passage cited from the *Opus postumum* argued that it cannot "be a property of matter to have an **intention**" because of the contrast between the unity of an intention and the compositeness of matter, there are other passages in these texts where Kant asserts the dependence of organic matter on an immaterial principle because of the purposiveness or intentionality of organisms without saying anything about indivisibility. Here are several such passages:

The first division of physical bodies is, thus, that into organic and inorganic. A physically organic body (in contrast to a mechanically organic body) is one, each of whose parts is by nature there in it for the sake of the other; in which, conversely, the concept of the **whole** also determines the form of the parts.... Such a formation indicates a natural cause, acting according to **purposes**.... One can seek the productive force of this inner form nowhere else than in a formative understanding—that is, seek it solely in a non-material cause...(*OP*, 22:283)

Zoönomy contains three vital powers: **nervous power**, as a principle of excitability [*incitabilitas*]; **muscular power** [*irritabilitas Halleri*]; and a **third one**, which brings both forces into active and reactive, constantly alternating, play: one all-penetrating, all-moving etc. material, of which heat is one phenomenon. (4) The force of organization in space and time, which contains a **nonmaterial** higher principle, namely an effectivity according to purposes. (*OP*, 22:301)

In the latter part of physics, the highest division of **bodies** (not just matter) is [into organic] and inorganic. The division can emerge *a priori* from concepts. For, the possibility of an organic body (that is, a body each of whose parts is there for the sake of the other, or which is so formed that the possibility of the parts and the form of their inner relations emerge only from its concept—a body which is thus only possible through purposes, which presuppose an immaterial principle which forms this substance either mediately or immediately) produces a teleological principle. (*OP*, 22:501)

The second of these passages confirms my claim that the *Opus postumum* rejects the third *Critique*'s argument against hylozoism by treating a number of organic processes as forms of the self-moving force of the ether, and thus as features that organic bodies have in *common* with all forms of matter. Then this passage, like the other two, suggests that what clearly distinguishes organic from inorganic matter is the presence of purposes in the former, thus that there is an essential connection between purposiveness as such and the immaterial. What this connection is, however, is not made clear.

Several other passages make the essential connection to the immaterial even more obscure when they link the immaterial principle of organisms not to purposes in general but to *desire*. For instance,

The principle of the spontaneity of the motion of the parts of our own body (as limbs), considering the latter as our own self, is a mechanism. Although this [spontaneity] is an absolute unity of the principle of motion from **desires** (thus not material), nevertheless, reason can do no other than to make general (if only problematically) the concept of a purposive mechanism of matter, under the name of organization, and to contrast it with inorganic matter. (*OP*, 21:212)

The idea of organic bodies is **indirectly** contained *a priori* in that of a composite of moving forces, in which the concept of a real **whole** necessarily precedes that of its parts—which can only be thought by the concept of a combination according to **purposes**. . . . How can we include such bodies with such moving forces in the general classification, according to *a priori* principles? Because man is conscious of himself as a self-moving machine, without being able to further understand such a possibility, he can, and is entitled to, introduce *a priori* organic moving forces of bodies into the classification of bodies in general. . . . He [must], however, generalize the concept of vital force and of the excitability of matter in his own self by the faculty of desire. (*OP*, 21:213)

These passages only deepen the mystery, however. First Kant says that the mere presence of purposes in organisms implies their dependence on some immaterial substance, without explanation. Then he suggests that it is the evidence of motion from *desire*, an example of which we have in the spontaneity of our own motion, that implies the connection of organisms to a distinctive and immaterial principle. But given everything that we standardly assume about Kant's moral philosophy and moral anthropology, our *desires* are just the sort of thing for which we assume there can be, at least in principle, a completely physiological and, we should have thought, mechanical explanation. *Desires* are just those stimuli of our own actions that we can include in the phenomenal world, as part of the seamless causal nexus of that world. How is the presence of *desire* in ourselves supposed to prove the presence of any immaterial principle in or connected to our own organism, which we might then extend to the case of other organisms, and from there to nature as a whole?

One can only conjecture that a step is being omitted from Kant's argument. And what could this be? Perhaps it is precisely that reflection on our own desires is what reveals to us the difference between those desires, as what is merely passive in us, and our freely adopted *purposes*, which are the expressions of a kind of spontaneity that we do *not* directly experience in nature, namely our purposes as set for us by reason, and by means of which we can actually constrain our own desires. It is the *contrast* between our mere desires and our rational purposes that reveals to us the fact of our own freedom, as something that cannot be included in the seamless causal web of the phenomenal world but is an intimation of another aspect of our existence. Of course, we know well that it is Kant's view from the *Critique of Practical Reason* onward that it is only our recognition of our obligation under the moral law that leads us to realize that we are always free in the determination of our purposes, no matter how passively determined our mere desires may be. Then what is not explicitly stated in Kant's remarks on purposes in the *Opus postumum* would be the fact that we infer the freedom of our own purposes from our moral obligation, and so it is reflection on *morality* that requires us to think of purposes as free in a way that is not compatible with a purely mechanical explanation of the powers of matter. His argument would then have to be that it is our obligation under moral law that requires us to conceive of our *own* purposes as having a principle other than the mechanism of matter, so that when we impute an immaterial principle to organisms in general because of their purposiveness, it is our own model of purposiveness that we are using. The overall form of his argument would then have to be that it may be theoretical difficulties in comprehending organisms that require us to conceive of them as products of purpose, but that it is our morally grounded conception of our own purposiveness as free that leads us to the further thought that purposiveness entails immateriality, thus that organisms and ultimately all of nature must have an immaterial ground. In other words, only through the twofold stance that we need to take on our own purposes would our experience of organisms as purposive entities lead us to take a twofold view of nature as a whole.

Kant certainly does not make this argument explicit in the *Opus postumum*. But if, as we have seen, Kant himself has undermined the original arguments for the special nature of organisms offered in the *Critique of Judgment*, and if the explicit new argument in the *Opus postumum* falls victim to the original critique of any paralogism of pure reason, it is hard to see where Kant could turn for an argument for the special nature of organisms except to our own purposes, distinctive because they are under the legislation of morality. Of course, such an argument could never be considered theoretically constitutive; instead, the special status of organisms would be more like that of a postulate of practical reason such as that of our own freedom than like anything else. But since Kant had argued since the *Critique of Pure Reason* that it is only as postulates of practical reason that metaphysical claims can have any force for us at all, this is precisely the result we should have expected all along.

# PART II

## The System of Freedom

# 6

# Kant on the Theory and Practice
# of Autonomy

We all know what Kant means by autonomy: "the property of the will by
which it is a law to itself (independently of any property of the objects of
volition)" (G. 4:440),[1] or, since any law must be universal, the condition
of an agent who is "subject **only to laws given by himself but still
universal**" (G. 4:432). Or do we know what Kant means by autonomy?
There are a number of questions here. First, Kant's initial definition of
autonomy itself raises the question of why the property of the will being a
law to itself should be equivalent to its independence from any property
of objects of volition. It is also natural to ask, how does autonomy as

This chapter was originally presented at a conference on autonomy at the Social
Philosophy and Policy Center, Bowling Green State University, and was first published
in Ellen Frankel Paul, Fred D. Miller, Jr., and Jeffrey Paul (eds.), *Autonomy* (Cambridge:
Cambridge University Press, 2003), pp. 70–98. It is reprinted here with permission of the
publisher.

An earlier version of this essay was presented at the Collegium Transatlanticum Philo-
sophicum at Emory University in January 2002. I thank Jeff Edwards and Laszlo Tengelyi
for their comments on that occasion. I also thank Fred D. Miller, Jr., and Ellen Frankel
Paul for the valuable comments that they made on this more recent version.

[1] Citations from most of Kant's works will be located by volume and page number of
the Akademie edition, *Kant's gesammelte Schriften*, edited by the Royal Prussian (succes-
sively the German and then Berlin–Brandenburg) Academy of Sciences (Berlin: Georg
Reimer, later Walter de Gruyter & Co., 1900– ). Citations from the *Critique of Pure
Reason* will be located in the traditional manner by the pagination of its first (A) and
second (B) editions.
Translations of the *Critique of Pure Reason* are from Immanuel Kant, *Critique of Pure
Reason*, ed. and trans. Paul Guyer and Allen W. Wood (Cambridge: Cambridge University
Press, 1998). Translations of Kant's published works in moral philosophy are from
Immanual Kant, *Practical Philosophy*, ed. and trans. Mary J. Gregor (Cambridge:
Cambridge University Press, 1996); those of *Religion* are from Immanuel Kant, *Religion
and Rational Theology*, ed. and trans. Allen W. Wood and George di Giovanni (Cam-
bridge: Cambridge University Press, 1996); and those of his lectures are from Immanuel
Kant, *Lectures on Ethics*, ed. Peter Heath and J. B. Schneewind, trans. Peter Heath
(Cambridge: Cambridge University Press, 1997). Since these three volumes reproduce
the Akademie pagination, separate page references for the translations will be omitted.
This is also true of Immanuel Kant, *Anthropology from a Pragmatic Point of View*, trans.
Mary J. Gregor (The Hague: Martinus Nijhoff, 1974). Unless otherwise attributed here in
note 1, all other translations are my own.

Kant conceives it relate to more familiar notions of freedom. For example, consider Locke's conception of freedom as the condition of a person "to think, or not to think; to move, or not to move, according to the preference or direction of his own mind," rather than according to the preference or direction of any other person.[2] What is the relation between autonomy and this traditional conception of freedom as the liberty of an agent? And what is the relation of autonomy to the traditional conception of freedom of the will; that is, the condition that obtains, as G. E. Moore puts it, if, "wherever a voluntary action is right or wrong...it is true that the agent **could**, in a sense, have done something else instead,"[3] or in Kant's own terms, "**freedom** in the transcendental sense, as a special kind of causality...namely a faculty of absolutely beginning a state, and hence also a series of its consequences" (*CPurR*, A 445/B 473)? Second, we can ask why does Kant think that we have an unconditional obligation to strive to achieve autonomy through a self-given law, or why "the **principle** of every human being as **a will giving universal law through all its maxims**...would be very well suited to be the categorical imperative" (*G.* 4:432). Third, we can ask how does Kant think that human beings can actually achieve autonomy in the empirical conditions of human life, which include, among other conditions, those of being subject to a wide range of inclinations, and of being able to gain control over those inclinations, if at all, only by a slow process of education and maturation.

As it addresses these questions, this essay accordingly consists of three major parts. Section I makes two claims: First, that Kant sees autonomy, or self-governance by universal law, as the condition that is necessary to achieve and maintain freedom in two ordinary and, as it turns out, related senses—namely, the independence of the choices and actions of a person not only from domination by other persons, but also from domination by his own inclinations. The second claim of Section I is that autonomy cannot simply be equated with freedom of the will, but must instead be understood as the aim that a person with free will must adopt if he is to preserve and promote his freedom of choice and action in an ordinary sense, which is something such an agent ought to do, and can do, but does not necessarily do. Section II of this essay considers a variety of arguments by means of which Kant attempted, at various points in his career, to ground the assumption that the achievement of autonomy is the funda-

---

[2] John Locke, *An Essay concerning Human Understanding*, ed. P. H. Nidditch (Oxford: Clarendon Press, 1975), bk. II, chap. XXI, sec. 8.
[3] G. E. Moore, *Ethics* (Oxford: Oxford University Press, 1965), 84. Originally published in 1912.

mental unconditional obligation for human beings, as it is for any finite rational beings who can, but do not automatically, act in accordance with pure practical reason. Sections I and II will thus comprise a study of Kant's theory of autonomy. Section III then examines Kant's conception of the practice of autonomy, first by considering his account of how human beings can actually gain control over their inclinations in the course of their maturation, and then by distinguishing the empirical realization of autonomy from other conditions with which it might be confused.

## I. FREEDOM, FREEDOM OF THE WILL, AND AUTONOMY

### A. Freedom and Autonomy

In a number of passages, notably in his lectures on ethics, Kant suggests a bipartite account of freedom in choice and action. On the one hand, freedom consists in a person's ability to determine his ends independently of domination by his own inclinations and desires; on the other hand, freedom consists in a person's ability to select and pursue his own ends independently of domination by other persons. Thus, in his lectures in 1785 on moral philosophy, Kant is reported to have said, first, that a person demonstrates his freedom by "employing the power he has, to rule over his strong inclinations" (Mrong., 29:617). Then, a moment later, he reportedly said: "Freedom consists in this, that everyone can act according to his own will, without being necessitated to act according to the will of another" (Mrong., 29:618). Eight years later, in the Vigilantius lectures on the metaphysics of morals, we likewise find both definitions, although not in such close proximity to one another. On the one hand, Kant states that a person "actually proves himself free, in that he thereby demonstrates an *independentia arbitrii liberi a determinationibus per stimulos*," or an "independence of his free will from determination by stimuli" (Vig., 27:520). On the other hand, Kant also states that freedom consists in the independence of one person from domination by another: "Freedom consists only in this, that the agent utilizes his powers at his own choice, in accordance with a principle of reason; now anyone who ceded himself, with all his powers, to the disposition of another, and thus voluntarily enslaved himself, would alienate this freedom" (Vig., 27:594). It seems natural to ask what is the relationship between these two conceptions of freedom, before asking what is the relation of either or both to autonomy.

In fact, an account of the relationship between freedom as independence from domination by one's own inclinations and as independence from domination by others will readily emerge if we begin by considering the relationship between the first of these forms of freedom and autonomy. In the Vigilantius lectures, some pages prior to his definition of freedom as the independence of the determination of one's will by stimuli or inclinations, Kant had already stated:

The concept of freedom . . . **negatively** consists in the independence of choice from all determination *per stimulos*; so often, that is, as reason is determined by itself, independently of all sensory drives; **positively**, however, it consists in spontaneity, or the ability to determine oneself by reason, without the need for triggers [*Triebfedern*] from nature. (Vig., 27:494)

This passage parallels a familiar one from the *Groundwork*, in the opening of its section III:

**Will** is a kind of causality of living beings insofar as they are rational, and **freedom** would be the property of such causality independently of alien causes **determining it,** just as **natural necessity** is the property of the causality of all nonrational beings to be determined to activity by the influence of alien causes.
  The preceding definition of freedom is **negative** and therefore unfruitful for insight into its essence; but there flows from it a **positive** concept of freedom, which is so much the richer and more fruitful. Since the concept of causality brings with it that of laws in accordance with which, by something that we call a cause, something else, namely an effect, must be posited, so freedom, although it is not a property of the will in accordance with natural laws, is not for that reason lawless but must instead be a causality in accordance with immutable laws but of a special kind. . . . (G, 4:446)

Why should the freedom of the determination of the will by one's own inclinations or sensory drives be possible only if the will is instead determined by reason in accordance with its own immutable laws; that is, why should freedom, negatively described, be possible only by the achievement of autonomy?

This question should not be overlooked, because Kant, at least sometimes—and notoriously—makes it sound as if one could obtain freedom from domination by one's own inclinations simply by abolishing those inclinations: "[T]he inclinations themselves, as sources of needs, are so far from having an absolute worth, that it must instead be the universal wish of every rational being to be altogether free from them" (G, 4:428). However, it is Kant's considered position not only that our inclinations cannot be abolished because of our finitude or imperfection, but also that, since we can undertake no particular actions without particular ends, and yet particular ends are always suggested, although not determined, only by our natural inclinations, we can have no coherent conception of our own agency, that is, our ability to act, whether in accord with the demands of morality or in violation of them, without inclinations. Thus, freeing the determination of our wills from domination by our own inclinations cannot consist in the abolition of those inclinations, but, rather, only in the regulation of their role in the determination of our ends, a regulation that must consist in the application of principles of pure practical reason to our inclinations.

That particular actions always have particular ends, that particular ends are given empirically (that is, by inclinations or sensory impulse), and that the exercise of pure practical reason must therefore consist in the application of laws of reason to empirical impulses (or the elevation of the objects of some of those inclinations into ends, in light of their permissibility or even necessity in the eyes of reason), are constant principles in Kant's theory of action from early to late. In the mid-1770s, for example, Kant wrote:

Moral philosophy is the science of ends, so far as they are determined through pure reason. Or of the unity of all ends (where they do not contradict themselves) of rational beings. The matter of the good is given empirically, its form *a priori*. ...(R 6820, 19:172)

The doctrine that the "form of the good" must be *a priori* was subsequently amplified into the view that not only must the form of the good be given by pure practical reason, in the form of the moral law, but also that this law must itself be the motivation for any morally estimable action. Yet it remained Kant's view that any particular action needs a particular end, so that the moral law, as both form and motive of morally praiseworthy action, must still be applied to particular ends. Thus, almost twenty years after the previous passage, Kant wrote in the 1793 preface to *Religion within the Boundaries of Mere Reason*:

In the absence of all reference to an end no determination of the will can take place in human beings at all, since no such determination can take place without an effect, and its representation, though not as the determining ground of the power of choice nor as an end that comes first in intention, must nonetheless be admissible as the consequence of that power's determination to an end through the law... without this end, a power of choice which does not add to a contemplated action the thought of either an objectively or subjectively determined object... instructed indeed as to **how** to operate but not as to the **whither**, can itself obtain no satisfaction. (*Rel.*, 6:4; see also *TP*, 8:279–80 n.)

Thus, it is clearly Kant's view that inclinations are to be regulated, not abolished. But what justifies his further claim that freedom from domination by our own inclinations can only be achieved by achieving autonomy, that is, by the subjection of our inclinations to a self-given but universal law in the selection of morally permissible and necessary ends?

Kant never spells out his argument for this claim, but his reasoning must have been something like this: Since all complete actions must seek to realize some end or other originally suggested by inclination, any regulation of the ends of action can be considered as the subordination of some inclinations to one or more other inclinations. Yet, if a person regulates his actions merely by subordinating all of his other inclinations to the pursuit of one or more inclinations, to the satisfaction of which he assigns priority, that would merely represent his domination by these dominant inclinations, unless they themselves have been selected in accordance with some principle other than inclination. What could such a principle be? If the principle is simply that one ought to subordinate the satisfaction of any or all of one's own inclinations to the satisfaction of those of one or more other persons, then that would not constitute an escape from domination by inclination. Indeed, he would still be dominated by inclinations, not only by the inclinations of the other person(s) to whom he would (barring the introduction of any other principle) be subordinating the satisfaction of his own inclinations, but also by his inclination to subordinate himself to the inclinations of others. For, unless some further ground is forthcoming, this would be all that could explain his apparent subordination of his own inclinations to those of other persons. The only way out of this dilemma would be to subordinate the satisfaction of his inclinations to an impartial principle, which privileges no inclination over any other, that is, no inclination of one person over any other of his own inclinations, nor any inclination of one person over that of any other person(s). Instead, an impartial principle would permit, and indeed prescribe, the satisfaction of only an interpersonally consistent set of inclinations. However, this is exactly the principle of autonomy, at least as it is given by the second of our opening definitions, namely, the principle that all of any individual's maxims must be part of a system of universal law (G, 4:432).

This argument also connects the two parts of Kant's bipartite characterization of freedom by revealing that the avoidance of domination by one's inclinations and the avoidance of domination by other persons are not two independent goals after all. Allowing oneself to be dominated by the inclinations of others depends upon allowing oneself to be dominated by one's own inclination to be dominated by others, and the principle that will allow one to avoid being dominated by this inclination also requires one to avoid domination by the inclinations of others. Of course, a condition in which no one is dominated, either by his own inclinations or by those of any other individuals, is not a situation in which no one acts to satisfy any of his own inclinations or any of the inclinations of anyone else. Rather, it is a condition in which, under normal circumstances, each person will work to satisfy some of his own inclinations and some of those of others, subject to the impartial principle of intra- and interpersonal consistency or compatibility among inclinations. But such a situation is precisely one in which no one is *dominated* by anyone's inclinations, neither his own nor those of anyone else. Instead, it is a situation in which everyone's pursuit of the satisfaction of inclinations is *regulated* by the principle of autonomy itself.

By means of the foregoing argument, adherence to the principle of autonomy can be shown to be the necessary condition for the realization of freedom from domination by both one's own inclinations and those of others, in the choice and pursuit of ends. At this point, I turn to the relation between Kant's concept of autonomy and his concept of transcendental freedom, which is his version of the traditional concept of freedom of the will.

## B. Freedom of the Will and Autonomy

Kant conceives of the freedom of the will as the ability to initiate a series of events, even when that series would appear to differ from what would be entailed by the conjunction of one's own history with the natural laws of human behavior: "a faculty of absolutely beginning a state, and hence also a series of its consequences" (*CPurR*, A 445/B 473). In the *Critique of Pure Reason*, Kant wrote that "**freedom in the practical sense**," that is, "the independence of the power of choice from **necessitation** by impulses of sensibility," which, as we have just seen, can only be achieved by adherence to the same principle that is also necessary and sufficient to establish freedom from domination by others, is "grounded" on "this **transcendental** idea of freedom" (*CPurR*, A 533–4/B 561–2). Kant certainly means that transcendental freedom is a necessary condition of practical freedom, or that the ability to free oneself from domination by one's sensory impulses presupposes the ability to initiate new series of actions, independent of natural laws, since he assumes that such laws would grant sensory impulses inexorable sway over our conduct.[4] Of course, he also assumes that the possibility of transcendental freedom can, in turn, be explained only by transcendental idealism, which is the doctrine that the history of our behavior in time, and the natural laws that hold sway there, are all a matter of appearance, and that, as we are in ourselves, we may always be able to initiate any course of action, regardless of the appearance of our histories and the natural laws of behavior. But does Kant also mean that transcendental freedom is a *sufficient* condition for practical freedom, that is, that any agent who is transcendentally free must, in fact, choose to liberate himself from domination by his own sensory impulses in the choice of his ends and actions? One might think that sensory impulses are all a matter of appearance, and thus that an act of choice that takes place outside the order of mere appearance must necessarily be free from domination by sensory impulses. Perhaps this is what Kant means by his statement that "every action, irrespective of the temporal relation in which it stands to other appearances, is the immediate effect of the intelligible character of pure reason; reason therefore acts freely, without being determined dynamically by external or internal grounds temporally preceding it in the chain of natural causes" (*CPurR*, A 553/B 581). But Kant does not explicitly commit himself in the first *Critique* to the claim that transcendental freedom is both a necessary and a sufficient condition for practical freedom.

In the *Groundwork*, however, he seems to commit himself precisely to this claim. In this work Kant asks, "What, then, can freedom of the will be other than autonomy, that is, the will's property of being a law to itself?" where the "proposition, the will is in all its actions a law to itself, indicates only the principle, to act on no other maxim than that which can also have as object itself as universal law" (*G*, 4:447). Here, adherence to this principle is sufficient to ensure practical freedom in both its parts. Kant's intended answer to this question is clearly that the freedom of the will cannot be anything other than autonomy. And this indeed follows from Kant's conception, in the *Groundwork*, of transcendental freedom: "although [it is]...not a property of the will in accordance with natural laws, [it is] not for that reason lawless but...instead...a causality in accordance with immutable laws but of a special kind" (*G*, 4:446). His assumption here is that, just as the phenomenal realm of appearances is thoroughly governed by natural laws, the noumenal realm

---

[4] See Allen W. Wood, "Kant's Compatibilism," in Allen W. Wood, ed., *Self and Nature in Kant's Philosophy* (Ithaca, NY: Cornell University Press, 1984), 73–101, esp. at 82–3, 85.

of the real self, where freedom of the will is exercised, must also be thoroughly governed by law, which can be nothing other than the law of pure practical reason itself. So a free will cannot but choose in accordance with the fundamental principle of pure practical reason, and thus, freedom of the will is not only a necessary but also a sufficient condition for the achievement of autonomy, understood as practical freedom, or as freedom from domination by one's own sensory impulses and, therefore, as freedom from domination by others as well.

However, Kant's position in the *Groundwork* is notoriously problematic. He simply appeals to general epistemological considerations for the distinction between the two "standpoints" (*G*, 4:450) of the phenomenal and noumenal, thus presupposing the soundness of his arguments for transcendental idealism in the first *Critique*, without adding anything to them. Worse yet, he justifies his assumption that the principle of pure practical reason is the causal law of the noumenal realm by what appears to be a blatant category mistake. He argues that, because the possession of reason is what distinguishes us from all other things *in the phenomenal realm*, it must also be what distinguishes our *noumenal selves* from our phenomenal selves! But, what is most problematic, as has often been pointed out, perhaps most famously by Henry Sidgwick a century after the publication of the *Groundwork*,[5] is that Kant's assumption that freedom of the will is not only necessary but also sufficient for autonomy would undermine our ordinary belief that we can impute responsibility to individuals for immoral actions (that is, choices that reflect heteronomous submission to impermissible inclinations, rather than the autonomous regulation of our inclinations by means of self-given, but universal, law). If the mere existence of freedom of the will were to entail the existence of autonomy, then, by the logical principle of contraposition, the commission of any immorally heteronomous action, as a failure of autonomy, could only imply the complete absence of freedom of the will. But, if the imputation of responsibility presupposes freedom of the will (that is, the ability to have chosen otherwise than one actually did—as we ordinarily assume), then the agent who fails to be autonomous, that is, to free himself from domination by his own inclinations or those of others, cannot be held responsible for his actions, because he could not in fact have chosen to do otherwise.

Kant was not much inclined to explicitly acknowledge his errors, but he clearly came to retract the thesis that freedom of the will entails

---

[5] Henry Sidgwick, "The Kantian Conception of Free Will," *Mind* 13 (1888), reprinted in Sidgwick, *The Methods of Ethics*, 7th ed. (London: Macmillan, 1907), 511–16.

autonomy. He is usually thought to have done so in the *Critique of Practical Reason*, which he produced just three years after the *Groundwork*, but the evidence for this view is actually less than decisive. In the second *Critique*, Kant begins by arguing that a will that is determinable by the moral law must be a transcendentally free will, because "the mere form of a law," which is the essence of the moral law, is "not an object of the senses and consequently does not belong among appearances," but can instead be apprehended and acted upon only by a transcendentally free will (*CPracR*, 5:28). This clearly implies that freedom of the will is a necessary condition of autonomy, but not that it is a sufficient condition for autonomy or that it necessarily entails it. Kant then claims, however, that the "lawgiving form" of the moral law is "the only thing that can constitute a determining ground of the will." Because "the matter of the will...can never be given otherwise than empirically"—that is, as an object of inclination—yet a free will "must nevertheless be determinable, a free will must find a determining ground in the law but independently of the **matter** of the law" (*CPracR*, 5:29). What this means depends on just what Kant means by a "determining ground": On the one hand, if he is assuming that the free will must have a determining ground in order to act rationally (that is, a determining ground that could only be the principle of autonomy), but that it need not act rationally, then he is not committed to the thesis that the free will is necessarily autonomous. On the other hand, if he is assuming that the free will must always have a sufficiently determining ground, which could only be the formal principle that suffices to establish autonomy, then he is assuming that freedom of the will entails autonomy, with all the problems such an assumption involves. So it is not clear whether the *Critique of Practical Reason* actually retracts the problematic claim of the *Groundwork*.

By the time of his *Religion within the Boundaries of Mere Reason*, however, Kant clearly does withdraw the thesis of the *Groundwork*, that the mere existence of freedom of the will is a sufficient condition for autonomy. The thesis of the *Religion* is that we have transcendental freedom to choose between making our fundamental maxim the priority of the moral law over the principle of self-love, or, conversely, making our fundamental maxim the priority of self-love over the moral law. Since, all too obviously, many human beings often choose the latter, we are clearly prone to evil, and since our evil is a reflection of our own choice of our fundamental maxim, when we are evil, our evil is radical. But since our choice of evil is an expression of the same freedom that we could also use to choose the moral law, we have the possibility of being radically good as well as radically evil, and the power of conversion from evil to good is always in our own hands. It does not depend upon the grace of a god or the suffering of a savior, for they are nothing more than symbols of our own capacity for goodness and self-redemption. What is crucial for our present purposes, however, is just Kant's construal of the character of the free choice between good and evil. First, Kant puts it beyond doubt that we must be able to choose either good or evil in order for evil, as well as good, to be imputable to us: The "subjective ground" of "the exercise of the human being's freedom in general" must "itself always be an act [*Actus*] of freedom (for otherwise the use or abuse of the human being's power of choice with respect to the moral law could not be imputed to him, nor could the good or evil in him be called 'moral')" (*Rel.*, 6:21). Kant no longer conceives of the moral law as the causal law of the noumenal self, but, rather, conceives of the noumenal self as absolutely free either to affirm or to reject the unconditional priority of the moral law. Second, Kant conceives of the free choice between the priority of the moral law and the priority of self-love precisely as the choice between autonomy, on the one hand, or domination by one's inclinations, that is, heteronomy, on the other. For a human's choice to be evil is simply the choice to be "dependent on the incentives of his sensuous nature," or "according to the subjective principle of self-love" to take "them into his maxim **as of themselves sufficient** for the deter- mination of his power of choice, without minding the moral law" (*Rel.*, 6:36). To choose evil is nothing more, and nothing less, than to give one's inclinations free reign over one's choice of ends, or to surrender one's autonomy to self-love. As the second *Critique* had already made clear, self-love is merely another name for the policy of determining one's choices by "material practical principles," or ends that are suggested by inclination alone (*CPracR*, 5:22).

So how does Kant ultimately conceive of the relationship between freedom of the will and autonomy? Clearly, he continues to conceive of freedom of the will, in the form of transcendental freedom, as a necessary condition for the achievement of autonomy. Without such freedom, he imagines, we would necessarily be subject to domination by our own inclinations and could not even entertain the possibility of realizing autonomy. But transcendental freedom is not a sufficient condition for, or guarantee of, the realization of autonomy: we can freely choose to give our inclinations free reign over us. So transcendental freedom and prac- tical freedom, that is, freedom of the will and autonomy, are not identi- cal. Rather, autonomy must be conceived of as a condition of mastery over our inclinations in our choice of ends and actions, and for that reason as a condition of cooperation with, but not domination by, others as well, a condition which we can freely choose to maintain, but which we can just as well freely choose to subvert. Autonomy is not identical with a noumenal "act" of freedom. Autonomy is a condition, dependent upon an *a priori* principle but realized in the empirical world, which we can freely choose to realize and maintain, or to subvert or destroy.

Do we need to accept Kant's theory of freedom of the will as transcendental freedom in order to understand and accept this normative ideal of autonomy? Of course not; we could also explain the possibility of autonomy by dismissing his assumption that the laws of nature, by themselves, would always produce domination by sensuous incentives, and instead allow that self-governance by reason, rather than domination by inclination, is possible within the domain of nature and in accordance with its laws. If we take that route, we are very likely to conclude that the freedom to be autonomous is something that human beings develop only over the course of an extended process of maturation and education, and only to a degree that might well vary over a lifetime and might vary for different people. Perhaps we are even likely to conclude that some human beings cannot and do not get very far in this process at all. I will suggest in the last section of this paper that, when he came to think concretely about the duty of self-development, Kant drew exactly such conclusions. First, however, I will consider the quite different question of how Kant attempted to establish the absolute value of autonomy.

## II. THE ABSOLUTE VALUE OF AUTONOMY

How does Kant argue for the unconditional obligation to use our freedom of the will in order to attain autonomy? Since the formula of autonomy is one of the "three ways of representing the principle of morality" that "are at bottom only so many formulae of the very same law" (G, 4:436), to ask this question could be to ask, How does Kant argue for the unconditional obligation to act in accordance with the moral law itself? That is, of course, too large a question to be answered in this essay. What I propose to do here is to look at two arguments for the fundamental value of autonomy that Kant tried out in connection with his bipartite conception of autonomy as freedom from domination, both by other persons and by one's own inclinations. I then intend to see what elements of these arguments might have survived in Kant's mature practical philosophy. Of course, the concepts of unconditional obligation and absolute value are not identical to one another, but it would not have been unlike Kant to think that an unconditional obligation could only be grounded in something of absolute value.

## A. Psychological Arguments for the Value of Autonomy

Chronologically, Kant's thought about the value of autonomy begins with what we may consider to be empirical, psychological arguments for the value of freedom from domination, by others and by one's own inclinations in the choice of one's ends. The earliest record of Kant's emerging conception of autonomy can be found in the notes that he made in his 1764 work *Observations on the Feeling of the Beautiful and the Sublime* shortly after its publication. Here, he remarks on the natural human abhorrence of domination by other people. For example:

The human being has his own inclinations, and by means of his capacity of choice a clue from nature to conduct his actions in accordance with these. Nothing can be more appalling than that the action of a human stand under the will of another. Hence no abhorrence can be more natural than that which a person has against servitude. On this account a child cries and becomes bitter if it has to do what another wants without one having made an effort to make that pleasing to him. And it wishes only to become a man quickly and to operate in accordance with its own will. (Rischmüller, 60)

A few pages later, Kant adds:

Find himself in what condition he will, the human being is dependent upon many external objects. He depends on some things because of his needs, on others because of his concupiscence, and because he is the administrator but not the master of nature, he must often accommodate himself to its compulsion, since he does not find that it will always accommodate itself to his wishes. But what is harder and more unnatural than this yoke of necessity is the subjection of one human being under the will of another. No misfortune can be more terrifying to one who has been accustomed to freedom, who has enjoyed the good of freedom, than to be delivered over to another creature of the same species and to see the latter compel him to do what he will (to give himself over to his will). (Rischmüller, 70–1)

It might be natural to interpret passages such as these as assuming that our happiness lies in the gratification of our own inclinations, and that domination by others is abhorrent to us because it is the chief obstacle to such happiness: Anyone in a position to dominate the choices of another individual would naturally attempt to use that power to gratify his own inclinations, rather than those of the other. But Kant does not explicitly state this, so these passages are at least consistent with a view that there is simply a special satisfaction in making our own choices, free from the interference of others—a satisfaction that is distinct from, and more profound than, the satisfaction of whatever particular inclinations we choose to gratify by means of our actions. This could, in turn, imply that our dissatisfaction at having actions imposed upon us by others is so great that it would outweigh any pleasure we might take even in the satisfaction of our own inclinations if that satisfaction is forced upon us by others. To avoid the frustration of being dominated by others and to experience, instead, the pleasure of making their own choices, human beings who live in circumstances in which they cannot avoid contact with others, or in which they even depend upon interaction with others—that is, all human beings in the empirical conditions of their actual existence —must figure out how to act in accordance with a principle of cooperation but nondomination, which is at least part of a principle of autonomy.

That Kant had recently read Rousseau is evident in these notes, and perhaps this emphasis on our love of freedom from domination by others can be traced to this source. But beginning in these notes, Kant also develops an account of our satisfaction in making choices free from the domination of our own inclinations, which seems original to him and to which he would return in his notes and lectures on both moral philosophy and anthropology for many years to come. At one point in these notes, Kant begins with a passage emphasizing our gratification in making choices freely, which might be read in the same vein as the passages that we have already seen:

We have gratification in certain of our perfections, but much more if we ourselves are the cause. We have the most if we are the freely acting cause. To **subordinate** everything to the free capacity for choice is the greatest perfection. And the perfection of the free capacity for choice as a cause of possibility is far greater than all other causes of good even if they have produced actuality. (Rischmüller, 107–8)

Here, he could be taken to be describing again the pleasure of making one's own choices, rather than having someone else make them for him. But as Kant continues, it becomes clear that he is now talking about a special satisfaction that lies in subordinating our own capacities other than the capacity for free choice to our own capacity of free choice:

Since the greatest inner perfection and the perfection that arises from that consists in the subordination of all of our capacities and receptivities to the free capacity for choice, the feeling for the **goodness** of the capacity of choice must be immediately much different and also greater than all the consequences that can thereby be actualized. (Rischmüller, 108–9)

During the 1770s, Kant would develop this thought into a fuller account of our satisfaction in regulating, rather than being dominated by, our own inclinations.

Here is Kant's idea as he further developed it. The fullest expression of life, and therefore the deepest source of our satisfaction, lies in free and unhindered activity. Such free activity precludes being ruled by inclination, both because we are, in principle, passive rather than active with respect to the occurrence of our inclinations, and also because, in practice, our inclinations can always come into conflict with one another, thus exposing the freedom of any activity that would be based on any particular inclination to limitation by another inclination at any time. In order to preserve and promote our full freedom of activity, we must, therefore, govern our activity by laws of reason, rather than being pushed around by whatever inclination happens to be strongest in us at any given time. Laws of reason, unlike particular inclinations, are impersonal and interpersonally valid, so to govern ourselves by reason, rather than by inclination, is necessarily to govern ourselves by universally valid laws. Yet to govern ourselves by reason cannot mean simply to eliminate all inclinations, for without inclinations suggesting desirable courses of action to us, we would have nothing to do, nothing for reason to govern. Rather, what the full enjoyment of our freedom requires is that we subject both our own inclinations and those of others to the regulation of reason in a way that, while respecting the freedom of all, leads to the pursuit of the satisfaction of an intersubjectively compatible set of inclinations, representing the union of the free choices of all who are involved.

This argument is briefly suggested in Kant's lectures on ethics, when he equates "the greatest use of freedom" with the "highest *principium* of life" itself, and then proposes that the conditions under which freedom can "be consistent with itself," rather than those under which "it comes into collision with itself," are precisely the conditions that must be satisfied in order to realize this "highest *principium* of life" (Col., 27:346). The argument is spelled out in a little more detail in Kant's notes and anthropology lectures from the 1770s. The first step in this argument is the premise that our deepest satisfaction lies in the promotion of life, which, in turn, consists in the maximally unhindered activity of all of our powers and capacities. Here is a representative statement from Kant's anthropology lectures from 1775–6:

The feeling of the promotion of life is gratification or pleasure. Life is the consciousness of a free and regular [*regelmäßigen*] play of all of the powers and faculties of the human being. The feeling of the promotion of life is that which is pleasure and the feeling of the hindrance of life is displeasure. (Friedländer, 25:559)

One page later Kant reiterates the point that what we enjoy in life is the exercise of our own activity, while he also introduces the second step in the argument, that the maximization of our activity requires our self-regulation by rules of reason:

The play of the mental powers [*Gemüths Kräfte*] must be strongly lively and free if it is to animate. Intellectual pleasure consists in the consciousness of the use of freedom in accordance with rules. Freedom is the greatest life of the human being, whereby he exercises his activity without hindrance. Through some hindrance of freedom life is restricted, since [then] freedom does not stand under the coercion of a rule. If this were the case, then it [our activity] would not be free, but since this introduces a lack of rule if the understanding does not direct it, while this lack of rule hinders itself, thus no freedom can please us except that which stands under the rule of the understanding. This is the intellectual pleasure, which leads to the moral. (Friedländer, 25:560)

A note from the beginning of the 1770s also quickly states the first two steps in Kant's argument:

Feeling is the sensation of life. The complete use of life is freedom. The formal condition of freedom as a use that is in complete concordance with life is regularity [*Regelmäßigkeit*]. (R 6870, 19:187)

Our deepest pleasure in life is activity itself, and freedom is equivalent to activity, but in order to maximize the use of our freedom, we must subject it to regulation by law.

As I mentioned above, each of these two steps in Kant's argument can also be found in Kant's notes on ethics from the 1770s. Several notes from the crucial period 1769–70 make the first step by contrasting the distinctive and superior quality of our pleasure in activity, rather than passivity, and explicitly associate the latter with the determination of our will by inclination. Kant's second claim, that the enjoyment of our free activity depends upon the subordination of that activity to rules rather than inclination, is made in a number of notes. He argues that it is only by the use of rules that the *unity* of our actions can be maintained, or conflicts avoided among actions inspired by competing inclinations, which would otherwise have the effect of restricting or reducing the scope of our free activity. The following note, probably from 1776–8, reiterates Kant's first claim and then makes the second in the form that I have just suggested:

In the end everything comes down to life; what animates (or the feeling of the promotion of life) is agreeable. Life is unity; hence all taste has as its *principio* the unity of the animating sensations.

Freedom is the original life and in its connection [*Zusammenhang*] the condition of the coherence [*Übereinstimmung*] of all life; hence that which promotes the feeling of universal life or the feeling of the promotion of universal life causes a pleasure. Do we feel good in universal life? The universality makes all our feelings agree with one another, although prior to this universality there is no special kind of sensation. It is the form of *consensus*. (R 6862, 19:183)

Here two thoughts are interwoven. Kant is assuming, first, that the primary source of satisfaction in life is the gratification of particular inclinations, but that the use of free choice is necessary to maximize such satisfaction by selecting a coherent set of inclinations as the object of our actions. He also assumes, second, that there is a "special kind" of satisfaction associated with the exercise of free choice, one that is connected with activity or life itself. This special satisfaction is the source of the priority that we give to the freedom of choice from domination by any particular inclination over the satisfaction of any particular inclination.

Kant's argument is thus that the deep satisfaction that we take in maximally free activity—a satisfaction that he equates with the feeling of life itself—is incompatible with simply acting on whatever inclinations present themselves to us. This is, in the first instance, because he takes the mere occurrence of inclination to be something with respect to which we are passive rather than active, and in the second instance, because he assumes that any of one's own inclinations can always conflict either with other inclinations of one's own or with those of other persons in such a way as to reduce the sphere of our free activity, or even to undercut any possibility of coherent activity at all. The only way to avoid this conflict is to govern our actions by rules of reason.

Of course, there is an obvious problem with Kant's observation that humans abhor being dominated by each other, and with his more elaborate argument that humans take a deep and distinct satisfaction in freely choosing which of their inclinations to satisfy, rather than simply being pushed to act by whatever inclinations happen to be strongest at any moment. The problem is simply that, first of all, these psychological claims are empirical and, thus, as far as we can tell, contingent, so they would not seem to be adequate premises for what the mature Kant demands, namely, a moral law that would "hold for all rational beings and **only because of this** be also a law for all human wills"—a law that states an unconditional obligation. These claims could yield only what he

rejects, namely, a principle "derived from the special natural constitution
of humanity—what is derived from certain feelings and propensities and
even, if possible, from a special tendency that would be peculiar to
human reason and would not have to hold necessarily for the will of
every rational being" (G, 4:425). Second, it should worry not only Kant
but also anyone that these claims might not be true even of all human
beings. To state it mildly, there is much in modern psychology and
modern history to suggest that many human beings are happy to be
dominated by whatever inclinations they happen to have, and are all
too ready to allow themselves to be dominated by other people and their
inclinations. If not for this second reason, then certainly for the first, the
project of providing a psychological foundation for the value of autonomy, and thus for our obligation to achieve it, disappears from Kant's
mature writings in moral philosophy. But Kant's early thoughts about
our love of the two forms of freedom hardly disappear without a trace. In
one of his last publications, his 1798 textbook for the anthropology
lectures that he had ceased to give the year before, Kant preserves the
love of freedom from domination by others in its original form as the
passion for "outer freedom," while suggesting that the love of freedom
from domination by one's own inclinations is the basis for moral feeling
itself: "It is not only the concept of freedom under moral laws that
arouses an affect, which is called enthusiasm; the mere sensuous idea of
outer freedom, by analogy with the concept of law, raises the inclination
to continue in it or extend it to the point of vehement passion" (APV,
§82; 7:269).

## B. A Metaphysical Basis for the Value of Autonomy

If Kant cannot use his psychological observations on our love of the two
forms of freedom that comprise the practice of autonomy in order to
ground its value and our obligation to achieve it, then what else can he
try? Other passages from his writings suggest that at various times he was
tempted by a metaphysical argument. In the following note from
1769–70, Kant grounds his view that the value of freedom is the source
of the unconditional validity of the moral law in a metaphysical conception of the essence, and thus the perfection, of the will:

There is a free capacity for choice, which has no proper happiness as its aim, but
rather presupposes one. The essential perfection of a freely acting being rests on
this, that this freedom is not subjected to inclination or to any foreign cause at
all. The primary rule of externally good actions is not that of agreement with the
happiness of others but that of agreement with their capacity for choice, and just

as the **perfection** of a subject does not rest on its being happy but on its **subordinating its state to freedom**, likewise the universally valid perfection rests on actions standing under universal laws of freedom. (R 6605, 19:105–6)

This form of argument does not depend upon empirical claims about human beings that must ultimately be confined to anthropology, and it could be true of other forms of rational beings, not just human beings. This form of argumentation may also be present in the *Groundwork's* conception of a "metaphysics of morals" that can derive a proper formulation of the moral law from the mere analysis of the concept of a rational will (*G*, 4:426–7). But as the *Groundwork* itself makes clear, the analytic derivation of the correct formulation of the moral law is not yet the necessary but synthetic proof of its validity (*G*, 4:444–5). At least in Section II of the *Groundwork*, Kant seems to be aware of Hume's prohibition of deriving a moral "ought" from a metaphysical "is"; thus, the strategy of deriving the obligation to achieve autonomy from a metaphysical conception of the perfection of the human will, or of rational wills in general, does not seem to be one that Kant can maintain. So, if he can appeal neither to psychology nor to metaphysics to demonstrate the absolute value of autonomy, then what is left?

## C. Respect for Autonomy

Kant's early arguments for the value of autonomy turn on the psychological and metaphysical superiority of activity over passivity. In his mature practical philosophy, I suggest, this fascination with the ideal of pure activity is transmuted into the normative premise that only what is the product of an agent's activity is suitable for moral evaluation, *a fortiori* for esteem or respect. Coupling this normative assumption with the theoretical premise that inclinations simply happen to us, and that we remain passive if we are dominated by them, but that we can be active in regulating them in accordance with the principle of autonomy, Kant reaches this conclusion: Only an agent's self-regulation of inclinations in accordance with the principle of autonomy, which entails freedom from domination by his own inclinations and those of others, is worthy of respect. Thus, only the achievement of such autonomy itself can be the source of all our unconditional obligations.

Kant's most famous assertion of the unique dignity of autonomy in the *Groundwork* makes explicit that acting in accordance with universal laws of reason is the only way to free oneself from subjection to mere laws of nature, and he suggests, for this reason, that lawgiving has unique dignity:

And what is it, then, that justifies a morally good disposition, or virtue, in making such high claims? It is nothing less than the **share** it affords a rational being **in the giving of universal laws,** by which it makes him fit to be a member of a possible realm of ends, which he was already destined to be by his own nature as an end in itself and, for that very reason, as lawgiving in the realm of ends—**as free with respect to all laws of nature** [emphasis added], obeying only those which he himself gives and in accordance with which his maxims can belong to a giving of universal law (to which he at the same time subjects himself). . . . **Autonomy** is therefore the ground of the dignity of human nature and of every rational nature. (G, 4:435–6).[6]

What the foregoing passage does not make explicit, however, is what the value of freeing oneself from subjection to mere laws of nature is. But much earlier in the *Groundwork*, Kant has revealed what I take to be the missing premise of the present argument and the underlying assumption of his entire view:

For an object as the effect of my proposed action I can indeed have **inclination** but **never respect,** just because it is merely an effect and not an activity of the will. In the same way I cannot have respect for inclination as such, whether it is mine or that of another; I can at most in the first case approve it and in the second sometimes even love it, that is, regard it as favorable to my own advantage. Only what is connected with my will merely as ground and never as effect, what does not serve my inclination but outweighs it or at least excludes it altogether from calculations in making a choice—hence the mere law for itself—can be an object of respect and so a command. (G, 4:400)

This passage alludes to the two forms of domination with which Kant had been concerned since the 1760s—domination by one's own inclinations and by those of others—and states that there can never be respect

---

[6] At the elision, I have omitted Kant's statement that "For, nothing can have a worth other than that which the law determines for it. But the lawgiving itself, which determines all worth, must for that very reason have a dignity, that is, an unconditional, incomparable worth; and the word **respect** alone provides a becoming expression for the assessment of it that a rational being must give." This passage suggests the interpretation, advocated by Christine Korsgaard and Allen Wood, that Kant argues for the value of autonomy by inferring from the objective value of particular objects of choice to the absolute value of the act of choice that confers the first sort of value; see Christine Korsgaard, "Kant's Formula of Humanity," in Korsgaard, *Creating the Kingdom of Ends* (Cambridge: Cambridge University Press, 1996), 106–32, and Allen W. Wood, *Kant's Ethical Thought* (Cambridge: Cambridge University Press, 1999), chap. 4, sec. 5, 124–32. (However, neither author actually cites this passage from Kant in the locations that I have cited.) But since this argument presupposes that we assign objective value to particular objects before recognizing the value of free choice itself, it would seem to run afoul of the *Groundwork*'s opening argument that nothing has unconditional value except the good will itself: the unconditional value of free choice could not, it seems, be inferred from the merely conditional value of any particular objects of the will.

for either, because neither is an "activity of the will." Only what is an activity of the will is even a candidate for respect, and the only form of pure activity of the will is making choices in accordance with "the mere law for itself," rather than by mere inclination. Thus, acting in accordance with the principle of autonomy is the only way to express the activity of the will and the only possible candidate for respect.

Now it might well seem as if the normative premise that a genuine action of the will is a necessary condition for moral evaluation or imputation is not sufficient to establish that activity of the will is sufficient for the positive evaluation of esteem; after all, heteronomy or evil-doing is also, by Kant's account of radical evil, a genuine expression of an action of the free will. So it might seem as if an additional normative premise must underlie the claim that autonomy is the proper object of moral esteem. However, although it is true that any evil act, considered by itself, is just as much an expression of the freedom of the will as is a good action, we have also seen that the condition of autonomy is precisely that in which a free action of the will preserves and promotes free activity itself, in the sense of preserving the possibility of further free acts on the part of both the agent of the particular act concerned, as well as other agents who might be affected by his actions. Compliance with the principle of autonomy is the only form of free action that preserves the possibility of further exercises of freedom. Thus, while the normative premise that a genuine activity of the free will is a necessary condition for imputation or moral assessment of a single action considered by itself does not seem to be sufficient to determine the character of actions that should be esteemed rather than reviled, reflection on the fact that only autonomous actions *preserve* the possibility of further free actions seems to point directly to autonomy as the necessary object of respect.

However, it might still seem natural to ask whether such an argument for autonomy as the basis of the normative theory of the *Groundwork* is consistent with Kant's insistence in the *Religion* that not only goodness or autonomy but also evil or heteronomy must be imputed to free choice. Kant's argument will be inconsistent with this premise if the activity that can only be expressed by adherence to the principle of autonomy is simply equated with the act of choosing a maxim for a single action. The activity of the will that necessarily deserves esteem, rather than blame, must be understood as the free choice of *continuing* freedom in the setting and pursuit of particular ends on the part of both oneself and others, which is a form of freedom in real time, so to speak, and which can be achieved and preserved only by adherence to the principle of autonomy, that is, a principle that can, in turn, be affirmed or rejected by an act of the transcendentally free will. In other words, Kant's notion of activity needs to become as complex as his notion of the will in order to preserve his conception of the value of autonomy.

## III. THE PRACTICE OF AUTONOMY

### A. *Autarky, Autocracy, and Autonomy*

What is it like to practice autonomy in the empirical conditions of human life? Kant's remark that "[o]nly . . . what does not serve my inclination but outweighs it or at least excludes it altogether from my calculations . . . can be an object of respect" (G, 4:400) might suggest that to be autonomous simply requires that we must exclude inclinations and the attempt to satisfy them from our lives altogether. As we have already seen, a few other comments in the *Groundwork* also suggest as much, such as Kant's statement that "the inclinations themselves, as sources of needs, are so far from having an absolute worth, as to make one wish to have them, that it must instead be the universal wish of every rational being to be altogether free from them" (G, 4:428). The complete elimination of inclinations as sources of needs would represent the extreme case of what Kant calls, in his lectures on ethics, *autarky* (*autarchia*), the "capacity to master oneself, to possess oneself, to be sufficient to oneself," giving rise to the "duty of being able to do without" (Vig., 27:653), or to "[s]eek independence from all things of nature, as needs, and likewise from other people" (Vig., 27:651).[7] Complete autarky might seem to guarantee the preservation of our autonomy, because it would remove every inclination that might tempt us to surrender our autonomy to ourselves or to others. But Kant could not have thought that complete autarky should be the moral ideal for human beings, because, as we have seen, he had made it plain, from early on in his lectures and notes, that human action requires a matter as well as a form: particular human actions always attempt to fulfill particular human needs, which are suggested by inclinations, although *which* inclinations are to be gratified

---

[7] In spite of its spelling, Kant's Latin term *autarchia* would have to be derived from the classical Greek *autarkeia*, meaning self-sufficiency, rather than from the later term *autarchia*, meaning politically self-governing. In his *Ethica Philosophica*, the textbook for Kant's lectures on ethics, Alexander Baumgarten had correctly used the former Greek term to connote the "status of a man . . . in which he is the sole and sufficient ground of his own felicity" (Baumgarten, *Ethica Philosophica*, sec. 277; in the Akademie edition of Kant's lectures on ethics, 27:948–9). The misspelling in Kant's lectures could be due, of course, either to Kant's own error or to the student transcriber of the notes.

must be regulated by reason. As he said in the mid-1770s, "The matter of the good is given empirically, its form *a priori*" (R 6820, 19:172). Complete autarky cannot be a goal for human conduct, because it would leave us with nothing whatever to do, and thus with no way in which to express our activity. And this conclusion is actually consistent with Kant's statement that it must be "the universal wish of every rational being to be altogether free from" inclinations, for a *wish* is not a *will*, and differs from the latter precisely in that we can wish for what is impossible, but we cannot will it.[8] Kant does not, in fact, suggest that we strive to realize autonomy by realizing complete autarky or the elimination of inclinations. Rather, he urges that we put the ideal of autonomy into practice by developing what he calls *autocracy* or "self-mastery," "the authority to compel the mind, despite all the impediments to doing so," involving "mastery over oneself, and not merely the power to direct" (Col., 27:363).

Kant describes the principle of self-mastery in bold terms:

The rule is this: Seek to maintain command over yourself, for under this condition you are capable of performing the self-regarding duties. There is in man a certain rabble element which must be subject to control, and which a vigilant government must keep under regulation, and where there must even be force to compel this rabble under the rule in accordance with ordinance and regulation. (Col., 27:360)

Kant does not suggest that this form of self-government can be achieved all at once by a single action. Instead, he clearly regards it as a condition that must be achieved and maintained by the cultivation and discipline of a number of capacities and practices, guided by the ideal of the moral law, that is, by the ideal of autonomy. This process of achieving autocracy, as the empirical realization of autonomy in the actual circumstances of human existence, is not only temporally extended, but also complex, for it requires, apparently, both that we directly strengthen the efficacy of the moral law on our conduct, and also that we learn techniques that indirectly support the reign of the moral law, by removing or diminishing impediments to its rule.

These two aspects of the cultivation of self-mastery are evident in Kant's initial discussion of moral feeling in his lectures. In his major published works, Kant often makes it sound as if moral feeling, in the form of the feeling of respect, is the immediate and automatic

---

[8] See *CPJ*, Introduction III, 5:177–8 n., in Immanuel Kant, *Critique of the Power of Judgment*, ed. Paul Guyer, trans. Paul Guyer and Eric Matthews (Cambridge: Cambridge University Press, 2000), 65.

consequence of consciousness of the moral law (See G, 4:401 n., and
*CPracR*, 5:75). But in his lectures he makes it clear that, while it is moral
feeling that gives "executive authority" to the moral law, that is, makes it
empirically efficacious in the etiology of our actions, this feeling must be
"cultivated," and this requires two different things. First, competing
incentives to action coming from sensibility must simply be "weakened
and overcome"; "we first have to discipline ourselves, i.e., to root out, in
regard to ourselves, by repeated actions, the tendency that arises from the
sensory motive." This can be understood simply as removing impediments to the efficacy of moral feeling. But second, "He who would
discipline himself morally must pay great attention to himself, and
often give an account of his actions before the inner judge, since then,
by long practice, he will have given strength to the moral motivating
grounds, and acquired, by cultivation, a habit of desire or aversion in
regard to moral good or evil" (Col., 27:361). These two statements
together suggest that humans have a natural disposition to moral feeling,
which can make the moral law efficacious in the regulation of our
conduct, but that we must do two things to make this disposition
effective: we must practice, by repeated actions, the suppression of
competing incentives, for they are not simply eliminated by a single act
of the will, at least in actual experience; and we must repeatedly attend to
the voice of moral feeling, or the inner judge within us, for to hear it once
is not enough to make it effective. Both the moral feeling and the
suppression of alternatives to moral feeling must be cultivated by attention and vigilance over time.

Beyond these general requirements for the development of self-mastery, Kant also recommends a number of particular techniques for the
realization of autocracy. His discussion aims to show how we can gain
autocracy over "the mental powers, insofar as they have a bearing on
morality," or develop "a capacity [*Vermögen*] for keeping them under
free choice and observation." The division of the mental powers on
which his discussion is based is not explicit, but can be understood
thus: since we are concerned with how the cultivation and discipline of
other mental powers bears on the use of the faculty of choice or desire
for the determination of conduct, it is these other mental powers, rather
than the faculty of desire itself, which is to be discussed. Using the
tripartite scheme that Kant accepted throughout his anthropology
lectures, and that would ultimately dictate his system of three critiques,
the mental powers other than the faculty of desire can be divided into the
cognitive powers and the capacity for feeling. Among the cognitive
powers, pure reason is excluded from the discussion, since its role is to

provide the principle of autonomy, the implementation of which is to be facilitated by the use of the other mental powers. This leaves the cognitive powers of imagination, understanding, and judgment, and Kant then advises how best to cultivate each of these in order to achieve self-mastery.

First, since the imagination—which is the general power to have images, thus including the senses—is a source of images of "sensual pleasures" that can tempt us to "vices that run contrary to nature, and extreme violations of the self-regarding duties," then "[a]utocracy should consist . . . in the person banishing his imaginings from his mind, so that the imagination does not work its spell of presenting objects that are unobtainable" or impermissible. But since the imagination, like the senses in general, tends to "dupe and also outwit the understanding," this can best be accomplished by our learning to "outwit them in turn, by trying to furnish the mind with another form of sustenance than that offered by the senses, and seeking to occupy it with ideal diversions, comprising all refined forms of knowledge" (Col., 27:364). In other words, in order to keep the imagination from presenting us with inappropriate temptations, we must occupy it with other things. This is a discipline that both can and must be learned. As Kant also stresses a few pages later in the same lecture notes, the trick is not simply to learn how to substitute morally appropriate for morally inappropriate images, but also to cultivate appropriate activities: "[W]e display autocracy by keeping our mind active and effective under the burden of work. . . . We must therefore have the resolve to stick firmly to what we have undertaken, and to carry it through regardless of the arguments for procrastination." To gain control over the imagination, we must not only develop alternative habits of imagination, but also develop the discipline to keep ourselves fully involved in meaningful activity. We must cultivate "the union and harmony of the mental powers evinced in carrying out our business. This is not, indeed, a thing for everyone, but depends upon talent. Yet it can be strengthened by practice" (Col., 27:366).

Second, we must apply the understanding in "the observation of oneself," not "eavesdropping on oneself," but learning "to observe ourselves through actions, and to pay attention to them." By this Kant seems to mean not the more general point that he has already made, that we must learn to be aware of the presence of moral feeling and the promptings of conscience in us, but, rather, that we must learn to pay attention to our particular tendencies to action, that is, "to examine our actions to see if they are good or bad," and thus to learn in which arenas of conduct we need to make special efforts in order to act in accordance with the general principle of autonomy. This, too, is not an ability that is simply given, but one that must be cultivated: a "person always has to get to know himself in a gradual way" (Col., 27:365).

Finally, autocracy "includes *suspensio judicii*," or the ability to defer decision on a proposed course of action until we have had time to consider it and its moral status fully. "In such judgment we must have enough autocracy to be able to defer it if we will, and not be moved to declare our judgment on [merely] persuasive grounds." For example, "if I receive a letter, and it has aroused anger in me on the spot; if I answer right away, I let my anger be very plain; but if I can put it off until the following day, I will see the matter from a very different standpoint" (Col., 27:365–6). In this case, Kant does not explicitly assert that the discipline to suspend judgment on a fraught matter is one that must be learned and cultivated over time, but perhaps that is too evident to need saying. Like the ability to control and divert the imagination, and like the practice of carefully attending to one's actions and motives in order to see where one needs to apply the greatest effort to comply with the demands of autonomy, the practice of not making hasty judgments is clearly something that both can and must be learned and strengthened over time.

After describing the techniques that we can and must use in order to develop autocracy in the use of our cognitive powers, Kant comments more briefly on how we must cultivate, for the sake of self-mastery, the faculty of feeling. Here, he first observes that there is a difference between "feelings and inclinations" [*Empfindungen und Neigungen*], on the one hand, and "emotions and passions" [*Affecten und Leidenschaften*] on the other—the former being natural and unavoidable states of mind that can be regulated, while the latter are momentary or enduring conditions that interfere with sound judgment and reasoning (see *APV*, §§73–4, 7:251–2). He then merely says: "In duty to ourselves, and for the dignity of mankind, the demand upon a person is that he have no emotions and passions at all; such is the rule, although it is another matter whether people can actually get as far as that." The suggestion is not that we have a duty to try to eradicate feelings and inclinations, but that we must try to prevent them from developing into emotions and passions. But Kant does not have very much to say about how we can actually do that; he merely says that a person "should be brave, orderly, and steadfast in his work, and guard against falling into the fever-heat of passions" (Col., 27:368). Apparently, each person will have to work out for himself what he needs to do in order to keep his feelings and inclinations from degenerating into emotions and passions, and thereby undermining his autonomy. But presumably, in whatever way people develop such discipline, it will take time for them to do so; and Kant's remark that it is a question how far anyone can get in this process surely presupposes that the development of such discipline is a temporally extended process.

Indeed, not one of Kant's recommendations for the development of autocracy is terribly specific, but they all clearly evince the recognition that, in the actual circumstances of human life, the moral ideal of autonomy is not something that can be achieved by a single act of the will, but something that can be implemented only over time, only with effort and discipline, and only to a certain degree. Autonomy is the goal, but a certain degree of autocracy is the most for which we can actually hope.

## B. *Fallback or Usual and Customary Means?*

How should we appraise the moral merit of such practices of autocracy as learning how to divert our imaginations from unsuitable objects, or learning how to suspend judgment until a cooler moment? Should we regard such practices as ways of getting ourselves to comply with the demands of duty that are alternatives to acting directly from respect for the moral law, that is, as techniques for acting in conformity with duty but not out of duty, which should as such be praised and encouraged, but which have no "true moral worth" and merit no real "esteem"? (See *G*, 4:398.) Or should we regard them as the usual means to the end of acting from duty, that is, the characteristic ways in which human beings, when motivated by respect for the moral law, can implement that respect, and thus as fully worthy of true esteem? Kant does not raise this question in his discussion of autocracy, but his comments in another context suggest his answer to it. In the "Doctrine of Virtue" of the late *Metaphysics of Morals*, Kant mentions two kinds of naturally occurring feelings that we have a moral duty to preserve and cultivate. The first kind are natural inclinations toward the beauty of nonhuman nature, and the second kind are natural feelings of sympathy toward other human beings. In light of Kant's apparent insistence that there is no moral merit in any actions, even actions in outward conformity to the requirements of duty, that are motivated by mere feelings (see, most famously, *G*, 4:398–9), it would seem as if such natural inclinations could at best be morally irrelevant. But Kant insists, with regard to the first of these natural feelings, that we have a duty to preserve and cultivate "a natural predisposition that is very serviceable to morality in one's relation with other people" (*MM*,

DV, §17, 6:443). Here his assumption is that how we treat nonhuman beings—"humanely" or "inhumanely," as we say—will affect how we treat human beings. With regard to the second—natural feelings of sympathy—he makes the following statements: "Nature has already implanted in human beings receptivity to these feelings. But to use this as a means to promoting active and rational benevolence is still a particular, though only a conditional, duty" (*MM*, DV, §34, 6:456), and

> While it is not in itself a duty to share the sufferings (as well as the joys) of others, it is a duty to sympathize actively in their fate; and to this end it is therefore an indirect duty to cultivate the compassionate natural (aesthetic) feelings in us, and to make use of them as so many means to sympathy based on moral principles and the feelings appropriate to them.—It is therefore a duty not to avoid the places where the poor who lack the most basic necessities are to be found but rather to seek them out, and not to shun sickrooms or debtors' prisons and so forth in order to avoid sharing painful feelings one many not be able to resist. For this is still one of the impulses that nature has implanted in us to do what the representation of duty alone [*für sich allein*] might not accomplish. (*MM*, DV, §35, 6:457)

It might seem natural to read the last sentence of this citation as saying that feelings of sympathy should be cultivated so that we will have a fallback when the representation of duty alone is insufficient to get us to do for others who are in need what we ought to do for them. In such a case, the performance of beneficent deeds would seem to be in conformity *with* duty, and therefore worthy of encouragement, but not to be *from* duty, and therefore not worthy of esteem. However, I do not think that such an interpretation is consistent with the rest of what Kant says here, for what his other statements suggest is that nature has implanted certain feelings in us as the means to execute the ends that duty requires of us. It is by cultivating these feelings and then acting on them in appropriate circumstances that we, constituted as we are, can do what respect for duty requires of us. The duty to cultivate such feelings is, as Kant says, indirect, because it cannot be a duty simply to have feelings that we do not naturally have (see *MM*, DV, §25, 6:449), but it can be a duty to preserve and cultivate tendencies to feeling that we do have, for such preservation and cultivation call for actions that are under the control of our wills. And the duty to use naturally occurring feelings as a "means to promoting active and rational benevolence" is a conditional duty, because we must only act on such feelings when the actions they would prompt are indeed actions called for by duty. The objects of our benevolence must be appropriate candidates for our help, and the occasion must be suitable, that is, we must not, in the particular circumstances at hand, have other, more pressing duties that need to be satisfied (for example, we cannot give to charity money that we need to repay a debt). But once these conditions are satisfied, then it is our duty to cultivate natural feelings that prompt us to perform beneficent or other acts that are required by duty, for it is through feelings that we human beings can act, and those feelings are the means that nature has granted us to fulfill the ends that duty imposes on us. On this account, that the representation of duty alone is insufficient for the fulfillment of our duties should not be taken to mean that the motive of duty is *sometimes too weak* to get us to do what we ought to do, but, rather, that it is *always incomplete*: it specifies the end, but not the means. We have to look to our nature to find what means we have available to realize this end.[9]

I suggest that the same analysis should be applied to the cultivation of techniques for self-mastery. Developing control over our imagination, using our understanding to comprehend our own proclivities, learning how to defer judgment, figuring out how to prevent our feelings from degenerating into irrational passions—these are not alternatives to willing to be autonomous out of respect for morality itself, but are simply the means by which human beings can implement the ideal of autonomy in the empirical circumstances of human life. Whether we think of the decision to make the cultivation of such forms of discipline our maxim and end, as the product of a free choice outside of time, as Kant does, or as the products of choice within time, with whatever sort of freedom is possible within time, as most of us now do, it remains the case that the cultivation of such forms of discipline over time, by the variety of techniques to which Kant alludes, is the naturally available means that we have to implement such a maxim and end. The achievement of autocracy by such means is thus not a fallback to genuine autonomy, worthy of grudging encouragement but not true esteem. Rather, it is the only means that human beings have to implement the ideal of autonomy, and thus it is fully worthy of genuine esteem.

There might seem to be a risk of a vicious regress here: namely, that if the motive to perform our duty out of respect for the moral law itself is

---

[9] I would also argue that the idea that natural feelings should be cultivated as a fallback to substitute for weak moral motivation, which is worthy of encouragement but not esteem, is actually incoherent. If these feelings are intentionally cultivated, so as to enable us to perform our duty regardless of other circumstances, then they are, presumably, cultivated out of recognition of the need always to be able to do what duty demands, that is, out of respect for duty itself. The very fact that such feelings have been cultivated is, therefore, itself worthy of esteem.

always incomplete, requiring for its implementation particular feelings to which we are naturally disposed, but which need cultivation, then we will not have a complete motive to cultivate these feelings themselves. It is perhaps in order to avoid such a regress that Kant himself distinguishes between a general "moral feeling," that is, "the susceptibility to feel pleasure or displeasure merely from being aware that our actions are consistent with or contrary to the law of duty" (*MM*, DV, Introduction, §XII, 6:399), and particular feelings of "[l]ove of human beings" (6:401). The former is the expression of our susceptibility to be moved by the moral law itself, while the latter, like aesthetic feelings of disinterested love toward nonhuman nature, are naturally occurring means that can be cultivated for the implementation of the general demands of morality, given that we are, in fact, motivated to fulfill these demands. However, it must also be noted that Kant explicitly says that our "obligation with regard to [general] moral feeling can only be to *cultivate* it and to strengthen it through wonder at its inscrutable source" (6:399). He clearly supposes that both general and particular moral feelings can and must be cultivated. Perhaps he thus imagines that our natural disposition to take pleasure in doing as morality commands us to do is strong enough to get us going on the project of cultivating that feeling, in order to make it strong enough to be efficacious in particular circumstances in which our commitment to morality will be put to the test, and then that our general commitment to morality, strengthened in that way, will also lead us to cultivate particular sorts of feeling, such as feelings of benevolence and sympathy, that can be useful in the implementation of the general demands of morality in the normal course of affairs. This does not seem to me to be an implausible moral psychology.

## CONCLUSION

In Section I of this essay, I argued that Kant's principle of autonomy should be understood as offering the means by which we can achieve freedom from domination by both our own inclinations and those of others, but that the achievement of autonomy should be understood as something that is only made possible, not made necessary, by the possession of free will. Contrary to Kant, I suggested that the extent to which we are free to achieve autonomy is a matter of degree, to be determined empirically, not an absolute that is given *a priori*. The particular techniques that Kant recommends in order to attain autocracy or self-mastery, which are described in Section III of this essay, would be entirely consistent with such an empirical, rather than transcendental, conception of freedom. Kant's early psychological argument for the value of autonomy, which is described in Section II, subsection A of this essay, would also be consistent with such a naturalistic approach to freedom of the will. It is clear that the Kant of the published writings in practical philosophy would not himself have been happy without both a transcendental guarantee of the existence of freedom of the will and an *a priori* argument for the unconditional obligation to be autonomous. But we might do better to settle for the empirical argument for the value of autonomy and the natural methods for the achievement of autocracy that Kant also provides.

# The Form and Matter of the Categorical Imperative

## I. HOW MANY FORMULAE?

In the *Groundwork for the Metaphysics of Morals*, Kant states that there are "three ways of representing the principle of morality" that "are at bottom only so many formulae of the very same law." There are three such formulae because all maxims have both a "form" and a "matter, namely an end", and there must also be "a complete determination of all maxims." Thus Kant writes that

All maxims have, namely,

(1) a form, which consists in universality; and in this respect the formula of the moral imperative is expressed thus: that maxims must be chosen as if they were to hold as universal laws of nature;

(2) a matter, namely an end, and in this respect the formula says that a rational being, as an end by its nature and hence as an end in itself, must in every maxim serve as the limiting condition of all merely relative and arbitrary ends;

(3) a complete determination of all maxims by means of that formula, namely that all maxims from one's own lawgiving are to harmonize with a possible kingdom of ends as with a kingdom of nature. A progression takes place here, as through the categories of the unity of the form of the will (its universality), the plurality of the matter (of objects, i.e., of ends), and the allness or the totality of the system of these. (*G*, 4:436)[1]

---

This chapter was originally presented as a plenary lecture at the Ninth International Kant Congress, and was first published in Volker Gerhardt, Rolf-Peter Horstmann, and Ralph Schumacher (eds.), *Kant und die Berliner Aufklärung. Akten des IX. Internationalen Kant-Kongresses* (Berlin: Walter de Gruyter, 2001), vol. i, pp. 131–50. It is reprinted here with permission of the publisher.

[1] Citations will be given parenthetically by an abbreviation of the title of the work cited and the location of passage cited in the Akademie edition of Kant's works, *Kant's gesammelte Schriften*, edited by the Royal Prussian (later German) Academy of Sciences (Berlin: Georg Reimer, later Walter de Gruyter, 1900– ). Unless otherwise indicated, translations

In the preceding pages, however, Kant has enumerated not three but four distinct formulations of the fundamental principle of morality or what he calls, in virtue of the way in which it presents itself to human beings, the categorical imperative. The first two formulations he has previously listed correspond to the first two he enumerates in the present list. Kant begins with what has come to be known as the formula of universal law,[2] **"Act only in accordance with that maxim through which you can at the same time will that it become a universal law"**, which, he claims, because of the very definition of the concept of nature as "the universality of law in accordance with which effects take place", can also be formulated as **"Act as if the maxim of your action were to become by your will** a universal law of nature" (*G*, 4:421).[3] Kant then proceeds to what has come to be known as the formula of humanity as an end in itself, **"So act that you use humanity, whether in your own person or in the person of any other, always at the same time as an end, never merely as a means"** (*G*, 4:429). These two versions of the categorical imperative clearly correspond to the two that Kant connects to the form and matter of maxims respectively. But Kant introduces two different candidates for the third formulation of the categorical imperative. First he states that the "present third formula of the principle" is "the idea of the will of every rational being as a **will giving universal law**", or "the **principle** of every human will as **a will giving universal law through all its maxims**"

are taken from Immanuel Kant, *Practical Philosophy*, translated and edited by Mary J. Gregor (Cambridge: Cambridge University Press, 1996). Translations from Kant's lectures on ethics will be taken from Immanuel Kant, *Lectures on Ethics*, edited by Peter Heath and J. B. Schneewind (Cambridge: Cambridge University Press, 1997). Translations from *Religion within the Boundaries of Mere Reason* are from Immanuel Kant, *Religion and Rational Theology*, translated and edited by Allen Wood and George di Giovanni (Cambridge: Cambridge University Press, 1996).

[2] This and the following designations for the several formulations of the categorical imperative were introduced, at least into Anglophone discussion of Kant, by H. J. Paton, in his commentary *The Categorical Imperative: A Study in Kant's Moral Philosophy* (London: Hutchinson, 1947), as well as in his translation, Immanuel Kant, *The Moral Law* (London: Hutchinson, 1948), republished as *Groundwork of the Metaphysics of Morals* (New York: Harper & Row, 1964).

[3] H. J. Paton famously argued that Kant introduces a teleological conception of nature by the addition of the words "of nature", and thus that the formula of the universal law of nature should be distinguished from the formula of universal law per se; see *The Categorical Imperative: A Study in Kant's Moral Philosophy* (London: Hutchinson, 1947), ch. xv, pp. 146–64. But Kant makes it plain that all he means by "nature" in this context is a condition in which a universal law is satisfied—"the universality of law in accordance with which effects take place constitutes what is properly called **nature** in the most general sense" (*G*, 4:421)—and this makes it clear that all that the formula of the universal law of nature adds to the formula of universal law is the thought of the satisfaction of the latter formula. I have argued this issue more extensively in Ch. 8 below.

(*G*, 4:432). He calls "this basic principle the principle of the **autonomy** of the will in contrast with every other, which I accordingly count as **heteronomy**" (*G*, 4:433). But then Kant claims that "The concept of every rational being as one who must regard himself as giving universal law through all the maxims of his will, so as to judge himself and his actions from this point of view, leads to a very fruitful concept dependent upon it, namely that **of a kingdom of ends**" (*G*, 4:433). Yet though Kant does go on to say that "A rational being must always regard himself as lawgiving in a kingdom of ends possible through freedom of the will" and that "Morality consists, then, in the reference of all action to the lawgiving by which alone a kingdom of ends is possible" (*G*, 4:434), he does not actually formulate a fourth version of the categorical imperative that would say something like "So act that a kingdom of ends is possible through the maxim of your action." So maybe there are only three formulations of the categorical imperative, the formulae of universal law, of humanity as an end in itself, and of autonomy, the latter of which somehow leads to the further concept of a kingdom of ends but not to a fourth imperative. However, in the enumeration with which we began, Kant does not list the formula of autonomy after the formulae of universal law and of humanity as an end in itself at all, but instead formulates what is clearly a fourth version of the imperative, the requirement "that all maxims from one's own lawgiving are to harmonize with a possible kingdom of ends as with a kingdom of nature", and he treats that formula of the kingdom of ends as the third formulation of the categorical imperative instead of the formula of autonomy. So Kant does seem to have four rather than three formulations of the categorical imperative, and to be confused about what should count as the canonical third formulation, that is to say, the formulation arrived at as or by "**a complete determination** of all maxims" (*G*, 4:436). What is going on here?

My proposal is that, as our opening passage itself makes clear, Kant is using two different conceptions of the matter or end of all moral maxims, and comes up with four rather than three different formulations of the categorical imperative because two different conceptions of the complete object of morality arise from applying the concept of "complete determination" to these two different conceptions of a moral end. One concept of end that Kant employs is that involved in the thought that humanity or rational being is itself an end that is to "serve as the limiting condition of all merely relative and arbitrary ends" (*G*, 4:436), and the "**principle** of every human will as **a will giving universal law through all its maxims**" (*G*, 4:432) is the principle that arises when the idea of complete determination is applied to this conception of the end, matter, or object of moral law: a universal system of legislation in which all the maxims of each are autonomously or freely legislated in harmony with all the maxims of all is what results when each agent is treated as an autonomous rational being who freely chooses his maxims in light of an intra- and interpersonal conception of rationality. But Kant also employs another concept of end, namely the particular object that any rational being has in view in choosing to perform a particular action. The maxim under which any action is intended must be consistent with the general constraint or "limiting condition" of treating every rational being as an end in itself, but must also have some particular content. A kingdom of ends is what results when every rational being is treated as an end in itself, to be sure, but also when the particular ends that each agent sets for himself are realized to the extent that this is consistent with treating each agent as an end in itself: a kingdom of ends is "a whole of all ends in systematic connection (a whole both of rational beings as ends in themselves and of the ends of his own that each may set himself)" (*G*, 4:433). Or, one could say, the idea that all rational beings must be treated as ends in themselves is included in the idea of a kingdom of ends, and the idea of a kingdom of ends thus includes the principle of autonomy, but the idea of a kingdom of ends also includes the idea of the realization of a consistent set of freely chosen particular ends of rational beings, and in this it goes beyond the principle of autonomy.

In the explication of the formula of humanity as an end in itself in our opening passage, to be sure, Kant appears to deny any moral significance to the particular "ends of his own that each may set himself", calling them "relative and arbitrary" (*relativen und willkührlichen*). But there are many passages in which Kant insists that every action must have an *a priori* and universal form but also an empirical and particular matter, a particular outcome that is intended to be realized by it, and that no sense can be made of the very idea of rational and moral agency except insofar as we recognize that in particular circumstances the universal principle of morality does not merely allow but even requires the adoption of particular ends.

My argument thus has the following steps. First, I show that it is Kant's view that every choice, even the choice of a fundamental maxim for the governance of all one's particular maxims, has both a form and matter, and that indeed the formula of humanity as an end in itself introduces the matter or object the value of which makes adherence to the formula of universal law rational. It is the idea of a complete and systematic application of this conception of humanity as an end in itself to all human beings that gives rise to the idea of a universal system of legislation envisioned in Kant's principle of autonomy. Then I argue that the further idea that every rational action must have a particular end, a positive conception of a determinate state of affairs to be realized as well as a limiting or negative and general conception of an end to be respected in all choice of actions and maxims, gives rise to the idea of a kingdom of ends as a systematic whole of particular as well as general ends. Finally, I argue that Kant's conception of the kingdom of ends as the ultimate object of morality is essentially identical with his conception of the highest good as the complete object of morality.[4] But since the idea of the kingdom of ends clearly includes the idea of the realization of the particular "ends of his own that each may set himself", that is, the realization of one's *own* particular ends as well as the particular ends of others, the idea of the kingdom of ends or the highest good as the ultimate object of morality thus makes the realization of one's own ends and therefore one's own happiness as well as the ends and the happiness of others part of the complete object of morality. The final stage of my argument is thus a brief examination of Kant's reasons for resisting the idea that the realization of one's own happiness can be any part of one's duty, and the rejection of this assumption in favor of the view that one's own happiness is a proper part of the kingdom of ends or the highest good.

## II. HUMANITY AS END IN ITSELF

Kant often derives the formulation of the categorical imperative as the command to act so that your maxim is at the same time universal law from the premise that a genuine practical law can only concern the "form" and not the "matter" or "effect" to be expected from the actions it commands. Thus in the *Groundwork* he states that

There is one imperative that, without being based upon and having as its condition any other purpose to be attained by certain conduct, commands this conduct immediately. This imperative is categorical. It has to do not with the

---

[4] Although Kant does not formally introduce the concept of the highest good into the *Groundwork*, he signals this equivalence when he appends this footnote to the reference to the kingdom of ends in our opening passage: "**Teleology** considers nature as a kingdom of ends, **morals** considers a possible kingdom of ends as a kingdom of nature. In the former the kingdom of ends is a theoretical idea for explaining what exists. In the latter, it is a practical idea for the sake of bringing about, in conformity with this very idea, that which does not exist but which can become real by means of our conduct" (*G*, 4:436 n.). That the kingdom of ends is an idea to be realized *in nature* identifies it with the idea of the highest good, which Kant typically characterizes in the same way.

matter of the action and what is to result from it, but with the form and the principle from which the action itself follows; and the essentially good in the action consists in the disposition, let the result be what it may. (*G*, 4:416)

Likewise, the *Critique of Practical Reason* insists that "practical universal laws" can only concern the form and not the matter of the actions they command: "If a rational being is to think of his maxims as practical universal laws, he can think of them only as principles that contain the determining ground of the will not by their matter but only by their form" (*CPracR*, 5:27). The basis for Kant's thesis is that a genuine imperative or universal practical principle must command universally and necessarily; its grip upon agents cannot depend upon a condition that is satisfied only contingently and perhaps intermittently. But in fact this means only that a universal practical principle cannot depend upon any *contingent* object of the will, not that it must exclude all reference to any object of the will whatever.

This is evident in Kant's arguments leading up to the first formulation of the categorical imperative. In the first section of the *Groundwork*, Kant's derivation of the principle of universal law from the analysis of the conditions of a good will turns precisely upon the necessity of eliminating the contingent effects of inclination, and excludes from the grounds for a principle of morality only those objects the attraction of which depends upon inclination:

Now, an action from duty is to put aside entirely the influence of inclination and with it every object of the will; hence there is left for the will nothing that could determine it except objectively the **law** and subjectively **pure respect** for this practical law, and so the maxim of complying with such a law even if it infringes upon all my inclinations ... But what kind of law can that be, the representation of which must determine the will, even without regard for the effect expected from it, in order for the will to be called good absolutely and without limitation? Since I have deprived the will of every impulse that could arise for it from obeying some law, nothing is left but the conformity of actions as such with universal law, which is alone to serve the will as its principle, that is, **I ought never to act except in such a way that I could also will that my maxim should become a universal law.** (*G*, 4:400–1, 402)

Kant repeatedly remarks that the moral law must be independent of anything contingent. Thus he states that "all moral concepts have their seat and origin completely *a priori* in reason ... that they cannot be abstracted from any empirical and therefore merely contingent cognitions" (*G*, 4:411), and that "everything empirical, as an addition to the principle of morality, is not only quite inept for this; it is also highly prejudicial to the purity of morals, where the proper worth of an absolutely good will ... consists just in the principle of action being free from all influences of contingent grounds" (G, 4:426). What particular inclinations any of us have is contingent, and so states of affairs that are suggested to us as objects of action because they promise to satisfy inclinations are also contingent. Therefore no genuine principle of morality can be founded upon the apparent desirability of objects of action suggested to us by inclination. That much is beyond dispute. However, what Kant assumes in leaping from this premise to the conclusion that the moral law can concern only the form of our maxims, their eligibility to serve as universal law alone, is that all objects of action are suggested to us by mere inclination. This is particularly clear in the *Critique of Practical Reason*, where Kant writes that "All practical principles that presuppose an **object** (matter) of the faculty of desire as the determining ground of the will are, without exception, empirical" (*CPracR*, 5:21), that "All material practical principles as such are, without exception, of one and the same kind and come under the general principle of self-love or one's own happiness", and thus that "All **material** practical rules put the determining ground of the will in the **lower faculty of desire**" (5:22). However, Kant's inference is invalid, because it fails to admit the possibility that there might be an object of the will that is not suggested by contingent inclination but that is in some sense necessary—that is not, as it were, suggested by the lower faculty of desire, but by a higher faculty of desire. Moreover, Kant's argument from the first to the second formulation of the categorical imperative, the formula of humanity as an end in itself, is based precisely on the assumptions that the rational will is always determined by the representation of an object or matter as well as by form, and thus that if the rational will is to be determined by a truly universal law it must have a necessary rather than contingent object which can be realized only by adherence to that law. Humanity as an end in itself with unconditional value is then introduced into Kant's argument as the necessary rather than contingent end or object of the will that can make adherence to the formula of universal law rational.

Kant introduces the formula of humanity as an end in itself as the result of a step into metaphysics, which consists in analysis of "the concept of the will of a rational being as such" (G, 4:426). What this analysis is supposed to reveal is that, first, "The will is thought as a capacity to determine itself to action in conformity with the **representation of certain laws**", but, second, "what serves the will as the objective ground of its self-determination is an end" (G, 4:427). Kant assumes that it is rational to act only for the sake of an end, and if it is rational to conform one's action to a law or principle that is because so doing is the way to realize that end. He then infers if a law is truly universal, or valid for all rational beings, that must be because adherence to it is the means to an end that "must hold equally for all rational beings", or an "objective end." He then observes that "Practical principles are **formal** if they abstract from all subjective ends, whereas they are **material** if they have put these, and consequently certain incentives, at their basis" (*G*, 4:427–8). Unlike the *Critique of Practical Reason*, then, this passage makes clear that principles are material not because they refer to any end at all, but only if they depend upon subjective ends, suggested by contingent inclination;[5] whereas a formal principle can and indeed must have an end, although this must be an objective end. Kant then asserts that there is a candidate for the role of objective end, namely humanity itself, and that it is only the unconditional value of this end that can serve as the ground for a rational will to determine itself in accordance with the formula of universal law:

> But suppose there were something the **existence of which in itself** has an absolute worth, something which as **an end in itself** could be a ground of determinate laws; then in it, and in it alone, would lie the ground of a possible categorical imperative, that is, of a practical law.
>
> Now I say that the human being and in general every rational being *exists* as an end in itself . . . (*G*, 4:428)

and this is what leads to the second formulation of the categorical imperative, "So act that you use humanity, whether in your own person or in the person of any other, always at the same time as an end, never merely as a means" (*G*, 4:429). This formulation specifies the end or object that is to be achieved by adherence to the formula of universal law.[6] To return to the terms of our opening quotation, then, the matter of the categorical imperative actually precedes and dictates its form, a fact that violates none of Kant's strictures on the derivation of a categorical

---

[5] On this point, see Allen W. Wood, "Humanity as an End in Itself", in Hoke Robinson, ed., *Proceedings of the Eight International Kant Congress*, vol. 1, part 1 (Milwaukee: Marquette University Press, 1995), pp. 301–19, reprinted in Paul Guyer, ed., *Kant's Groundwork of the Metaphysics of Morals: Critical Essays* (Lanham, Md.: Rowman & Littlefield, 1998), pp. 165–87, especially p. 167, and Wood, *Kant's Ethical Thought* (Cambridge: Cambridge University Press, 1999), p. 112.

[6] I first argued for this point in "The Possibility of the Categorical Imperative", *Philosophical Review* 104 (1995): 353–85, reprinted in Guyer, ed., *Kant's Groundwork of the Metaphysics of Morals: Critical Essays*, pp. 215–46, and in Guyer, *Kant on Freedom, Law, and Happiness* (Cambridge: Cambridge University Press, 2000), ch. 5. See also Wood, "Humanity as an End in Itself", in Guyer, *Kant's Groundwork*, pp. 176–7, and *Kant's Ethical Thought*, pp. 113–14.

imperative as long as we recognize that there can be a necessary and objective end of action as well as contingent and subjective ends.

I will not delve here into the difficult question of how, if at all, Kant proposes to argue for his claim that humanity is an, indeed the only end in itself with absolute worth.[7] My present project concerns instead the question of how Kant gets from the second formulation of the categorical imperative to not one but two further formulations of it, and the consequences of those further formulations. To begin to address those issues, the first thing we need is an account of what Kant means by the concept of humanity. In the *Groundwork* we can only glean this from Kant's illustrations of the classes of duties to which the formula of humanity as an end in itself is supposed to give rise. What these examples suggest is that humanity is nothing other than the capacity to choose ends. This is particularly clear in Kant's second example, where making promises one does not intend to keep is argued to violate the requirement always to treat humanity as an end and never merely as a means because "he whom I want to use for my purposes by such a promise cannot possibly agree to my way of behaving toward him, and so contain the end of this action"; conversely, to value others as ends in themselves is to treat them "as beings who must also be able to contain in themselves the end of the very same action", that is, who have the capacity to choose their own ends and to agree to actions only if they are consistent with their own choice of ends (*G*, 4:429–30).

Kant's equation of humanity with the capacity freely to choose one's own ends, implicit in the *Groundwork*, is made explicit in other works. In his lectures on ethics from 1793–4, Kant defines humanity as "the totality of all the properties of the human being, considered as an intelligent being, and whereby he is set in contrast to the *homo brutus* in his animality" (Vig., 27:671). But what sets us apart from other animals above all is what Kant identifies as humanity in the *Metaphysics of Morals*, three years later: humanity is "that by which [the human being] alone is capable of setting himself ends" (*MM*, 6:387). "The capacity to set oneself an end—any end whatsoever—is what characterizes humanity (as distinguished from animality)" (*MM*, 6:392).[8] On this

---

[7] A contemporary classic on this subject is Christine M. Korsgaard, "Kant's Formula of Humanity", *Kant-Studien* 77 (1986): 183–202, reprinted in her *Creating the Kingdom of Ends* (Cambridge: Cambridge University Press, 1996), pp. 106–32. I have suggested some criticisms of her approach in "The Value of Reason and the Value of Freedom", *Ethics* 109 (1998): 22–35. See also Wood, *Kant's Ethical Thought*, pp. 124–32.

[8] In *Religion within the Boundaries of Mere Reason* (1793), Kant defines human nature in terms of three predispositions: the predisposition to animality, which is the source of

definition of humanity, then, the first condition for treating humanity whether in our own person or that of others as an end and never merely as a means is that each of us must choose maxims of action that are compatible with our own freedom to set our ends and with the freedom to set their own ends of everyone else who might be affected by our own choice of maxims. Morality's fundamental constraint on the freedom of choice of each of us is that we use it in ways that are compatible with the freedom of choice of all of us. On any given occasion one might exercise her freedom of choice in a way that would destroy or limit the possibility of her own free choice on other occasions, and on many occasions any one of us might use her freedom of choice in a way that would destroy or limit the freedom of choice of others. So recognizing our freedom, under the name of our humanity, as an end in itself that has absolute rather than contingent worth gives real point to the formal requirement of acting on maxims that can be universal law: it requires that our maxims can be accepted by all as preserving the freedom of all.

Kant directly explicates this first way in which freedom itself functions as an end of action in his earlier lectures on ethics. These lectures might appear to introduce an independent conception of humanity by holding that the exercise of freedom of choice must be compatible with the achievement of some independently specified essential human ends: "The prime rule whereby I am to restrict freedom is the conformity to the essential ends of mankind" (Col., 27:345). However, Kant explains that "The conditions under which alone the greatest use of freedom is possible, and under which it can be self-consistent, are the essential ends of mankind. With these freedom must agree" (Col., 27:346). The essential ends of mankind are not some independent set of goods, suggested by inclination or anything else, to which our use of freedom must conform; the essential ends of mankind are nothing other than self-consistency in the use of freedom or the greatest possible use of freedom, because humanity itself is nothing but the capacity freely to choose our ends and the principles of action by means of which we can realize those ends.

inclinations that we share with other animals, such as those based in the drives for the preservation of the individual and the species; the predisposition to humanity, which "can be brought under the general title of a self-love ... and yet **involves comparison**", that is, a tendency to love oneself because one thinks one is better than others; and finally, a predisposition to personality as "the susceptibility to respect for the moral law **as of itself a sufficient incentive to the power of choice**" (*Rel.*, 6:26–7). What he calls humanity in the Vigilantius lectures and the *Metaphysics of Morals* subsumes both humanity and personality as defined in *Religion*, because according to that work we are exercising our capacity for free choice equally when we select either self-love or the moral law as our fundamental maxim, that is, the principle that is always sufficient for our power of choice.

I suggest, then, that Kant arrives at his first candidate for the third formulation of the categorical imperative, the formula of autonomy, by applying the requirement of "complete determination" to the idea of humanity as an end in itself, thus concluding that *each* rational agent in the manifold of rational agents—the world containing not just one but many rational agents in which practical reasoning actually takes place— must be acknowledged to be an agent who freely chooses his own ends and his own principles in light of respect for the humanity in his own person and the person of every other. That means that each person conceives of himself as an agent capable of freely choosing principles of action that preserve and promote his own capacity to choose his ends freely, and that he conceives of all other persons as agents capable of choosing their principles of action so as to preserve and promote the freedom of every one to choose their ends freely. This is, I take it, what is conveyed by Kant's characterization of the third formula as "the **prin- ciple** of every human will as **a will giving universal law through all its maxims**" (*G*, 4:432), or the "concept of every rational being as one who must regard himself as giving universal law through all the maxims of his will" (*G*, 4:433): since each human being must regard the humanity of every human being as an end and never merely a means, and humanity is the capacity to choose ends and appropriate principles for the realization of those ends, each person must regard the preservation of this capacity in himself and everyone else as his primary obligation in his choice of all his maxims. What it is to be an autonomous legislator in a realm (*Reich*) of such legislators, "a systematic union of various rational beings through common laws" (*G*, 4:433), is to choose all of one's maxims in a way that respects the humanity in oneself and every other person, thus the freedom of oneself and everyone else freely to choose their own principles and their own ends.

## III. THE KINGDOM OF ENDS

But why does Kant introduce not only the formula of autonomy but also the formula of the kingdom of ends, which dictates that we strive to achieve not only "a whole ... of rational beings as ends in themselves" but also a whole or systematic connection "of the ends of his own that each may set himself" (*G*, 4:433)? For the simple reason, I suggest, that since humanity is the capacity freely to set ends for oneself, our duty to make humanity, whether in our own person or that of others not merely a means but always an end, requires us not only to preserve and promote the capacity of all freely to choose their ends but also to promote the realization of the particular ends that all freely set for themselves, so far as to do so is within our power and consistent with our underlying obligation to preserve and promote the capacity for the free choice of ends in every human being. While a realm of autonomous legislators is one in which each person's right to determine his own principles in a way consistent with the right of all is fully recognized, in a kingdom of ends not only is that condition satisfied but also the freely chosen ends of each are promoted to the extent that so doing is compatible with promoting the ends of all. This is what it means that the kingdom of ends is "a whole both of rational beings as ends in themselves and of the ends of his own that each may set himself" (G, 4:433). The goal of a kingdom of ends is thus reached by applying "complete determination" to the particular ends that free agents set for themselves as well as to those free agents themselves as ends in themselves.

It may seem strange to propose that the fundamental principle of morality can be formulated in a way that commands the promotion of particular ends, not just respect for end-setters, given Kant's repeated insistence that the fundamental principle of morality must be a law that determines the will "even without regard for the effect expected from it" (G, 4:402). But throughout his writings, Kant makes it clear that every action must have a matter as well as a form, a particular end or objective as well as a principle to which it conforms, thus that there is no agency at all without particular ends of actions, and that to promote agency naturally includes promoting the particular ends freely set by agents, at least under appropriate circumstances. This is compatible with the idea that the principle of morality must be adopted independently of the desirability of particular objectives; a principle adopted in such a way can still command the promotion of particular ends as its consequence.

Kant's conception of agency is presupposed in his derivation of the duty of beneficence from the formula of humanity as an end in itself: this assumes that humanity as an end in itself is a general end and limiting condition that might by itself give rise to certain prohibitions, but that we cannot derive any positive duties of commission except through the recognition that in making humanity itself our end we also make the particular ends freely chosen in the exercise of humanity our ends:

Humanity might indeed subsist if no one contributed to the happiness of others but yet did not intentionally withdraw anything from it; but there is still only a negative and not a positive agreement with **humanity as an end in itself** unless everyone also tries, as far as he can, to further the ends of others. For, the ends of a subject who is an end in itself must as far as possible also be **my** ends, if that representation is to have its **full** effect on me. (G, 4:430)

Numerous passages elsewhere make explicit the conception of agency that underlies this passage. In the late *Metaphysics of Morals*, Kant states that "no free action is possible unless the agent intends an end (which is the matter of choice)" (*MM*, 6:389): we cannot choose, that is, exercise our freedom of choice to set our own ends, without choosing something, that is, setting some particular end. This is the premise of Kant's argument that there must be some ends that are also duties—which is also to say that there must be some duties that are also ends. As Kant puts it,

For since there are free actions there must also be ends to which, as their objects, these actions are directed. But among these ends there must be some that are also (i.e., by their concept) duties.—For were there no such ends, then all ends would hold for practical reason only as means to other ends; and since there can be no action without an end, a **categorical** imperative would be impossible. (*MM*, 6:385)

Since there can be no rational action without an end, actions commanded as duties must also be actions aimed at ends; but if the ends aimed at were themselves always ends that lie outside the purview of morality, then all duties would be commands to perform actions meant to realize ends that are not duties. That is incoherent, so at least some of the ends of our actions must be included within the purview of duty.

Thus pure practical reason, by placing absolute value on humanity as freedom, determines a general end for us, but this by itself is not enough to determine us to perform particular actions, because particular actions require particular ends. These ends can in turn be suggested to us only by naturally occurring inclinations, because pure reason itself defines only a general end. Inclination proposes objects to the faculty of desire, but the pursuit of such objects is not merely permitted if it is consistent with treating freedom as an end, but is actually commanded out of respect for humanity itself once those naturally suggested objects of desire have been made into ends of free human choice.

Kant can be seen as having reached this conclusion by combining the distinction between the form and matter of choice with a distinction between *a priori* and empirical sources of choice. Such a model is found in Kant's early notes:

Moral philosophy is the science of ends; so far as they are determined through pure reason. Or of the unity of all ends (where they do not contradict themselves) of rational beings. The matter of the good is given empirically, its form *a priori* ... (R 6820 [1776–8? 1778–1780s?], 19:172)

This suggests that pure reason can supply only the form of action, not the matter; the matter must be supplied empirically, which can only mean by inclinations proposing specific objects of desire to the faculty of desire. We cannot imagine any other source for the matter of action:

We understand nothing of merely moral happiness or blessedness. If everything material that the senses provide to our will were removed, what would become of rectitude, goodness, self-mastery, which are only forms for ordering all of these materials in ourselves? Since we can thus understand happiness and the true good only in this world, we must believe that we would overstep the bounds of our reason if we would paint for ourselves a new and higher kind of perfection. (R 6883 [1776–8? 1778–9?], 19:191)

Without actions suggested by inclinations, human beings would simply have nothing to do, and would not be agents at all. Unless treating humanity always as an end and never merely as a means includes promoting particular objects of action suggested by desire but transformed into ends by free and rational choice, it will be the denial of humanity rather than its promotion. Kant makes the same point in his final lectures on ethics. That our actions accord with the possibility of universal law is "the essential condition of the form of the action", and is the basis of rectitude; "If, on the other hand, we consider duties and their grounds of determination in regard to matter, then the action has need of an object to which it is related", or an "end of the action." Thus he concludes that "Apart from the freedom of the action, there is thus another principle present, which in itself is enlarging, in that, while freedom is restricted by the determination according to law, it is here, on the contrary, enlarged by the matter or end thereof" (Vig., 27:542–3).

As my earlier reference to the duty of beneficence suggests, that morality commands the promotion of particular ends chosen by human beings as well as the general end of the freedom that constitutes their humanity is also implied by Kant's classification of duties. Kant first introduces this classification in the *Groundwork* in order to confirm his formulations of the categorical imperative by showing that they give rise to the essential classes of duty that anyone would acknowledge. The four classes of duty he illustrates are generated by combining the distinction between perfect and imperfect duties, that is, narrow duties or duties of omission that proscribe specific forms of conduct, and broad duties or duties of commission that prescribe general policies of conduct without being able to detail all the specific acts that could fulfill those policies, with the distinction between duties to oneself and duties to others. Thus, Kant's example of a perfect duty to oneself is the prohibition of suicide; his example of a perfect duty to others is the prohibition of false promises; his example of an imperfect duty to oneself is the duty to cultivate some talents and capabilities for which one has natural predispositions, which could make one into "a human being useful for all sorts of purposes" (G, 4:423); and his example of an imperfect duty to others is the duty to find appropriate ways to contribute to their welfare. Taken together, what these duties describe is a complex requirement for "the **preservation** of humanity as an end in itself" and "the **furtherance** of this end" in both oneself and others (G, 4:430), where humanity is understood precisely as the capacity to set and pursue our ends freely. Thus, the perfect duties are duties regarding humanity as a general end, namely, duties not to destroy the existence and the possibility of the exercise of freedom in oneself or others, while the imperfect duties are duties to develop the capacities on which the successful pursuit of the particular ends freely chosen in the exercise of humanity depends and even directly to promote the realization of such ends.

Kant's examples of perfect duties to oneself and to others are examples of duties to preserve the existence and the possibility of the exercise of free choice. In his clearest treatments of suicide, Kant prohibits it on the ground that it is a free act, but one that would destroy the free agent who performs it and thus the possibility of any further free acts by that agent: "So far, then, as anyone destroys his body, and thereby takes his own life, he has employed his choice to destroy the power of choosing itself; but in that case, free choice is in conflict with itself" (Col., 27:369). Kant could have chosen homicide, the freely chosen destruction of the life of another free agent, as his example of a perfect duty of omission to others, but to make a further point he instead chooses the prohibition of false promises. What this duty prohibits is not the destruction of another's free agency itself but rather the restriction of his exercise of it. If someone to whom I would make a false promise really understood my intentions, then he could not "possibly agree to my way of behaving toward him, and so himself contain the end of this action" (G, 4:429–30): What you do when you make a false promise to another is to deny him the opportunity to choose his own response freely in full knowledge of the real circumstances and consequences of his action.

Kant's example of an imperfect duty to oneself is the duty to cultivate some of one's natural predispositions to talents in order to further one's own humanity. This is necessary because "as a rational being [one] necessarily wills that all the capacities in him be developed, since they serve him and are given to him for all sorts of possible purposes"

(*G*, 4:423). Making humanity one's end requires not just freely choosing ends but also taking steps to assure the successful accomplishment of those ends. This is an imperfect rather than a perfect duty because there is no mechanical way to specify which talents one could successfully develop, which among all those that one could develop one should develop, and how far one should go to develop them. There will also be occasions on which acting to develop a talent for future use may have to give way before a more immediately pressing duty. But within these limits, one has a general obligation freely to cultivate means to the successful accomplishment of one's freely chosen ends.

Finally, as we have already seen, Kant argues that one has a duty to assist others in the pursuit of their freely chosen ends because "there is still only a negative and not a positive agreement with **humanity as an end in itself** unless everyone also tries, as far as he can, to further the ends of others" (*G*, 4:430). Kant does not argue that one must assist others for the prudential reason that doing so might increase the likelihood that they will then help one in the pursuit of one's own ends (even though such a strategy could actually be required by one's duty to oneself to cultivate means to the realization of one's own ends). Instead, his idea is simply that insofar as the ends of others are freely chosen, one has a duty to help them realize those ends just because of the value of their free choice itself. Again, this duty is broad rather than narrow: in assisting another, one must not violate any of one's other duties or help the other to violate one of his duties;[9] and, Kant stresses, "I cannot do good to anyone in accordance with **my** concepts of happiness . . . thinking to benefit him by forcing a gift upon him; rather I can benefit him only in accordance with **his** concepts of happiness" (*MM*, 6:454). To attempt to benefit another in accordance with my conception of his happiness rather than his own would be precisely to rob him of the freedom of choice from which my obligation to assist him in the pursuit of his happiness arises in the first place.

Thus, the fundamental principle of morality rests on the duty to make humanity itself our end, but the duty to make humanity itself our end implies the duty to promote the realization of the particular ends that human beings freely choose, at least under appropriate circumstances. Applying the requirement of complete determination to both humanity

[9] Barbara Herman famously argued that the duty of beneficence does not extend to helping another with a heavy burden that is in fact a stolen object, and that for this reason the duty of beneficence cannot be based simply on a naturally occurring feeling of sympathy or benevolence, which cannot itself draw the rational distinction between well-placed and misplaced assistance; see *The Practice of Moral Judgment* (Cambridge, Mass.: Harvard University Press, 1993), chapter 1, pp. 4–5.

as end in itself as well as to the particular ends freely chosen in the exercise of humanity is what gives rise to the two different, or less and more inclusive, formulae of autonomy and the kingdom of ends. Understanding the distinction between these two results is crucial not just for explaining why Kant ends up with four rather than three formulations of the moral law, but also for explaining the place of happiness in Kant's ethics: because a kingdom of ends requires the satisfaction of particular ends in a way that the mere idea of autonomy does not, and the satisfaction of particular ends is of course the source of happiness, it is through the formula of the kingdom of ends alone that happiness is directly connected to the fundamental principle of morality.[10]

[10] Before exploring that connection, however, I want to conclude the present section with a comment on an important distinction that Kant draws within the sphere of our imperfect duties to others. In his important treatment of the formula of humanity, Allen Wood has stressed that it is this formula that Kant typically uses to derive specific duties, and that the derivations of such duties proceeds by showing that particular forms of action or omission are necessary in order to *express* respect for humanity as an end in itself. This is entirely correct if understood in the sense in which Wood intends it, as the claim that "the expression of respect for humanity [is] the *fundamental reason* why we should conform to moral laws and pursue moral ends" (Wood, "Humanity as End in Itself", in Guyer, ed., *Kant's Groundwork*, p. 177 of this edition. The same account is given in Wood, *Kant's Ethical Thought*, pp. 141–2). We have a duty to promote particular ends freely chosen by human beings under the appropriate circumstances because their choice of such ends is an expression of their humanity itself, which is of absolute value. But it would be unfortunate if Wood's characterization of our duties to others as "expressive" because our fundamental reason for fulfilling them is our duty to express respect for humanity itself were to be understood to limit our obligations to others to expressions of respect for them in an everyday sense. In his treatment of our imperfect duties to others in the "Doctrine of Virtue" of the *Metaphysics of Morals*, Kant himself distinguishes between duties of *love*, which flow not from "feeling" but from the "maxim of **benevolence** (practical love), which results in beneficence", and duties of respect, which are duties to limit "our self-esteem by the dignity of humanity in another person" (*MM*, DV, §25, 6:449). Duties of love are duties such as those to help the sick and needy, while duties of respect are duties to avoid self-aggrandizement and the demeaning of others, and Kant's point is that our general obligation to express respect for the humanity in others, although the reason for all our moral actions, can manifest itself in two different forms: by the advancement of their particular ends, or by other forms of action that do not actually advance their particular ends, but in some more abstract way preserve their humanity intact. Now, Kant himself assumes that "a duty of free respect toward others is, strictly speaking, only a negative one" (*loc. cit.*), and the examples of duties of respect he gives are indeed all examples of duties of omission, such as the duties to refrain from expressions of arrogance, defamation and ridicule (*MM*, DV, §41, 6:465), while duties of love are all assumed to be positive or duties of commission. As Wood's examples show, there can be positive duties of respect as well, such as the duty to doff one's hat before a national or religious symbol or shrine, even if not one's own, in order to show respect for others (Wood, "Humanity as End in Itself", pp. 169, 177; *Kant's Ethical Thought*, pp. 141–2). This means that the distinction between duties of love and respect is not strictly congruent with that between duties of commission and omission. (This in turn raises the question of why Kant classifies the duties of respect as imperfect rather than perfect duties to others,

## IV. THE KINGDOM OF ENDS AND THE HIGHEST GOOD

Each of Kant's three critiques culminates in the conception of the highest good and the doctrine of the postulates of pure practical reason, above all the postulate of the existence of God as the condition of the possibility of the realization of the highest good. *Religion within the Boundaries of Mere Reason* does not end with the doctrine of the highest good, but instead begins with it (*Rel.*, 6:3–6). Almost alone among Kant's major works, the *Groundwork* makes no reference to the highest good. But I suggest that the conception of the kingdom of ends in the *Groundwork* is equivalent to the concept of the highest good in Kant's other works. The *Critique of Practical Reason* for instance, characterizes the highest good as the "whole, the complete good" of a "possible world" (*CPracR*, 5:111), while the *Groundwork*, as we have seen, introduces the kingdom of ends as the ultimate formulation of the "complete determination" of the maxims of morality. I believe that these are the same notions.

This may not be immediately apparent, of course, because the concept of the highest good is formulated as a conjunction of virtue and happiness, while Kant's description of the kingdom of ends explicitly mentions neither of these. The highest good is characterized as "happiness distributed in exact proportion to morality" (*CPracR*, 5:110), while the kingdom of ends, as we have seen, is characterized as the "systematic" "whole both of rational beings as ends in themselves and of the ends of his own that each may set himself" (*G*, 4:433). But from the thesis of the first section of the *Groundwork* that virtue consists in being motivated by respect for the moral law alone (*G*, 4:400) and the second

when the perfect duties typically seem to be negative duties or duties of omission. Kant does not address this question, but the answer must be that duties of respect are included among duties of virtue because unlike some other negative or perfect duties to others, such as the duties to refrain from injuring, killing, or robbing them, the duties to avoid defaming or mocking them are not appropriate subjects for coercive enforcement, and thus for inclusion among duties of right. Since the "Doctrine of Virtue" has no special category for non-coercively enforceable perfect duties to others, Kant includes them among the imperfect duties to others.) Even once this is noted, however, it must still be emphasized that in many cases the duty to express respect for the humanity in others will not just require an expression of respect in an everyday sense, whether by refraining from a gesture of disrespect or performing a gesture of respect, but will also require the performance of an action meant to promote or assist in the realization of someone's particular end. Respect for humanity as an end in itself is the reason for performing a duty of love, but the characterization of such a performance is not exhausted by description of it as an expression of respect.

formulation of the moral law as requiring the treatment of all humanity, whether in your own person or in the person of any other, as an end and never merely as a means, it follows that what virtue requires is nothing other than the treatment of all humanity as a whole of "rational beings as ends in themselves." And since happiness consists in nothing other than the satisfaction of particular ends, whatever they may be, a systematic whole "of the ends of his own that each may set himself", insofar as that is consistent with the systematic whole of rational beings as ends in themselves, is surely nothing other than the happiness of all insofar as that is consistent with the requirements of virtue. The imperative to realize the kingdom of ends as the complete determination of all maxims is thus equivalent to the imperative to realize the highest good as the complete object of morality.

An objection to this equation could be grounded in the facts that the happiness intended in the conception of the highest good would seem to be the happiness of an individual, not of the whole of all humankind, and the relation between virtue and happiness that is intended seems to be that of proportionality, according to which the virtuous should be rewarded with happiness while the vicious should be deprived of it. The kingdom of ends, however, seems to be an ideal condition, in which everyone treats everyone as an end in himself, so all are virtuous, and in which the ends that each may set himself consistent with this are realized, so that all are happy—one's object in attempting to bring about the kingdom of ends is surely not one's own happiness, and since it is an ideal there is not even room for the thought that happiness might ever have to be limited in proportion to less than perfect virtue. However, in spite of the language with which Kant introduces the conception of the highest good in the second *Critique*—"virtue and happiness together constitute possession of the highest good in a person, and happiness distributed in exact proportion to morality...constitutes the **highest good** of a possible world"—neither of the assumptions I have mentioned plays any role in Kant's arguments from the highest good to the postulates of pure practical reason, particularly the postulate of the existence of God. Kant never argues that God is necessary to ensure that all and only the just are happy; he argues only that God is necessary to ensure that the laws of nature are such that happiness can indeed result from virtue (see especially *CPracR*, 5:124–5).[11] And he takes great pains to

---

[11] On the issue of whether the notion of proportionality is central to Kant's conception of the highest good, see Andrews Reath, "Two Conceptions of the Highest Good in Kant", *Journal of the History of Philosophy* 26 (1988): 593–619. See also Guyer, *Kant on Freedom, Law, and Happiness*, chapter 10.

explain that the happiness included in the conception of the highest good is not the happiness of an individual agent alone, but the happiness of all.

The last point is particularly clear in Kant's 1793 essay "On the Common Saying: That May Be Correct in Theory, but it is of No Use in Practice." In the first section of this work, Kant rebuts Christian Garve, who had construed Kant's account of the highest good in the *Critique of Practical Reason* to mean that an individual agent could be motivated to comply with the moral law only by the promise of his personal happiness as a reward for his virtue. Garve found this idea abhorrent, and Kant agreed, but also insisted that it had never been his idea at all. Instead, Kant explained, his position was that no thought of happiness, whether one's own or everyone's, was any part of morally praiseworthy *motivation* (TP, 8:282 n.), but that the concept of duty itself makes the collective happiness of mankind the *object* of our morally motivated action. In Kant's words, "this concept of duty does not have to be grounded on any particular end but rather **introduces** another end for the human being's will, namely to work to the best of one's ability toward the **highest good** possible in the world (universal happiness combined with and in conformity with the purest morality throughout the world)" (TP, 8:279). There is no hint here that someone's happiness should merely be made proportionate to virtue, whatever his level of virtue happens to be; rather, the argument is that both virtue and happiness must be maximized, and that to maximize the former, by treating everyone as an end in himself, is in fact also to maximize the latter.

Kant argues that the "need to assume, as the final end of all things, a good that is the **highest good** in the world . . . is a need not from a deficiency in moral incentives", but rather depends simply on the fact that "without some end there can be no **will**" (TP, 8:279 n.). This is Kant's premise that there is no rational action without some end in the second of its applications: the particular free choices that are to be preserved and promoted by respect for humanity as a general end are choices of particular ends, and promoting these choices means promoting the realization of their ends as well, which is precisely what produces happiness. Kant stresses that "not every end is moral", thus the choice of "one's own happiness" alone would not be moral, but a moral end must be an "unselfish one"; thus he concludes that

With the human being too, accordingly, the incentive which is present in the idea of the highest good possible in the world by his cooperation is not his own happiness thereby intended but only this idea as end in itself, and hence compliance with it as duty... But a determination of will which limits itself and its aim of belonging to such a whole to this condition is **not selfish**. (TP, 8:280 n.)

Kant's claim is that because every rationally chosen action must have an end, the very idea of preserving and promoting rational action itself defines a universal rather than selfish idea of happiness as the object of action motivated by the thought of duty alone. One's own happiness is neither the motive nor the object of action so motivated, although of course one's own happiness must be included in the object that is so defined, universal happiness.

This conclusion raises an obvious question about the equation I have suggested. How can the kingdom of ends be equivalent to the highest good as the complete object of morality if that means that it includes one's own happiness as part of the object of morality, given all that Kant says against the idea that morality has anything to do with happiness, let alone one's own happiness? This question requires a long answer; here I will only focus on two specific points among Kant's many qualms about linking morality and happiness, and show that neither of these in fact gives rise to objections to his conceptions of the highest good and the kingdom of ends.

In the introduction to the "Doctrine of Virtue" in the *Metaphysics of Morals*, Kant argues that one's own happiness cannot be an end that is also a duty, for while "**his own happiness** is an end that every human being has (by virtue of the impulses of his nature)... What everyone already wants unavoidably, of his own accord, does not come under the concept of **duty**, which is **constraint** to an end adopted reluctantly" (*MM*, DV, IV, 6:386). Simply because one wants it naturally, one has no need to impose a concern for one's own happiness on oneself as a duty. This little argument is unsound, however. For while one may have the various particular impulses and desires that one has from moment to moment naturally and unavoidably, one does not in the same way naturally have a concern for one's own happiness in the sense of a conception of the desires one could consistently fulfill over a lifetime—that is an object of reason, not nature alone, and one may well need to compel oneself to pay due regard to such a conception of one's own happiness as contrasted to a mere passing impulse. Kant himself recognizes this in his well-known example of the gouty man who has to distinguish between short-term satisfaction of a desire for rich food or drink and his long term health and happiness (*G*, 4:399). This example shows that one's own happiness is not a mere object of desire, but an object of reason.[12]

In the "Doctrine of Virtue", Kant almost immediately qualifies his initial rejection of one's own happiness as an end that is a duty by admitting that "Adversity, pain, and want are great temptations to violate one's own duty", and inferring that one may therefore have an indirect rather than direct "duty to promote **one's own** happiness and not just the happiness of others", at least to the extent of making sure that one can avoid any adversity, pain, and want that might tempt one to violate one's own duty, although not for the sake of one's own happiness but as a means to the fulfillment of one's duty. "But then", Kant says, "the end is not the subject's happiness but his morality, and happiness is merely a means for removing obstacles to his morality" (*MM*, DV, V, 6:388). Apart from the contingent fact that unhappiness would be a temptation to immorality, one would still have no moral reason to take a concern for one's own happiness. Later in the work, however, Kant tacitly concedes the illogic of his initial position when he states that

Since all **others** with the exception of myself would not be **all** ... the law making benevolence a duty will include myself, as an object of benevolence, in the command of practical reason. This does not mean that I am thereby under obligation to love myself (for this happens unavoidably ...); it means instead that lawgiving reason, which includes the whole species (and so myself as well) in its idea of humanity as such, includes me as giving universal law along with all others in the duty of mutual benevolence, in accordance with the principle of equality... (*MM*, DV, §27, 6:451)

Just as I must treat humanity as an end in itself whether in the person of others or in myself, so I must treat happiness, as the satisfaction of ends rationally chosen, as an object of morality whether in others or myself, and indeed I must do so because that is part of what it is to treat humanity as an end in itself. Only if I include my own happiness, conceived as an object of reason and not of mere passing desire, as part of the systematic whole of the ends that each may set himself, do I truly conceive of this as a systematic whole.

An objection that Kant makes to any attempt to *ground* the principle of morality on the desire for happiness is that anyone's conception of happiness is often indeterminate and even contradictory: one cannot know in advance everything that would make one happy, various things

---

[12] See Christine M. Korsgaard, "Motivation, Metaphysics, and the Self: A Reply to Ginsborg, Guyer, and Schneewind", *Ethics* 109 (1998): 49–66, at pp. 57–9, and Guyer, *Kant on Freedom, Law, and Happiness*, chapter 2.

that one might expect would make one happy would conflict with one another, and certainly there can be conflicts between what would make one person happy and what would make another happy, even when there is superficial agreement between them (*CPracR*, 5:28). For these sorts of reasons, one cannot define a determinate and consistent ideal of happiness and derive a principle of morality *from* that. However, Kant's model of a kingdom of ends as the complete determination of moral maxims does not require that anyone be able to specify such an ideal of happiness in advance of the formulation and adoption of the principle of morality. The fundamental principle of morality requires that we work *toward* a kingdom of ends in which the ends that each person freely sets himself must be promoted because they are products of the free choice in which the humanity of each consists and insofar as they express that humanity. This means that those ends the choice of which is discovered to be consistent with the humanity of each and with the humanity of all, and the realization of which could thus give rise to a systematic form of happiness within the limits set by respect for the humanity in each and all, must be promoted. But there is no requirement that the content of those choices be known in advance of individual acts of choice. Indeed, since the particular ends of each are of value only as expressions of the free choice of each, they can be revealed only as those choices are themselves made over time. Thus one does not and cannot have to know in advance what particular ends will be promoted in a kingdom of ends in order to know what one has to do to help realize the kingdom of ends, namely promote the realization of those ends of oneself and others that are expressions of the free choice of all made with respect to the humanity of each.

Because the humanity that is the general end and limiting condition of all moral maxims is nothing other than the capacity to choose and pursue particular ends in our actions, a complete determination of our maxims must respect universal autonomy but also result in a kingdom of ends. Kant's confusion over how to count his formulations of the categorical imperative cannot mask his clear understanding of its implications.

# 8

## Ends of Reason and Ends of Nature: The Place of Teleology in Kant's Ethics

I

In his classical commentary on Kant's *Groundwork of the Metaphysics of Morals*, H. J. Paton argued that Kant's conception of the fundamental principle of morality is teleological virtually from the outset. Kant's initial formulation of the moral law as what Paton termed the "Formula of Universal Law," namely the categorical imperative "Act only in accordance with that maxim through which you can at the same time will that it become a universal law," is "concerned only with the form of moral obligation."[1] This law obligates us independently of the desirability of any particular ends we might expect to achieve by means of action in accordance with it. As Kant says in the *Critique of Practical Reason*, "If a rational being is to think of his maxims as practical universal laws,

This chapter was originally presented as an H. J. Paton Lecture in the Department of Moral Philosophy at the University of St Andrews. It was first published in the *Journal of Value Inquiry*, 36 (2002), 161–86. Copyright held by Kluwer Academic Publishers BV; reprinted with their permission.

[1] Immanuel Kant, *Groundwork of the Metaphysics of Morals*, Ak 4: 421, and H. J. Paton, *The Categorical Imperative: A Study in Kant's Moral Philosophy* (London: Hutchinson, 1947), p. 135. Citations of Kant's works are from the volume and page number of their appearance in the so-called Akademie edition: *Kant's gesammelte Schriften*, ed. Royal Prussian Academy of Sciences, 29 vols. (Berlin: Georg Reimer (later Walter de Gruyter), 1900– ). Translations from Kant's published works in moral philosophy are from Immanuel Kant, *Practical Philosophy*, trans. and ed. Mary J. Gregor (Cambridge: Cambridge University Press, 1996). Translations from Kant's lectures on ethics are from Immanuel Kant, *Lectures on Ethics*, ed. Peter Heath and J. B. Schneewind (Cambridge: Cambridge University Press, 1997). Translations from *Religion within the Boundaries of Mere Reason* are from Immanuel Kant, *Religion and Rational Theology*, trans. and ed. Allen Wood and George di Giovanni (Cambridge: Cambridge University Press, 1996). Translations from Immanuel Kant, *Critique of the Power of Judgment* are from the edition trans. Paul Guyer and Eric Matthews (Cambridge: Cambridge University Press, 2000). The only exception to this is the *Critique of Pure Reason*, which is cited, in customary passage, by the page numbers of the first (A) and second (B) editions of 1781 and 1787; translations are from Immanuel Kant, *Critique of Pure Reason*, ed. and trans. Paul Guyer and Allen W. Wood (Cambridge: Cambridge University Press, 1998).

he can think of them only as principles that contain the determining ground of the will not by their matter"—objects of desire the attainment of which promises happiness—"but only by their form."[2] However, Paton argued, as soon as Kant reformulates this principle as the "Formula of the Law of Nature," namely, "act as if the maxim of your action were to become by your will a universal law of nature," he introduces teleological assumptions into his moral philosophy through the concept of a law of nature itself.[3] In fact, Paton argues, Kant makes two teleological assumptions. First, when human nature is conceived of as part of nature in general it becomes "an essential characteristic of human nature to set purposes before itself."[4] But Kant also holds that in nature "no organ, no faculty, no impulse . . . is either superfluous or disproportionate to its use, but . . . everything is exactly adapted to its purpose in life."[5] Further, according to Paton, Kant inescapably relies upon the second of these assumptions in deriving determinate duties from the fundamental principle of morality, as when he argues that suicide is prohibited because in it the feeling of self-love, which is destined by nature for one purpose, namely self-preservation, is used for a contrary purpose, namely self-destruction. Thus, for example, Kant argues that suicide is prohibited because it destroys a "harmony of purpose, a harmony between the ends proposed by the maxim when universalized as a law of nature, and what [Kant] calls 'purposes of nature'."[6]

Paton was right to suppose that Kant recognizes that rational human action must always have an end intended to be realized in nature, but wrong to suppose that the derivation of duties in Kant's ethics crucially depends upon the assumption that everything in nature has one and only one proper purpose. Kant does prominently assume this principle in his first discussion of suicide in the *Groundwork*, but it is not necessary for him to appeal to this principle to explain what is wrong with suicide, nor does he have any justification for importing this regulative principle of theoretical inquiry into his account of practical reasoning. Indeed, as Paton himself notes, Kant's use of this principle in his argument against suicide makes it the "weakest" of his four examples of duty following the initial formulation of the categorical imperative.[7]

While Paton's second claim should be rejected, his first claim may be refined, and, as we will see, Kant's moral theory is teleological in no fewer than four ways. First, Kant recognizes that the rationality of

---

[2] Kant, *Critique of Practical Reason*, 5:27; cf. 5:21.
[3] Kant, *Groundwork of the Metaphysics of Morals*, 4:421.
[4] Paton, op. cit., p. 149.
[5] Ibid., p. 150.     [6] Ibid., p. 154.     [7] Ibid.

adherence to the moral law itself presupposes that such adherence must serve an ultimate end. This end is humanity itself; thus Kant's second formulation of the categorical imperative, the "Formula of Humanity as an End in Itself," introduces the end to which adherence to the first formulation, the Formula of Universal Law, is the means. But this is a formal end, and does not provide determinate objectives for specific rational actions without material ends for those actions.[8] However, this problem raised by the conception of humanity as an end is also solved by the fact that humanity itself is nothing other than the capacity freely to set particular ends. Thus the first teleological element of Kant's theory, the fundamental moral principle to make humanity itself our end, leads to its second teleological aspect, the moral requirement that we preserve and promote human capacities to choose and realize particular ends. These two conclusions then lead to two further teleological dimensions of Kant's thought: the recognition that both the cultivation of freedom in the choice of ends and the realization of human ends, in the systematic and collective form that Kant calls the highest good, must be conceived of as possible within nature. Kant sometimes suggests that both human freedom and human happiness can be seen as the ends of nature, although we will see that there are reasons for taking such claims cautiously and restricting him to the claim that the realization of these ends of reason must be compatible with the laws of nature. Once we have understood this, we will then see that what Paton considered the second main element of Kant's moral teleology, the principle that every natural organ and capacity has one and only one proper use, has no fundamental normative role within Kant's moral philosophy, although it may serve without harm as a heuristic principle of meta-ethics, as it serves Kant generally for a heuristic principle of metaphilosophy. Kant makes use of the principle in the argument of Section I of the *Groundwork*, when he argues that the proper purpose of human reason does not seem to be the realization of individual human happiness, but it must have some proper purpose, which must instead be the realization of the good will or human virtue.[9] This parallels Kant's more general teleological argument in the *Critique of Pure Reason* that the proper purpose of human reason cannot be theoretical knowledge of the soul, the world, and God, for it cannot provide such knowledge, yet it must have a proper purpose, which can only be found in its practical use instead.[10] Although Kant does use this

[8]  See John Silber, "The Importance of the Highest Good in Kant's Ethics," *Ethics*, 28 (1963), p. 186.
[9]  See Kant, *Groundwork of the Metaphysics of Morals*, 5:395–6.
[10]  See Kant, *Critique of Pure Reason*, A 642–3/B 670–1.

principle, not only in some of his arguments against suicide but also in some aspects of his treatment of human sexuality, he has no justification for doing so. Any suggestion that nature itself sets certain ends for us seems incompatible with Kant's insistence upon both the unrestricted force and the unconditional value of human freedom, and indeed Kant himself ultimately recognizes that we cannot allow the ends of nature to override the exercise of human freedom in the choice of ends even in his treatments of suicide and sexuality.

2

In the first section of the *Groundwork*, Kant derives the fundamental principle of morality from the premise that such a principle must be one upon which we can act independently of any inclination in behalf of any action it might require of us. It is to support this premise that Kant introduces the notorious example of the philanthropist who has lost all natural inclination to help others but can still do so out of respect for duty alone: only if the principle of morality is independently of inclination can such a person act upon it.[11] Because the principle of morality must obligate us independently of our inclination in behalf of any object of desire, Kant then infers that it must be formal in the sense of requiring of us nothing less than that the maxims of our actions have the form of universal law:

> But what kind of law can that be, the representation of which must determine the will, even without regard for the effect expected from it, in order for the will to be called good absolutely and without limitation? Since I have deprived the will of every impulse that could arise for it from obeying some law, nothing is left but the conformity of actions as such with universal law, which alone is to serve the will as its principle, that is, I ought never to act except in such a way that I could also will that my maxim should become a universal law.[12]

Kant assumes that the independence of the moral law from any object of inclination that is required to make room for the apathetic philanthropist entails the independence of this law from any object of the faculty of desire altogether. However, what is actually required for this purpose is only that the possibility of fulfilling our obligation under the moral law not depend upon anything that would be made into an object of desire only by contingent inclination; the possibility is left open that there might

---

[11] Kant, *Groundwork of the Metaphysics of Morals*, 4:398.
[12] Ibid. 4:402.

be a necessary object of the will furnished to the faculty of desire by something other than mere inclination, and that the rationality of our adherence to the moral law might depend upon this necessary end.[13]

Kant does not explicitly acknowledge this gap in his argument. He nevertheless fills it in when he goes on to argue there must be something that is an "end in itself" with an "absolute worth" that could serve as the ground of a practical law, an end that would make it rational for a rational being to adhere to such a law: "But suppose there were something the existence of which in itself has an absolute worth, something which as an end in itself could be a ground of determinate laws; then in it, and in it alone, would lie the ground of a possible categorical imperative, that is, of a practical law."[14]

Kant applies an assumption of means-end rationality, namely that it is never rational to act without an end in view, to the rational act of choosing to adhere to the fundamental principle of morality itself. Thus he infers that if it is rational for us to ignore all of our particular, contingent inclinations and act only on maxims that conform to the ideal of universal law, this must be because acting in accordance with this ideal is the means to an end that has an absolute rather than merely contingent worth.

But if all ends suggested by inclination have already been excluded as grounds for the adoption of a universal moral law because of their contingency, what sort of end could be such a necessary end to which adherence to the moral law is the means? Kant's claim is that the end in itself that has absolute value can be nothing other than our humanity itself, so that, "The practical imperative will therefore be the following: So act that you use humanity, whether in your own person or in the person of any other, always at the same time as an end, never merely as a means."[15]

Kant's moral philosophy is thus teleological from the outset insofar as it is founded upon the argument that the adoption of any principle without an end to which adherence to this principle would be the means would be irrational; that a universally valid principle or practical

---

[13] See Paul Guyer, "The Possibility of the Categorical Imperative," *Philosophical Review* 104 (1995), reprinted in Paul Guyer, ed., *Immanuel Kant: The Groundwork of the Metaphysics of Morals: Critical Essays* (Lanham, Md.: Rowman & Littlefield, 1998), pp. 215–46, esp. pp. 226–8; and in *Kant on Freedom, Law, and Happiness* (Cambridge: Cambridge University Press, 2000), pp. 172–206; see also "The Derivation of the Categorical Imperative: Kant's Correction for a Fatal Flaw," *Harvard Review of Philosophy*, 10 (2002), pp. 64–80.

[14] Kant, *Groundwork of the Metaphysics of Morals*, 4:428.

[15] Ibid. 4:429.

law requires a universally valid end, or an end with absolute worth; that particular ends contingently suggested by inclination obviously do not have absolute worth; and that the only alternative to them is humanity itself, which must have absolute worth and must be the end advanced by adherence to the moral law.

3

But Kant himself stresses that this "humanity" is only a negative end, an end that "must never be acted against."[16] Why should Kant's ethical theory be seen as teleological in the second way, as requiring the preservation and promotion of the human capacity to choose and realize particular ends—precisely the sort of ends that would seem to be suggested only by inclination? This question is answered by what Kant means by "humanity." In fact, what Kant means by this term is nothing other than the capacity freely to choose ends of actions that in his view distinguishes humankind from all other animals. To make humanity always our end and never merely a means thus requires that we make the human capacity freely to choose ends itself our end and never merely a means. In turn, Kant assumes that making the capacity freely to choose our ends our ultimate end and never merely a means requires the preservation and promotion of the capacity to choose and realize particular ends. The requirement that we preserve the capacity to choose ends might still be a merely negative end, but the requirement that we promote the capacity to choose and realize particular ends, together with the further recognition that such particular ends are in fact suggested by inclination and thus by nature, certainly introduces a second teleological dimension to Kant's ethics: Kant's fundamental principle of morality requires not only that we recognize and preserve the formal end of human freedom itself, but also that, at least under suitable circumstances, we promote the particular objectives that are suggested to us by nature through mere inclination but are transformed into ends only by the exercise of our capacity for free choice, which makes some but usually not all of these objectives into our ends.

This argument depends upon the equation of our humanity with our capacity freely to choose our own ends. Kant does not always define humanity in this way, but he does do so in crucial places. In his lectures on ethics from 1793–4, Kant defines humanity as "the totality of all the

---

[16] Kant, *Groundwork of the Metaphysics of Morals*, 4:437.

properties of the human being, considered as an intelligent being, and whereby he is set in contrast to the *homo brutus* in his animality."[17] But what sets us apart from other animals above all is what Kant identifies as humanity in *The Metaphysics of Morals*, three years later: humanity is "that by which [the human being] alone is capable of setting himself ends."[18] "The capacity to set oneself an end—any end whatsoever—is what characterizes humanity (as distinguished from animality)."[19]

On this definition of humanity, the first condition for treating humanity whether in our own person or that of others as an end and never merely as a means is that each of us must choose maxims of action that are compatible with our own freedom to set our ends and with the freedom to set their own ends of everyone else who might be affected by our own choice of maxims. The fundamental constraint of morality on the freedom of choice of each of us is that we use it in ways that are compatible with the freedom of choice of all of us. On any given occasion any person might exercise her freedom of choice in a way that would destroy or limit the possibility of her own free choice on other occasions, and on many occasions any of us might use our freedom of choice in a way that would destroy or limit the freedom of choice of others. Recognizing our freedom, under the name of our humanity, as an end in itself that has absolute rather than contingent worth gives real point to the formal requirement of acting on maxims that can be universal law: it requires that our maxims can be accepted by all as preserving the freedom of all.

Kant directly explicates this first way in which freedom itself functions as an end of action in his earlier lectures on ethics. These lectures might appear to introduce a teleological element by holding that the exercise of freedom of choice must be compatible with the achievement of some independently specified essential human ends: "The prime rule whereby I am to restrict freedom is the conformity to the essential ends of mankind."[20] However, Kant explains that, "The conditions under which alone the greatest use of freedom is possible, and under which it can be self-consistent, are the essential ends of mankind. With these freedom must agree."[21] The essential ends of mankind are not some independent set of goods, suggested by inclination or anything else, to which our use of freedom must conform; the essential ends of mankind are nothing

---

[17] Kant, *Kant on the Metaphysics of Morals: Vigilantius's Lecture Notes*, 27:671.
[18] Kant, *The Metaphysics of Morals*, 6:387.
[19] Ibid. 6:392. See also Kant, *Religion within the Boundaries of Mere Reason*, 6:26–7.
[20] Kant, *Moral Philosophy: Collins's Lecture Notes*, 27:345.
[21] Ibid. 27:346.

other than self-consistency in the use of freedom or the greatest possible use of freedom.

But how do we get from here to the further claim that morality actually requires the promotion of the realization of particular ends? This is the subject of dispute between Hannah Ginsborg and Christine Korsgaard. Ginsborg argues that the idea that morality actually endorses nonmoral ends is incoherent because the incentives furnished by inclination and those furnished by morality itself are two competing incentives, and the principles to act on the incentives of inclination and to act on the incentives of morality are two competing principles. The principle of morality can at best be understood as a principle of permissibility, allowing us to act on incentives of inclination when so doing does not conflict with any requirements of morality, but that still does not mean that morality itself endorses nonmoral motives.[22] Korsgaard objects to Ginsborg's model of inclinations as themselves incentives or motives; rather, she argues, "The faculty of inclination" by itself "only alerts us to incentives, or possible reasons, for action, while reason has the function of deciding whether to act as we are inclined to or not."[23] It is always reason that transforms an inclination into a motive for action, and it can do this by adopting either the principle of morality or self-love; but in neither case is the inclination alone ever the motive for the action. Korsgaard uses Kant's distinction between the form and matter of action to make this point: "we are not god-like to the extent that we do not ourselves generate the matter on which that form is imposed" by reason.[24] However, Korsgaard's refutation of Ginsborg could be made even stronger than it is by appealing to the Formula of Humanity as an End in Itself, as we will see: the moral law is not simply a law of permissibility because it directly requires that we preserve and promote the capacity to choose and realize particular ends. It does not merely permit us to pursue particular ends, but under appropriate circumstances it requires us to do so under the name of humanity.

Let us now return to the question concerning the claim that morality actually requires the promotion of the realization of particular ends. The answer to this question lies in the simple fact that the freedom of choice in which our humanity consists is the freedom to set particular ends for our actions, and it is unreasonable to suppose that we could place

[22] Hannah Ginsborg, "Korsgaard on Choosing Nonmoral Ends," *Ethics*, 109 (1998), pp. 9–12.
[23] Christine Korsgaard, "Motivation, Metaphysics, and the Value of the Self," *Ethics*, 109 (1998), p. 51.
[24] Ibid., p. 57.

absolute value on this ability without also valuing our freedom to pursue and our ability to realize the ends we freely set. Making freedom our absolute value thus makes our ability to set and pursue our ends in a way that is consistent with the greatest possible use of freedom our ultimate end. This is why Kant's principle of the absolute value of humanity immediately gives rise to the idea of a kingdom of ends, "a systematic union of rational beings through common objective laws" that would give rise to "a whole of all ends in systematic connection (a whole both of rational beings as ends in themselves and of the ends of his own that each may set himself)."[25] To realize a kingdom of ends requires the fulfillment of the freely chosen ends of each rational being as well as the treatment of each rational being as an absolute end.

Kant makes this clear by an analysis of the concept of free action as well as by the system of duties through which he makes concrete what it means to make freedom our end and never merely a means. Let us begin with the analysis of the concept of free action. In *The Metaphysics of Morals*, Kant states that "no free action is possible unless the agent intends an end (which is the matter of choice)."[26] We cannot choose or exercise our freedom of choice to set our own ends, without choosing something, thereby setting some particular end. This is the premise of Kant's argument that there must be some ends that are also duties inasmuch as there must be some duties that are also ends. As Kant puts it:

For since there are free actions there must also be ends to which, as their objects, these actions are directed. But among these ends there must be some that are also (i.e., by their concept) duties.—For were there no such ends, then all ends would hold for practical reason only as means to other ends; and since there can be no action without an end, a categorical imperative would be impossible.[27]

Kant's thought is that since there can be no rational action without an end, actions commanded as duties must also be actions aimed at ends; but if the ends aimed at were themselves always ends that lie outside the purview of morality, then all duties would be commands to perform actions meant to realize ends that are not duties. That is incoherent, so at least some of the ends of our actions must be included within the purview of duty.

Thus pure practical reason, by placing absolute value on humanity as freedom, determines a general end for us, but this by itself is not enough to determine us to perform particular actions because particular actions

---

[25] Kant, *Groundwork of the Metaphysics of Morals*, 4:433.
[26] Kant, *The Metaphysics of Morals*, 6:389.
[27] Ibid. 6:385.

require particular ends. These ends can in turn be suggested to us only by naturally occurring inclinations, because they are the only alternative to reason, which defines only a general end. Inclination proposes objects to the faculty of desire, the pursuit of which may then be endorsed if it is consistent with treating freedom as an end and not merely as a means and is even enjoined once those naturally suggested objects of desire have been made into ends of free human choice.

Kant formulated this model of action by combining his distinction between the form and matter of choice with a distinction between *a priori* and empirical sources of choice. Such a model is found throughout Kant's notes and lectures, early and late: "Moral philosophy is the science of ends, so far as they are determined through pure reason. Or of the unity of all ends (where they do not contradict themselves) of rational beings. The matter of the good is given empirically, its form *a priori*."[28] This suggests that pure reason can supply only the form of action, not the matter; the matter must be supplied empirically, which can only mean by nature, in the form of inclinations proposing specific objects of desire to the faculty of desire. We cannot imagine any other source for the matter of action than the nature with which we are empirically acquainted:

We understand nothing of merely moral happiness or blessedness. If everything material that the senses provide to our will were removed, what would become of rectitude, goodness, self-mastery, which are only forms for ordering all of these materials in ourselves? Since we can thus understand happiness and the true good only in this world, we must believe that we would overstep the bounds of our reason if we would paint for ourselves a new and higher kind of perfection.[29]

Without actions suggested by inclinations, human beings would simply have nothing to do, and would not be agents at all. Unless treating humanity always as an end and never merely as a means is to include support for the pursuit of ends endorsed by pure practical reason, it will be the denial of rational agency rather than the promotion of rational agency. In his lectures, Kant makes this explicit for the case of duties regarding ourselves:

Let us consider those actions of human beings that relate to themselves, and contemplate freedom there. They arise from impulses and inclinations, or from maxims and principles. It is therefore necessary for a person to resort to maxims, and restrict his self-regarding actions by rules, and these are rules and duties that are directed to himself.[30]

[28] Kant, *Reflexion* 6820 [1776–1778? 1778–1780s], 19:172.
[29] Kant, *Reflexion* 6883 [1776–1778? 1778–1779?], 19:191.
[30] Kant, *Moral Philosophy: Collins's Lecture Notes*, 27:345.

Naturally occurring inclinations have to be regulated: those that are consistent with the greatest use of freedom can be acted upon, while those that are not so consistent cannot be acted upon. But without naturally occurring inclinations, human beings would have nothing to do at all.

In his last lectures on ethics, Kant makes the same point. That our actions accord with the possibility of universal law is "the essential condition of the form of the action," and is the basis of rectitude. "If, on the other hand, we consider duties and their grounds of determination in regard to matter, then the action has need of an object to which it is related," or an "end of the action." Thus he concludes that, "Apart from the freedom of the action, there is thus another principle present, which is itself enlarging, in that, while freedom is restricted by the determination according to law, it is here, on the contrary, enlarged by the matter or end thereof."[31]

That morality must be able to endorse particular ends chosen by human beings as well as the general end of the freedom that constitutes their humanity is also implied by Kant's classification of duties. Kant first introduces this classification in the *Groundwork* in order to confirm his formulations of the categorical imperative by showing that they give rise to the essential classes of duty that anyone would acknowledge. The four classes of duty he illustrates are generated by combining the distinction between perfect and imperfect duties, narrow duties or duties of omission that proscribe specific forms of conduct and broad duties or duties of commission that prescribe general policies of conduct without being able to detail all the specific acts that could fulfill those policies, with the distinction between duties to ourselves and duties to others. Thus, Kant's example of a perfect duty to ourselves is the prohibition of suicide; his example of a perfect duty to others is the prohibition of false promises; his example of an imperfect duty to ourselves is the duty to cultivate some talents and capabilities for which we have natural predispositions, which could make an agent into "a human being useful for all sorts of purposes"; and his example of an imperfect duty to others is the duty to find appropriate ways to contribute to their welfare.[32] Taken together, what these duties provide is a complex requirement for "the preservation of humanity as an end in itself" and "the furtherance of this end" in both ourselves and others, where humanity is understood precisely as the capacity to set and pursue our ends freely.[33] Thus, the perfect duties

---

[31] Kant, *Kant on the Metaphysics of Morals: Vigilantius's Lecture Notes*, 27:542–3.
[32] Kant, *Groundwork of the Metaphysics of Morals*, 4:423.
[33] Ibid. 4:430.

are duties not to destroy the existence and the possibility of the exercise of freedom in ourselves or others, while the imperfect duties are duties to develop the capacities on which the successful pursuit of freely chosen ends depends and even directly to promote the realization of such ends.

Kant's examples of perfect duties to ourselves and to others are examples of duties to preserve the existence and the possibility of the exercise of free choice. In the treatment of suicide that we find in Kant's lectures rather than in the *Groundwork*, Kant prohibits it on the straightforward ground that it is a free act, but one that would destroy the free agent who performs it and thus the possibility of any further free acts by that agent: "So far, then, as anyone destroys his body, and thereby takes his own life, he has employed his choice to destroy the power of choosing itself; but in that case, free choice is in conflict with itself. If freedom is the condition of life, it cannot be employed to abolish life, since it then destroys and abolishes itself."[34]

This argument depends on the supposition that life is the condition of freedom as well as the fact, which Kant emphasizes, that freedom is the condition of life: freedom is the condition of life in that it is what gives life its value, but life is the condition of freedom in that it is what makes freedom possible.

Kant could have chosen homicide, the freely chosen destruction of the life of another free agent, as his example of a perfect duty of omission to others, but to make a further point he instead chooses the prohibition of false promises. What this duty prohibits is not the destruction of another's free agency itself but rather the restriction of his exercise of it. What you do when you make a false promise to another person is to deny him the opportunity to choose his own response freely in full knowledge of the real circumstances and consequences of his action. If someone to whom I would make a false promise really understood my intentions, then he could not "possibly agree to my way of behaving toward him, and so himself contain the end of this action."[35] When I deceive someone into agreeing to an action that he would not agree to if he knew my real intentions, I deprive him of the possibility of exercising his freedom of choice, at least under circumstances he would choose.

Kant's example of an imperfect duty to ourselves is the duty to cultivate some of our natural predispositions to talents in order to further our own humanity. This is necessary because "as a rational being [a person] necessarily wills that all the capacities in him be developed, since they

---

[34] Kant, *Moral Philosophy: Collins's Lecture Notes*, 27:369.
[35] Kant, *Groundwork of the Metaphysics of Morals*, 4:429–30.

serve him and are given to him for all sorts of possible purposes."[36] Making humanity in the form of freedom our end requires not just freely choosing ends but also taking steps to assure the successful accomplishment of those ends. Of course, this is an imperfect rather than perfect duty because there is no mechanical way to specify which talents we could successfully develop, which among all those that we could develop we should develop, and how far we should go to develop them. There will also be occasions on which acting to develop a talent for future use may have to give way before a more immediately pressing duty. But within these limits, we have a general obligation freely to cultivate means to the successful accomplishment of our freely chosen ends.

Finally, Kant argues that we have a duty to assist others in the pursuit of their freely chosen ends because "there is still only a negative and not a positive agreement with humanity as an end in itself unless everyone also tries, as far as he can, to further the ends of others."[37] Kant does not argue that we must assist others for the prudential reason that doing so might increase the likelihood that they will then help us in the pursuit of our own ends, even though such a strategy could be endorsed or even required by our duty to ourselves to cultivate means to the realization of our own ends. Instead, Kant's idea is simply that insofar as the ends of others are freely chosen, we have a duty to help them realize those ends just because of the value of their free choice itself. Again, this duty is broad rather than narrow: in assisting another person, we must not violate any of our other duties or help the other to violate one of his duties; we must not rob ourselves of happiness in attempting to bring happiness to others, because the happiness of all others with the exception of myself would not be the happiness of all.[38] Above all, Kant stresses, "I cannot do good to anyone in accordance with my concepts of happiness ... thinking to benefit him by forcing a gift upon him; rather I can benefit him only in accordance with his concepts of happiness."[39] To attempt to benefit another person in accordance with my conception of his happiness rather than his own would be precisely to rob him of the freedom of choice from which my obligation to assist him in the pursuit of his happiness arises in the first place.

---

[36] Ibid. 4:423.
[37] Ibid.
[38] Kant, *The Metaphysics of Morals*, 6:451; see also 6:393. See also Barbara Herman, *The Practice of Moral Judgment* (Cambridge, Mass.: Harvard University Press, 1993), ch. 1, pp. 4–5.
[39] Kant, *The Metaphysics of Morals*, 6:454.

Thus, both Kant's general analysis of action and his fourfold classification of our duties show that his ethics is teleological in a twofold sense: the fundamental principle of morality rests on the duty to make humanity itself our end, but the duty to make humanity itself our end implies the duty to promote the realization of the particular ends that human beings freely choose, at least under appropriate circumstances. Once we have come this far, however, we can see that Kant's ethics is teleological in two further senses: it requires that both human freedom and human happiness, again appropriately conceived, be able to be seen as ends realizable within nature. This is particularly evident in the case of the duty to promote the realization of particular ends: if the ends are suggested by inclination, but inclination occurs only in nature, then the ends can only be fulfilled within nature. Thus although reason cannot permit all inclinations to be fulfilled, the inclinations that it does permit to be fulfilled can only be fulfilled within nature. It is through his conception of our duties as including the duty to promote the realization of particular freely chosen ends that Kant reaches the conclusion that the highest good is the complete object of morality.

4

At this point we must proceed cautiously for two distinct reasons. First, Kant sometimes makes it sound as if both human freedom and human happiness are ends of nature, ends determined for us by nature to which we must, whether grudgingly or not, conform our own choice. Even before he published the *Groundwork*, Kant suggested in the 1784 essay on the Idea for "a Universal History" that human freedom and human happiness as the product of human freedom can themselves be seen as the ends of nature:

Nature has willed that man should produce entirely by his own initiative everything that goes beyond the mechanical ordering of his animal existence, and that he should not partake of any other happiness than that which he has procured for himself without instinct and by his own reason. Nature gave man reason, and freedom of will based upon reason.[40]

Here Kant may give priority to freedom over happiness among the ends set for us by nature: "It seems that nature has worked more with a view to man's rational self-esteem than to his mere well-being"; but he never-

---

[40] Kant, "Idea for a Universal History from a Cosmopolitan Point of View", 8:19.

theless treats both human freedom and human happiness as ends determined by nature.[41] But certainly the idea that human happiness is an end
of nature is both empirically and morally problematic. It is empirically
problematic because, as Kant takes some relish in arguing in the *Critique
of the Power of Judgment*, there is no evidence that nature in fact has any
special regard for human happiness: "it is so far from being the case that
nature has made the human being its special favorite and favored him
with beneficence above all other animals, that it has rather spared him
just as little as any other animal from its destructive effects, whether of
pestilence, hunger, danger of flood, cold, attacks by other animals great
and small, etc."[42] It is morally problematic because, as even the passage
from the essay on history suggests, it is not human happiness *per se* but
human happiness as the product of human reason that could conceivably
be the end of nature. Yet human reason, at least in the form of practical
reason, does not seem to be an agency of nature at all, but a mani-
festation of human freedom. Thus it would seem to be only human
freedom and not nature that could make human happiness, in any
form, into an end.

Yet there also seems to be a problem in the idea that human freedom
should make human happiness an end of reason. Kant notoriously com-
mences both the *Groundwork* and the *Critique of Practical Reason* with
an onslaught upon the idea that the goal of happiness has anything to do
with morality at all, and even when he does introduce the idea of the
highest good later in the second *Critique* Kant makes it seem as if this is a
grudging concession to the human desire for happiness which is ineliminable but has its origins elsewhere than in morality itself.[43] Kant makes it
sound as if the highest good is a compound of two independent ends, the
end of reason, which is the development of virtue without regard to
happiness, and the end of nature, which is the realization of our own
happiness without regard to virtue. On such a conception, the highest
good would then be the compound object of a compound being, the
natural pursuit of personal happiness restricted by the moral requirements to fulfill duties and to achieve virtue as the condition for worthiness to be happy. This at least may be suggested when Kant states that
virtue is "not yet the whole and complete good as the object of the faculty
of desire of rational finite beings; for this, happiness is also required."[44]

---

[41] Ibid. 8:19–20.
[42] Kant, *Critique of the Power of Judgment*, §83, 5:430.
[43] See Kant, *Groundwork of the Metaphysics of Morals*, 4:393–6 and 416–19; and
Kant, *Critique of Practical Reason*, 5:25–9.
[44] Ibid. 5:110.

This makes it sound as if virtue is our sole object as rational beings, but happiness our object of desire as finite beings, for which virtue must, somehow yet somewhat grudgingly, make room.[45]

However, this is not Kant's considered conception of the highest good. Instead, his view is that since the duty to preserve and promote humanity itself includes the duty to promote the realization of the freely chosen ends not of ourselves alone but of all human beings so far as to do so lies within our power and is consistent with our other duties, and happiness is simply the condition that results from the successful pursuit of our ends, the promotion of happiness, not our personal happiness alone but the happiness of all insofar as that is compatible with the freedom of each is part of our duty under the moral law. Happiness is not simply restricted by virtue, but under appropriate circumstances prescribed by it. Furthermore, since human happiness can be realized only in nature, where the inclinations that suggest even our freely chosen ends arise and must be fulfilled, the object of virtue can therefore be realized only in nature. Since it would be irrational to pursue any object, even virtue, which we know to be impossible, the rationality of virtue itself requires that the highest good be, if not the end of nature, at least compatible with the laws of nature. To the extent that a conception of the laws of nature as compatible with the goals of human reason can be considered teleological, then in this third sense too Kant's morality is teleological.

The two elements of this conception of the highest good, that the goal of human happiness is prescribed by morality itself and that this goal must be realizable within nature and thus compatible with the laws of nature for morality to be rational, are manifest in many of Kant's discussions of the concept. The "Canon of Pure Reason" of the *Critique of Pure Reason* first introduces "the ideal of the highest good, as a determining ground of the ultimate end of pure reason."[46] Here Kant defines a "moral world" as "the world as it would be if it were in conformity with all moral laws (as it can be in accordance with the freedom of rational beings and should be in accordance with the necessary laws of morality)."[47] He then goes on to state that,

Now in an intelligible world, i.e., in the moral world, in the concept of which we have abstracted from all hindrances to morality (of the inclinations), . . . a system of happiness proportionately combined with morality can also be thought as necessary, since freedom, partly moved and partly restricted by moral laws,

---

[45] See Lewis White Beck, *A Commentary on Kant's Critique of Practical Reason* (Chicago: University of Chicago Press, 1960), pp. 242–5.

[46] Kant, *Critique of Pure Reason*, A 804/B 832.

[47] Ibid., A 805/B 833.

would itself be the cause of the general happiness, and rational beings, under the guidance of such principles, would themselves be the authors of their own enduring welfare and at the same time that of others.[48]

Kant stresses that this "system of self-rewarding morality is only an idea," because in the actual rather than intelligible world not everyone does conform to the laws of morality, and nature also does not always seem to pay much attention to the happiness of even the virtuous. But our immediate concern is only Kant's idea that under ideal circumstances morality would be "self-rewarding." There would be no reason to think this if happiness were simply a natural goal. The idea makes sense only if it is morality itself, through its command that we promote the accomplishment of freely chosen ends, that prescribes happiness as the product of virtue.

Of course, such a conception of the highest good is possible only if the happiness it prescribes is not our own happiness as the object of a merely natural desire, but the collective happiness that would be the result of the realization of the particular ends freely chosen by all human beings and promoted by each, to the extent that this is possible, because of the value of free choice itself. Kant makes this clear in his essay "On the Common Saying: That May Be Right in Theory, but it is of No Use in Practice." In the first section of this work, Kant rebuts Christian Garve, who had construed Kant's account of the highest good in the *Critique of Practical Reason* to mean that an individual agent could be motivated to comply with the moral law only by the promise of his personal happiness as a reward for his virtue. Garve found this idea abhorrent, and Kant agreed, but insisted that it had never been his idea at all. Instead, he explained, his position was that no thought of happiness, whether our own or everyone's, was any part of morally praiseworthy motivation, but that the concept of duty itself makes the collective happiness of mankind the object of our morally motivated action.[49] In Kant's words, "this concept of duty does not have to be grounded on any particular end but rather introduces another end for the human being's will, namely to work to the best of our ability toward the highest good possible in the world (universal happiness combined with and in conformity with the purest morality throughout the world)."[50] Kant argues that the "need to assume, as the final end of all things, a good that is the highest good in

---

[48] Ibid., A 809/B 837.
[49] Kant, "On the Common Saying: That May Be Correct in Theory, but it is of No Use in Practice," 8:282 n.
[50] Ibid. 8:279.

the world...is a need not from a deficiency in moral incentives," but depends simply on the fact that "without some end there can be no will."[51] This is Kant's premise that there is no rational action without some end in what we earlier saw to be its second application: the particular free choices that are to be preserved and promoted by respect for humanity as a general end are choices of particular ends, and promoting these choices means promoting the realization of their ends as well, which is precisely what produces happiness. Kant stresses that "not every end is moral," thus the choice of "one's own happiness" alone would not be moral, but a moral end must be an "unselfish one"; thus he concludes:

With the human being too, accordingly, the incentive which is present in the idea of the highest good possible in the world by his cooperation is not his own happiness thereby intended but only this idea as end in itself, and hence compliance with it as duty.... But a determination of will which limits itself and its aim of belonging to such a whole to this condition is not selfish.[52]

Thus Kant's view is that because every rationally chosen action must have an end, the very idea of preserving and promoting rational action itself defines a universal rather than selfish idea of happiness as the object of action motivated by the thought of duty alone. Our own happiness is neither the motive or the object of action so motivated, although of course our own happiness must be included in the object that is so defined, universal happiness.

That the object of morality is a collective or unselfish form of human happiness means that this end is not simply set for us by natural inclination, but is an end of reason. Yet this end can be realized only in nature, because that is where happiness as the realization of those human inclinations that are transformed into ends by free choice can alone occur. That means that for morality itself to be rational, this form of happiness must be compatible with the laws of nature even if it cannot properly be conceived of as the end of nature. This may not be apparent in Kant's initial discussion of the highest good in the *Critique of Pure Reason*, where Kant describes the moral world as an intelligible world, which might seem a nonnatural world that can be apprehended only by pure reason, not the senses, and where he also seems to suggest, at least in passing, that the postulate of a future life is a condition of the possibility not only of the perfection of virtue but also of the completion of happiness.[53] But even here Kant stresses that "Pure reason...contains—not in

[51] Kant, "On the Common Saying: That May Be Correct in Theory, but it is of No Use in Practice," 8:279 n.

[52] Ibid. 8:280 n.          [53] Kant, *Critique of Pure Reason*, A 811/B 839.

its speculative use, to be sure, but yet in a certain practical reason...
—principles of the possibility of experience, namely of those actions in
conformity with moral precepts which could be encountered in the
history of humankind."[54] In the *Critique of Practical Reason*, even
though it begins by suggesting a composite rather than unitary conception of the highest good, Kant nevertheless goes on to make it clear
precisely that what the possibility of the highest good as the object of
morality requires is that the realization of this object be compatible with
the laws of nature, and thus the postulate that the author of the laws of
nature have written them with an eye to the moral law as well. Here Kant
writes that since "we ought to strive to promote the highest good," it
"must therefore be possible."

Accordingly, the existence of a cause of all nature, which contains the ground of
this connection, namely of the exact correspondence of happiness with morality,
is also postulated.... The highest good in the world is possible only insofar as a
supreme cause of nature having a causality in keeping with the moral disposition
is assumed.... Therefore the supreme cause of nature, insofar as it must be
presupposed for the highest good, is a being that is the cause of nature by
understanding and will (hence its author), that is God. Consequently, the postulate of the possibility of the highest derived good (the best world) is likewise
the postulate of the reality of a highest original good, namely of the existence of
God.[55]

Kant recognizes that if morality itself commands the realization of a
universal rather than selfish form of happiness, and if happiness is
something that can be realized only in the natural world, then the
possibility of morality itself depends upon the possibility of realizing
happiness in the natural world. This is the third aspect of Kant's
teleology.


5


If human happiness is an object of morality only because morality places
absolute value on the capacity for free choice by which the ends the
fulfillment of which constitutes human happiness are elected, we should
consider whether human freedom itself can coherently be understood as
an end of nature. This seems dubious, for Kant often defines human
freedom precisely by the absence of the sort of causal law that is in turn

---

[54] Ibid., A 807/B 835.
[55] Kant, *Critique of Practical Reason*, 5:125.

definitive of nature, as when the *Groundwork* defines "freedom as...causality...that can be efficient independently of alien causes determining it, just as natural necessity is the property of the causality of all nonrational beings to be determined to activity by the influence of alien causes."[56] But then how could nature ever make it its end that human beings realize their freedom?

The most obvious thing to say would be that human freedom cannot literally be the end of nature, for nature can at most bring human beings to the water of freedom but it cannot make us drink it. By such natural mechanisms as unsocial sociability nature can make us see the rationality of freely choosing to govern our actions by the moral law rather than self-love, but in the end we must make the free choice to do so and cannot be forced into this by any natural mechanisms. Precisely this would seem to be Kant's position in such a work as *Towards Perpetual Peace*, where he argues that even a race of devils can see the necessity of governing themselves by the laws of a just republic but that only moral politicians can freely choose to maintain such a form of government.[57] At the same time, however, it is not only fundamental to Kant's moral philosophy to argue that human freedom must be compatible with the causality of nature, which he accomplishes, whether we like it or not, through the dualistic theory of transcendental idealism; Kant also argues that there must be a form of human freedom that is realizable not outside of, or alongside of, but within nature, and that we must even be able to see at least this form of freedom as the end of nature.

This argument is found in the *Critique of the Power of Judgment*. In the grand and complex second half of this work, the "Critique of Teleological Judgment," Kant argues that the relationship between organisms and their parts cannot be understood within the limits of our ordinary conception of efficient causation, and instead leads us to conceive of organisms as if they were the product of intelligent design. Once we do that, however, two further ways of looking at nature inevitably suggest themselves to us. First, once we have introduced the idea of design and thus a designer for part of nature, it is inevitable that we will at least attempt to conceive of a design and a designer for all of nature. Second, once we have introduced the idea of a design and a designer for all of nature, it is then inevitable for us to form the idea of a purpose for nature, or what Kant calls an ultimate end, or *letztes Zweck*, for nature. But the

---

[56] Kant, *Groundwork of the Metaphysics of Morals*, 4:446.

[57] See Paul Guyer, "Nature, Morality, and the Possibility of Peace," in Guyer, *Kant on Freedom, Law, and Happiness* (Cambridge: Cambridge University Press, 2000), pp. 408–34.

only thing that can play the role of an ultimate end for nature, even though such an ultimate end must be realizable within nature, is something that is a final end, or *Endzweck*, something that is an end in itself of absolute value. Kant's argument is then that this can be nothing other than humanity in itself, precisely because of its freedom:

Now we have in the world only a single sort of beings whose causality is teleological, i.e., aimed at ends and yet at the same time so constituted that the law in accordance with which they have determined ends is represented by themselves as unconditioned and independent of natural conditions but yet as necessary in itself. The being of this sort is the human being... the only natural being in which we can...cognize...a supersensible faculty (freedom)... together with the object that it can set for itself as the highest end (the highest good in the world).[58]

Although in this argument, unlike Kant's argument from the concept of the highest good, it is scientific inquiry rather than practical reason that sets us the task of conceiving of an ultimate end for nature, the conclusion is that only morality can supply the conception of this ultimate end through its own conception of freedom as the final end of humanity.

What is crucial for our present purposes is that while Kant calls the freedom that makes humanity the only fit candidate for the final end of a purposive creation a supersensible faculty, he also argues that we must conceive of at least a form or aspect of freedom that can be realized within nature in order to serve as the ultimate end of nature. This is what Kant calls the culture of discipline, the liberation of the will from domination by desires through the development of mastery over desires. Kant argues that "only culture can be the ultimate end that one has cause to ascribe to nature in regard to the human species (not its own earthly happiness...)," but also that "not every kind of culture is adequate for this ultimate end of nature"; what can be the ultimate end of nature is not the mere culture of skill for achieving our particular ends, but "the culture of training (discipline)," which "consists in the liberation of the will from the despotism of desires," by which "we turn into fetters the drives that nature has given us merely for guidance."[59] Just as desires occur within nature, so the discipline of desires must be a form of freedom that can take place within nature. It can thus be seen as a morally valuable end of nature, whether it is theoretical inquiry or moral reasoning itself that forces us to find a moral end even more fundamental than happiness that can be realized within nature.

[58] Kant, *Critique of the Power of Judgment*, §84, 5:435.
[59] Ibid., §83, 5:431–2.

Even in this argument, Kant calls freedom a "supersensible faculty," and thus it might seem that the freedom of discipline can be only a sensible consequence of a free act of the will that must take place behind the veil of appearance that constitutes nature. On such an account, nature might teach us to see the unhappiness into which our unfettered desires lead, but the true freedom to choose not to be governed by desires would not be part of nature and could thus not literally be the end of nature. As in the case of happiness, the laws of nature must be compatible with the laws of freedom, but freedom cannot actually be the end of nature. This is undoubtedly Kant's predominant view. However, there is at least one line of argument in Kant that actually implies that discipline must not be merely a natural consequence of a freedom of the will lying beyond nature, but rather that it must be a consequence of a choice of a fundamental maxim of self-conduct that itself takes place within nature and yet is free in any sense that morality can require. The two key premises in such an argument would be, first, that discipline, or what in his moral writings Kant typically calls self-mastery, can only be a consequence of the choice of the fundamental principle of morality as our primary maxim, and that, second, the duty of self-knowledge is our primary duty to ourselves because self-knowledge of our motivation is a necessary condition of a proper choice of fundamental maxim; the possibility of fulfilling the duty of self-knowledge as the precondition of self-mastery would then imply the possibility of knowledge of what our motivation really is, and that would in turn imply that our motivation must be empirically accessible, or part of nature rather than transcendent to it.

Kant scattered the premises of such an argument throughout his moral writings. In the *Religion within the Boundaries of Mere Reason* he claimed that discipline cannot be achieved through any techniques short of the proper choice of principles: "a human being's moral education must begin, not with an improvement of mores, but with the transformation of his attitude and the establishment of a character, although it is customary to proceed otherwise and to fight vices individually."[60] But years before, in his early lectures on ethics, Kant had already argued that the proper choice of principles requires self-knowledge:

Man has a general duty to himself, of so disposing himself that he may be capable of observing all moral duties, and hence that he should establish moral purity and principles in himself, and endeavor to act accordingly. This, then, is the primary duty to oneself. Now this entails self-testing and self-examination, as to whether the dispositions also have moral purity. The sources of those

---

[60] Kant, *Religion within the Boundaries of Mere Reason*, 6:48.

dispositions must be examined, to see whether they lie in honor or delusion, in superstition or pure morality.[61]

Finally, in *The Metaphysics of Morals* Kant drew the conclusion that our first duty to ourselves as moral beings, our first duty to ourselves beyond the duty to preserve our life and physical well-being as the instrument of our free choice is the duty to

'know (scrutinize, fathom) yourself', not in terms of your natural perfection (your fitness or unfitness for all sorts of discretionary or even commanded ends) but rather in terms of your moral perfection in relation to your duty. That is, know your heart—whether it is good or evil, whether the source of your actions is pure or impure.... Moral cognition of oneself, which seeks to penetrate into the depths (the abyss) of one's heart which are quite difficult to fathom, is the beginning of all human wisdom.... (Only the descent into the hell of self-cognition can pave the way to godliness.)[62]

But such a duty makes sense only if self-knowledge is something that can be achieved by empirical means, for such are the only means to knowledge available to us, and thus if the object of self-knowledge—our choice of fundamental principle—is something that takes place within nature, not beyond it. If this is so, then discipline or self-mastery is not merely the concomitant of a free act beyond nature, but rather the product of a self-knowledge and choice of principle that must take place within nature, and thus could be the ultimate end of nature.

Let us consider the conclusion that Kant's conception of freedom as the abstract object of human morality requires that freedom be compatible with the laws of nature, just as his conception of the collective happiness included in the highest good as the more concrete object of human morality requires the assumption that the achievement of such happiness is compatible with the laws of nature. What neither of these teleological conclusions entails or even permits, however, is the assumption that nature can set specific goals for us in the way assumed by the principle that each natural organ or capacity has one and only one proper purpose which is thereby automatically morally obligatory for us.

6

Thus the proposition that is most commonly identified as the teleological element in Kant's ethics has no foundation within Kant's ethical theory at

[61] Kant, *Moral Philosophy: Collins's Lecture Notes*, 27:348.
[62] Kant, *The Metaphysics of Morals*, 6:441.

all, and is ultimately inconsistent with the full scope of human freedom. This premise is assumed in two of Kant's most notorious arguments, his argument that suicide is prohibited because it is contrary to the laws of nature, where Paton noticed it, but also in one of Kant's arguments that the only permissible form of sexual activity is heterosexual sex for the purposes of procreation within the confines of marriage.

Kant's argument against suicide the first time he treats it in the *Groundwork* is that to "make it my principle, from self-love, to shorten my life when its longer duration threatens more troubles than it promises agreeableness," could not also give rise to a universal law of nature because "a nature whose law it would be to destroy life itself by means of the same feeling whose destination it is to impel toward the furtherance of life would contradict itself."[63] This is not a straightforward argument about universalizability as requiring "practical consistency": it does not assert that it would defeat my purposes in attempting to commit suicide if everyone were to do it.[64] Instead, the argument depends specifically upon the assumption that a law of nature can only have us ascribe a single purpose to a natural phenomenon: the feeling of self-love can have only a single function, that of prolonging life, not a dual purpose, such as prolonging life in some circumstances but shortening it in others. Kant makes clear the role of the assumption that everything in nature has a single purpose when he recapitulates this argument in *The Metaphysics of Morals* with the simple statement that "love of life is destined by nature to preserve the person."[65]

Kant employs the same teleological premise when he proceeds from the prohibition of suicide to the prohibition of all forms of sexual activity other than heterosexual sex for the purpose of procreation within marriage—self-stimulation and masturbation, or what he so sternly calls self-defilement, as well as homosexuality and bestiality. The clause just quoted is actually part of a longer sentence:

Just as love of life is destined by nature to preserve the person, so sexual love is destined by it to preserve the species; in other words, each of these is a natural end, by which is understood that connection of a cause with an effect in which, although no understanding is ascribed to the cause, it is still

---

[63] Kant, *Groundwork of the Metaphysics of Morals*, 4:422.

[64] See Onora O'Neill, *Acting on Principle: An Essay on Kantian Ethics* (New York: Columbia University Press, 1975), pp. 63–81; and Christine M. Korsgaard, "Kant's Formula of Universal Law," in Korsgaard, *Creating the Kingdom of Ends* (Cambridge: Cambridge University Press, 1996), pp. 77–105, esp. pp. 92–101.

[65] Kant, *The Metaphysics of Morals*, 6:424.

thought by analogy with an intelligent cause, and so as if it produced human beings on purpose.[66]

Kant reiterates his assumption when he states that "Nature's end in the co-habitation of the sexes is procreation, that is, the preservation of the species."[67] In these claims, Kant does not assume that through sexual inclination nature suggests a variety of desires, some of which we may transform into freely chosen ends if they are consistent with the general end of preserving and promoting freedom itself; rather, he suggests that nature has already determined a single end for the use of our sexual capacities, just as it has determined a single end for the feeling of self-love, and that it would be immoral to use our sexual capacities for any purpose other than the one intended by nature simply because it is immoral to adopt an end other than that which nature intends for us. However, there is no justification for such a moral principle in Kant's account of the role of teleological principles in scientific inquiry or in any of the genuinely teleological aspects of his moral philosophy we have previously encountered. Furthermore, Kant ultimately reveals such an assumption to be incompatible with his fundamental principle of the unconditional value of human freedom.

The arguments for the wrongness of suicide and non-procreative sex that we have just examined are by no means Kant's only arguments for these prohibitions. Prior to stating that what is wrong with suicide is that it contradicts nature's intention for the feeling of love of life, Kant in *The Metaphysics of Morals* offers the alternative argument that "To annihilate the subject of morality in one's own person is to root out the existence of morality itself from the world, as far as one can, even though morality is an end in itself."[68] This claim can be explicated in turn by the analysis from Kant's lectures, cited earlier, that if a person "takes his own life, he has employed his choice to destroy the power of choosing itself; but in that case, free choice is in conflict with itself."[69] Kant's insistence that only heterosexual marital sex with the aim of procreation is consistent with nature's intention regarding our use of our sexual capacity is but one strand in a much more complicated analysis of the rights and wrongs of sex, in which Kant argues that sexual desire for another is a desire to consume the other, thus to treat the other as an object, hence as a means rather than an end, a destruction of the personality of the other and a surrender of our own that can only be made good by the recreation of personality within the framework of complete legal and moral

---

[66] Ibid.     [67] Ibid., 6:426.     [68] Ibid., 6:423.
[69] Kant, *Moral Philosophy: Collins's Lecture Notes*, 27:369.

recognition of the reciprocal rights of each partner that is a proper marriage.[70] This account is based on the wild assumptions that in wanting to have any sort of sex I reduce myself to an object for pleasure and that in wanting to have sex with another I reduce the other to a passive object for consumption. This account also leads to revolutionary conclusions, such as that only complete sharing of economic rights satisfies the moral burden on marriage, thus that morganatic marriage is nothing but legalized prostitution.[71] But any adequate exploration of Kant's fascinating melange of absurdity and insight on the subject of sex is beyond the scope of this study.[72]

Let us return to Kant's teleological premise that every natural organ or capacity has one and only one natural end, which is *eo ipso* a moral end. Why does this have no justification in Kant's theoretical or moral teleology, and is ultimately inconsistent with this moral teleology? Kant's treatment of teleology in natural science is obscure, but one main line of his thought seems to be this. As we have seen, organisms display a kind of reciprocity between part and whole that defies comprehension on our usual model of efficient causation: the parts of an organism contribute to the structure and function of the whole in the way that defines mechanical explanation, but the ultimate character and function of the whole also seems to determine the antecedent structure and function of the parts in a way that cannot be so explained. In order to comprehend organisms at all, therefore, we must conceive of them as if their parts were the product of an antecedent design of the whole and then in turn produce the actual whole; such a three-staged process, analogous to human intentional artistic production even though we have no theoretical ground for assuming that organisms are a product of intentional production, would fit within our standard model of efficient causation.[73] However, in order to think of a design for organisms, we have to think of a designer, and this sets us off to look for a design and hence a purpose for nature as a whole: "this concept necessarily leads to the idea of the whole of nature as a system in accordance with the rule of ends."[74] That is Kant's path from the need of science to the necessity of morality. But the actual scientific role of the idea of a design and hence a function for organisms and their parts is apparently purely heuristic: "It is self-evident

---

[70] See Kant, *The Metaphysics of Morals*, §§24–6, 6:277–9.
[71] Ibid. 6:279.
[72] See Lara Denis, "Kant on the Wrongness of 'Unnatural Sex'," *History of Philosophy Quarterly*, 16 (1999), pp. 225–48.
[73] Kant, *Critique of the Power of Judgment*, §§64–5, 5:369–76.
[74] Ibid., §67, 5:378–9.

that this is not a principle for the determining but only for the reflecting power of judgment, that it is regulative and not constitutive, and that by its means we acquire only a guideline for considering things in nature."[75] Specifically, Kant's idea seems to be that positing functions for specific parts or behaviors of organisms can help us in ultimately finding mechanical explanations for such parts or behaviors. Hence Kant states that the teleological assumption is actually a principle "for extending natural science... yet without harm to the mechanism of nature," while "it is by no means determined by this whether something that we judge in accordance with this principle is an intentional end of nature."[76]

Thus, Kant argues that the teleological assumption that everything in nature has a purpose, *a fortiori* a single purpose, is only a heuristic principle. How strictly such a principle may hold seems open to experience, and Kant never argues that it is non-defeasible, that we cannot encounter anything in experience that would prove to be without purpose. It might seem likely that nothing in experience could conclusively be shown to lack a purpose, given that we can apparently always discover something more about almost anything we can experience, but this is hardly an *a priori* proof of the non-defeasibility of the teleological assumption. Furthermore, there do in fact appear to be limits to the principle that everything in nature has a purpose. Kant himself admits that such parts of organisms as skin, hair, and bones may not require teleological explanation even if there must still be an account of the organism's use of them.[77] Contemporary scientists go much further in questioning the assumption that everything in nature makes a positive contribution to the well-being of the individual or the species. Contemporary evolutionary theorists recognize traits that have no adaptive benefit to the individual or species or are even contrapurposive but are carried along with other traits that do have a benefit by accidents of mechanical causation; both traits express the same protein. Contemporary researchers recognize that an organism will allow some cell-lines to continue as long as they contribute to the well-being of the larger organism but kill them off when they are no longer beneficial. Such a trait would seem analogous to a feeling of love of life that would prolong the life of the organism as long as that life is worth living but curtail it when it no longer is, which is precisely what Kant claims is contradictory to the idea of a law of nature itself. There certainly seem to be limits to the heuristic value of Kant's teleological principle.

[75] Ibid. 5:379.    [76] Ibid.    [77] Ibid., §66, 5:377.

But the moral import of the assumption that everything in nature has one and only one purpose is even more questionable. First, of course, we can simply ask why any theoretical principle should automatically be given moral force. Furthermore, we can note Kant's own insistence that "it is by no means determined" even by the proven heuristic value of his teleological principle in theoretical inquiry "whether something that we judge in accordance with this principle is an intentional end of nature."[78] Most important, however, it is Kant's own argument that we cannot find any determinate purpose in anything in nature until we appeal to something that has unconditional value in itself as a moral end, human freedom itself. But this means that the only morally significant question that we can ask about the use of any natural organ or capacity is whether it can be used in a way that preserves or promotes the end of human freedom.

In fact, Kant ultimately recognizes this in his treatments of both suicide and sexuality. In *The Metaphysics of Morals*, he concedes that it is at least a question whether "hurl[ing] oneself to certain death . . . in order to save one's country" should count as "murdering oneself," or suicide; and in his lectures, he actually seems to admit that suicide might be a virtue in the case of Cato, who "killed himself [that] the Romans might yet dedicate their final efforts to the defense of their freedom."[79] Thus his position must be that while in most cases suicide is simply a destruction of my own further freedom, and must be prohibited on that ground, in some cases suicide might be the only means to the continued existence of freedom—not my own, of course, but that of others—and in that case it might be meritorious or even mandatory. Such an argument ignores any concern about whether the prolongation of life is the sole end of a natural capacity, and takes the only morally significant question about suicide to be whether or not it preserves or promotes the end of human freedom.

Kant recognizes the role of human freedom in evaluating the morality of sexual activity in an even more surprising argument in his late lectures on ethics. While continuing to maintain that "nature, in implanting the sexual impulse in humankind, has assuredly had [the] end [of procreating the species] in view," and that this end in turn requires the institution of marriage, he also argues that it would actually be an unnecessary abrogation of the human freedom to select our own ends to restrict sex within marriage to the purpose of procreation or to maintain that marriage can continue only as long as procreation remains a possibility. "This would

---

[78] Kant, *Critique of the Power of Judgment*, §67, 5:379.
[79] Kant, *Moral Philosophy: Collins's Lecture Notes*, 27:370.

all represent a debasement of our personhood. . . . This bond must therefore absolutely rest on the conformity of the natural impulse with the
moral law."[80] Nature does not determine what is moral; morality determines what desires suggested by nature are consistent with human freedom. It is always up to human freedom to transform objects of desire
suggested by nature into ends of reason.


7


This then is the full sense in which Kant's ethics is teleological: the moral
law requires an end with absolute worth, namely human freedom, but
human freedom cannot be exercised without more particular ends, which
can only be suggested by nature. Both the general end of human freedom
and the particular choices made by human freedom must be compatible
with the laws of nature if pursuit of them is to be rational. But
neither human freedom nor human happiness can literally be ends of
nature, for nature itself can never make anything our end: only our free
choice, governed above all by concern for the consistency of our particular choices with the value of freedom itself, can transform a natural
object of desire, even the desire to preserve ourselves or our species,
into a moral end.

[80] Kant, *Kant on the Metaphysics of Morals: Vigilantius's Lecture Notes*, 27:640.

# 9

# Kant's Deductions of the Principles of Right

## I. ARE KANT'S PRINCIPLES OF RIGHT DERIVED FROM THE SUPREME PRINCIPLE OF MORALITY?

In the 'Doctrine of Right', Part I of his 1797 *Metaphysics of Morals*, Kant appears to derive his 'universal principle of right'—'Any action is **right** if it can coexist with everyone's freedom in accordance with a universal law, or if on its maxim the freedom of choice of each can coexist with everyone's freedom in accordance with a universal law' (*MM*, DR, Introduction, §C, 6:230)[1]—from the fundamental principle of morality, which presents itself to us in the form of the Categorical Imperative. He appears simply to apply that fundamental principle's requirement that we use our power of free choice and of action upon our choice in accordance with the condition that the maxims upon which we choose to act be universalizable (e.g. *G*, 4:402, 421) to the external use of our freedom—that is, to our physical actions in so far as they can affect other persons, in order to derive the rule that we act only in ways that leave others a freedom of action equal to our own, regardless of our purposes in and our motives for so acting, those being subjects for ethical but not legal rules. He then seems to derive further, more specific principles of right from the universal principle of right by additional arguments. In particular, he seems to

This chapter was first published in Mark Timmons (ed.), *Kant's Metaphysics of Morals: Interpretative Essays* (Oxford: Oxford University Press, 2002), pp. 24–64.

I would like to thank Bernd Ludwig, Mark Timmons, Kenneth Westphal, and Allen Wood for helpful comments on an earlier draft of this paper.

[1] Quotations from *The Metaphysics of Morals* as well as the *Groundwork, Critique of Practical Reason*, and 'Theory and Practice' follow the translation by Mary Gregor from Immanuel Kant, *Practical Philosophy*, ed. and trans. Mary Gregor (Cambridge: Cambridge University Press, 1996), with a few modifications; I also follow Gregor's rather than the Akademie's numbering of sections in *The Metaphysics of Morals*. Translations from Vigilantius are from Immanuel Kant, *Lectures on Ethics*, ed. Peter Heath and J. B. Schneewind (Cambridge: Cambridge University Press, 1997). Translations from the *Critique of Pure Reason*, are from Immanuel Kant, *Critique of Pure Reason*, ed. and trans. Paul Guyer and Allen W. Wood (Cambridge: Cambridge University Press, 1998). Translations from Kant's preparatory notes for *The Metaphysics of Morals*, printed in volume 23 of the Akademie edition, are my own.

derive the principle that violations of right may be prevented or punished by coercion through the supposition that the proposition that a hindrance to a hindrance of an effect itself promotes that effect is true by the law of non-contradiction, or is an analytic truth, in which case it follows that 'Right and authorization to use coercion therefore mean one and the same thing' (*MM*, DR, Introduction, §E, 6:232). And he presents the central principle of 'private right'—that is, the principle that it must be possible for persons to acquire property rights, including rights to land, to movable objects upon the land, to specific performances by others in the fulfilment of promises and contracts, and to the long-term services of others within the family and household—as a 'postulate of practical reason with regard to rights' that, although itself a 'synthetic *a priori* proposition', is also supposed to follow from the universal principle of right, 'in a practical respect, in an analytic way' (*MM*, DR, §6, 6:250). Even more specific rights, such as the right to acquire property in land by 'first appropriation', are said to follow from the more general principles by a 'deduction' (*MM*, DR, §17, 6:268). Kant seems to have promised such a derivation of the principles of right from the supreme principle of morality four years prior to *The Metaphysics of Morals*, in the 1793 essay 'On the Common Saying: That May Be Correct in Theory, but it is of No Use in Practice', which had stated that 'the concept of an external right as such proceeds [*geht... hervor*] entirely from the concept of **freedom** in the external relationship of people to one another' (*TP*, 8:289), and then to have confirmed his delivery on that promise in the 'Doctrine of Right', which states that 'we can know our own freedom (from which all moral laws, and so all rights as well as duties proceed), only through the **moral imperative**, which is a proposition commanding duty, from which the capacity for putting others under obligation, that is, the concept of a right, can afterwards be developed [*entwickelt*]' (*MM*, DR, Introduction, 'Division of the Metaphysics of Morals as a Whole', 6:239).[2] Surely this means that the Categorical Imperative, the form in which the supreme principle of morality presents itself to creatures such as ourselves, whose power of choice can also be tempted by inclination, is both the means by

---

[2] In his edition of *The Metaphysics of Morals*, Bernd Ludwig has suggested that this 'Division' belongs in the general introduction to *The Metaphysics of Morals*, following 6:221, rather than in the specific Introduction to the 'Doctrine of Right'. See Immanuel Kant, *Metaphysische Anfangsgründe der Rechtslehre: Metaphysik der Sitten*, pt. 1, ed. Bernd Ludwig (Hamburg: Felix Meiner, 1986), 31–4, also pp. xxxi–xxxii. The word *entwickelt*, which Gregor translated as 'explicated', is one of those words that makes Kant's arguments in this late work so obscure. It is hardly clear from this term whether Kant thinks that rights and duties can be derived from the concept of freedom or from the Categorical Imperative by straightforward analysis or by some other method of argument.

which we know of our freedom and also the principle by means of which we must restrict our freedom in order to determine both our legally enforceable rights against one another as well as our ethical duties to ourselves and to one another.

Several writers have recently challenged this natural interpretation and argued that Kant did not intend to derive the principles of right from the fundamental principle of morality at all but, instead, intended them to stand on their own as rational but not moral principles of human conduct. Allen Wood has argued that 'Kant very explicitly discredits the whole idea that the principle of right could be derived from the fundamental principle of morality',[3] and Marcus Willaschek has argued that Kant supposes, at least part of the time, that 'the fundamental laws of the realm of right are expressions of human autonomy akin to, but independent from, the moral domain'.[4] These authors have based their surprising conclusion precisely on what seems like part of the evidence for the ordinary view that Kant's philosophy of right is derived from his supreme principle of morality—namely, his claims that the connection of coercion to right is *analytic* and his designation of the principles of acquired right as a *postulate* of practical reason. Thus, Wood says that Kant discredits the idea of a derivation of the principles of right from morality simply 'by declaring that the principle of right, unlike the principle of morality, is *analytic*',[5] and Willaschek seconds that claim, while adding that Kant's statement that 'the 'universal law of right' is 'a postulate that is incapable of further proof [*keines Beweises weiter fähig*]" (6:231) . . . would be astonishing if Kant held that this law was a special instance of a more general principle whose validity Kant, on his own account, had proven in the *Critique of Practical Reason*'.[6] To reach their conclusion, both authors must assume that an analytic proposition, because it is true in virtue of the containment of its predicate in its subject concept and the law of non-contradiction, neither needs nor can receive any sort of justification beyond the analysis of the concepts that comprise it. Willaschek must also assume that anything Kant calls a postulate cannot have a foundation in any more fundamental principle, such as the supreme principle of morality.

---

[3] Wood, 'The Final Form of Kant's Practical Philosophy', in Timmons (ed.), *Kant's Metaphysics of Morals*, 7.

[4] Marcus Willaschek, 'Why the *Doctrine of Right* does not Belong in the *Metaphysics of Morals*', *Jahrbuch für Recht und Ethik*, 5 (1997), 205–27, at 208.

[5] Wood, 'The Final Form of Kant's Practical Philosophy', 7.

[6] Willaschek, 'Why the *Doctrine of Right* does not belong in the *Metaphysics of Morals*', 220.

Strictly construed, the claim that Kant's universal principle of right is not derived from the Categorical Imperative, understood as the requirement to act only on maxims that can also serve as universal law, is correct because the principle of right concerns only the compatibility of our actions with the freedom of others, and does not concern our maxims at all, *a fortiori* their universality. However, any broader claim that the principle of right is not derived from the fundamental principle of morality, in the sense of the fundamental concept of morality, is surely implausible. The foundational assumption of Kantian morality is that human freedom has unconditional value, and both the Categorical Imperative and the universal principle of right flow directly from this fundamental normative claim: the Categorical Imperative tells us what form our maxims must take if they are always to be compatible with the fundamental value of freedom, and the universal principle of right tells us what form our actions must take if they are to be compatible with the universal value of freedom, regardless of our maxims and motivations. Thus the universal principle of right may not be derived from the Categorical Imperative, but it certainly is derived from the conception of freedom and its value that is the fundamental principle of Kantian morality.[7]

At the same time, Kant's suggestion that the universal principle of right flows directly from the concept of freedom should not be taken to suggest that this principle, the connection of coercion to right, or the postulate of

---

[7] In maintaining that the universal principle of right is not derived from the Categorical Imperative but is derived from the concept of freedom as the fundamental principle of morality, I am differing from the position of Allen D. Rosen, *Kant's Theory of Justice* (Ithaca, NY: Cornell University Press, 1993), 50–5. I am also thereby suggesting that the structure of Kant's argument in the 'Doctrine of Right' of *The Metaphysics of Morals* is similar to that of the 'Doctrine of Virtue'. As Allen Wood has pointed out, in the latter part of the work Kant almost never derives the duties of virtue from the Categorical Imperative as the Formula of Universal Law, but almost always derives these duties directly from the concept of humanity, or our obligation to preserve and promote humanity as an end and never merely as a means; see Allen W. Wood, 'Humanity as an End in Itself', in Hoke Robinson (ed.), *Proceedings of the Eighth International Kant Congress*, vol. 1, pt. 1 (Milwaukee, WI: Marquette University Press, 1995), 301–19, repr. in Paul Guyer (ed.), *Kant's Groundwork of the Metaphysics of Morals: Critical Essays* (Lanham: Rowman & Littlefield, 1998), 165–87, and Allen Wood, *Kant's Ethical Thought* (Cambridge: Cambridge University Press, 1999), Conclusion, especially 325–33. If freedom—the freedom to set and pursue our own ends—is the defining characteristic of humanity (see e.g. the Introduction to the 'Doctrine of Virtue', 6:387), then the duties of right are simply the coercively enforceable subset of our duties to preserve humanity, while the duties of virtue include those duties to preserve humanity that are not coercively enforceable as well as all duties to promote humanity. See also Paul Guyer, 'Moral Worth, Virtue and Merit', in Guyer, *Kant on Freedom, Law, and Happiness* (Cambridge: Cambridge University Press, 2000), ch. 9.

right regarding property stand in no need of further justification or what Kant sometimes calls deduction. While the characterization of an analytic judgement as one that is true in virtue of its concepts and the laws of logic alone seems like a textbook definition of the analytic (see *CPuR*, A 6–10/B 10–14), Kant himself does not assume that the logical character of analytic judgements relieves us from all further obligation to justify them. On the contrary, both in the *Critique of Pure Reason* and in polemical writings from the beginning of the 1790s, closer to the period of *The Metaphysics of Morals*, Kant consistently maintains that even analytic judgements have no cognitive value without a proof of the 'objective reality' of the subject concepts on which they are based— that is, a proof that such concepts describe real objects or real possibilities for objects. And it is by no means obvious that by calling a principle a postulate Kant means to imply that it cannot be derived from a more fundamental principle. It certainly is his view that one synthetic *a priori* judgement can be derived from another, so by calling the principle of acquired right synthetic *a priori* Kant cannot mean to imply that it is not derivable from the general principle of right and through that from the supreme principle of morality. Moreover, those propositions that Kant most prominently labels postulates—the postulates of pure practical reason asserting the existence of freedom, God, and the immortality of the soul—are clearly subject to elaborate proofs. So, by calling a principle of right a postulate, Kant may mean to suggest something about *how* such a proposition must be proved, but not that it cannot be proved.

My plan for this chapter is the following. First, I examine some of Kant's general claims about analytic judgements and postulates in order to show that Kant's application of these concepts to principles of right does not by itself imply that those principles are independent from the fundamental concept of morality. Then I examine some of Kant's specific claims about the principles of right in order to show that Kant by no means intends to imply that these principles can stand independently of the fundamental concept of morality, but rather that he intends to deduce them from that concept. I then discuss two of Kant's central claims: the allegedly analytic proposition that right and the authorization to use coercion mean one and the same, and the postulate of practical reason with regard to the right to acquire property, showing that Kant attempts to establish the conditions of both the moral and theoretical possibility of these claims by arguments that can only be considered deductions. Whether Kant's arguments fully satisfy his own expectations for deductions or ours is probably impossible to answer, given how many ways he used the term 'deduction' and the debates that have raged in recent years about the nature of transcendental arguments. So I will not attempt to answer such questions.

## II. ANALYTIC JUDGEMENTS AND THEIR JUSTIFICATION

On Kant's conception of analytic judgements, the claim that a principle of right is analytic is hardly incompatible with the assumption that it flows from the concept of freedom as the supreme principle of morality. Further, for Kant the truth of an analytic proposition depends upon the justification of the concept that it analyses; in the case of a principle of right, its truth thus depends upon the objective reality of the fundamental concept upon which the supreme principle of morality depends, the concept of freedom. The present section comments on Kant's general concept of analyticity; more specific observations about just what propositions about right Kant claims to be analytic and what they presuppose will be offered later.

Kant's conception of analyticity is not as simple as it may seem. Kant famously introduces his concept of analytic judgements by claiming that in such judgements 'the predicate *B* belongs to the subject *A* as something that is (covertly) contained in this concept *A*' and thus that they are judgements 'in which the connection of the predicate is thought through identity' (*CPuR*, A 6–7/B 10–11).[8] This is usually interpreted to mean that an analytic judgement, or, as we would say, an analytic proposition, is one that is *true* in virtue of what is contained in its subject concept and the laws of logic alone. But Kant does not say anything about truth in this passage; he only says, vaguely, that in an analytic judgement the 'connection' between subject and predicate is 'thought' through a logical law. Whether this is supposed to be enough to explain or justify the truth of the proposition is far from obvious; it certainly leaves open the possibility that a full justification for belief in the truth of an analytic proposition may require some sort of justification for the subject concept itself. It is

---

[8] It has sometimes been thought that Kant offers two different concepts of or criteria for analyticity, one in which a judgement is analytic if the predicate is contained in the subject concept and another in which it is analytic if it depends on the law of identity or some related principle of logic; see e.g. Lewis White Beck, 'Can Kant's Synthetic Judgments Be Made Analytic?', *Kant-Studien*, 67 (1955), 168–81; repr. in Beck, *Studies in the Philosophy of Kant* (Indianapolis: Bobbs-Merrill, 1965), 74–91 (see esp. 74–81). It is clear from Kant's text that he does not intend two different conceptions or criteria, but rather supposes that an analytical judgement can be 'thought' through the law of identity *because* its predicate is contained in its subject concept.

certainly not obvious that the subject concept of an analytic judgement cannot itself be derived from some more fundamental source, some more fundamental intuition, concept, or principle that would be part of the basis for the truth of the analytic judgement built upon that subject concept.

Following his introduction of the concept of an analytic judgement, Kant does make it clear that the fact that a proposition may be *proved* by means of an inference or chain of inferences proceeding strictly in accordance with laws of logic is *not* enough to show that the proposition—presumably, the truth of the proposition—is *known* by means of logic alone, or even that the proposition is actually analytic. He says that prior philosophers failed to recognize that 'Mathematical judgements are all synthetic':

> For since one found that the inferences of the mathematicians all proceed in accordance with the principle of contradiction (which is required by the nature of any apodictic certainty), one was persuaded that the principles could also be cognized from the principle of contradiction, in which, however, they erred; for a synthetic proposition can of course be comprehended in accordance with the principle of contradiction, but only insofar as another synthetic proposition is presupposed from which it can be deduced, never in itself. (*CPuR*, B 14)

This says that provability in accordance with the law of contradiction, and, presumably, by any other purely logical principle, such as the law of identity,[9] is not enough by itself to establish analyticity. The status of a proposition ultimately depends upon the status of the premises of its proof: if they are synthetic, then the conclusion is synthetic even though reached by purely logical inferences. If it always takes a synthetic proposition to establish the justifiability of any concept that could be used as a premiss in a logical inference, this would actually imply that all propositions that can be known to be true are really synthetic. Kant does not draw this conclusion in the first *Critique*, although, as we will see momentarily, that may be his ultimate position. But, even apart from that conclusion, the present argument is enough to establish that the mere fact that one proposition can be proven from another in accordance with the law of identity or contradiction is hardly enough to establish that the subject concept of a proposition and with it the truth of the

---

[9] In his earliest philosophical work, the *New Elucidation of the First Principles of Metaphysical Cognition* of 1755, Kant had argued that the principle that all identities are true and the principle that all contradictions are false are actually two separate logical principles (1:389; see David Walford (ed.), *Immanuel Kant: Theoretical Philosophy 1755–1770* (Cambridge: Cambridge University Press, 1992), 7). In the *Critique of Pure Reason*, Kant tends to treat the principles of identity and of contradiction interchangeably.

proposition do not depend upon something more fundamental. Thus, even if Kant says that a principle of right is provable in accordance with the principle of identity or of contradiction, that by itself hardly implies that this principle can be known to be true without appeal to some more fundamental concept or principle, and may not even by itself actually imply that the principle is analytic.

Before leaving the first *Critique*, we should also look at Kant's introduction of the concept of a deduction. Kant introduces the concepts of deduction in general and of transcendental deduction in particular in the 'Transcendental Logic' in order to explain our knowledge of synthetic *a priori* cognitions that go beyond those explained solely by appeal to our *a priori* intuition of space and time; thus, a transcendental deduction is needed to explain our cognition of the universal principle of causation, for example, as contrasted to a mathematical theorem. But Kant does not say that only synthetic *a priori* propositions need a deduction; in fact, he says that *any* concept the use of which cannot be justified by an immediate appeal to experience needs a deduction. In fact, he introduces the concept of deduction by none other than the example of rights, arguing that claims of right always need a deduction:

Jurists, when they speak of entitlements and claims, distinguish in a legal matter between the question about what is lawful (*quid juris*) and that which concerns the fact (*quid facti*), and since they demand proof of both, they call the first, that which is to establish the entitlement of the legal claim, the **deduction**. We make use of a multitude of empirical concepts without objection from anyone... because we always have experience ready to hand to prove their objective reality. But there are also concepts that have been usurped, such as **fortune** and **fate**... and then there is not a little embarrassment about their deduction because one can adduce no clear legal ground for an entitlement to their use either from experience or from reason. (*CPuR*, A 84/B 116–17)[10]

This implies that any concept the 'objective reality' of which cannot be established by a straightforward appeal to experience of an object that satisfies it needs a deduction of some kind. And, as Kant's example implies, claims of right, as opposed to mere descriptions of fact, can never establish their objective reality by a direct appeal to experience. While particular claims of right are not the same as principles of right, of course, surely this suggests that, if the principles of right are to be shown

---

[10] Dieter Henrich has emphasized the legal origins of Kant's notion of deduction in a number of articles; see 'Kant's Notion of a Deduction and the Methodological Background of the first *Critique*', in Eckart Förster, *Kant's Transcendental Deductions: The Three 'Critiques' and the 'Opus postumum'* (Stanford: Stanford University Press, 1989), 29–46.

to have binding force for us, which can hardly be shown by an appeal
to experience, the concepts on which they are based must have
their objective reality established by some form of deduction.
Thus, even if certain principles of right do have the logical structure
of analytic judgements, it seems unlikely that Kant intended that
the principles of right can be known to be valid by analysis of their
concepts alone.

Kant further expounded his view about analyticity in a polemical
exchange with the Halle Wolffian Johann August Eberhard, who in a
series of publications from 1788 to 1792 attempted to show that Kant's
claim that mathematical propositions are synthetic *a priori* is false, and
that, as he took Leibniz to have already shown, all mathematical results
can be proven by purely logical inferences from appropriate definitions,
such as definitions of number, and hence are analytic.[11] In response to
this charge, Kant insisted upon the point already made in the first
*Critique* that a proposition may have a strictly analytical *proof*, which
proceeds by unpacking the predicates contained in a concept, but the
objective reality of the concept, that is, its application to anything real,
and thus the *truth* of everything that follows from it, even in the strictest
accordance with the laws of logic, can never be established by analysis
alone, but always needs to be established by some other, and thus
synthetic method—this is what Kant had meant by his statement that
analysis always presupposes synthesis (see *CPuR*, B130). Indeed, Kant
argues, by suitable definitions *any* proposition might be given an analytical proof, but such a proof implies the truth of nothing unless the
construction of the definition itself can be justified. Kant had already
implied this in the first *Critique* when he stated that 'Prior to all analysis
of our representations these must first be given, and no concepts can arise
analytically as far as **the content is concerned**. The synthesis of a manifold ... first brings forth a cognition' (*CPuR*, A77/B103). But the point is
made even more clearly in the debate with Eberhard. In Kant's main
publication in the debate, *On a Discovery according to which any New*
Critique of Pure Reason *has been Made Superfluous by an Earlier One*,
Kant focuses on the case of mathematics, basing his argument on the
insight that real progress in mathematics was made only when mathematicians realized that 'the objective reality of [a] concept, i.e. the
possibility of the existence of a thing with these properties, can be proven

---

[11] Eberhard's articles were published in the first four volumes of the journal *Philosophisches Magazin*, edited by himself, J. G. Maaß, and J. E. Schwab. For a description of his
attack, see Henry E. Allison, *The Kant–Eberhard Controversy* (Baltimore: Johns Hopkins
University Press, 1973), 6–45.

in no other way **than by providing the corresponding intuition**';[12] that is, no matter what they could prove from the concept of an object, the mathematicians had first to prove that the object itself could exist in order to assign any truth to the results of their proofs. In a further reply to Eberhard, Kant's disciple Johann Schultz stated the point more generally:

If one wishes to decide about a judgment, one must in each case know previously what should be thought under the subject as well as the predicate.... Let one place just so many marks in the concept of the subject that the predicate, which he wishes to prove of the subject, can be derived from its concept through the mere principle of contradiction. This trick does not help him at all. For the *Critique* grants him without dispute this kind of analytic judgment. Then, however, it takes the concept of the subject itself into consideration, and it asks: how did it come about that you have placed so many different marks in this concept that it already contains synthetic propositions? First prove the objective reality of your concept, i.e. first prove that any one of its marks really belongs to a possible object.[13]

No matter what you can prove from a definition, the reality of the object defined and the suitability of the definition to the object must first be proved if genuine knowledge is to result from the logical exercise of analysis.

Given Kant's statement in the first *Critique* that any proposition proved by logical methods is ultimately synthetic if the initial premisses of its proof are, his position in this debate with Eberhard may imply that there are, in the last analysis, no genuinely analytic judgements.[14] But even if that conclusion is not drawn, the application to practical philosophy of the Kantian position in its most fundamental form, summed up in the axiom that analysis always presupposes synthesis, surely means that normative principles can never be established by an analysis of definitions that may turn out to be arbitrary inventions, but must be shown to have a foundation in something justifiable or even inescapable. The justification of practical propositions cannot, of course, take

---

[12] *On a Discovery*, 8:191; Allison, *Kant–Eberhard*, 110.

[13] Schultz's review of Maaß's discussion of the analytic/synthetic distinction, 20:408–9; Allison, *Kant–Eberhard*, 175. This passage was famously cited by Lewis White Beck in his article showing that Kant had prefigured some of the objections of Willard Quine and Morton White to the logical positivist's use of the analytic/synthetic distinction, in which he argued that the issue important to Kant survived their critique; see Beck, 'Can Kant's Synthetic Judgments Be Made Analytic?'

[14] See Beck, 'Can Kant's Synthetic Judgments Be Made Analytic', 168–81. Essentially, Beck argues that, while Kant has room for purely analytic judgements in uninterpreted formal systems, on his account even those mathematical propositions that may be logically derived from adequate definitions are synthetic if interpreted as knowledge claims about objects.

precisely the same form as that of theoretical propositions: practical propositions state what ought to be, not what is, so their concepts may not need objective reality in precisely the same sense as theoretical concepts do.[15] But they clearly need a foundation in something real. For the principles of right, the only non-arbitrary foundation available is the concept of freedom, the proof of the objective reality of which is in turn the fundamental issue for Kant's practical philosophy, ultimately solved by the validation of our assumption of our freedom through our awareness of the binding force of the Categorical Imperative. The task for the philosophy of right must then be to show that principles of right have an indisputable foundation in the reality of freedom, and that the scope of these principles is precisely delimited by what is required for the preservation of freedom. Whatever may be analytically 'developed' out of the concept of right has no force unless the concept of right itself can be shown to be grounded in the nature and reality of freedom.

## III. POSTULATES AND PROVABILITY

Let us now consider possible implications of Kant's characterization of some or all of the principles of right as 'postulates'. In different passages, Kant suggests, first, that *all* practical laws are or are like postulates; second, that the *general* principle of right is a postulate; and, third, that the particular principle of right that states that it must be right to acquire property is a postulate. It will be useful to have his statements before us.

First, on practical laws in general, Kant writes:

The simplicity of the [Categorical Imperative] in comparison with the great and various consequences that can be drawn from it must seem astonishing at first, as must also its authority to command without appearing to carry any incentive with it. But in wondering at an ability of our reason to determine choice by the mere idea that a maxim qualifies for the universality of a practical law, one learns that just these practical (moral) laws first make known a property of choice, namely its freedom, which speculative reason would never have arrived at, either on *a priori* grounds or through any experience whatever, and which, once reason has arrived at it, could in no way be shown theoretically to be possible, although these practical laws show incontestably that our choice has this property. It then seems less strange to find that these laws, like mathematical postulates, are **incapable of being proved** and yet **apodictic,** but at the same time to see a

---

[15] See *CPuR*, A 633/B 661: 'theoretical cognition [is] that through which I cognize **what exists**, and practical cognition [is] that through which I represent what **ought to exist.**'

whole field of practical cognition open up before one, where reason in its theoretical use, with the same idea of freedom ... must find everything closed tight against it. (*MM*, Introduction, III, 6:225)

Even without detailed analysis, two points are obvious in this passage. First, within two sentences Kant can say that practical laws are like mathematical postulates and yet are also consequences drawn from the Categorical Imperative, which Kant is here equating with the fundamental principle of morality; evidently, the way in which practical laws are like mathematical postulates does not preclude their being derived from a more fundamental principle of morality. Second, Kant's analogy between practical laws and mathematical postulates does not seem to mean that they are incapable of proof altogether, but rather that there is some sense in which these laws, or the fact of our freedom on which they depend and which they reveal, is a matter for *practical* rather than *theoretical* cognition. In other words, by calling practical principles postulates Kant apparently does not intend to imply that such laws admit of no proof at all, but rather to say something about the kind of proof of which they do admit.

Next, Kant calls the universal principle of right a postulate. This comes in the course of his comment that right requires only legality, not morality—that is, for purposes of right it is sufficient that we act in accordance with the universal principle of right even if we are not actually motivated by it as our maxim:

Thus the universal law of right, so act externally that the free use of your choice can coexist with the freedom of everyone in accordance with a universal law, is indeed a law that lays an obligation on me, but it does not at all expect, far less demand, that I **myself should** limit my freedom in these conditions just for the sake of this obligation; instead, reason says only that freedom **is** limited to these conditions in conformity with the idea of it and that it may also be actively limited by others: and it says this as a postulate that is incapable of further proof. (*MM*, DR, Introduction, §C, 6:231)[16]

---

[16] In correspondence, Allen Wood has objected that my account of the derivation of the principle of right from the fundamental concept of morality runs the risk of making individual motivation a fit subject for juridical legislation, a result that Kant surely and rightly wished to avoid. But this objectionable result certainly does not follow from my approach. As he does in section one of the *Groundwork*, Kant can use his account of the pure character of morally praiseworthy moral motivation to identify the necessarily formal character of the fundamental principle of morality (see esp. *G*, 4:402), yet that principle, once identified, can still require certain actions or omissions of us as obligations that must be fulfilled regardless of our motivation for doing so. The duties of right are precisely obligations that flow from the fundamental concept of morality that we must fulfil even if our motivation for so doing is not our respect for the fundamental principle of

Here Kant states that the universal principle of right is a postulate incapable of further proof *while* stating that the principle expresses the restriction of the use of freedom to the condition of its consistency with a like use by others, and indeed perhaps he means that the principle of right is a postulate just *because* it expresses the restriction of the use of freedom to the condition of its consistency with a like use by others. Thus, Kant apparently does not mean that the principle of right is not derived from a more fundamental principle of the supreme moral value of freedom; rather, he seems to mean that the principle of right needs no *further* proof just *because* it is derived directly from the application of the most fundamental concept of morality to the case of external action— that is, the case in which one person's use of his freedom to act has the potential to limit or interfere with other persons' use of their freedom to act.

Finally, Kant calls the principle that 'It is possible for me to have any external object of choice as mine' a 'postulate of practical reason with regard to rights', or also, in the next paragraph, a 'presupposition of practical reason' (*MM*, DR, §6, 6:250). Yet Kant immediately proceeds to supply an argument for this 'postulate', and this argument, in the form of a *reductio*, begins by asking what would follow 'If it were nevertheless not within my **rightful** power to make use of it, that is, if the use of it could not coexist with the freedom of everyone in accordance with a universal law.' In other words, the postulate of practical reason with regard to rights is to be *derived* from the universal principle of right by a proof that the acquisition of property is consistent with and indeed required by the general principle that each person's external use of freedom be consistent with everyone else's. So whatever Kant means by calling the principle of property a postulate, it *cannot* be that this principle is not derivable from a more general principle of right, and thereby from the even more fundamental supreme principle of morality.

So what can Kant mean by calling moral laws in general, the universal principle of right, and the particular principle of right that licenses the acquisition of property—the 'permissive law of practical reason' (*MM*, DR, §6, 6:257)—postulates? Here it may be helpful to recall that there are three other kinds of propositions that Kant calls postulates: the 'postulates of empirical thinking in general' in the 'System of the Principles of Pure Understanding'; mathematical postulates, which he dis-

---

morality itself; that is just why there is typically nothing praiseworthy about fulfilling the obligations of right. Again, see Guyer, 'Moral Worth, Virtue and Merit'.

cusses in order to elucidate the postulates of empirical thinking in general; and the postulates of pure practical reason.

We can consider the first two sorts of postulates together, since Kant explains what he means by mathematical postulates in order to explain the 'postulates of empirical thinking in general'. The latter are the principles governing the application of the modal categories of possibility, actuality, and necessity, which are derived from analysis of the logical functions of judgement, to the objects of human experience: thus, calling an object possible implies that its concept is consistent with the pure forms of human intuition and conceptualization; calling an object actual means that sensation, as the matter of intuition, provides evidence of the objective reality of its concept; and calling an object necessary means that it is subsumed under causal laws (see *CPuR*, A 217–18/B 265–6). Kant does not explain why he calls these principles or as he also says 'definitions' of the modal concepts 'in their empirical use' (*CPuR*, A 219/B 266) 'postulates' until the end of the section expounding them; but then what he says is that he calls them 'postulates' *not* because they are 'propositions put forth as immediately certain without justification or proof' (*CPuR*, A 232/B 285), but rather because, like postulates in mathematics, they do not add to the content of a concept but rather 'assert . . . the action of the cognitive faculty through which [the concept] is generated'. 'In mathematics a postulate is the practical proposition that contains nothing other than the synthesis through which we first give ourselves an object and generate its concept' (*CPuR*, A 234/B 287). The postulate for a mathematical concept is thus the principle telling us how to construct an object that instantiates the concept in intuition, like the rule that a circle can be drawn by keeping a single curved line on a plane equidistant from a single centre point; a postulate for a modal concept is a principle telling us how to use such a concept, such as the rule that a concept may be called actual if the predicates included in its concept are not only consistent with our forms of intuition but are also instantiated in our sensation.

By calling such a principle a postulate Kant does not mean that it cannot be proved; on the contrary, he says explicitly that, if postulates 'could claim unconditional acceptance without any deduction, merely on their own claim, then all critique of understanding would be lost'. Thus for any postulate 'if not a proof then at least a deduction of the legitimacy of its assertion must unfailingly be supplied' (*CPuR*, A 233/B 285–6). Rather, what may not be subject to further proof, at least in the case of a mathematical postulate, is the possibility of the action *through which* the concept is provided with its construction, for it is the construction itself that is the proof of the possibility of the concept of a given figure. Kant's view thus seems to be that a postulate is the assertion of the possibility, actuality, or necessity of a concept, and that it *needs* to be proved, but that the proof can be given only through a construction, as in the case of a mathematical postulate, or something more like the description of the general conditions for a construction or verification, as in the case of the postulates of empirical thinking in general. But, whatever the details, Kant makes it plain that by calling a principle a postulate he hardly means to imply that it needs no proof or deduction; rather, by so doing he means to say something about the kind of proof that it permits.

The third and most prominent context in which Kant ordinarily uses the term 'postulate' is, of course, that of the postulates of pure practical reason. In his most extensive treatment of the postulates of pure practical reason, Kant introduces two such postulates—namely, those of the immortality of the soul and of the existence of God (*CPracR*, 5:122–3, 124–32) (although often he also speaks of the existence of freedom as a postulate of pure practical reason, and thus proceeds as if there are three such postulates). In introducing the postulates of immortality and the existence of God, Kant states that a postulate of pure practical reason is 'a **theoretical** proposition, though one not demonstrable as such, insofar as it is attached inseparably to an *a priori* unconditionally valid **practical** law' (*CPracR*, 5:122). On this definition, a postulate of practical reason is not a moral law or command itself, but an existential proposition, thus a proposition with the form of a theoretical proposition although not demonstrable as such, that is connected with a moral law or command. Kant does not make clear in this definition what sort of 'connection' he has in mind. But his very first mention of the doctrine of the postulates of pure practical reason, which was in fact already introduced in the first *Critique*, does spell out what connection he has in mind:

Now if it is indubitably certain, but only conditionally, that something either is or that it should happen, then either a certain determinate condition can be absolutely necessary for it, or it can be presupposed as only optional and contingent. In the first case the condition is postulated (*per thesin*), in the second it is supposed (*per hypothesin*). Since there are practical laws that are absolutely necessary (the moral laws), then if these necessarily presuppose any existence as the condition of their **binding** force, this existence has to be **postulated**, because the condition from which the inference to this determinate condition proceeds is itself cognized *a priori* as absolutely necessary. (*CPuR*, A 633–4/B 661–2)

This makes clear that a postulate is a theoretical proposition asserting the existence of an object or state of affairs that is a condition of the possibility of the binding force of a moral command. The binding force of a moral command depends upon the possibility of carrying it out; so the theoretical condition of the possibility of the binding force of a moral command is whatever entity or state of affairs must exist in order to explain how what the moral law commands can be carried out.

As is well known, Kant then reaches the postulates of immortality and the existence of God as the conditions of the possibility of the moral law through the concept of the highest good, and this is in fact why Kant does not initially treat the existence of our own freedom as a postulate of pure practical reason, although later he often lumps freedom in with the other two: immortality and the existence of God are necessary not in order to explain the binding force of the moral law as such—for that, the presupposition of our freedom suffices—but in order to explain the possibility of the attainment of the *object* of the moral law—that is, the state of affairs that the moral law commands us to realize. This is what Kant calls the 'highest good', or the attainment of the greatest happiness possible consistent with the conscientious observation of the moral law. There are different interpretations of the meaning of Kant's concept of the highest good: many interpret him to assume that the pursuit of happiness is a natural tendency of human beings that has no foundation in the moral law and simply has to be constrained by it; I believe that Kant's view is not so dualistic, but is rather that the fundamental principle of morality itself, by commanding us always to preserve and promote human freedom, and thereby to treat ourselves and others always as ends and never merely as means, actually requires us to promote the realization of the ends of all humans in so far as they are consistent with each other, and that such a realization would be precisely the realization of the greatest happiness consistent with the observation of the moral law.[17] But the details of how Kant introduces the highest good as the object of morality need not concern us here; what interests us is the connection between the highest good and the postulates of immortality and the existence of God. Briefly, Kant's argument is this: the realization of both virtue and happiness requires the perfection of our moral disposition, or virtue, on the one hand, and the maximal fulfilment of lawful human ends, or happiness, on the other. The perfection of the human moral disposition, Kant supposes, would require an indefinitely long lifespan, or immortality, in order to overcome the propensity to evil that is otherwise natural to human beings. The maximal fulfilment of human ends, however, is

[17] See Guyer, 'From a Practical Point of View', in Guyer, *Kant on Freedom, Law, and Happiness*, ch. 10 and ch. 8 in this volume.

something that can happen only in nature (because it is only in nature that the human desires that may be transformed into legitimate ends can be fulfilled), but we can have reason to believe that nature is suitable for the fulfilment of human purposes only if we believe that the laws of nature have been written to be compatible with the moral law—something we cannot ascribe to our own power but only to that of God as the author of nature. As Kant puts it,

> Therefore the supreme cause of nature, insofar as it must be presupposed for the highest good, is a being that is the cause of nature by **understanding** and **will** (hence its author), that is, **God**. Consequently, the postulate of the possibility of the **highest derived good** (the best world) is likewise the postulate of the reality of a **highest original good**, namely of the existence of God. (*CPracR*, 5:125)[18]

Kant's reasoning is thus as follows. The moral law commands the realization of the highest good (literally, the 'highest derived good'), so, since the binding force of an obligation depends upon the possibility of its realization ('ought implies can'), for the moral law even to have binding force requires that the realization of the highest good be *possible*. But for the highest good to be possible, we must suppose that both immortality and the existence of God (the 'highest original good') are *actual*. The possibility of the binding force of the supreme principle of morality, as a moral command, thus requires us to believe in the truth of certain theoretical propositions, that is, assertions of the existence of some object or state of affairs, even though these theoretical propositions can have no theoretical proof. Purely theoretical consideration can and indeed must be able to show them to be free of inconsistency, thus to possess what Kant calls 'logical possibility'; but only moral considerations can give us reason to believe that the concepts employed in these theoretical propositions have any objective reality, or what Kant also calls 'real possibility'.

Besides containing a clear statement of what Kant means by a postulate of pure practical reason, the first *Critique* also contains a clear statement of what he means by his claim that such a postulate is theoretically indemonstrable but practically certain. Kant says:

> Of course, no one will be able to boast that he **knows** that there is a God and a future life; for if he knows that then he is precisely the man I have long sought.... No, the conviction is not **logical** but **moral** certainty; and, since it depends on subjective grounds (of moral disposition), I must not even say 'It is morally certain that there is a God', etc., but rather 'I **am** morally certain', etc.

---

[18] Kant uses the same formula at *CPuR*, A 811/B 839.

That is, the belief in a God and another world is so interwoven with my moral disposition that I am in as little danger of ever surrendering the former as I am worried that the latter can ever be torn away from me. (*CPuR*, A 828–9/B 857–8)

There can be no theoretical proof of the existence of such things as immortality and God, Kant has argued throughout the first *Critique*, because such objects could not be presented within the limits of human intuition. But it is nevertheless necessary for us to believe in the existence of these objects because it would be incoherent for us to attempt to fulfil the command of morality to bring about the highest good without also believing in these objects—even the possibility of realizing the highest good depends on their actuality. Thus our belief in the existence of these objects has the same grip upon us as the moral law itself.

One last point should be noted. In the last passage cited from the *Critique of Practical Reason* (5:125) Kant used the word 'postulate' not once but twice: he said that the postulate of the possibility of the highest derived good, the highest good in its ordinary sense, is 'likewise' the postulate of the reality of the highest original good, the existence of God. Both of the postulates referred to here could be understood as theoretical propositions affirmed on practical grounds: the real possibility of the highest good could be understood as the condition of the possibility of the binding force of the moral law, and the actuality of God in turn as the condition of the real possibility of the highest good. Earlier on that page, however, Kant employed a twofold use of the term that might be taken differently. Here he wrote:

There is not the least ground in the moral law for a necessary connection between the morality and the proportionate happiness of a being belonging to the world as part of it. . . . Nevertheless, in the practical task of pure reason, that is, in the necessary pursuit of the highest good, such a connection is postulated as necessary: we **ought** to strive to promote the highest good (which must therefore be postulated). Accordingly, the existence of a cause of all nature, distinct from nature, which contains the ground of this connection, namely of the exact correspondence of happiness with morality, is also **postulated**. (*CPracR*, 5:125)

In the last sentence of this quotation, Kant clearly means to use the term 'postulate' to characterize the affirmation on moral grounds of the theoretical proposition asserting the existence of God as the cause of nature. In what precedes, however, he uses the term to characterize the assertion of the *necessity* rather than the *possibility* of the highest (derived) good itself. But since Kant never supposes that the *existence* of the highest good is necessary, but only that it is possible, he must here be suggesting that the postulate of the highest good is necessary as a practical *command* following from the moral law rather than a theoretical *condition* of the possibility of the binding force of that law. In other words, in this instance Kant may be using the term 'postulate' to characterize the status of one moral command, the command that we seek to realize the highest good, as depending upon a more fundamental moral command—namely, the supreme principle of morality itself. In this sense, of course, a practical postulate could not be a practical principle that is independent of the fundamental principle of morality; on the contrary, such a postulate would be so called precisely because of its dependence on the most fundamental moral principle.

Three conclusions follow from this discussion. First, as far as theoretical postulates are concerned, mathematical postulates are so designated simply because the objective validity of their concepts must be established by a construction in pure intuition, or depends upon the possibility of an action of construction. It may seem natural to suppose that mathematical postulates are also fundamental in the sense of not being derivable from any more fundamental propositions—that they are not theorems that are proven, but axioms from which theorems are proven; but Kant does not actually say that. In turn, the more general postulates of empirical thinking are so called solely in virtue of one point of analogy with mathematical postulates: as mathematical postulates depend upon construction in pure intuition for demonstration of the objective reality of their concepts, so the postulates of empirical thought in general describe the kinds of constructions in or relations to pure and empirical intuition that can verify the objective possibility, actuality, or necessity of concepts of objects. Kant never says that these postulates themselves cannot be derived from anything more fundamental; on the contrary, he says they do need a deduction, and they receive that deduction precisely by being derived from the application of certain of the functions of judgement to the forms of human intuition.

Secondly, in its most usual sense a postulate of pure practical reason is not a moral command at all, let alone an underivable or primitive one, but a theoretical proposition asserting the existence of the conditions necessary for the possibility of fulfilling a moral command, our confidence in which, however, is based not on any theoretical proof but solely on our confidence in the binding force of the moral command itself. If there are postulates of pure practical reason with regard to rights in this sense, it would be natural to think of such postulates as concerning the conditions of the possibility of the binding force of those principles of right: a postulate of practical reason regarding a right would then be the assertion that the conditions for the realization of that right obtain. Pursuing the analogy with mathematical postulates further, Kant might even mean that a postulate of practical reason with regard to a right is the construction of the conditions under which the right may be realized. Such a construction might be practical rather than theoretical in virtue of demonstrating that there is a consistent idea of the use of freedom that would realize such a right rather than proving that such a use of freedom ever has been, is currently, or will in the future be realized. But the key idea would be not that the principle of right cannot itself be derived from a more fundamental moral principle, but rather that the conditions of its realizability must be shown to be possible.

Finally, if in the context of principles of right Kant uses the term 'postulate' in the last of the senses we have considered, he might not mean by a postulate of practical reason with regard to a right a proposition asserting the possibility of the realization of the right, but the principle or command of right itself; but, even so, if his usage in this case is to be analogous to that in the *Critique of Practical Reason*, by calling such a principle a postulate he would not mean that it is not derivable from a more fundamental moral law, but precisely that it is, just as the postulate of moral necessity of the highest derived good is derived by the application of the supreme principle of morality to the human pursuit of ends. Such a principle could still be called a postulate because the principle from which it is derived is not provable by theoretical means, but only practically. In this sense, a principle of right might be derivable from the fundamental principle of morality yet still be called a postulate.

I now turn directly to what Kant says about the principles of right themselves in order to argue that, while Kant has certain reasons for calling them analytic and postulates—where he does—he still intends them to 'proceed from' or be deduced from the supreme principle of morality.

## IV. ARE ALL PRINCIPLES OF RIGHT ANALYTIC?

To begin, we must be careful in drawing inferences from Kant's statements about the analyticity of principles of right, because Kant in fact applies the analytic/synthetic distinction to principles of right in a number of different ways, and the same principle may be analytic by one criterion but synthetic by another.[19] And, if this is so, then, even apart from Kant's general argument that the objective reality of the subject concept analysed in an analytic judgement itself needs a deduction, there can still be something about a principle of right that obviously needs a deduction—namely, whatever it is that makes it synthetic on one way of drawing the analytic/synthetic distinction—even if there is something else that may not need proof—namely, what makes it analytic on another way of drawing the distinction.

Specifically, Kant sometimes says that all principles of right are analytic, in contrast to principles of ethics—that is, principles commanding duties of virtue—which are all synthetic; yet he also says that it is only the principle of the innate right to freedom—that is, freedom of the person—which is analytic, while all principles of acquired right—that is, all principles of property rights—are synthetic. And even when he says the former, what Kant means is that principles of right flow directly from the fundamental moral requirement that we use our freedom only in universally acceptable ways, whereas principles of ethics depend upon the additional assumption that we necessarily will certain ends. We find Kant saying this several times in his preparatory notes for *The Metaphysics of Morals*. In one passage, he writes that 'All laws of right (concerning what is mine and yours) are analytic (on account of freedom)—all laws of ends are synthetic. . . . The duties of right follow from external freedom analytically; duties of virtue follow from internal freedom synthetically' (*Loses Blatt Erdmann*, Cl, 23:246). In another note, Kant expands upon this cryptic comment:

The doctrine of right is that which contains what is consistent with the freedom of the power of choice in accordance with universal laws [*was mit der Freyheit der Willkühr nach allgemeinen Gesetzen bestehen kann*].

The doctrine of virtue is that which contains what is consistent with the necessary ends of the power of choice in accordance with a universal law of reason.

The former are negative and analytic in their internal and external relationship and contain the internal as well as the external conditions of possible external laws.

The second are affirmative and synthetic in the inner and outer relationship, and no determinate law can be given for them.

The first duties are *officia necessitatis* and the second are *officia charitatis*. (*Loses Blatt Erdmann*, 50, 23:306–7)

---

[19] This point is noted in passing by Leslie Mulholland; see Mulholland, *Kant's System of Rights* (New York: Columbia University Press, 1990), 243.

On this account, principles of right are analytic because they simply state the conditions under which freedom can be used in accordance with universal law—that is, the conditions under which multiple persons can exercise their individual freedom of choice consistently with each other—while principles of ethics are synthetic because they assume that human beings have necessary ends and state the conditions under which the use of our power of choice is consistent with the realization of those ends. The proof of a principle of ethics must therefore appeal beyond the concept of freedom itself to a necessary end of mankind, while the proof of a principle of right need demonstrate only that a relationship among persons is one that is consistent with the concept of freedom itself. Of course, to say the latter is to say precisely that a principle of right *is* derived from the concept of freedom and expresses the conditions necessary for the instantiation of the concept of freedom in relations among persons. Thus Kant's claim that principles of right are analytic is itself a claim that such principles 'proceed from' and therefore can be proven by appeal to the concept of freedom.

Kant makes the same point in the 1793–4 lectures on the metaphysics of morals transcribed by Johann Friedrich Vigilantius by using his ever-handy distinction between the formal and the material rather than the distinction between the analytic and the synthetic. Here he says that we arrive at duties of right by considering merely the formal consistency of our use of freedom, while we arrive at ethical duties by considering the consistency of the object, purposiveness, or 'matter' of our actions with the formal requirement of freedom. In his words:

If we consider the use of our freedom merely under a formal condition, the action is lacking in a determinate object that might essentially contribute a determination thereto, or we abstract from all objects. The determinate form points to a limitation of freedom, namely to the universal legitimacy of the action.... For this formal condition has reference to strict right, or duty of right....

If, on the other hand, we consider duties and their grounds of determination in regard to matter, then the action has need of an object to which it is related. This object, or the matter in this determination of duty, is the end of the action... there is an end that we **ought** to have in view when performing our duties, and which must thus be so constituted that the condition of universal rectitude can coexist with it. So in this principle also, right and obligation are present, but if the action is judged solely according to the material principle, the latter stands *in oppositio* to strict right in the purposiveness of the action. Apart from the freedom of the action, there is thus another principle present, which in itself is enlarging [*erweiternd*], in that, while freedom is restricted by the determination according to law, it is here, on the contrary, enlarged by the matter or end thereof, and something is present that has to be acquired. (Vig., 27:542–3)

Kant's use of the term 'enlarging' (*erweiternd*) indicates that this is another way of saying that the principles of right are analytic and the principles of ethics of duties of virtue synthetic, because a synthetic judgement is one that enlarges or amplifies its subject concept while an analytic judgement merely clarifies its subject concept (see *CPuR*, A 7/B 11). Again, Kant's point is that principles of right are derived by the limitation of freedom to the conditions of the universal consistency of its use, whereas principles of ethics state how certain ends may be pursued consistently with the universal realization of freedom. But again, for Kant to make this contrast is also for him to state that the principles of right are derived from the fundamental moral concept of freedom by considering how it must be limited or restricted among any population of interacting persons not in order to pursue any particular ends but simply for the sake of its own universalization. The *formality* of principles of right does not suggest the independence of the principles of right from the fundamental principle of morality, but their direct dependence upon it.[20]

While Kant thus uses the analytic/synthetic distinction to contrast duties of right and ethical duties, he also uses it to draw a contrast *within* the domain of principles of right. This is the contrast between the innate right to freedom of the person and acquired rights to property. Kant makes this contrast in the 'Doctrine of Right' by using his contrast between 'empirical possession', or physical detention of an object— holding it in one's hands or sitting on it—and 'intelligible' or 'noumenal possession', a right to control its use and disposition that does not depend upon current physical detention of it, but instead ultimately consists in an agreement among possible users of the object concerning who will have the right to it. Kant's argument is that one (ordinarily) has the right to control one's own body without any special consent from others, thus

[20] Kant's use of the analytic/synthetic distinction to draw the distinction between duties of right and ethical duties is clearly connected to his contrast between the Categorical Imperative as testing for contradictions in the *conception* of the universalization of maxims and contradictions in *willing* the universalization of maxims in the *Groundwork* (G, 4:424). However, this distinction in the *Groundwork* is equated with the distinction between perfect and imperfect duties, and that then raises the question of why Kant does not include all the perfect duties, the duties that arise from the Contradiction in Conception test, among the duties of right, which include none of the perfect duties to oneself and only some of the perfect duties to others. The substantive reason for this is that only some duties to others are morally appropriate candidates for coercive enforcement; Kant struggles for the right way to say this in the Vigilantius lectures, but explicitly draws a contrast between coercive and non-coercive strict duties at least once (Vig., 27:581–2). For further discussion of this issue, see Guyer, 'Moral Worth, Virtue and Merit'.

that forcible removal of an object from one's bodily grasp or of one's body from an object on which it currently sits would be interference with a right to freedom that does not depend upon the concurrence of others; but that the removal of an object from one's intelligible but not physical possession can only be a wrong if there is a prior agreement that one has a right to it. In Kant's words:

All propositions about right are *a priori* propositions.... An *a priori* proposition about right with regard to **empirical possession** is **analytic,** for it says nothing more than what follows from empirical possession in accordance with the principle of contradiction, namely that if I am holding a thing (and so am physically connected with it), someone who affects it without my consent (e.g., snatches an apple from my hand) affects and diminishes what is internally mine (my freedom)....

On the other hand, a proposition about the possibility of possessing a thing **external to myself**... goes beyond those limiting conditions; and since it affirms possession of something even without holding it, as necessary for the concept of something external that is mine or yours, **it is synthetic.** Reason then has the task of showing how such a proposition, which goes beyond the concept of empirical possession, is possible *a priori.* (*MM*, DR, §6, 6:250)

On this account, the innate right to freedom of the person is analytic precisely because it flows from the concept of freedom itself, while the possibility of acquired rights needs a deduction—which will presumably consist in showing the compatibility of possession without detention with the concept of freedom, or even the necessitation of the possibility of such a form of possession by the concept of freedom.

What will be involved in the latter deduction is suggested in one of Kant's notes for *The Metaphysics of Morals,* which even bears the contrasting propositions that 'The principle of all propositions of innate right is analytic' and 'The principle of an acquired right is synthetic' as its title. Here Kant argues that to establish the right to freedom of the person—that is, the right to maintain or change one's own body or mind as one pleases as long as so doing does not impinge upon others—one does not have to go beyond the concept of freedom itself, whereas to explain the possibility of a right in something other than one's own body and mind one has to bring in further factors, in particular, the nature of the *other thing* that one proposes to control and the will of *other persons* who might also control that other thing:

For in the case of propositions of the first sort we do not proceed beyond the conditions of freedom (we do not supply the power of choice with any further object), the condition, namely, that the power of choice must be consistent with the freedom of everyone in accordance with a universal law....

In the case of propositions of the second kind I supplement the power of choice with an external **object** which by nature belongs to no one, i.e., which is not innate and therefore cannot be deduced [*gefolgert*] analytically from freedom as the object of the power of choice.

   The synthetic *a priori* principle of acquired right ... is the correspondence of the power of choice with the idea of the united will of those who are restricted by that right. For since all right that is not innate is an obligation (to do or refrain from doing something) on another on whom it is not laid innately, but this cannot be done by another person alone, since that would be opposed to the innate freedom, and thus it can only happen in so far as his will is in agreement with it ... thus only through the united will can a right be acquired. (*Loses Blatt Erdmann*, 12, 23:219–20)[21]

As Kant also says, 'The synthetic principle of external right cannot be anything other than: all distinction of mine and yours must be able to be derived from the compatibility of the possession with the idea of a communal choice under which the choice of everyone else with regard to the same object stands' (*Loses Blatt Erdmann*, 11, 23:215). Kant's idea is that we do not have to appeal to anything other than the idea of freedom itself in order to justify the innate right to freedom of the person—that is what freedom in the external use of the power of choice *means*. However, to explain the possibility of rights to property that go beyond one's own person we have to explain how the exercise of freedom in control of an external object is consistent both with the nature of the object and with the freedom of the other persons who could, at least as far as their own innate right to freedom would seem to imply, also use or control the object. Providing such an explanation is the task of Kant's theory of acquired right or property. It is certainly a deduction of the possibility of acquired right, in the form of an explanation of the conditions of possibility of acquiring property consistently with the freedom of all who might be able to use the object acquired or who could be affected by the acquisition of it.

   Before examining more fully Kant's deduction of the possibility of acquired right, however, we must first pause over the suggestion that the principle of innate right is analytic. We shall see that, while Kant does believe that the universal principle of right flows directly from freedom as the fundamental concept of morality, this by no means frees him from the burden of providing a deduction of a proposition that is at least intimately connected with the universal principle of right.

---

[21] For many similar passages, see *Vorabeiten zur Rechtslehre*, 23:227, 235, 297, 303, 309, and 329.

## V. THE UNIVERSAL PRINCIPLE OF RIGHT AND THE AUTHORIZATION TO USE COERCION

Kant's most basic claim in the general introduction to *The Metaphysics of Morals* is that 'The concept of **freedom** is a pure rational concept', and that 'On this concept of freedom, which is positive (from a practical point of view), are based unconditional practical laws, which are called **moral**' (*MM*, Introduction, III, 6:221). Moral laws, in turn, as Kant has already made plain, include both the principles of right as well as the laws of ethics:

In contrast to laws of nature, these laws of freedom are called **moral** laws. As directed merely to external actions and their conformity to law they are called **juridical** laws; but if they also require that they (the laws) be the determining grounds of actions, they are ethical laws.... The freedom to which the former refer can be only freedom in the **external** use of choice. (*MM*, Introduction, II, 6:214)

Kant argues that the *reality* of freedom is not proven from the concept of freedom itself, but is rather proven through our consciousness of the binding force of the 'moral concepts and laws [that] have their source' in the reality of our freedom (*MM*, Introduction, III, 6:221). But this means that there is one way in which all moral laws, not only the principles of right which do not refer to any particular ends of human beings but also the ethical laws that do, must be synthetic, because they presuppose the reality of freedom.[22] This is so, even though by the criterion of reference to necessary ends, the principles of right are analytic.

In the further introduction to the 'Doctrine of Right', Kant clearly has the dependency of the principles of right upon the *concept* of freedom in mind when he writes that in the case of right 'All that is in question is the **form** in the relation of choice on the part of [multiple persons], in so far as choice is regarded merely as **free**, and whether the action of one can be united with the freedom in accordance with a universal law', and thus when he concludes that 'Right is therefore the sum of the conditions under which the choice of one can be united with the choice of another in accordance with a universal law of freedom' (*MM*, DR, Introduction, §B, 6:230). But in fact Kant does not specifically use the language of analyticity at this point in his exposition, and thus does not explicitly assert that the universal principle of right is analytic. Rather, he explicitly raises the flag of analyticity only at the next step, his assertion

---

[22] This point has been stressed by Mulholland, *Kant's System of Rights*, 171.

that the fulfilment of obligations under the laws of right, unlike those under ethical laws, may be coercively enforced. In fact, it is only in making *this* claim that Kant first explicitly uses the language of postulation as well as that of analyticity. First he says that 'reason says only that freedom **is** limited to those conditions in conformity with the idea of it and that it may also be actively limited by others; and it says this as a postulate that is incapable of further proof' (*MM*, DR, Introduction, §C, 6:231); next he says that 'there is connected with right by the principle of contradiction an authorization to coerce someone who infringes upon it' (*MM*, DR, Introduction, §D, 6:231); and finally he says that 'Right and authorization to use coercion therefore mean one and the same thing' (*MM*, DR, Introduction, §E, 6:232). None of these claims suggests that the content and scope of the principles of right are proven independently of the fundamental moral concept of freedom, nor that the binding force of the principles of right is independent of the binding force of the supreme principle of morality itself; they claim only that 'no further proof' is needed *for the right to enforce legal obligations coercively* because the concept of right and that of coercion are connected 'by the principle of contradiction' or 'mean one and the same thing'. Kant's claim about the analyticity of the principles of right, then, seems to come down to the assertion that the connection between right and coercion is analytic.

Is Kant right to make even this limited claim? His argument for this claim is as short as it is famous:

Resistance that counteracts the hindering of an effect promotes this effect and is consistent with it. Now whatever is wrong is a hindrance to freedom in accordance with universal laws. But coercion is a hindrance or resistance to freedom. Therefore, if a certain use of freedom is itself a hindrance to freedom in accordance with universal laws (i.e., wrong), coercion that is opposed to this (as a **hindering of a hindrance of freedom**) is consistent with freedom in accordance with universal laws, that is, it is right. (*MM*, DR, Introduction, §D, 6:231)

If one use of coercion would interfere with or destroy an exercise of freedom that is in accordance with universal law, then another use of coercion, designed to prevent the first instance of coercion, will preserve the possibility of the originally intended use of freedom, and in that regard is consistent with it and actually promotes it. Is this an analytic judgement, true by the law of (non-) contradiction? Kant supposes that it is, and most commentators have followed him without questioning his claim. However, the very language of Kant's argument seems to undermine any suggestion that the connection of coercion to right is merely analytic: Kant says not that a hindrance to a hindrance to freedom is simply identical with the lawful use of freedom, but rather that a hindrance to a hindrance of freedom 'promotes this effect' (*ist eine Beförderung dieser Wirkung*), or actually secures or produces freedom. This sounds like the language of *real causality*, not that of *logical identity*; but real causality is a synthetic connection, needing an explanation. In particular, in order to avoid the obvious objection that two wrongs simply *cannot* make a right, Kant seems to need to show that the use of coercion against coercion *can* cause the desired effect—namely, the preservation of freedom in accordance with a universal law; and to prove this would certainly be to prove a synthetic rather than an analytic proposition. For Kant to think otherwise would be for him to commit what he had diagnosed as one of the cardinal sins of philosophy as early as 1763, when he warned against confusing logical and real relations, for instance, confusing the logical relation of contradiction with the real opposition of forces[23] or the logical relation of ground and consequence with the real relation of cause and effect.[24] If he is not to make such a mistake, Kant needs to explain *how* the use of coercion can preserve freedom and *why* only it can do so. Thus, the claim about rights that Kant most explicitly says is analytic, at least within the 'Doctrine of Right', even if it is itself analytic, certainly depends upon a synthetic proposition and needs a deduction.

In fact, a variety of Kant's comments reveal that he at least tacitly recognizes that the deduction of the authorization to use coercion must ultimately contain both a theoretical and a moral element—that is, that it must show that there is a use of coercion that can cause a state of universal freedom in a way that respects the rights of all involved. The first comment about his argument that Kant makes shows that he recognizes that this purportedly analytic proposition needs the kind of proof he ordinarily gives to one kind of synthetic *a priori* proposition, even if not the kind needed by a causal proposition, and thus that it needs a theoretical deduction. He claims that the *concept* of right must be supplemented by a demonstration of the possibility of a *construction* of a sphere of right, analogous to the kind of construction of a mathematical object that is necessary to demonstrate the objective reality of a mathematical concept:

---

[23] See *Attempt to Introduce the Concept of Negative Magnitudes into Philosophy*, Ak. 2:165–204, at 2:171–2.
[24] *Negative Magnitudes*, Ak. 2:201–2.

The law of a reciprocal coercion necessarily in accord with the freedom of everyone under the principle of universal freedom is, as it were, the **construction** of that concept, that is, the presentation of it in pure intuition *a priori*, by analogy with presenting the possibility of bodies moving freely under the law of **equality of action and reaction.** In pure mathematics we cannot derive the properties of its objects immediately from concepts but can discover them only by constructing concepts. Similarly, it is not so much the **concept** of right as rather a fully reciprocal and equal coercion brought under a universal law and consistent with it, that makes the presentation of that concept possible. (*MM*, DR, Introduction, §E, 6:232–3)

Kant continues with the mathematical analogy by noting that, just as mathematical constructions are carried on by means of straight and curved lines whose relations to each other can be precisely determined, so a condition of right requires the determination of 'what belongs to each...with mathematical exactitude', a determination that indeed is not just analogous to mathematical construction, but that is actually based in one of the most fundamental forms of applied mathematics— namely, surveying. However, this is an anticipation of a point that, as we shall see in the next section, should only come into the final stage of Kant's deduction of the acquired right to property. What Kant needs here is rather a more general proof of the real consistency of a legal system of coercion with the preservation of universal freedom: only this would be the construction of a 'law of a reciprocal coercion necessarily in accord with the freedom of everyone', the proof of the objective reality of a concept of freedom that can be coercively enforced.

Such a construction cannot be purely mathematical (any more than the proof of the equality of action and reaction can be purely mathematical), because, by Kant's own account, freedom (just like action and reaction) is a kind of causality: the causality by means of which changes in our intentions can effect changes in our bodies and the world around them, and, in the case of the external use of freedom that is relevant to the concept of right, the causality to effect changes in the circumstances of other persons affected by our actions. As Kant himself had stated in the *Groundwork*, freedom, 'although it is not a property of the will in accordance with natural laws, is not for that reason lawless but must instead be a causality in accordance with immutable laws but of a special kind' (*G*, 4:446). The point is undeniable in the case of right, because the condition of right is defined causally from the outset, in so far as it is defined as a condition in which the actions or external use of the power of choice of each leaves all others an equal freedom; and coercion is equally clearly a causal concept, the concept of an action of one person that can cause a change in the intentions of another through the latter's representation of what has happened or will happen to him because of the action of the former.[25] Thus what Kant must demonstrate in order to prove the objective reality of the concept of right, even if, or more precisely, *just because* the concept of authorized coercion means the same thing as the concept of right, is that it is theoretically possible to use coercion in a way that can actually cause a universal condition of right.

Does Kant ever provide such a proof? Most commentators accept Kant's claim that the connection of right and the authorization to use coercion is analytic without recognizing that even on Kant's own account the objective reality of the subject concept in an analytic judgement needs a deduction. Mary Gregor, for instance, claims that the connection stands by itself because the concept of right requires the restriction of freedom to the condition of its accordance with universal law, and coercion just *is*, as Kant says, the 'active' institution of that restriction.[26] But such a claim still presupposes that it is possible for an action to count as both the coercion of another and yet as a preservation of freedom. Bernd Ludwig, by contrast, holds that Kant recognizes the need to prove the *moral* possibility of coercion, but then argues that this is not much of a challenge for Kant because, since an unprovoked use of coercion would not itself be an instance of the lawful exercise of freedom—that is, of the use of freedom in accordance with a universal law—it is itself outside the protected sphere of right, and another coercive act aimed against it therefore *could not* be incompatible with the lawful use of freedom.[27] But this argument, which in any case fails to address the issue of the theoretical possibility of coercion *promoting*, that is, causing freedom, assumes that the freedom of the *perpetrator* of an act of unprovoked coercion can simply be ignored as unlawful, thus that the freedom of the perpetrator does not have to be preserved at all. However, this is not compatible with Kant's idea that principles of right can preserve a truly *universal* condition of freedom. To show that this is possible, Kant needs to prove that, although an unprovoked and unanswered act of coercion would certainly destroy the freedom of its *victim*, the further use of

[25] This is particularly clear in Hume's famous account of how the 'constancy and fidelity' of a prisoner's executioners constitute just as reliable a natural force as 'the operation of the ax or wheel'; see *A Treatise of Human Nature*, bk. II, pt. III, sect. i.

[26] See Mary Gregor, *The Laws of Freedom: A Study of Kant's Method of Applying the Categorical Imperative in the* Metaphysik der Sitten (Oxford: Basil Blackwell, 1963), 43.

[27] Bernd Ludwig, *Kants Rechtslehre, Kant Forschungen*, ii (Hamburg: Felix Meiner, 1988), 97.

coercion as a hindrance to such coercion can itself preserve the freedom of *everyone*, including the would-be perpetrator as well as his victim. This requires a proof that coercion can actually be an effective cause of universal freedom.

To be sure, Kant does sometimes try to establish what is clearly the *moral* possibility of coercion for the sake of freedom, although by an argument different from the one that Ludwig suggests. Thus, in the Vigilantius lectures, he states the following:

The right to resist the other's freedom, or to coerce him, can only hold good insofar as my freedom is in conformity with universal freedom. The ground for that is as follows: the universal law of reason can alone be the determining ground of action, but this is the law of universal freedom; everyone has the right to promote this, even though he effects it by resisting the opposing freedom of another, in such a way that he seeks to prevent an obstruction, and thus to further an intent. For in the coercion there is presupposed the rectitude of the action, i.e., the quality that the agent's freedom accords with universal freedom. The other, however, obstructs the action by his freedom; the latter I can curtail and offer resistance to, insofar as this is in accordance with the laws of coercion; so *eo ipso* I must thereby obstruct universal freedom by the use of my own. From this it follows that I have a right to all actions that do not militate against the other's right, i.e., his moral freedom; for to that extent I can curtail his freedom, and he has no right to coerce me. (Vig., 27:525–6)

Several pages later, Kant again emphasizes that the 'right of coercion' depends on the condition that 'my action (the freedom of my action, that is) is directed according to universal law, and thus effects no abridgement of universal freedom' (Vig., 27:539). In these passages, Kant directs our attention not to the fact that the *perpetrator* of a crime would use his freedom lawlessly and thus step outside the protection of the law, but rather to the fact that one who would use coercion *against* such a crime must do so in accordance with universal freedom and thereby without militating against the right—that is, the moral freedom—of the other. However, this specification of the proper moral position for the use of coercion still seems to presuppose that in the proper circumstances the use of coercion can bring about the condition of universal freedom. So it looks as if it still needs to be shown that this can actually be done,—that is, that it is theoretically possible for one person to exercise coercion against another without depriving the latter of his right or his part in universal freedom.

In at least one case, Kant clearly does recognize that the possibility of a law depends upon the theoretical possibility of a causally effective use of coercion to achieve its intended end. Kant implies that a proposed use of coercion as a hindrance to coercion must be shown to be causally effective in his discussion of the so-called right of necessity. In the case of a shipwreck, he argues, one person has no right to push another off a floating piece of wreckage in order to save his own life, yet there can be no penal law against such an act because in such circumstances there can be no effective use of coercion as a hindrance to coercion: the threat of possible capture and punishment, no matter how severe, can hardly outweigh the certainty of drowning that faces the person willing to save his own life at the cost of another's, and therefore it cannot modify his behaviour. In this case 'a penal law.... could not have the effect intended' (*MM*, DR, Introduction, Appendix II, 6:235–6), and so while there is no right to self-preservation in such a case there can also be no right to punish such an attempt. Here Kant recognizes that there is a *factual* question whether an act of coercion against coercion could preserve the freedom it is intended to (in this case, the freedom of the unlucky soul pushed off the wreckage), and thus that here the proposition that the use of coercion *can* be a hindrance to a hindrance to freedom is synthetic, not analytic. Yet it is not clear from this that Kant recognizes that a general proof that a hindrance to a hindrance to freedom can preserve or promote freedom must actually be a proof of a causal and therefore synthetic proposition.

Perhaps in spite of his clear recognition that the objective reality of the concept of right needs a deduction, thus that the analysis of the concept of right must, like any analysis, presuppose a synthesis, Kant was distracted by his focus on the mathematical aspect of the *determination* of claims of right (what is necessary to make them precise) and thereby failed to provide the necessary argument that coercion can ever contribute to a condition of universal freedom. Yet it should not have been hard for him to provide the necessary argument or 'construction'. It could go something like this: while one person who would commit an unprovoked act of coercion against another would certainly deprive the latter of his use of freedom—for a short period, a long period, or permanently, depending upon the nature of the injury he would inflict—the judicial threat and even use of coercion against such a would-be perpetrator does not deprive him of his freedom in the same way that he would deprive his victim of his. When the laws and the sanctions for breaking them are known, it can be argued, anyone who chooses between conforming to them and breaking them can make his own choice freely. If he chooses to conform his behaviour to the law, he may have to give up his particular desire to do violence to another, but at least he does so freely; and, if he chooses to break the law, he does that freely too, and can then even be said to suffer the consequences of his action freely, though undoubtedly not gladly. The point is that while in either case there are ways in which his freedom is limited, he is not simply deprived of it in the way that the victim of a crime is. His freedom is limited—indeed, this is what it means for freedom to be limited to the conditions of its own universality, that is, compatibility with the freedom of others—but unlike his victim's it is not destroyed.[28]

If Kant needs an argument like this, then his connection of right and the authorization to use coercion not only needs but also can have a deduction that establishes the theoretical condition for the rightful use of coercion—namely, that it can actually bring about a condition of universal freedom, as well as specifying the moral constraints on the use of coercion. Perhaps Kant was never completely clear that the argument required for the deduction of the authorization to use coercion for the sake of right must have both a theoretical and a practical component. In the case of the postulate of practical reason regarding the acquired right to property, however, he does seem to recognize clearly that establishing the possibility of the rightful acquisition of property involves both a moral inference from the concept of freedom as well as theoretical and clearly synthetic premises about the conditions of the possibility of our experience as well. Let us now see how he supplies such a complex deduction while still calling the principle of acquired right a postulate.

## VI. THE DEDUCTION OF THE POSTULATE OF PRACTICAL REASON WITH REGARD TO ACQUIRED RIGHT

I now turn to Kant's theory of acquired right. Although Kant centres his account of property rights around a 'postulate of practical reason', he makes it abundantly clear that such a postulate rests upon synthetic propositions and therefore needs a deduction. He provides such a deduction in the form of an extended demonstration that the conditions for the possibility of a rightful acquisition of property can be satisfied in our

---

[28] This argument seems open to the objection, pressed upon me by Mark Timmons, that even the would-be perpetrator of a crime leaves his victim a choice, and thus freedom: 'Your money or your life!', after all, leaves the victim a choice. But here the criminal places his victim in a situation or forces upon him a choice that is not necessitated as a condition of preserving the universality of freedom, its maximal distribution to all consistent with the equal freedom of each, while the choice offered by a penal code—'Refrain from this crime or suffer the lawful penalties for committing it'—is a restriction of choice justified by the need to preserve the universality of freedom.

relations to physical objects and to each other in space and time. This argument is meant to show that it is possible to acquire property in a way consistent with the universal principle of right or the preservation of universal freedom in the external use of our power of choice and to show that the institution of the state is necessary for rightful property claims actually to be acquired. It seems clearer here than in the case of the authorization of coercion that Kant intends his argument to demonstrate both the moral and the theoretical possibility of rightful property claims, and in this case the two aspects of the deduction can even be associated with particular stages of Kant's exposition: in the first chapter of 'Private Right', 'How to Have Something External as One's Own' (*MM*, DR, 6:245), Kant explains the moral condition for the rightful acquisition of property, and in the second chapter, 'How to Acquire Something External' (*MM*, DR, 6:258), Kant establishes the theoretical conditions for the rightful acquisition of property, which must ultimately be realized in the state, before finally arguing that the establishment of the conditions for the rightful acquisition of property is actually a moral necessity.

Kant introduces the postulate of practical reason with regard to acquired rights or property in §6 of the 'Doctrine of Right', immediately following the contrast between the analyticity of the principle of empirical possession and the syntheticity of the principle of intelligible possession that was cited in Section IV. Kant's initial statement of the 'Postulate of practical reason with regard to rights' might initially appear to be simply a statement of a theoretical possibility: 'It is possible for me to have any external object of my choice as mine, that is, a maxim by which, if it were to become a law, an object of choice would **in itself** (objectively) have to **belong to no one** (*res nullius*) is contrary to right' (*MM*, DR, §6, 6:246).[29] However, that the possibility of property is to be established by showing that its denial would be contrary to right suggests that Kant intends to show that its assertion is compatible with right, so what is ultimately to be proved seems to include the moral as well as the theoretical possibility of property. The moral side of the claim seems predominant a page or two later when Kant states that the postulate of practical reason with regard to rights is 'that it is a duty of right to act towards others so that what is external (usable) could also become someone's'

---

[29] I translate Kant's term *rechtswidrig* as 'contrary to right' rather than 'contrary to rights', as Gregor does (*Practical Philosophy*, 405); I see no syntactical basis for her use of the plural, and it seems misleading to me, as it suggests that the denial of the possibility of acquiring property would be contradictory to particular and therefore already established rights, which is tautologous, rather than contrary to the principle of right, which is what Kant's ensuing argument clearly intends to establish.

(*MM*, DR, §6, 6:252); indeed, the second formulation of the postulate appears to tells us it is a duty of right to establish claims to property, while the first appears to tell us it is a duty of right to establish claims to property, while the first appears to tells us only that such claims are morally permissible. In fact, Kant's complete deduction of the postulate attempts to prove both of these claims as well as to prove the theoretical possibility of the rightful acquisition of property. First, Kant will show under what conditions the acquisition of property can be compatible with the principle of universal freedom—this is the establishment of what Kant calls a 'permissive law of practical reason' (*MM*, DR, §6, 6:247).[30] Then, Kant demonstrates the theoretical possibility of the rightful acquisition of property. Finally, Kant will argue that we actually have a duty to establish determinate property claims, which can only be done by means of the state or civil condition, when the particular empirical circumstances of our existence are such that we cannot otherwise avoid conflict with other people—under these circumstances the establishment of property rights is a moral necessity and not merely a moral and theoretical possibility. Kant's complete account of the application of the universal principle of right to the actual circumstances of human existence thus includes both a permissive law and a duty concerning property. Given this elaborate argument, Kant's designation of the principle of property as a postulate can hardly be meant to obviate the need for a deduction of it from the general principle of right and through that from the supreme principle of morality.

Yet in calling the principle of property a postulate, Kant might seem to imply that the theoretical possibility of property cannot be proved except by inference from its moral necessity. Thus, in introducing the second statement of the postulate just quoted, he writes that 'The possibility of this kind of possession, and so the deduction of the concept of non-empirical possession, is based' upon this postulate (*MM*, DR, §6, 6:252). Here he seems to mean that the theoretical possibility of the acquisition of property is problematic and can be inferred from the moral necessity of acquired right only by means of an 'ought-implies-can' argument: 'There is, however, no way of proving of itself the possibility of nonphysical possession or of having any insight into it (just because it is a rational concept for which no corresponding intuition can be given); its possibility is instead an immediate consequence of the postulate referred to' (*MM*, DR, §6, 6:252). This is clearly an echo of Kant's central

---

[30] This passage has been moved from §2 to §6 by Ludwig and Gregor, and thus actually succeeds the first formulation of the postulate at 6:250.

argument that the reality of the freedom of the will can be inferred only from our awareness of the binding force of the Categorical Imperative. Kant reiterates the claim several pages later when he states that 'we cannot see how intelligible possession is possible and so how it is possible for something external to be mine or yours, but must infer it from the postulate of practical reason' (*MM*, DR, §7, 6:255). These passages suggest that we need to be precise in how we characterize the second stage of Kant's extended argument: perhaps we should say that in this stage Kant expounds the conditions that make it possible to acquire property consistently with the general principle of right given the fundamental conditions of actual human existence—namely, in the spatiotemporal circumstances of life on the surface of a naturally undivided sphere—without attempting to prove that such conditions can actually be fulfilled otherwise than by means of the practical certainty provided by the moral possibility and indeed necessity of the acquisition of property. It should still seem reasonable to characterize this part of Kant's argument as a deduction of the theoretical rather than the moral possibility of property.

It cost Kant a great deal of effort to sort out the stages of his argument, and perhaps he never signposted them for us as clearly as we would have liked. Yet I believe it is ultimately possible to discern the outlines of the kind of complex deduction that has been described in the first seventeen sections of 'Private Right'. This argument consists of four main steps, the first two focusing on the moral possibility of property, the third on the conditions that are necessary for satisfying the moral constraints on property given the general structure of our physical circumstances, and the fourth showing that it is actually a moral necessity to establish determinate property rights in the particular empirical circumstances of our existence, which include unavoidable contact with other people. At the first stage of this deduction, Kant argues that there can be no objection from the side of *objects* to our acquisition of property rights in them. Second, he argues that it is possible for all who might use any object to agree to the assignment of the right to it to a particular person, via a *general will* or multilateral agreement to assign unilateral rights to the object, and that only the consent of the general will to individual rights to property can make those individual rights compatible with universal freedom. Third, he argues that there is actually a way for an individual to acquire a right to an object in space and time as we experience them, either through first acquisition of a previously unowned object or through voluntary transfer of an already owned object from its previous owner to a new one, consistent with the general terms for individual ownership laid down by the general will. Finally, he argues that, in the actual circumstances of our existence, where contact and potential conflict with others cannot be avoided, the rightful acquisition of property can take place only within a civil condition subject to a rule of law that can both make property claims determinate and enforce them, or at least in anticipation of such a state—only a person willing to submit to the rule of a state can rightfully claim property and forcibly require others to recognize his claim.

I will hardly have room here to analyse convincingly all the details of this argument, let alone consider its normative implications.[31] I will simply try to provide some of the evidence for the key steps in Kant's argument that can be found in the published text as well as in Kant's preparatory notes, which never give a consecutive statement of Kant's whole argument but sometimes illuminate its individual steps.[32]

Following his initial statement of the postulate in §6, Kant takes the first step of his argument by arguing that it would be a contradiction in practical reason itself to deny ourselves the use of objects: 'freedom would be depriving itself of the use of its choice with regard to an object of choice, by putting **usable** objects beyond any possibility of being **used**; in other words, it would annihilate them in a practical respect and make them into *res nullius*' (*MM*, DR, §6, 6:246). This presupposes the canon of rationality that underlies all of Kant's claims about contradictions in willing, the presupposition that if it is rational to will an end then it must also be rational to will the means (see *G*, 4:417). But, just as that principle must always be restricted by the permissibility of using an object in question as a means—the restriction most obviously exemplified in Kant's second formulation of the Categorical Imperative as the requirement that we always be able to treat humanity as an end and never merely as a means (*G*, 5:429)—so here too the argument that it would be irrational to deny ourselves the use of something that could be useful as a means must be supplemented by the premiss that it is permis-

---

[31] I have tried to provide some suggestions in that direction in 'Kantian Foundations for Liberalism', *Jahrbuch für Recht und Ethik*, 5 (1997), 121–40, and 'Life, Liberty and Property: Rawls and the Reconstruction of Kant's Political Philosophy', *Recht, Staat und Völkerrecht bei Immanuel Kant*, eds. Dieter Hüning and Burkhard Tuschling (Berlin: Duncker & Humblot, 1998), 273–91, repr. as chs. 7 and 8, respectively, of my *Kant on Freedom, Law, and Happiness*.

[32] Among commentators I have read, Leslie Mulholland, I believe, comes closest to appreciating the full complexity of Kant's complete deduction of acquired right; see *Kant's System of Rights*, chs. 8 and 9. But though I have learned more from Mulholland than from any other commentator, I think the reconstruction I will give makes it easier to see the outlines of Kant's argument than Mulholland's does. However, I do not pretend to engage Mulholland here on the many difficulties he finds in the details of Kant's argument.

sible to treat an external object merely as a means. Kant recognizes the need for this additional assumption in one of his notes:

That one person should restrict another in the use of external objects...to the limits of their physical possession would contradict the use of freedom in consensus with the freedom of others in accordance with universal laws and hence with the rights of mankind in general, for in that case freedom in accordance with laws of freedom would make itself dependent upon objects, which would presuppose either the representation of an obligation toward objects (just as if they also had rights) or a principle that no external object should be mine or yours, either of which, as a principle robbing freedom of its use, is self-contradictory. Thus the principle of freedom in the idea of a collective and united power of choice of itself (*a priori*) extends rightful possession beyond the limits of physical possession. (*Loses Blatt Erdmann*, 33, 23:288)

The moral possibility of property rights rests, in the first instance, on the assumptions that it would be irrational to deny ourselves the use of objects that can be used as means to our ends and that, at least in the case of physical objects, the objects themselves have no rights, or we have no obligations to them, that would block this use.[33] Kant assumes this is obvious in the case of non-human physical objects (although contemporary advocates of animals' rights might not take it to be obvious). In the case of rights against other persons in the form of contracts for specific performances and long-term relations of servitude, the point of Kant's further arguments is to show that these rights are limited but not excluded by the humanity of those who are obligated, because they can be instituted in ways that do not reduce the obligees to mere means who are not also ends. Kant's argument also makes the major assumption that the usefulness of objects presupposes long-term individual control or intelligible possession of them, which he never spells out.[34]

The second main step of Kant's argument, already hinted at in the last sentence of the last quote, is that, since any property right restricts the freedom of others who might also have been able to use the object in question, such a right can be rightfully acquired only under conditions in which all could freely and rationally agree to the individual acquisition of the right. Kant expresses this condition in the 'Doctrine of Right' by

---

[33] See also Mulholland, *Kant's System of Rights*, 250.

[34] Mulholland argues that Kant may not have been attempting to prove that *individual* possession of property is necessary, since some forms of common possession, such as by nomadic bands, seem to work perfectly well and to be compatible with Kant's general claim that it would be irrational to deny ourselves the use of objects as far as the objects are concerned; see *Kant's System of Rights*, 275. But the whole issue of whether property rights must be private certainly needs more of an airing than Kant gives it.

arguing that, since 'a unilateral will cannot serve as a coercive law for everyone with regard to possession that is external and therefore contingent, since that would infringe upon freedom in accordance with universal laws', it 'is only a will putting everyone under obligation, hence only a collective general (common) and powerful will, that can provide everyone this assurance' (*MM*, DR, §8, 6:256). But this almost immediately conflates the moral condition that others be able to agree to the property right with the theoretical condition that there must be a means to enforce this collective agreement, which is part of the deduction of the empirical conditions of the possibility of property that belongs only later in Kant's argument. The continuation of Kant's note just cited may clarify his statement of the condition for the moral possibility of property, although it too quickly moves on to the theoretical condition as well:

The possibility of such a principle, however, lies in the presupposition that with regard to corporeal things outside us the free power of choice of all must be considered as united and indeed as originally so, without a juridical [*rechtlich*] act, and indeed because it is related to a possession which is original but communal, in which the possession of each...cannot be determined except in accordance with the idea of the consensus of all with a possible aggregate choice. The possibility of merely rightful possession is, as given *a priori*, the rightful determination of it, but is not possible through the individual choice of each, but only through external positive laws, thus only in the civil condition. (*Loses Blatt Erdmann*, 33, 23:288)

This note, however, clearly states the moral condition by itself:

With regard to the possession of a thing external to me I cannot, according to the laws of freedom, exercise any coercion against others unless all others to whom I might stand in this relation can agree with me about it, i.e., through the will of all of them united with my own, for in that case I coerce them through their own wills in accordance with laws of freedom. For all, the concept of a right is a concept of reason which through the idea of a united will grounds all external mine and yours. (*Loses Blatt Erdmann*, 6, 23:277–8)

This passage also makes the point clearly:

An exclusion of all others through my own power of choice alone, however, is a categorical imperative for others to consider such objects as belonging to me. Thus such an imperative actually exists, as it were an obligation can be laid upon the objects to obey only my will, and freedom in regard to corporeal things is a ground of external coercive laws and indeed without a *factum iniustum* [doing an injustice] to others.... But this law is a law of the communal [*gemeinschaftlichen*] power of choice for without this it would rob itself of the use of external things.—Thus it is the communal will together with the communal original possession that makes external things in whose possession I am by nature into my own. (*Loses Blatt Erdmann,* 32, 23:286–7)

Since any property right is a restriction of the freedom of others, and indeed one that may ultimately be coercively enforced, it cannot be right unless it is one that others could freely agree to. This is the moral condition that property rights must be compatible with the universality of freedom in its external use, or the condition that the so-called postulate of acquired right must itself be derivable from the general principle of right.

The next stage of Kant's argument is what we may consider the deduction of the theoretical possibility of property, the explanation of 'How to acquire something external' in a way that is consistent not only with the moral requirements of the general principle of right but also with the physical conditions of our existence. Kant begins the second chapter of 'Private Right' with a recapitulation of the two distinct steps in the first part of his deduction:

The principle of external acquisition is as follows: that is mine which I bring under my **control** (in accordance with the law of outer **freedom**); which, as an object of my choice, is something that I have the capacity to use (in accordance with the postulate of practical reason); and which, finally, I **will** to be mine (in conformity with the idea of a possible united **will**). (*MM,* DR, §10, 6:258)

The first two parenthetical clauses express what I have been calling the first stage of Kant's moral deduction, and the last expresses the second. Kant then embarks upon the theoretical portion of his deduction. This is essentially the following argument, appealing to the most general features of the spatiotemporal conditions of human existence: all rightful possession of property must, given the temporal nature of our experience, originate in a rightful act of acquisition of the property. Such an act could be either a rightful transfer of the property from one owner to another or a rightful first appropriation of the property. There would be an infinite regress if only the former were possible, so the latter must also be possible. But, since the spherical surface of the earth is not naturally divided into lots (this expresses the spatial condition of our experience (see *MM,* DR, §13, 6:262)), any original appropriation of land (the 'substance' which is the basis for all movable property as 'accidents' (see *MM,* DR, §12, 6:261)) must be an individual appropriation from a previously undivided common. Yet if such an appropriation is to confer a rightful title, it must begin from a condition of rightful ownership, so it must be conceived of as a transfer of an original rightful possession of the undivided commons to a rightful possession of a divided portion of the whole. Kant does not conceive of this transfer from the undivided whole as a historical event. 'Original possession in common is, rather, a practical rational concept which contains *a priori* the principle in accordance with which alone people can use a place on the earth in accordance with principles of right' (*MM*, DR, §13, 6:262). That is, to ask whether a people as a whole that possessed the land as a whole could freely and rationally agree to a particular system for the distribution of individual property rights is a test of the rightfulness of such a system, which is required by both the moral condition set by the general principle of right and the theoretical condition set by the physical circumstances of our existence.

In his notes, Kant clearly labels this argument a 'Deduction of the right to an original appropriation of the land'. Here is a compact version of it:

It is grounded on a *factum* which is original, i.e., not derived from any rightful act, namely the original community in the land.

The original appropriation of the land must be independent [*eigenmächtig*], for if it were grounded on the approval [*Einwilligung*] of others it would be derived.

However, the right of the appropriator cannot stand in an immediate relation to things (here, to the land), for to the right there corresponds **immediately** the obligation of others; but things cannot be made to have obligations. Thus the appropriation of a piece of land is possible only through a **rightful act**, i.e., it is possible not through one whereby the appropriator is immediately connected to the land, but only through one whereby the appropriator is **mediately** connected to the land, namely by means of the determination of the will of one person to oblige every other negatively in accordance with universal laws to refrain from the use of a certain piece of land, which restraint is possible only in accordance with universal laws of freedom (i.e., in accordance with laws of right ... ).

In this respect, however, the appropriator can only take possession of a piece of land in order to have it as his own through his private choice, i.e., independently, by means of a rightful act, for otherwise he would place an obligation on everyone through his own merely unilateral will, consequently only as the consequence of a possession in which he finds himself originally (prior to any rightful act), and this also as a common possession by all who could make claim to the same land, i.e., a possession that can unite all possible possession on the land of the earth through one will, which contains an original community (*communio originaria*) of the entire land of the earth, on which alone the act of first taking possession is grounded. (*Loses Blatt Erdmann*, 56, 23:316)

Kant may seem to contradict himself, saying first that original possession cannot be a rightful act and then that it must be a rightful act of taking a piece of property out of the undivided commons with the consent of all or through the will of all. But the contradiction can be avoided if we interpret him to mean that, although historically the initial appropriation of property may or even must precede the organization of any public entity to license it, morally such an appropriation can create a right only if it is possible to see the individual possession of property as one that could be agreed to through a common or united will by all who could also claim it. It is through such a rational idea that both the theoretical and the moral constraints on the acquisition of property can be satisfied.

That both moral and historical, thus theoretical, constraints must be satisfied in the deduction of the possibility of property is also evident in the final stage of Kant's argument, in which he argues that historically property must be acquired in the state of nature and thus prior to the existence of the civil condition in the form of an organized juridical system, because securing the possession of property is the reason for the creation of a civil entity, yet that, because only the expression of the common will through a juridical entity can make the possession of property legitimate as well as secure, the acquisition of property in the state of nature must be 'provisional' and can only be rendered 'conclusive' through the creation of a civil state (*MM*, DR, §15, 6:264). Kant's argument for this final claim depends on both moral and theoretical considerations, and leads to the final, moral conclusion of 'Private Right', that we actually have a duty to leave the state of nature and enter the civil condition. The moral argument is that, since the '**rational title**' of acquisition can lie only in the idea of a will of all united *a priori*', and 'the condition in which the will of all is actually united for giving law is the civil condition', therefore 'something external can be **originally** acquired only in conformity with the idea of a civil condition, that is, with a view to its being brought about' (*MM*, DR, §15, 6:264). The theoretical argument, however, is that the state is what we might think of as both a mathematical and a psychological condition of the possibility of secure property claims. The mathematical argument is that, since property claims extend beyond the body of the individual, yet beyond the body of the individual there are no other naturally defined boundaries, the state is necessary to introduce determinate boundaries between claims; thus the surveying of boundaries and the recording of deeds to property are among the most basic functions of the state. The psychological argument is that, since no one can reasonably expect to enjoy a claim to property unless others are also allowed to do so as well, but also that no one can reasonably be expected to confine his claims to his own property unless others can also be expected to do so, a system for the public enforcement of the boundaries of properties claims is as necessary as a public system for defining them. Thus the office of sheriff is as basic to the state as is that of the recorder of deeds.

Kant tends to stress the second of these two theoretical conditions in the published text of the 'Doctrine of Right', as when he writes that 'it is only a will putting everyone under obligation, hence only a collective general (common) and powerful will, that can provide everyone this assurance' (*MM*, DR, §8, 6:256). Again, however, passages in his notes clearly reveal his fuller argument. A passage like this one expresses the role of the state in creating determinate boundaries between property claims: a person 'rightfully possesses a piece of land that he does not occupy . . . not through his own power of choice . . . only insofar as he can necessitate others to unite with him into a common will in order to draw the boundaries for each' (*Loses Blatt Erdmann*, 32, 23:285). And one like this explicitly refers to both the surveying and the enforcement functions of the state:

Every human being has an innate right to be some place on the earth, for his existence is not a *factum* [deed] and therefore not *iniustum* [unjust]. He also has the right to be in several places at once *incorporealiter* if he has specified them for his use, though not through his own will alone. But since every one else also has this right, the *prior occupans* has the provisory right to coerce each who would hinder him to enter into a contract to determine the boundaries of the permissible possession and to use force against the refusal [to accept them]. (*Loses Blatt Erdmann*, 10, 23:279–80)

This passage also points to the moral aspects of Kant's thesis that conclusive possession of property can exist only in a civil condition. On the one hand, Kant holds that, since it is both morally and theoretically possible to acquire property consistent with the universal principle of right, thus that property can be claimed consistently with universal freedom, everyone has a right to claim property, and therefore has a right to coerce others into joining with him to form a state in order to establish property rights. At the same time, since property rights are coercive, they can be rightful only if they are claimed with an eye to the creation of a civil condition. 'Therefore something external can be **originally** acquired only in conformity with the idea of a civil condition, that is, with a view to it and to its being brought about, but prior to its realization (for otherwise acquisition would be derived)' (*MM*, DR, §15, 6:264). But, since the psychological and physical conditions of our existence are such that we inevitably will attempt to claim property rights in circumstances where that will bring us into conflict with others, we also have a *duty* to claim such rights with an eye to the civil condition and in turn to bring about that civil condition. Thus Kant concludes his exposition of 'Private Right' and makes the transition to 'Public Right', his deduction of the conditions necessary for the rightful existence of the state, by means of a complement to the postulate of acquired right— namely, 'the postulate of public right':

From private right in the state of nature there proceeds the postulate of public right: when you cannot avoid living side by side with all others, you ought to leave the state of nature and proceed with them into a rightful condition, that is, a condition of distributive justice.—The ground of this postulate can be developed analytically from the concept of **right** in external relations, in contrast with **violence**. (*MM*, DR, §42, 6:307)

This passage can also stand as one last reminder that Kant cannot mean postulates with regard to right to be principles that stand independently of any deduction. On the contrary, the postulate of public right proceeds from the postulate of private right, just as the postulate of private right has proceeded, by what turns out to be a complex deduction involving both moral and theoretical arguments, from the universal principle of right, which itself proceeds from the supreme moral principle of the absolute value of freedom in its external as well as its internal use.

To sum up this long argument, as has recently been emphasized, there are certainly contexts in which Kant calls some principles of right 'analytic' and contexts in which he calls some of them 'postulates'. But we have to be careful about what he means, since he uses each of these terms in a variety of ways. Further, Kant's general philosophy makes it clear that both analytic propositions and postulates ultimately need a deduction of the objective reality of their key concepts. Finally, Kant's philosophy of right, as expounded in both the 'Doctrine of Right' in the published *Metaphysics of Morals* as well as in the many preparatory notes for this work that have come down to us, clearly recognizes the need for such deductions and at least in the case of the principles of private right provides an extensive exposition of such a deduction. Kant's deduction of the objective reality of a concept of right that authorizes its coercive enforcement may be sidetracked by his misleading comparison of such a deduction with a mathematical construction, but there can be no mistaking the key steps by which he expounds the conditions of the possibility of the right to acquire property, even though he calls the principle of such a right a 'postulate'. As in the less complete argument that Kant gives in the case of the authorization to use coercion, the deduction of acquired right involves both moral and theoretical components. The fundamental argumentative strategy of Kant's philosophy of right is thus to argue that the key principles of right, even if for various reasons they are called analytic and designated as postulates, are consistent with and required by the most basic moral and theoretical conditions of human existence.

# 10

# Kant's System of Duties

## 1. A SYSTEM OF DUTIES?

The idea of systematicity is clearly central to Kant's moral philosophy. His culminating formulation of the categorical imperative in the *Groundwork for the Metaphysics of Morals* is that 'All maxims from one's own lawgiving are to harmonize with a possible realm of ends, as with a realm of nature' (*G*, 4:436), where a 'realm' is in turn understood as 'a systematic union of various rational beings through common laws' and a 'realm of ends' more specifically as 'a whole of all ends in systematic connection (a whole both of rational beings as ends in themselves and of the ends of his own that each may set himself' (*G*, 4:433).[1] This adds to the requirement that we treat ourselves and all other rational beings possibly affected by our actions—that is, as far as we know, all but only all other human beings—as equal members of a whole, which is expressed in Kant's formulation of the categorical imperative as the requirement to 'So act that you use humanity, whether in your own person or in the person of any other, always at the same time as an end, never merely as a means' (*G*, 4:439), the further requirement that we regard a systematic connection or union of the particular ends set by such

---

[1] Citations in Kant's works are located by volume and page number of the Akademie edition, i.e. *Kant's gesammelte Schriften*, edited by the Royal Prussian (later German, then Berlin–Brandenburg) Academy of Sciences (Berlin: Georg Reimer, later Walter de Gruyter & Co., 1900– ). Translations from Kant's writings in practical philosophy are taken from Immanuel Kant, *Practical Philosophy*, ed. trans. Mary J. Gregor (Cambridge: Cambridge University Press, 1996), although occasionally modified (here I have translated *Reich* as 'realm' rather than 'kingdom'). Translations from the *Critique of Pure Reason* are from the edition by Paul Guyer and Allen W. Wood (Cambridge: Cambridge University Press, 1998), and are located by the pagination of the first (A) and second (B) editions rather than by Akademie pagination. Translations from Kant's lectures are from Immanuel Kant, *Lectures on Ethics*, ed. Peter Heath and J. B. Schneewind (Cambridge: Cambridge University Press, 1997). The quotation from the First Introduction to the *Critique of the Power of Judgment* is from Immanuel Kant, *Critique of the Power of Judgment*, ed. Paul Guyer, trans. Paul Guyer and Eric Matthews (Cambridge: Cambridge University Press, 2000).

human beings in the exercise of their humanity as the mandatory object of our actions.[2] But Kant also indicates that it is not just the objects of our duties—that is, the domain of agents and their ends towards whom we have duties—that must be dealt with systematically; he also clearly supposes that our duties themselves must comprise a system. The very first lines of the Preface to the 'Doctrine of Virtue' of the *Metaphysics of Morals* raise the question of whether our duties comprise a system:

A **philosophy** of any subject (a system of rational cognition from concepts) requires a system of **pure rational** concepts independent of any conditions of intuition, that is, a **metaphysics**.—The only question is whether every **practical** philosophy, as a doctrine of duties, and so too the **doctrine of virtue** (ethics), also needs **metaphysical first principles**, so that it can be set forth as a genuine science (systematically) and not merely as an aggregate of precepts sought out one by one (fragmentarily). (*MM*, DV, Preface, 6:375).

This question is obviously rhetorical, to be answered in the affirmative by the text that follows; and Kant accordingly starts the Introduction to the 'Doctrine of Virtue' with the statement that 'The system of the doctrine of duties in general is now divided into the system of the **doctrine of right** (*ius*), which deals with duties that can be given by external laws, and the system of the **doctrine of virtue** (*Ethica*), which treats of duties that cannot be so given' (*MM*, DV, Introduction, 6:379). This implies that the duties of right, that is, those duties that may be coercively enforced through political and juridical institutions, comprise a system; that those of our obligations which, for whatever reason, cannot be so enforced, also comprise a system; and that those two systems of duties in turn comprise a single system. But just what constraint is Kant placing upon moral philosophy when he assumes that each of its two main parts must comprise a system and that those two parts together must also comprise a system? Kant does not expli-

---

[2] Kant defines 'rational nature' or 'humanity' as the capacity to set ends in both the *Groundwork* and the 'Doctrine of Virtue' of the *Metaphysics of Morals*: 'Rational nature is distinguished from the rest of nature by this, that it sets itself an end' (*G*, 4:437); 'The capacity to set oneself an end—any end whatsoever—is what characterizes humanity (as distinguished from animality)' (*MM*, DV, Introduction, VIII, 6:392; see also 6:387). For the argument that treating humanity as end in itself naturally involves promoting the particular ends chosen in the exercise of humanity, as expressions of that humanity and therefore entitled to the respect which is due to humanity itself, see my 'Ends of Reason and Ends of Nature: The Place of Teleology in Kant's Ethics', *Journal of Value Inquiry*, 36 (2002), 161–86; this volume, Ch. 8.

citly address this question, and neither have the leading commentators on his moral philosophy.[3] I propose to do so here.

## 2. KANT'S CONCEPT OF A SYSTEM

Kant's most explicit discussion of the concept of a system occurs in the first section of the Appendix to the Transcendental Dialectic in the *Critique of Pure Reason*, entitled 'On the Regulative Use of the Ideas of Pure Reason' (*CPuR*, A 642–68/B 670–96). This text and associated passages suggest that Kant's conception of a system of concepts comprises three requirements, and thus that we should expect a system of duties to satisfy these three requirements as well. The first and most obvious requirement, virtually identical with the basic condition of philosophical or scientific knowledge itself, is that all of the subsidiary members of a system of concepts or laws be derivable from a single fundamental principle or fundamental set of principles, although preferably the former. Kant unequivocally states the requirement that the members of a system be derivable from a single principle at the outset of the Appendix: 'If we survey the cognitions of our understanding in their entire range, then we find that what reason quite uniquely prescribes and seeks to bring about concerning it is the **systematic** in cognition, i.e., its interconnection based on one principle' (*CPuR*, A 645/B 673). Several subsequent statements leave open the possibility that a system may not be derivable from a single principle, but from several: thus he writes that 'a certain systematic unity of all possible empirical concepts must be sought insofar as they can be derived from higher and more general ones', and that while this is a 'logical principle, without which there could be no use of reason... that such unanimity is to be encountered even in nature is something the philosophers presuppose... It is thereby said that the nature of things themselves offers material for the unity of reason' (*CPuR*, A 652/B 680; see also A 648/B 676); in

---

[3] Mary J. Gregor, in her still indispensable commentary on the *Metaphysics of Morals*, *Laws of Freedom: A Study of Kant's Method of Applying the Categorical Imperative in the Metaphysik der Sitten* (Oxford: Basil Blackwell), repeatedly uses the phrases 'system of duties' (e.g. pp. 64, 69, 85) and 'a system of pure rational ends,' stating that the latter 'is the implicit theme of the work and dominates Kant's derivation of ethics as a system of duties' (p. 91), but does not provide any analysis of the concept of a system of duties. Leslie A. Mulholland entitles his study of Kant's political philosophy and its foundation in his moral philosophy *Kant's System of Rights* (New York: Columbia University Press, 1990), but likewise provides no explicit analysis of the concept of a system of rights, that is to say, coercively enforceable duties.

other words, when we systematize our body of empirical concepts or laws of nature, we cannot suppose that the fundamental concept or principle from which we derive them is just a subjective convenience or an intersubjective convention, but must assume that it is itself true and the source of the truth of what is derived from it. Presumably a similar requirement would hold in the case of a system of moral principles. In the moral case, further, Kant clearly presupposes that there is a single fundamental principle from which all subsidiary principles are to be derived, not a group of fundamental principles. So the first constraint on a system of duties is surely that all of our duties be derivable from a single fundamental and objectively valid principle of morality.

Of course, Kant is also explicit that although this fundamental principle must be entirely *a priori*, the particular subsidiary duties for human beings to which it gives rise will also depend on certain basic but empirical facts about such beings:

Just as there must be principles in a metaphysics of nature for applying those highest universal principles of a nature in general to objects of experience, a metaphysics of morals cannot dispense with principles of application, and we shall often have to take as our object the particular **nature** of human beings, which is cognized only by experience, in order to **show** in it what can be inferred from universal moral principles. (*MM*, Introduction, I, 6:216–17)

The difference between a *groundwork for the metaphysics of morals* and the *metaphysics of morals* itself is precisely that while the former appeals only to *a priori* grounds to derive the fundamental principle of morality, the latter adduces certain basic but empirical—although also incontrovertible—facts about human nature to derive from that general principle the concrete duties of human beings.[4]

The second requirement for systematicity that Kant lays down is perhaps already implicit in his use of the term 'interconnection' (*Zusammenhang*) in his exposition of the first, but is made explicit when he follows that statement with the further claim that 'This unity of reason always presupposes an idea, namely that of the form of a whole of cognition, which precedes the determinate cognition of the parts and

---

[4] Ottfried Höffe in particular has stressed the proper role of key empirical assumptions in the systematic derivation of duties from the fundamental principle of morality; see 'Der moralische Begriff des Rechts', in his *'Königliche Völker': Zu Kants kosmopolitischer Rechts-und Friedenstheorie* (Frankfurt am Main: Suhrkamp, 2001), 119–46, esp. 125–32. Höffe argues that Kant's duties are 'synthetic but non-pure *a priori*' (p. 129); that concept in turn goes back to Konrad Cramer, *Nicht-reine synthetische Urteile a priori. Ein Problem der Transzendentalphilosophie Immanuel Kants* (Heidelberg: Carl Winter Universitätsverlag, 1985).

contains the conditions for determining *a priori* the place of each part and its relation to the others' (*CPuR*, A 645/B 673). The same thought is suggested three pages later when Kant states that 'systematic unity or the unity of reason' creates 'unanimity (*Einhelligkeit*) among its various rules under one principle (the systematic) and thereby interconnection, so far as this can be done' (A 648/B 676). These statements require that the relations among the members of a genuine system of concepts or rules be fully determinate, and that they be determined on the basis of the *a priori* principle that is the foundation of the system. In the case of a system of duties, I propose, this means that the fundamental principle of morality on which the system is based must give rise to determinate relations of priority, providing an *a priori* basis for the resolution of apparent conflicts among duties. Finding an adequate *a priori* basis for the resolution of such conflicts is the fundamental challenge for an interpretation of Kant's system of duties that has not been taken up by previous commentators, but that will be addressed in this paper.[5]

In the Appendix to the Transcendental Dialectic in the *Critique of Pure Reason*, these first two requirements for systematicity are expressed as the requirements of 'homogeneity' and 'affinity'. The first of these requires '**sameness of kind** in the manifold under higher genera', that is, the derivation of more concrete principles from more abstract ones, and ultimately the derivation of all from the most fundamental principle, ideally at least a single fundamental principle; the second requires a hierarchical order among the members of the system, or 'a continuous transition from every species to every other through a graduated increase of varieties' (*CPuR*, A 657–8/B 685–6). There Kant also includes a third requirement of systematicity, what he calls 'specification' or 'a principle of the **variety** of what is the same in kind under lower species' (A 657/B 685). This requires that the system include a level of subspecies of its concepts approximating although not identical to the 'actual **infinity**' of particular objects to which the system as a whole is to apply (A 656/B 684). In the case of a system of duties, this could be understood as the requirement that the system should ideally include concrete principles of duty for every morally significant situation or context of action that can

---

[5] I do not of course mean that no previous commentators have addressed the issue of conflicts of duties in Kant; Barbara Herman recurs to it repeatedly in her *The Practice of Moral Judgment* (Cambridge, Mass.: Harvard University Press, 1993), esp. ch. 8, 'Obligation and Performance', pp. 159–83, and Höffe discusses it in 'Universalistische Ethik und Urteilskraft', in *'Königliche Völker'*, ch. 2, pp. 63–82, esp. pp. 82–7 ('Prinzipienkonflikte'). What I mean is that this issue has not been considered as part of a systematic discussion of Kant's conception of a system of duties.

be encountered in human life. Of course, Kant stresses that such completeness is only a regulative ideal in the case of a system of theoretical cognition, and presumably he would hold the same view in the case of a system of moral duties.

In his other chief discussion of the ideal of systematicity, in the two versions of the Introduction to the *Critique of the Power of Judgment*, Kant offers what we might consider an alternative version of the third requirement of systematicity, namely a general requirement that a system apply to all the individual objects in its domain. In the first draft of the Introduction to the third *Critique*, he writes:

> We have seen in the critique of pure reason that the whole of nature as the totality of all objects of experience constitutes a system in accordance with transcendental laws...For that very reason, experience, in accordance with general as well as particular laws...must also constitute (in the idea) a system of possible empirical cognitions. For that is required by the unity of nature, in accordance with a principle of the thoroughgoing connection of everything contained in the totality of all appearances. To this extent experience in general in accordance with transcendental laws of the understanding is to be regarded as a system and not as a mere aggregate. (FI, 20:208–9)

Just as the second condition for systematicity requires determinate relations among all of the concepts, rules, or laws of the system, founded upon the *a priori* principle of the system, this version of the third condition can be seen as requiring that the system specify determinate relations among all the *objects* of the system, whether those be movable bodies, as in the case of the system of natural laws, or human agents, as in the case of the system of duties. A system of duties must therefore not only fix determinate relations among the various types of duties that we have, but must also specify our obligations toward every other human being who could possibly be affected by our own choices of maxims or actions. Again, of course, as Kant's parenthetical expression 'in the idea' implies, such completeness will only be a regulative ideal: no one is ever actually in a position to know who all the others who may be affected by his choice of maxims or actions are, nor what all the consequences of his choices for all those others will actually be. But a genuine system of duties must at least strive for completeness in its application to the whole of humankind as well as for determinacy in the relations among our various duties to this whole of humankind.

A genuine system of duties, therefore would be one in which all the classes of duty are derived from a single fundamental principle; one in which there is a clear hierarchy or, to borrow John Rawls's term,[6] a lexical ordering among all those classes of duty, which is itself based on that fundamental principle; and one which in principle or ideally determines any human being's duties with regard to all other human beings. Kant himself, as well as other commentators, has clearly devoted the most attention to the first of these requirements, and I will devote considerable attention to it here as well, though I can hardly discuss it in all its detail. But it is far less clear how Kant proposes to satisfy the latter two of these requirements, so I must reserve space for them. Between these two requirements, Kant's position on the hierarchy or ordering of duties is less clear than his position on the universal scope of our duties, so I will save that issue for last. In what follows, I will therefore first comment on the derivation of Kant's system of duties from the fundamental principle of morality, then make some brief comments on the universal scope of our moral obligations in Kant's view, and only then make a proposal for the lexical ordering of our various classes of duty on the basis of Kant's fundamental principle of morality.

## 3. THE PRINCIPLE OF THE SYSTEM OF DUTIES

Two questions about Kant's practical philosophy that have been intensely debated are whether his several formulations of the categorical imperative in the *Groundwork* are coextensive variations of a single principle or substantively different principles, thus whether Kant's system of duties can be derived from a single fundamental principle or only from a set of principles, and whether the juridical duties expounded by Kant depend upon his fundamental principle or principles of morality in the same way that his ethical duties obviously do, thus whether his juridical and his ethical duties constitute a single system of duties or at best two separate systems.[7] Here I will describe my position on these

---

[6] See John Rawls, *A Theory of Justice*, rev. edn. (Cambridge, Mass.: Harvard University Press, 1999), 37–40, 53–4.

[7] The literature on the former issue is vast; for my own discussion of the question and assessment of some of the previous literature, see 'The Possibility of the Categorical Imperative', *Philosophical Review*, 104 (1995), 353–85, repr. in my *Kant on Freedom, Law, and Happiness* (Cambridge: Cambridge University Press, 2000), 172–206 and elsewhere; for another important discussion of this issue, see Allen W. Wood, 'The Moral Law as a System of Formulas', in H. F. Fulda and J. Stolzenberg (eds.), *Architektonik und System in der Philosophie Kants* (Hamburg: Felix Meiner Verlag, 2001), 287–306, and his *Kant's Ethical Thought* (Cambridge: Cambridge University Press, 1999), chs. 3–5, pp. 76–190. For a set of papers debating the latter issue, see Allen Wood, 'The Final

issues only in the most general terms. First, for a variety of reasons, including Kant's own statement that it is only through this that 'the ground of a possible categorical imperative' is revealed (G, 4:428), I take Kant's formulation of the categorical imperative as 'So act that you use humanity, whether in your own person or in the person of any other, always at the same time as an end, never merely as a means' (G, 4:429) to be his most basic formulation of the categorical imperative, that is, the form in which the fundamental principle of morality presents itself to us human beings, and thus as a formulation from which all of his other versions of the categorical imperative can be derived. In this formulation, I take the concept of humanity to stand for the only case of rational being with which we are actually familiar, and thus as for all practical purposes interchangeable with it. Next, in the *Groundwork* Kant states that 'Rational nature is distinguished from the rest of nature by this, that it sets itself an end' (G, 4:437), and in the *Metaphysics of Morals* he states that 'The capacity to set oneself an end—any end whatsoever—is what characterizes humanity (as distinguished from animality)' (MM, DV, Introduction, VIII, 6:392). But he also immediately infers from this a duty to 'procur[e] or promot[e] the *capacity* to realize all sorts of possible ends' (ibid.), so I take him to mean that it is actually the *ability to set our own ends and the capacity to realize or successfully pursue them* that should always be treated as an end and never merely as a means in both ourselves and all others. The ability to set our own ends is clearly the fundamental form of the exercise of the freedom of choice, and the capacity to realize or pursue our freely chosen ends is equally clearly the fundamental form of the freedom of action. So I take the command always to treat humanity as an end and never merely as a means as the recognition of the unconditional value of freedom itself, that is, of the recognition that, as Kant says in his lectures on ethics,

Form of Kant's Practical Philosophy'; Paul Guyer, 'Kant's Deductions of the Principles of Right'; Marcus Willaschek, 'Which Imperatives for Right? On the Non-Prescriptive Character of Juridical Laws in Kant's *Metaphysics of Morals*'; and Thomas W. Pogge, 'Is Kant's *Rechtslehre* a "Comprehensive Liberalism"?', all in Mark Timmons (ed.), *Kant's Metaphysics of Morals: Interpretative Essays* (Oxford: Oxford University Press, 2002), 1–22, 23–64, 65–88, and 133–58 (my essay in this debate is reprinted in this volume, Ch. 9). Otfried Höffe has vigorously defended the view that juridical duties have a common moral foundation with ethical duties in a number of writings, especially 'Der moralische Begriff des Rechts' and the essays in part I of his *Categorical Principles of Law: A Counterpoint to Modernity*, trans. Mark Migotti (University Park: Pennsylvania State University Press, 2002), 17–102. His coinage '*kategorische Rechtsimperative*' is meant to connote precisely that the principles of right or juridical duty are indeed derived from the categorical imperative as the general principle of morality.

'freedom according to a choice that is not necessitated to act' is 'the inner worth of the world' (Col., 27: 344).[8] Thus the most general form of our moral obligation is to preserve and promote the possibility of freedom of both choice and action in both ourselves and others.

As Allen Wood has often stressed, it is to the formula of humanity as an end in itself that Kant most frequently appeals in deriving his list of the duties of virtue.[9] But I believe it can readily be seen that Kant's duties of right as well as his duties of virtue are grounded on this fundamental principle. Kant formulates the 'Universal Principle of Right' thus: 'Any action is **right** if it can coexist with everyone's freedom in accordance with a universal law, or if on its maxim the freedom of choice of each can coexist with everyone's freedom in accordance with a universal law' (*MM*, DR, Introduction, §C, 6:230). A page later Kant restates this principle as 'so act externally that the free use of your choice can coexist with the freedom of everyone in accordance with a universal law' (6:231), making it clear by the terms 'act externally' and 'free use of your choice' that it is the expression of one's choice in one's actions that is to be constrained by this principle, and it seems only natural to assume that what the principle requires is that your expression of your freedom of choice in your freedom of action be compatible with a like expression of their freedom of choice in their freedom of action by all others who could in any way be affected by your choice of action. Further, while, as we have just seen, the principle requires the consistency of the freedom of one's actions with the freedom of the actions of others 'in accordance with a universal law',[10] and thus it might seem as if the duties of right to be derived from the universal principle of right are ultimately derived from the formulation of the categorical imperative as the requirement that one's maxims be able to serve as universal law (*G*, 4:421), rather than as the requirement that they always treat humanity as an end and never merely as a means, it should be clear that the requirement for the consistency of one's own actions with the actions of all others in accordance with a universal law itself follows immediately from the requirement that humanity in the form of freedom of choice and its expression in freedom of action always be treated as an end and never merely as a

---

[8] Translation from Kant, *Lectures on Ethics*, ed. Heath and Schneewind, 125.

[9] See Allen W. Wood, 'Humanity as an End in Itself', *Proceedings of the Eighth International Kant Congress*, i/1 (Milwaukee: Marquette University Press, 1995), 301–19, repr. in Paul Guyer (ed.), *Kant's Groundwork of the Metaphysics of Morals* (Lanham, Md.: Rowman & Littlefield, 1998), 165–87, and Wood, *Kant's Ethical Thought*, 139–41.

[10] At 6:230 Kant also immediately glosses the universal principle of right as the requirement that 'my action or my condition generally can coexist with the freedom of everyone in accordance with a universal law'.

means in oneself *and others*. The requirement of universal validity is just a more formal expression of what the formula of humanity implies.

Kant stresses that the universal principle of right is indifferent to anyone's *motivation*:

It cannot be required that this principle of all maxims be itself in turn my maxim, that is, it cannot be required that **I make it the maxim** of my action; for anyone can be free so long as I do not impair his freedom by my **external action**, even though I am quite indifferent to his freedom or would like in my heart to infringe upon it. That I make it my maxim to act rightly is a demand that [only] ethics makes on me. (6:231)

The principle of right requires simply that our *actions* do not restrict the freedom of *action* of others, and does not concern the motivations we may use in order to get ourselves to comply with this requirement. It is because of this indifference to motivation that juridical duties derived from the universal principle of right can admit an 'incentive other than the idea of duty', thus an incentive drawn from '**pathological** grounds of determination' for the will (*MM*, Introduction, IV, 6:219), specifically coercion or the threat of coercion. It is at least in part because of this indifference to motivation that some commentators think that the universal principle of right is not itself founded on the fundamental principle of morality. But if the most fundamental form of the principle of morality is that which requires that humanity always be treated as an end and never merely as a means, and if humanity is equivalent to freedom of both choice and action, then the requirement to preserve the possibility of freedom of action for everyone else in one's own exercise of that freedom can be derived directly from the unconditional value of that freedom, and the command not to use one's own freedom in a way that unnecessarily restricts the freedom of others is itself a moral command.

It is, to be sure, a *negative* command, and as such compliance with it will earn one no special *commendation*, although breach of it will earn one *demerit* and possibly punishment as well (see *MM*, Introduction, III, 6:227-8). Demerit can be avoided as long as one complies with a prohibition, regardless of what one's motivation for so complying is, even if merit or commendation can only be earned by complying with the prohibition for a special reason, such as having made the moral law itself one's maxim. For that reason the universal principle of right can be indifferent to motivation and admit of external, pathological incentives. But that does not mean that it is not itself a moral law, or derived from the fundamental principle of morality; it is just a consequence of the fact that it is a moral *prohibition*.

The foundation of the universal principle of right on the fundamental principle of morality is also suggested by Kant's justification for the coercive enforcement of the former and thus of the juridical duties derivable from it. This is Kant's famous argument that 'Resistance that counteracts the hindering of an effect promotes this effect and is consistent with it,' that 'coercion is a hindrance or resistance to freedom', and that 'Therefore if a certain use of freedom is itself a hindrance to freedom in accordance with universal laws (i.e., wrong), coercion that is opposed to this (as a **hindering of a hindrance to freedom**) is consistent with freedom in accordance with universal laws, that is, it is right' (*MM*, DR, Introduction, §D, 6:231). The gist of this argument is that coercion is justified when and only when it is necessary to preserve the possibility of the exercise of *freedom in accordance with universal laws*. But if it is the unconditional value of the exercise of freedom in accordance with universal laws that is the basis of morality as such, then this is clearly a *moral* justification of coercion. Thus the argument for the permissibility of enforcing the universal principle of right by an external rather than an internal incentive is itself a *moral* argument. There would be no need to provide a moral argument for the coercive enforcement of the principle of right if that were not itself a moral principle.[11]

In demanding that humanity always be treated as an end and never merely as a means, the fundamental principle of morality requires that freedom of both choice and action be both preserved and promoted in both oneself and others. The fundamental principle of morality thus gives rise to both negative and positive commands, the command not to destroy or restrict freedom and the command to promote the conditions for its successful exercise. This idea was hardly novel to Kant; as the textbook that he used for his course on political philosophy put it, 'Since moral obligation is either positive or negative, the *moral law* divides into a law that *commands* and one that *prohibits*.'[12] The general prohibition against violating the freedom of action of others in the exercise of one's own may at least in some cases be enforced by the threat and imposition of coercive sanctions, while for several reasons the positive command to promote the successful exercise of freedom in both oneself and others may not, and therefore can be reliably motivated only by the agent's respect for morality itself. This is the basis for Kant's derivation of both

[11] Kant's moral justification of the juridical use of coercion is discussed more fully in my 'Kant's Deductions of the Principles of Right' (Ch. 9 in this volume), sect. v.

[12] Gottfried Achenwall and Johann Stephan Putter, *Anfangsgründe des Naturrechts (Elementa Iuris Naturae)*, ed. and trans. Jan Schröder (Frankfurt am Main: Insel Verlag, 1995), §106, pp. 44–5.

duties of right and duties of virtue from the fundamental principle of morality as well as for the distinction between them.

Unfortunately, Kant complicates this straightforward analysis. In the Introduction to the *Metaphysics of Morals* as a whole, he states clearly that both juridical laws and ethical laws are '**moral** laws', the difference between them being only that the former are 'directed merely to external actions and their conformity to law' or to 'freedom in the **external** use of choice', while the latter refer to 'freedom in both the external and the internal use of choice, insofar as it is determined by laws of reason', and that because the former concern only the external use of freedom, they allow the possibility of external incentives, but since the latter also concern the internal freedom of choice, they can 'also require that they (the laws) themselves be the determining grounds of actions' (*MM*, Introduction, II, 6:214). In the Introduction to the 'Doctrine of Virtue', however, Kant further claims that juridical duties concern only 'the **formal** condition of outer freedom (the consistency of outer freedom with itself if its maxim were made universal law', while ethical duties go 'beyond this and provide a **matter** (an object of free choice), an **end** of pure reason which it represents as an end that is also objectively necessary, that is, an end that, as far as human beings are concerned, it is a duty to have' (*MM*, DV, Introduction, I, 6:380). Kant goes on to argue that there are only two ends that are also duties, namely one's own perfection and the happiness of others (IV, 6:385–6). Both of these are obviously general ends that could be promoted in an indefinite number of particular ways on an indefinite number of occasions; the duties to promote them are therefore what Kant calls imperfect duties, where 'the law can prescribe only the maxim of actions, not the actions themselves' (VII, 6:390), in contrast to perfect duties, where particular actions can be prescribed or, more typically, proscribed. The implication here is that all ethical duties or duties of virtue are imperfect duties, while all perfect duties are juridical duties or duties of justice. Yet neither the suggestion that all duties of virtue are imperfect duties and all perfect duties are duties of right nor the suggestion that all duties of virtue can be motivated only by the moral law itself while all perfect duties admit of external, coercive sanctions squares with Kant's actual division of duties of right and duties of virtue. Does this mean that Kant's classification of these duties is completely unsystematic? No; it just means that the principle of division Kant actually uses needs to be stated somewhat more carefully than Kant himself manages to do.

In order to understand the actual basis for Kant's most fundamental division in his systematic classification of duties, it will be helpful to use a classification of duties that Kant had suggested prior to the *Metaphysics of Morals*. I refer to the classification that generates the famous four examples of duties which are discussed after the first and second formulations of the categorical imperative in the *Groundwork*. Kant's aim with these examples is clearly to confirm his account of the categorical imperative by showing that it gives rise to all the main kinds of commonly recognized moral duties. To do this, he chooses his examples from 'the usual division of [duties] into duties to ourselves and to other human beings and into perfect and imperfect duties' (*G*, 4:422 n.) (thereby omitting without comment the traditional category of duties towards God, although he has much to say against that category elsewhere).[13] He then offers one example from each of the four classes that arise from these two divisions: as an example of (1) a perfect duty towards oneself, he adduces the proscription of suicide; as an example of (2) a perfect duty towards others, he uses the duty not to make false promises, that is, promises one has no intention of keeping; as the example of (3) imperfect duty towards oneself, he offers the duty to cultivate one's natural predispositions for skills and talents; and for (4) imperfect duty towards others he instances the duty of beneficence or mutual aid (*G*, 4:422–4, 429–30).

If we recall Kant's definition of humanity as the capacity both freely to set and to pursue particular ends, we can derive these examples of duties from the general requirement always to treat humanity as an end and never merely as a means in the following way. (1) The duty to refrain from suicide is obviously a case of the more general duty not to destroy a being capable of free choice, a duty that would obviously proscribe homicide as well as suicide, that is, the destruction of a free agent other than oneself. (2) Since Kant analyses a false promise as one that compromises the free choice of another by inducing him to adopt as his own an end that he would not endorse if he were properly informed of the promiser's real intention (*G*, 4:429–30), the proscription of such promises is an example of the general duty not to compromise the exercise of free agency or destroy the possibility of its exercise on a particular occasion, rather than the duty not to destroy a free agent. There will of course be other examples of this general class of duty, including cases of such a duty towards oneself rather than towards others; for example, the duty to avoid drunkenness (*MM*, DV, §8, 4:427) can be understood as a duty not to compromise one's ability to exercise one's own freedom of choice during a period of intoxication (although of course driving under

---

[13] See e.g. Col. 27:327–34, in *Lectures on Ethics*, ed. Heath and Schneewind, 112–17; Vig., 27:712–29, ibid. 436–50; *MM*, DV, §18, 6:443–4; and *Rel.* esp. book 3, sect. V, 6:102–9, and book 4, Second Part, 6:167–202.

the influence can lead not just to temporary impairment but also to the death of oneself or others in an automobile accident, so the duty to avoid drunkenness could also be understood as the duty not to risk the destruction of a free being, either oneself or another). (3) Kant's example of the duty to cultivate one's talents, 'fortunate natural predispositions' which if developed can serve one 'for all sorts of possible aims' (G, 4:423), can be understood as a duty to develop general conditions that will facilitate the realization of the particular ends that one may freely set for oneself in the exercise of one's humanity. One might have such a duty with regard to others as well, for example the duty to educate one's children or to contribute to the education of the children of others by paying one's taxes. Finally, (4) the duty of beneficence can be understood as the duty to assist others in the realization of particular ends they have freely set for themselves: as Kant puts it, 'there is still only a negative and not a positive agreement with **humanity as an end in itself** unless everyone also tries, as far as he can, to further the ends of others' (G, 4:430). We might also think that treating one's own humanity as an end in itself would entail a duty to further the particular ends that one freely sets for oneself, although this could begin to sound like a duty to promote one's own happiness, an idea towards which Kant is generally hostile.[14]

Summing up, we can take Kant's analyses of his examples of the four commonly accepted classes of duty to imply the following comprehensive interpretation of the duty always to treat humanity as an end and never merely as a means: this consists of the duties (1) not to destroy human beings *qua* agents capable of free choice, (2) not to compromise the possibility of their exercise of their freedom of choice and action, (3) to cultivate general capacities that will facilitate the successful pursuit of the ends that they freely set for themselves, and (4), as circumstances warrant and allow, to take particular actions in order to facilitate the realization of the particular ends that they freely set for themselves. It is not clear what a formal completeness-proof for a classification of duties

---

[14] In the Introduction to the 'Doctrine of Virtue' Kant argues that one cannot have a direct duty to make oneself happy, because duty requires overcoming an aversion but one has no aversion to one's own happiness, although he also concedes that one might have an indirect duty to make oneself sufficiently happy in order to avoid temptation to doing something immoral (V, 6:387–8). But he eventually acknowledges that 'all **others** with the exception of myself would not be **all**' (§27, 6:451), and that therefore the duty to promote the realization of the freely chosen ends of human beings and thereby their happiness must include the promotion of my own ends and therefore my own happiness. In practice, of course, taking the steps necessary for one's own long-term happiness requires considerable constraint of one's current inclinations in so many cases that examples are hardly necessary, so the premiss of Kant's initial argument that one's own happiness cannot be a duty because one simply desires it naturally is obviously false.

would look like, but this schema seems exhaustive of the kind of steps we can take in order to preserve and promote humanity, and thus appears to be an adequate derivation of a comprehensive system of duties from a single principle. This may seem even clearer when we add one further consideration that we can derive from Kant's discussion of 'private right', that is, the right to property, from the 'Doctrine of Right'. The underlying empirical assumption of Kant's theory of property rights is that we are embodied creatures who can function only by means of the movement of our bodies—this gives rise to what Kant calls the 'innate right to freedom' (*MM*, DR, Introduction, 6:237–8)—and the use of bodies other than our own, including the use of non-human bodies, such as land, minerals, vegetables, and non-human animals, and also other human bodies, such as those of servants, other employees, contractors, and spouses—this is what gives rise to the various categories of what Kant calls 'acquired right'. The preservation of our own humanity and that of others as well as the pursuit of the freely chosen ends of ourselves and others will require us to be able to move our own bodies freely and to control and use various other bodies as well. Of course, the free movements of our own bodies as well as the free use of other bodies, whether non-human or human, can come into conflict with the free use of their own bodies and other bodies by other persons, and thus the general duty to treat humanity, that is, the capacity for freedom of choice and action, as an end and not merely as a means in both ourselves and others means that we will have to find ways to regulate the movements of our own bodies and the use of other bodies in order to preserve freedom not only in ourselves but also in others. The general duties to preserve free beings and the possibility of their exercise of their freedom as well as to promote the success of such exercise and the realization of particular freely chosen ends will all require the regulation of the use of both our own bodies and other bodies in ways designed to respect the humanity of all.

Against this background, we can now enumerate the classes of juridical and ethical duties that Kant deploys in the *Metaphysics of Morals*. Juridical duties are stated at the outset to be those that permit of coercive enforcement. There are three classes of them, although the first is only mentioned in the Introduction and only the latter two receive extended discussion in the two main sections of the 'Doctrine of Right'. The class of duties mentioned in the Introduction is that arising from the innate right to freedom, by which presumably Kant means freedom of the person to perform actions not using external objects or other persons as essential means. This innate right would therefore include freedom from restriction of or violence against the person, giving rise to prohibitions against kidnapping, assault, homicide, and other obvious attacks upon bodily existence, integrity, and motion, but also to rights such as freedom of speech.

The second main class of juridical duties, discussed under the rubric of 'Private Right', includes the rights to acquire property in things, rights towards specific performances by other persons through contracts, and rights towards other persons as if they were things, that is, long-term rights against others such as the rights of spouses regarding each other; the juridical *duties*, of course, are the enforceable duties to respect these *rights*. The clear purpose of Kant's discussion is precisely to explain how such rights can be acquired consistently with the general moral obligation to treat each person as an end and never merely as a means—to explain, for example, how one person can claim exclusive right to control a piece of property that others might also use in a way consistent with the freedom of others, or how a husband can claim rights over a wife consistent with her own status as an end in herself.

Kant then argues that a *state* is necessary in order to make all these rights both determinate and secure, and that our moral freedom to claim these rights therefore creates a moral obligation to institute and preserve a state (see *MM*, DR, §§8–9, 41–2). The third main class of rights and duties, expounded under the rubric of 'Public Right', are then those necessary to ensure that the state can perform its allotted role. The gist of Kant's argument here is that only a republican government, characterized by the division of powers and the denial to rulers of proprietary rights in the land and offices of the nation, can fulfil the purpose for which the state exists, and therefore that all, but especially the rulers of a state, however they have come to power, have an obligation to institute and maintain republican government.[15]

Now comes a problem. In spite of Kant's introductory characterization of ethics as involving only ends that are also duties, namely one's own perfection and the happiness of others, Kant's actual list of the duties of virtue is not restricted to these two headings but includes all of the specific obligations (*Tugendpflichten*) that we have that cannot be coercively enforced as well as the general and purely moral obligation (*Tugendverpflichtung*) to fulfil our specific duties out of our sense of duty (*MM*, DV, Introduction, XVII, 6:410). (This last obligation is one that can apply to juridical duties as well as to specific ethical duties, which would be difficult to understand if juridical duties were not themselves derived from the fundamental principle of morality; it is

---

[15]  See esp. TP, part II, and 'Toward Perpetual Peace', First Definitive Article, 8:349–53.

also a duty the failure to satisfy which produces no sanction, but the fulfilment of which entitles one to the highest form of esteem.) Thus Kant's actual list of ethical duties includes perfect duties prohibiting specific actions that would destroy or damage the humanity of oneself or others as well as imperfect duties to promote the capacity and conditions for the successful exercise of humanity by oneself and others. Kant's prohibitions of suicide (*MM*, *DV*, §6), self-defilement (§7), and self-stupefaction in the form of drunkenness and gluttony (§8) are perfect duties not to destroy, damage, or misuse the physical basis of one's capacity for freedom, not duties to *promote* one's own perfection; his prohibitions of lying (§9), avarice (§10), and servility (§11) are perfect duties towards oneself as a 'moral being', or duties not to *undermine* one's freedom of choice directly rather than through its physical basis. What Kant calls 'duties of respect' towards others are likewise perfect duties not to show disrespect towards the moral being of others through arrogance, defamation, and ridicule (§§42–4), not imperfect duties to promote their happiness. Of course, one has imperfect duties towards oneself that are duties to promote one's own perfection: these include the duty to improve the physical and mental capacities on which one's successful pursuit of one's freely chosen ends depends (§19), which is obviously the successor to the duty to cultivate one's talents mentioned in the *Groundwork*, but also include the duty to perfect one's moral judgment and disposition itself (§21).[16] And because in Kant's view one cannot directly contribute to the moral perfection of another, our imperfect duty to perfect the happiness of others is confined to the 'duties of love', specifically the duties of beneficence, gratitude, and sympathy (§§29–35), which flesh out the duty of beneficence used as the example of this category in the *Groundwork*. Here it is hard to refrain from observing that Kant's discussion of what one can and should do for others is radically incomplete: while it is of course true that people cannot make free choices for each other, and therefore that no one can perfect the moral being of another, one certainly can contribute to the development of the knowledge, skill, and judgment of others in which their capacities to pursue ends in general as well as to make moral choices in particular depend, and thus it seems that there is a large category of

---

[16] The 'human being's duty to himself as his own innate judge', that is, the duty to cultivate moral judgment and listen to one's conscience (§§13–15), which Kant discusses under the rubric of perfect duty towards oneself, should presumably be included under imperfect duty towards oneself as a moral being, since this duty is clearly an open-ended prescription of wide obligation, rather than a narrow proscription of specific violations of one's humanity.

potential imperfect duties which Kant omits, namely, obligations to contribute to the general education or development of natural capacities of others as well as to their moral education.

That criticism apart, the duties to cultivate one's own talents and moral judgment and to be beneficent to others are clearly duties of wide obligation either to promote the capacity to realize particular ends freely chosen in the exercise of one's own humanity or to directly promote the realization of particular ends freely chosen by another. They thus fit Kant's insistence that ethical obligations are duties that are also ends. The general obligation to fulfil all of one's duties out of respect for the moral law itself can also be construed as the obligation to make duty itself one's overarching end. But such duties as the duty not to commit suicide or not to defame others are not open-ended obligations to promote particular ends; they are narrow obligations not to destroy, damage, or disrespect a person who is a moral being or the humanity of such a person. They are thus duties to treat persons, whether oneself or others, as ends in themselves, but not duties to promote any particular or general ends. Does that mean that there is no systematic basis for Kant's collection of duties under the rubric of duties of virtue? No: the common principle of all duties of virtue is simply that among all the duties derivable from the general principle of morality they, unlike juridical duties, are not coercively enforceable.

Kant does not spell out a general theory of why none of the duties of virtue are coercively enforceable; and it seems as if there would be a variety of reasons why specific duties of virtue would not be so enforceable. In some cases, there is clearly a physical or even logical barrier to the coercive enforcement of a duty of virtue. The duty to develop and hearken to one's conscience, for example, could not be coercively enforced simply because coercive enforcement affects one's outer actions through fear of consequences, not one's inmost dispositions or character. In other cases, it might be the case that while a duty could be coercively enforced, no one has the moral or legal standing necessary to do so: there are sanctions that might prevent suicide for example, such as the threat of the confiscation of a suicide's estate or his burial outside of hallowed ground, but the fact that the would-be suicide's action injures no one but himself (not really always a fact, of course) may mean that no one else has the right to threaten or enforce these sanctions against him. Kant's predecessors such as Achenwall spelled out these considerations by maintaining that the coercive enforcement of any obligation requires both a logical and/or physical possibility of successful coercive enforcement as well as a moral possibility, capacity, or title for such enforcement.[17] Kant does not explicitly mention these conditions, perhaps because he could take them for granted. But he in fact assumes them. Thus, for example, in explaining why even though there is not a moral right to self-preservation at the cost of the life of an innocent there cannot be a legal prohibition of it—he refers to the alleged 'right of necessity', such as the right to push another off a floating piece of shipwreck in order to save oneself—he argues simply that there could not be an effective sanction to enforce such a prohibition: the threat of drowning is more immediate and certain than juridical sanction that might be threatened (*MM*, DR, Introduction, Appendix II, 6:235–6). In this case he thus assumes that a coercive sanction requires a physical possibility of efficacy. His general argument in behalf of the coercive enforcement of juridical duties, however, turns, as we earlier saw, on the claim that hindrances to hindrances of freedom are 'consistent with freedom in accordance with universal laws' (*MM*, DR, Introduction, §D, 6:231). This is clearly an attempt to provide the *moral* title for coercive sanctions (although an attempt that is woefully incomplete: it needs to be supplemented with an explanation of how a coercive sanction can ever preserve the freedom it is supposed to protect, as well as an account of how the general moral title to exercise coercive sanctions passes into the hands of the specific agents who are to exercise these sanctions).[18]

On this account, then, juridical duties would simply be those of our obligations arising from the fundamental principle of morality that satisfy the criteria for coercive enforcement, and ethical duties would be those that fail to satisfy these criteria. On such an account there would thus be a systematic derivation of all duties as well as a systematic basis for their division. And indeed, the basis for the division of duties would ultimately be the same as the basis for their derivation, namely the fundamental principle of morality itself. The requirement that there be a moral basis for the exercise of any coercive sanction, specifically the requirement that such a sanction actually preserve freedom itself, obviously derives directly from the principle that the freedom of every person is to be an end in itself. But the further requirement that there can be a coercive sanction only when there can be an effective sanction can also be regarded as part of morality itself, at least if the principle that 'ought implies can' is regarded as part of the foundation of morality—as Kant clearly regards it.[19] In other words, the division between coercively

[17] See e.g. Achenwall and Putter, *Elementa Iuris Naturae*, §145.
[18] Again, see my 'Kant's Deductions of the Principles of Right' (Ch. 9 in this volume), sect. V.
[19] See esp. *Rel.*, e.g. 6:45, 47, 49 n., 50, 62, and 66.

enforceable duties and duties that cannot be coercively enforced but can only be motivated by respect for duty is itself required by morality.

In this way Kant's system of duties satisfies his first requirement for systematicity, that both the basic concepts of the system and their most basic division be derived from a fundamental principle. Let us now turn to his remaining requirements for a system of duties.

## 4. THE EXTENSION OF THE SYSTEM OF DUTIES

The second of the requirements for a system of duties that I want to discuss (although the third enumerated in my original list of features) is the requirement that the system apply to every object in its possible domain. Of course, when Kant states that the fundamental principle of morality is always to treat humanity as an end in itself, 'whether in your own person or in the person of any other', he is making it clear that this principle and therefore every duty derivable from it applies to every human being. But what does this imply in practice? Does it mean that you must apply each of your duties to every human being, and thus, for example, not only not murder any human being but also promote the lawful ends of every other human being, in the name of the duty of beneficence? The latter would seem to impose an impossible task on every human being, and Kantian morality never says that you ought to do more than you actually can (although of course what you actually can do may be a lot more than you may be selfishly tempted to think you can do). So one natural thing to think might be that your perfect negative duties apply to every other human being—after all, it seems to be within your power to refrain from murdering, assaulting, or defrauding any and therefore every other human being—but that you can confine your fulfilment of imperfect and positive duties to something less than the whole of humanity—in principle, that is, in some imaginable circumstances, any other human being may have a claim on your beneficence, but since you cannot in practice benefit every other human being, you will have to find some practical way to limit the actual claims of others on your beneficence.

In a general way, this approach to the requirement of completeness in the application of the system of duties is no doubt correct, but when we begin to think about the more particular duties that Kant has included in his system, we see that it needs some refinement. I will discuss first some refinements that are needed in the case of the juridical duties founded on the conditions for the rightful acquisition of property. Issues regarding other forms of duty bring us into the territory of conflicts of duties, a subject naturally discussed in response to the question of whether Kant's set of duties constitutes a systematic hierarchy or lexically ordered set. So those issues will be saved for the next and final section of the chapter.

Since duties regarding property are coercively enforceable juridical duties, one might assume they are perfect duties, thus imposing on us constraints of restraint towards every other human being as other perfect duties do. This is partly right, although it has an implication that deserves to be stated explicitly; but there is also a way in which our duty regarding property blurs the line between perfect and imperfect duty, and that too needs comment.

I have discussed Kant's theory of property elsewhere,[20] so my account here will be brief. The basis of Kant's theory of property is the idea that a property right cannot consist simply in the physical grasp of an object or occupation of a place (what he calls 'sensible possession' at MM, DR, §1, 6:245)—because our property rights can extend far beyond what we can hold in our hands or cover with our feet—or in any other immediate, empirical relation between a single person and the property he claims— such as the Lockean candidate of having mixed one's labour with an object[21]—because the rightfulness of any such relation presupposes that one has a rightful claim to do anything with that object in the first place (see §17, 6:268–9). Instead, a property right consists in a relation *among* wills, *regarding* an object, namely the consent of all those persons who *could* control and use an object that *one* among them *can*. As Kant puts it, 'By my unilateral choice I cannot bind another to refrain from using a thing, an obligation he would not otherwise have; hence I can do this only through the united choice of all who possess it in common' (§11, 6:261). Because a property right really consists in an agreement regarding the control of an object that is a relation among wills rather than a simple relation between one will and the object, Kant calls it 'intelligible' or even 'noumenal' rather than merely 'sensible' or 'phenomenal' possession (see §1, 6:245; §5, 6:249; §6, 6:250; §7, 6:253).

Now in fact the consent of others to one person's control of some object could be gained in either of two ways: by sheer force, that is, the

---

[20] See my 'Kantian Foundations for Liberalism', in *Jahrbuch für Recht und Ethik*, 5 (1997), 121–40, and 'Life, Liberty, and Property: Rawls and Kant', in Dieter Hüning and Burkhard Tuschling (eds.), *Recht, Staat und Völkerrecht bei Immanuel Kant* (Berlin: Duncker & Humblot, 1998), 273–91; both repr. in my *Kant on Freedom, Law, and Happiness* (Cambridge: Cambridge University Press, 2000), 235–86, and 'Kant's Deductions of the Principles of Right' (Ch 9 in this volume).
[21] See John Locke, *Second Treatise of Government*, ch. v, §28.

physical power of one person to enforce his claim over the others out of his own resources and the fear of that force on the part of others; or by the consent of the others that is freely given by them under conditions that make it seem reasonable to them to do so. A *moral* right to property must clearly depend upon the latter rather than the former, however, so Kant stresses that property can *rightfully* be claimed only in a way to which others would freely consent: only because my will to use an object 'does not conflict with the law of outer freedom' can 'an obligation [be] laid upon all others, which they would not otherwise have, to refrain from using the object' (*MM*, DR, §7, 6:253). More fully,

When I declare (by word or deed) that I will that something external is to be mine, I thereby declare that everyone else is under an obligation to refrain from using that object of my choice, an obligation no one would have were it not for this act of mine to establish a right. This claim involves, however, acknowledging that I in turn am under an obligation to every other to refrain from using what is externally his; for the obligation here arises from a universal rule having to do with external rightful relations. (§8, 6:255)

What Kant stresses in his ensuing discussion is that it is reasonable for all concerned to consent to a system of property rights only if each participant can be given some practical assurance that his own rights will be honoured, and therefore that rightful property requires the existence of a state, a 'collective general (common) and powerful will, that can provide everyone this assurance' (6:256). That property rights can be merely provisional prior to the institution of a state and are conclusive only within a state (§9, 6:257) is the basis of Kant's political philosophy.[22] But a reasonable person does not merely require assurance that his own property will be respected; a reasonable person will also require that a system of property rights to which he is to freely consent be in his own interest as well as in the interest of the others who will benefit from it. In other words, a reasonable person will consent to a system of property rights only if he sees it as sufficiently *fair* (which of course does not necessarily mean *egalitarian* in all possible respects). So if a *rightful* system of property must be consistent with the universality of external freedom, and reasonable persons would only freely consent to a system of property that meets some minimal standard of fairness, then a rightful system of property must meet some such standard.

[22] The fact that nature provides no boundaries for property claims beyond the limits of our own skins, although we clearly claim property beyond the limits of our own skins, means that the state is necessary to make the boundaries between properties *determinate* as well as *secure*. The licensing of surveys is thus as essential to the primary function of the state as is the recording and enforcing of deeds.

For my larger argument I want to stress two implications of this analysis, both of which are in fact ultimately brought out by Kant, although only the first is immediately emphasized. This first implication is that since it is another inescapable empirical fact about the human condition that we all live on the finite surface of a sphere any point of which can be reached from any other and therefore no individual or people can completely avoid contact with any others (*MM*, DR, §13, 6:262), the potential users of any object whose consent one person must rightfully gain are not just his immediate neighbours in some currently existing state, whether small or large, whose borders are never more than accidental: in principle, any human being anywhere on earth might be able to raise a claim to the use of any object anywhere on earth, so any rightful system of property must ultimately honour a *global* claim of fairness as well providing a global assurance of possession. We must test the fairness of any system of property by imagining that 'all human beings on the earth' originally held the earth in common and then divided it up in a way to which all could freely give their consent: 'Original possession in common is . . . a practical rational concept which contains *a priori* the principle in accordance with which alone people can use a place on the earth in accordance with principles of right' (ibid.) This is why Kant eventually argues that a worldwide system of republics, each maintaining a rightful and therefore at least minimally fair system of property[23] within itself and all maintaining rightful relations among each other, is not merely the ultimate condition of *prudence* but rather the ultimate requirement of *justice*. 'Only in a universal **association of states** (analogous to that by which a people becomes a state) can rights come to hold **conclusively** and a true **condition of peace** come about' (§61, 6:350), and 'establishing universal and lasting peace constitutes not merely a part of the doctrine of right but rather the entire final end of the doctrine of right within the limits of mere reason' (*MM*, DR, Conclusion, 6:355). So Kant clearly argues that the rightfulness of the system of property must ultimately extend across the face of the earth to all of the people upon earth. This is the basis for Kant's argument that perpetual peace is the ultimate duty of justice.

---

[23] I use the vague expression 'system of republics' here to evade discussion of the contested issue of whether Kant ultimately advocates a non-coercive world *league* of republics or a more coercive *federation* or even *republic* of republics. For a few of the many discussions of this issue, see Otfried Höffe, 'Völkerbund oder Weltrepublik', in his *'Königliche Völker'*, 221–37, and Pauline Kleingeld, 'Kants Argumente für den Völkerbund', in Herta Nagl-Doeckal and Rudolph Langthaler (eds.), *Recht—Religion— Geschichte* (Berlin: Akademie Verlag, 2004) pp. 99–111.

The second point I want to make here is that although it might seem as if any juridical duty must be a negative duty not to destroy others or injure their freedom in some way, the line between negative and positive obligations is not so clear when it comes to the requirements of rightful property. For our obligation is not just to take property in a way that leaves others free to claim some as well—in the terms of Locke's famous proviso, 'that every man should have as much as he could make use of... without straitning any body' else.[24] Rather, maintaining a system of property claims that is fair enough for all affected by it to freely and therefore reasonably consent to it will inevitably require *affirmative* steps towards maintaining an at least minimally fair distribution of resources and opportunities for a variety of disadvantaged classes of persons. Kant argues this point only in passing and only in the terms of his own time:

To the supreme commander there belongs **indirectly**, that is, insofar as he has taken over the duty of the people, the right to impose taxes on the people for its own preservation, such as taxes to support organizations providing for the **poor, foundling homes** and **church organizations**, usually called charitable or pious institutions. (*MM*, DR, General Remark C, 6:325–6)

Now at least some of us would deny that the duty of the people to maintain all its members can constitutionally be carried out through 'faith-based' institutions at all, and would prefer to see this duty realized through a social safety net, regulation of big businesses, labour and equal employment laws, and many other developments of the modern state. But the basic lesson remains the same: that maintaining the fairness of the system of property rights which is the *raison d'être* of the state requires a range of measures, from not violently abrogating existing claims but using the courts when seeking to modify unfair ones, to paying taxes meant to support all sorts of governmental functions, to working to improve the fairness of governmental provisions for justice from within the government or political system, to working for social justice around the limits of government through non-governmental organizations and the like. As we traverse this spectrum, the line between negative and positive duties, thus the line between where our duty is well defined and we can be faulted for failing to fulfil it and where it is less well defined and we should be praised for special efforts to fulfil it, becomes blurry. Our general duty to claim property rights only within a system that maintains justice both locally and globally really involves both perfect and imperfect duty.

---

[24] Locke, *Second Treatise of Government*, ch. v, §36.

## 5. CAN CONFLICTS OF DUTIES BE SYSTEMATICALLY RESOLVED?

Now we can return to Kant's requirement of 'unanimity' (*Einhelligkeit*) among all the members of a system. Kant clearly presupposes this requirement in the Introduction to the *Metaphysics of Morals* when he famously argues that there cannot be a genuine conflict of duties:

A **conflict of duties** (*collisio officiorum s. obligationum*) would be a relation between them in which one of them would cancel the other (wholly or in part).— But since duty and obligation are concepts that express the objective practical **necessity** of certain actions and two rules opposed to each other cannot be necessary at the same time, if it is a duty to act in accordance with one rule, to act in accordance with the opposite rule is not a duty but even contrary to duty; so a **collision of duties** and obligations is inconceivable (*obligationes non colliduntur*). However, a subject may have, in a rule he prescribes to himself, two **grounds** of obligation (*rationes obligandi*), one or the other of which is not sufficient to put him under an obligation (*rationes obligandi non obligantes*), so that one of them is not a duty.—When two such grounds conflict with each other, practical philosophy says, not that the stronger obligation takes precedence (*fortior obligatio vincit*) but that the stronger **ground of obligation** prevails (*fortior obligandi ratio vincit*). (MM, Introduction, III, 6:224).

To strengthen Kant's argument here, one might add to his claim that actual duties cannot conflict because statements of duty are necessary truths and there cannot be contradictory necessary truths. The further claim that since the statement of our actual duty in any given circumstance must be necessarily true, the choice between competing grounds of obligation in such a situation cannot be arbitrary, left up to, for example, mere inclination or a toss of a coin, for in that case what turns out to be our particular duty would be contingent rather than necessary. There must be a principled, unique way to resolve such conflicts among grounds of obligation. It therefore seems natural to expect that a genuine system of duty must be able to resolve conflicts among competing grounds of obligation by including a hierarchical or lexical ordering of its duties, and that this hierarchy will be based on the foundational principle of the system. It is in this way that Kant's system of duties would manifest its satisfaction of the condition that a genuine system create 'unanimity among its various rules under one principle (the systematic) and thereby interconnection, so far as this can be done' (A 648/B 676) precisely by resolving conflicts among grounds of obligation on the basis of its fundamental organizing principles.

It might also seem natural to suppose that Kant intends such conflicts to be resolved by subordinating the fulfilment of imperfect duties, which are in any case only prescriptions of general ends or policies that leave us with a range of choices of concrete actions and occasions for those actions, to the satisfaction of perfect duties, which are proscriptions of particular types of action that apparently leave us no options. If our perfect duties to ourselves and others strictly prohibit suicide, homicide, fraud, or lying, then surely we know what to do when faced with a situation where we might fulfil an imperfect duty only by choosing to commit such an action: we just cannot do the latter, so we must find some other occasion and other way in which to fulfil our imperfect duty. However, such a strategy for resolving conflicts among grounds of obligation will not take us very far, because there can be conflicts within the class of perfect duties or the class of imperfect duty as well as between them, as well as competing claims under the rubric of a single type of duty, whether perfect or imperfect.

In fact, Kant's own examples of potential conflicts of duty are not typically conflicts between one perfect and one imperfect duty which could be readily resolved by the strategy thus far considered, but rather conflicts within the same class of duty (perfect or imperfect) or even conflicts between competing ways in which to fulfil a single duty. Thus, in illustrating what he means by the 'wide obligation' or 'playroom (*latitudo*) for free choice' characteristic of imperfect duties, Kant says that 'a wide duty is not to be taken as permission to make exceptions to the maxim of actions' on the basis of any sort of preference 'but only as permission to limit one maxim of duty by another (e.g. love of one's neighbour in general by love of one's parents), by which in fact the field for the practice of duty is widened' (*MM*, DV, Introduction, VII, 6:390). What he means by 'love' here is not emotional or as he calls it 'pathological' love, but 'practical' love, that is, simply, benevolence from principle rather than inclination (see *MM*, DV, §25, 6:449–50), so what Kant is suggesting here is that a conflict could arise even among alternative ways in which one might fulfil a particular imperfect duty, as in a situation where one has to choose between being beneficent to one's parents or to one's neighbours because one cannot do both; and it would seem that a genuine system of duties should include a principle for the resolution of conflicts of this sort.

Kant gives another example of conflict in raising a 'casuistical question' about suicide, a perfect duty to self that we might have thought could brook no casuistical questions. He asks whether it is in fact suicide or 'murdering oneself to hurl oneself to certain death (like Curtius) in order to save one's country?—or is deliberate martyrdom, sacrificing oneself for the good of all humanity, also to be considered an act of heroism?' (*MM*, DV, §6, 6:423). Kant was clearly puzzled about this case. In another mention of it in his classroom lectures just a few years earlier, he had unequivocally stated that when Curtius, a legendary hero who had been told by an oracle that the Roman people could be saved only if he were to hurl himself fully armed into a chasm in the forum, did so, 'he is acting contrary to duty' (Vig., 27:629);[25] but a decade or so earlier, in discussing the real case of the historical Marcus Porcius Cato Uticensis (95–46 BCE), he had written:

Suicide can also come to have a plausible aspect, whenever, that is, the continuance of life rests upon such circumstances as may deprive that life of its value; when a man can no longer live in accordance with virtue and prudence, and must therefore put an end to his life from honorable motives. Those who defend suicide from this angle cite the example of Cato, who killed himself once he realized that, although all the people still relied on him, it would not be possible for him to escape falling into Caesar's hands; but as soon as he, the champion of freedom, had submitted, the rest would have thought: If Cato himself submits, what else are we to do? If he killed himself, however, the Romans might yet dedicate their final efforts to the defense of their freedom. (Col., 27:370)[26]

Think of this not as a case of one man committing suicide in order to preserve his own virtue, as Kant initially suggests, but as a case of one man freely choosing to destroy his own continued existence as a free agent in order to encourage many others to make the supreme effort to preserve their existence as free agents, or at least their ability to exercise their freedom rather than suffer the tyranny of Caesar, as Kant subsequently suggests. Then we have a conflict between the duty to preserve the existence of freedom in one's own case and the duty to preserve it in the case of others, both of which seem to fall within the sphere of perfect duty, even under a single perfect duty to preserve the existence of free human beings. Once again the initial thought that we might resolve conflicts among competing grounds of obligation simply by subordinating the fulfilment of imperfect duties to the satisfaction of perfect duties will not solve our problem.

If Kant's classification of duties is a genuine system, then it ought to provide a basis for the resolution of these sorts of conflicts too. Does it? Kant does not explicitly explain how it can, but he does offer hints and materials that can be developed for this purpose. First, recall our earlier

---

[25] *Lectures on Ethics*, ed. Heath and Schneewind, 370.
[26] Ibid. 145.

discussion of the examples of the prohibitions of suicide and deceitful promises and the prescriptions of the cultivation of one's talents and the practice of beneficence from the *Groundwork* (Section 3 above). There we saw that these four examples could be understood not only as illustrations of the general categories of perfect duties to oneself, perfect duties to others, imperfect duties to oneself, and imperfect duties to others, but also as illustrations of the following four types of duties: (1) duties to preserve the existence of humans as free rational beings, (2) duties to preserve their ability to exercise their humanity on particular occasions, (3) duties to develop the capacities by means of which human beings can successfully pursue the particular ends they freely set for themselves in the exercise of their humanity, and finally (4) the duty to directly promote the realization of particular ends that humans have freely set for themselves. Now suppose that this list actually expresses a lexical ordering of the general classes of our duties, with the satisfaction of antecedent duties on the list being the condition for the satisfaction of subsequent ones. In this case, our first duty would be to preserve the existence of human beings *qua* rational beings, whether ourselves or others. Conditional upon our ability to satisfy that first duty, we are then obliged to preserve the ability of people to freely choose their ends on particular occasions, although if doing that in some particular circumstance would require the sacrifice of the existence of a free human being, then the second ground of obligation would have to give way to the first. Our next duty would be to develop our own capacities to pursue freely chosen ends successfully and, as Kant should have recognized, to assist others in the development of their capacities to do that too; but we could take particular actions towards this general end only when they do not conflict with either of the two grounds of obligation that precede them. Finally, when we have satisfied all the preceding grounds of obligation, then we would be free to perform particular acts of beneficence.

Before I say anything more, I want to acknowledge that this lexical ordering of duties could well suggest a different solution to the question whether 'it would be a crime to lie to a murderer who has asked whether a friend of ours whom he is pursuing has taken refuge in our house' than the one Kant proposes in his notorious late essay 'On a Supposed Right to Lie from Philanthropy' (September 1797). Kant's controversial answer to this question is that it would be a crime to do so, because although one does not owe anything to the murderer in particular, the duty to be truthful in general is an unconditional duty. Kant writes that 'Truthfulness in statements that one cannot avoid is a human being's duty to everyone, however great the disadvantage to him or to another that may result from it; and although I indeed do no wrong to him who unjustly compels me to make the statement if I falsify it, I nevertheless do wrong in the most essential part of duty **in general** by such a falsification,' because by so doing 'I bring it about, as far as I can, that statements (declarations) in general are not believed... and this is a wrong inflicted upon humanity generally' (8:426). Thus 'To be **truthful** (honest) in all declarations is... a sacred command of reason prescribing unconditionally, one not to be restricted by any conveniences' (8:428). (In the 'Doctrine of Virtue', published earlier the same year, Kant offers a different analysis, arguing there that lying under any circumstances is a violation of a duty to oneself rather than to humanity in general, 'directly opposed to the natural purposiveness of the speaker's capacity to communicate his thoughts, and... thus a renunciation by the speaker of his personality'; §9, 6:429.) Kant further argues that when one breaks a law, one is legally imputable for all of the consequences of one's breach, whether foreseen or not, so that if unknown to you your friend has actually left your house, and the murderer, successfully turned away from your door by your lie, precisely because of that succeeds in finding and murdering him, his death will be on your head, whereas if you had 'kept strictly to the truth, then public justice can hold nothing against you, whatever the unforeseen consequences might be' (8:427). One might also defend Kant's position by saying that the duty to help your friend is only an instance of the imperfect duty of beneficence, and therefore properly gives way to the perfect duty not to tell a lie, in spite of the unfortunate result.[27] However, the lexical ordering of duties I have proposed suggests an alternative resolution of this problem: we might think that we have an unconditional duty to do everything in our power to preserve the existence of a bearer of humanity, in this instance by saving the life of our friend, and that our duty to preserve the ability of human beings to exercise their capacity for free choice in light of truthful information on particular occasions must give way to this prior duty. After all, we can ordinarily suppose that neither the murderer nor anyone else will lose his life if I tell the lie (in spite of Kant's worry that my friend might sneak out of my house just as I am telling my lie to his pursuer), although if I do not my friend may well lose his. And if everyone lives, then everyone will have other occasions on which to exercise their humanity freely, even if some are deprived of that ability in the present situation. (To be sure, this analysis does not address Kant's concern that we are open to legal liability

---

[27] This possibility is suggested by Christine Korsgaard in 'The Right to Lie: Kant on Dealing with Evil', *Philosophy and Public Affairs*, 15 (1986), 325–49, repr. in her *Creating the Kingdom of Ends* (Cambridge: Cambridge University Press, 1996), 133–57, at p. 145, although she does not conclusively endorse it.

any time we break a law but saved from liability as long as we adhere to the law, nor his claim that we undermine general confidence in declarations any time we tell a lie. But the latter certainly seems implausible as long as we lie only to put off would-be murderers.)

I would like to think that the solution I have proposed to Kant's problem about the well-meant lie is more plausible than his own, and that it lends some confirmation to the method of lexical ordering of duties that I have extrapolated from Kant's examples in the *Groundwork*. But it should also be clear that this hierarchy by itself cannot solve all conflicts among grounds of obligation. It entails that some perfect duties should be given priority over others, and that all perfect duties should be given priority over imperfect duties, but it is not clear that it solves problems that arise when there are competing grounds of obligation within a single class of duty, nor that its implication that the imperfect duty to develop general capacities to realize particular ends should always be given priority over the imperfect duty to assist in the realization of particular ends. With regard to the latter, it may well seem implausible to maintain that one should always give priority to developing capacities that might help in the realization of possible but unknown ends in the future when there are particular human needs that could be met and projects that could be promoted right now; and both of Kant's own examples that were earlier mentioned, the case of Cato's suicide and the case of competing demands on one's beneficence, are actually cases where there are competing grounds of obligation within a single category of duty, thus where the lexical ordering of classes of duty cannot help. The question in the Cato case can be represented as the question whether it is right to sacrifice the existence of humanity in one person in order to preserve the existence of many other instances of humanity, and the question in the other case is whether particular human relations such as that between parent and child can or even should be allowed to determine the direction of one's concrete efforts to satisfy a single general kind of duty, namely the imperfect duty of beneficence. How can these sorts of conflicts be resolved?

It is obvious that we need more than the lexical ordering of the general categories of duty here, and not obvious that Kant offers us anything more than the barest of hints about what we might use to bring about this final stage of the systematization of duties. But maybe he does offer at least a hint. Take the Cato case: here one might think that if Kant is suggesting an argument in defence of Cato's suicide at all, it must be simply that by sacrificing his own existence he will preserve the existence of many others—the whole Roman people—*qua* free agents. In other words, *the numbers count*—faced with an inescapable choice between preserving one instance of humanity and preserving many, choose the latter. While one might think that numbers count only in consequentialist moral theories such as utilitarianism, there is in fact no reason why they should not count in a theory like Kant's. After all, Kant's fundamental principle that we should treat humanity whether in our own person or in the person of any other already deals with *instances* of humanity; it does not say that we should treat some universal, humanity in general (whatever that would mean), as an end in itself, but that we should treat each and every *instance* of humanity as an end in itself. Unfortunately, there are circumstances in which we cannot preserve the existence of every human being as an end in herself; but in such cases it may be plausible to propose that we can show our respect for humanity as an end in itself by preserving as many *instances* of humanity as we can, and therefore more instances—more people—rather than fewer.[28]

The numbers might well count in the realm of imperfect duty as well. Certainly it will sometimes be better and perhaps mandatory to choose an act of beneficence that will benefit more people rather than fewer, or to help develop talents in more people rather than fewer—for example, to pay one's local school taxes, for the education of many, rather than to contribute to a private school that educates far fewer. And sometimes it will be pretty obvious that one should in fact devote one's resources and efforts to the imperfect duty of beneficence rather than to the imperfect duty of cultivating talents, whether one's own or others'—it may be better or more mandatory to help many in concrete need now than to spend time and money cultivating a talent that may be useful in some indeterminate future. But as Kant's example suggests although does not assert, prioritizing one's efforts towards the fulfilment of imperfect duties may involve other factors than sheer numbers: your duty of beneficence towards your own parents or children, for example, may well trump your duty of beneficence to your neighbours, even if you have more neighbours than parents or children, and there are presumably explanations for such priorities. What could such other factors be? A variety suggest themselves. To one's parents, one may have specific obligations of gratitude, and for one's children, whom one has voluntarily brought into existence, one may have specific obligations of responsibility. So one's

---

[28] For a general argument that the numbers can count even within non-consequentialist theories, see Rahul Kumar, 'Contractualism on Saving the Many', *Analysis*, 61 (2001), 165–70. For discussion of this problem in Kant, see David Cummiskey, *Kantian Consequentialism* (New York: Oxford University Press, 1996), ch. 8, 'The Sacrifices of the Innocent', esp. pp. 141–3.

grounds of obligations towards specific persons may in fact be complex, and the sum of such grounds of obligations towards one group of persons may outweigh that towards another group, even if the latter group is numerically larger than the former. There may also be considerations of efficiency: it may be an empirical fact of human nature that one can be more effective in helping one's parents or children than one can be in helping one's neighbours, and therefore such facts as well as the sheer numbers of people involved must be considered in thinking about how much one can do towards satisfying the open-ended demand of any particular imperfect duty or the open-ended demands of competing imperfect duties. Sometimes empirical probabilities should also count as well: while in some cases it might be improbable that cultivating some talent of one's own will ultimately benefit more human beings than performing some direct act of beneficence now will, in other cases it might be quite probable that one can later do more good by now cultivating a talent (for example, spending the next four years in medical school) rather than practising beneficence now (spending the next four years volunteering in a soup kitchen).

These last observations suggest that at least when it comes to imperfect duties, a variety of empirical factors may affect our derivation of concrete actions from the indeterminate ends these duties prescribe, and that we ultimately need well-informed and well-practised empirical judgment as well as an *a priori* principle and hierarchy in order to resolve conflicts among grounds of obligations and thereby arrive at a fleshed-out system of duties. In fact, Kant is always insistent that a complete system of concepts is only a regulative ideal, and in particular that a system of concepts can only approach the determinacy of the vast domain of its objects asymptotically without ever completely exhausting it. Presumably this limitation on the completeness of any system must apply to a system of duties as well. Nevertheless, I hope I have succeeded here in showing that Kant's account of our duties is genuinely systematic by showing how both of the two main classes of our duty, duties of right and of virtue, may be derived from his single fundamental principle of morality; that he takes all of our duties to extend in principle to all of their proper domain, namely all of humanity; and that he suggests a lexical ordering of our duties of virtue in particular that, like any *a priori* principle, needs to be applied with sound empirical judgment, but which nevertheless suggests a real strategy for resolving conflicts among grounds of obligation and thereby assigning our duties determinate positions with respect to one another.

# PART III

The System of Nature and Freedom

# The Unity of Nature and Freedom: Kant's Conception of the System of Philosophy

### I

In the last stage of his last attempt at philosophical work, the "First Fascicle" of the *Opus postumum*, Kant was apparently trying to unify his theoretical and practical philosophy into a single system of the ideas of nature and freedom. In this work, Kant seems to have wanted to show that the constitution of nature through our forms of intuition and understanding must be compatible with the content of the moral law and our capacity to act in accordance with it, as represented by our idea of God as supreme lawgiver, because both the concept of nature and the idea of God have their common ground in human thought itself. One of the many drafts of a title page that Kant wrote for this never-completed work suggests his intent:

THE HIGHEST STANDPOINT OF
TRANSCENDENTAL PHILOSOPHY
IN THE SYSTEM OF THE TWO IDEAS
BY
GOD, THE WORLD, AND THE SUBJECT WHICH
CONNECTS BOTH OBJECTS,
THE THINKING BEING IN THE WORLD.
GOD, THE WORLD, AND WHAT UNITES BOTH
INTO A SYSTEM:
THE THINKING, INNATE PRINCIPLE OF MAN IN
THE WORLD (*MENS*).
MAN AS A BEING IN THE WORLD,
SELF-LIMITED THROUGH NATURE AND DUTY.

(*OP*, I.III.4, 21:34; Förster, p. 237)[1]

This chapter was originally presented at a conference at Dartmouth College, and first appeared in Sally S. Sedgwick (ed.), *The Reception of Kant's Critical Philosophy* (Cambridge: Cambridge University Press, 2000), pp. 19–53. It is reprinted here with permission of the publisher.

[1] Elements of citations from the *Opus postumum* are, first, fascicle, sheet, and page numbers, and then volume and page number of the text in the Akademie edition (*Kant's*

Some commentators[2] have interpreted texts like this to mean that in his final years Kant undertook a radical revision of his previous critical philosophy. On this view, Kant's earlier "critical idealism,"[3] which argued that human beings could and must impose on a single experience grounded on an unknowable external reality two different but compatible frameworks, the theoretical and practical points of view defined by the forms of intuition and understanding on the one hand and the formal principle of practical reason on the other, would be replaced by a more dogmatic metaphysical doctrine in which the natural and moral worlds would be seen as two products of a single common substratum, human thought itself. This new metaphysical doctrine would be akin to Spinoza's conception of the orders of nature and thought as two modes of the single substance God, a conception that was enjoying a revival in the 1790s among the emerging German idealists such as Schelling and his followers. I will argue, however, that Kant's final attempt to unify the *ideas* of nature and God in the common substratum of human thought was a project continuous with his earlier view that the laws of theoretical and practical reason, or of nature and of morality, must be unifiable within a theory of *reflective* judgment, or a theory of the necessities of *human* thought that claims no validity beyond the human point of view. Kant's numerous references to Spinoza in his final writings are only meant to emphasize the *difference* between his own theory of the systematicity of human thought as a product of reflective judgment and what he took to be the dogmatic monistic metaphysics of Spinoza as

*gesammelte Schriften*, edited by the Royal Prussian (later German) Academy of Sciences, Berlin: Walter de Gruyter [and predecessors], 1900– ); these are then followed by the page number from the translation by Eckart Förster and Michael Rosen, *Immanuel Kant: Opus postumum* (Cambridge: Cambridge University Press, 1993), referred to as "Förster." Other Kantian works will be cited by references to the volume and page numbers in the Akademie edition, except in the case of the *Critique of Pure Reason*, where, as is customary, the pagination of its first and second editions is used. Unless otherwise indicated, translations from these works are my own.

[2] See Burkard Tuschling, in a series of papers including "The Concept of Transcendental Idealism in Kant's *Opus postumum*," in *Kant and Critique: New Essays in Honor of W. H. Werkmeister*, ed. R. M. Dancy (Dordrecht: Kluwer, 1993), pp. 151–67; "Die Idee des transzendentalen Idealismus im späten *Opus postumum*," in *Übergang: Untersuchungen zum Spätwerk Immanuel Kants*, ed. Forum für Philosophie Bad Homburg (Frankfurt: Vittorio Klostermann, 1991), pp. 105–45; and "System des transzendentalen Idealismus bei Kant? Offene Fragen der—und an die—*Kritik der Urteilskraft*," *Kant-Studien* 86 (1995): 196–210; and Jeffrey Edwards, "Spinozism, Freedom and Transcendental Dynamics in Kant's Final System of Transcendental Idealism," In *The Reception of Kant's Critical Philosophy*, ed. Sally S. Sedgwick (Cambridge: Cambridge University Press, 2000), pp. 54–77.

[3] See *Prolegomena to any Future Metaphysics*, 4:294.

revived by Schelling and his followers. The philosophers of Schelling and his generation may have acquired their taste for a single all-embracing philosophical system of reality from Kant, but rebelled against his restriction of such a system to the realm of reflective judgment or mere "ideas."

Some well-known statements from Kant's three *Critiques* might suggest that he had originally considered the concepts and laws of theoretical and practical reason to constitute two compatible but independent systems of thought rather than the single system of ideas contemplated in the *Opus postumum*, and thus that Kant's late work represents a radical change in his views. This remark from the published Introduction to the *Critique of Judgment* is often invoked in defense of the interpretation of Kant's critical philosophy as an insuperable dichotomy of theoretical and practical viewpoints: There is "an incalculable abyss fixed between the domain of the concept of nature, as the sensible, and the domain of the concept of freedom, as the supersensible, so that no transition is possible from the first to the second (thus by means of the theoretical use of reason)" (*CPJ*, Introduction II, 5:175–6). Although the paragraph from which this remark is taken immediately proceeds to argue that there must be some way to bridge this gulf, the subject matter of the ensuing body of the work, the realm of the aesthetic on the one hand and of a methodological conception of teleological judgment on the other, seems to imply that any unification of the two realms of theoretical and practical thought can only take place in the highly subjective realms of analogy, symbolism, methodological principles, and so on, and that the theoretical and practical must remain two essentially distinct forms of thought.

I will argue, however, that there is much less difference between the conception of the systematic unity of nature and freedom in Kant's three *Critiques* and the conception to which he was apparently working in his final days as a functioning philosopher than may initially meet the eye. In fact, Kant had always insisted that the systems of nature and freedom, of theoretical and practical reason, must themselves be able to be conceived as comprising a single system of nature and freedom, although this conception would itself be valid only "from a practical point of view" —precisely as the citation from the *Critique of Judgment* suggests, which after all denies only that the gulf between the domains of nature and freedom can be bridged *by means of the theoretical use of reason*. Although Kant worked at refining his characterization of the practical point of view to the end, there are no arguments in his last writings to suggest that he had fundamentally revised the fundamental content of this conception. Specifically, I will defend the following theses:

(1) In all three *Critiques*, Kant argues that we must be able to conceive of *nature*, and not any other realm, as receptive to the realization of the intended outcome of morality, in the form of the *highest good*, and thus be able to conceive of the realms of nature and freedom as constituting a single system, although such a conception of the single system of nature and freedom is held to be valid only from a practical point of view.

(2) In the *Opus postumum*, Kant suggests that it is the possibility of the recognition and performance of *duty* that must be reconciled with the universality and necessity of natural law by seeing both as having a common ground in human thought; but in my view this represents more of a change of emphasis than a fundamental change in doctrine, not only because the compatibility between nature and duty is already insisted upon in the second *Critique*, but also because there is an essential and intrinsic connection between the concepts of duty and of the highest good. The latter is not a hybrid concept of the merely natural end of happiness as constrained by the moral condition of duty, but is rather a conception of the *object* or intended *outcome* of duty, although not an appropriate characterization of the morally praiseworthy *motivation* for the performance of duty.

(3) Throughout the three *Critiques*, Kant suggests that the concept of the highest good is a necessary and sufficient ground, from a moral point of view, for the postulation of the existence of God as an author of nature distinct from ourselves. In the *Opus postumum*, he states that the idea of God is nothing but a representation of our own capacity to give ourselves the moral law and act in accordance with it, an "idea, the product of our own reason" (e.g. *OP*, VII.X.1, 22:117, Förster 201). Yet this does not constitute a fundamental change in dogma, only a clarification of the subjective significance of the idea of God that had always been part of the meaning of Kant's claim that the postulation of the existence of God was valid only from a practical point of view.

(4) Finally, even if the conception of nature and God as constituting a single system because grounded in the single substratum of human thought did represent a fundamental departure from the earlier conception of the realms of nature and human freedom as constituting a single system because grounded in a single author of nature, this would hardly count as a move *toward* Spinozism, on which nature and human thought are merely two modes of a real God. Rather, it would be an even more radical statement of the

theoretical and practical anthropocentrism to which Kant had been working throughout his mature philosophy.

In what follows, I will argue for these theses by a commentary upon key arguments of the three *Critiques*, followed by a commentary upon some representative notes from the final stages of the *Opus postumum*, the Seventh and First Fascicles.

## II

Kant's first introduction of the concept of the highest good as well as his first statement of the argument that this concept can serve as the ground for the conception of God is found in the "Canon of Pure Reason" of the "Doctrine of Method" of the *Critique of Pure Reason*.[4] By a "canon," Kant means the "sum-total of the *a priori* principles of the correct use of certain cognitive faculties in general" (*CPuR*, A 796/B 824),[5] or a set of positive rules that can serve as grounds for further thought or action rather than a mere critique of unfounded thoughts or actions. The point of the section is to argue that while sensibility and understanding supply a canon for theoretical inquiry and judgment, theoretical reason does not, furnishing instead only metaphysical illusions; it is only reason in its practical use that can supply a canon, in the form of the pure principles of reason that are the foundation of morality and the further assumptions necessary for us to act on these principles. This thesis is stated in the first section of the "Canon," which announces that "the ultimate end of our pure use of reason" is grounded "uniquely and solely in its practical interest" (A 797/B 825). After providing an initial statement of his theory

[4] All our evidence is that at the time of the composition and publication of the first edition of the *Critique of Pure Reason*, Kant intended to proceed immediately to the composition of his long-intended metaphysics of nature and metaphysics of morals, and thus that he conceived of the preliminary statement of the foundations of his moral philosophy provided in the "Canon" as all that would be necessary before he proceeded to the substantive exposition of his normative moral philosophy. The publication of the *Groundwork of the Metaphysics of Morals* in 1785, the *Critique of Practical Reason* in 1788, and even the extensive "Doctrine of Method" in the "Critique of Teleological Judgment" of 1790 before he finally published the *Metaphysics of Morals* in 1797 clearly show that he changed his mind about the adequacy of the "Canon" as the foundation for his moral philosophy; but none of these works, I suggest, radically revised the concept of the highest good and its use in the "Canon"; the major changes in the subsequent works have to do with the exposition of the fundamental principle of morality and the theory of freedom, not the highest good or the system of nature and freedom.

[5] For extensive although inconclusive discussion of what Kant meant by "canon," see Giorgio Tonelli, *Kant's Critique of Pure Reason within the Tradition of Modern Logic*, ed. David H. Chandler (Hildesheim: Georg Olms, 1994), esp. pp. 92–8 and pp. 110–18.

of freedom in this first section, Kant goes on in the second to give his first account of "the ideal of highest good, as a determining ground of the ultimate end of pure reason" (A 804/B 832): Suggesting that he will abjure detailed discussion of the question "What should I do?" as purely practical (although he does not entirely do so), he proposes to discuss the highest good in answer to the question "If I do what I should, what may I then hope?" as "simultaneously practical and theoretical" (A 805/B 833). The key points about the highest good that Kant makes in the "Canon" are themes that will remain constant throughout the rest of his career: First, that the maximal happiness that it includes should be conceived of as the appropriate outcome of virtuous action; second, although there is some ambivalence about this, that this happiness must be conceived of as realizable in nature, thus as requiring a unity of the systems of nature and freedom and their ground in a common author; but, third, that this postulation of the realizability of the highest good and thus of the reality of the single system of nature and freedom and of their author can only be conceived to be valid from a practical point of view.

    1. Kant begins the discussion by drawing a firm distinction between the practical law that has *happiness* as its *motive*, which would be merely "pragmatic," and the practical law that has *worthiness to be happy* as its sole motive, which would be "moral" (*CPuR*, A 806/B 834). But he proceeds to suggest that happiness in accord with moral laws must be conceived to be possible because such happiness would be the intended although not motivating *outcome* of virtuous action, and it would be incoherent to undertake such action if its intended outcome were impossible. Kant defines "the world as it would be if it were in conformity with all moral laws" as a "moral world," and says that in the first instance the conception of the moral world is also the conception of an "intelligible world, since abstraction is made therein from all conditions (ends) and even from all hindrances to morality in it." Yet he also states that this idea of a moral world should be conceived to have "objective reality, not as pertaining to an object of an intelligible intuition . . . but as pertaining to the world of the senses" (A 808/B 836). In other words, the idea of a moral world does not give us theoretical knowledge of a world existing independently of or beyond the sensible world; rather, it gives us a practical ideal for the guidance of our conduct in the same sensible world that we know by means of the senses and the understanding.

    Next, Kant claims that "in an intelligible world," "a system of happiness proportionately combined with morality also can be thought as necessary, since freedom, partly moved and partly restricted by moral laws, would itself be the cause of the general happiness, and rational beings, under the guidance of such principles, would themselves be the authors of their own enduring welfare and at the same time that of others" (*CPuR*, A 809/B 837). Kant's subsequent works will suggest that this claim is grounded on the following argument: (i) since what the law of pure practical reason to which we should be motivated to conform by the virtuous desire to be worthy of happiness rather than by the merely natural desire for happiness itself requires us to do is to respect rational agency in ourselves and others, and (ii) since what making rational agency in both ourselves and others our ultimate end in this way requires is that we do what we can to preserve and promote the necessary conditions for ourselves and others realizing our other ends, whatever they may be, and even strive for the realization of those ends, to the extent that so doing is compatible with the general respect for rational agency itself,[6] yet (iii) since happiness is just the term for the maximal collective satisfaction of the ends of agents, which can in fact be brought about only under the condition of this general respect for agency itself, therefore (iv) the respect for rational agency itself would in fact bring about maximal collective happiness under the ideal circumstances in which each agent acted in conformity with this ideal and no natural conditions external to these agents intervened between their actions and their intended outcomes that would disrupt those outcomes. Under these conditions, a group of agents all motivated by respect for rational agency and the desire to be worthy of being happy would produce their own maximal collective happiness, even though that outcome of their actions would not be the motive of their actions.[7] Kant is quick to observe that no individual is relieved from his obligation under the moral law by anyone else's failure to live up to it, but at the same time he continues to maintain that the connection between "the hope of being happy [and] the unremitting effort to make oneself worthy of happiness" is "necessary" (*CPuR*, A 810/B 838). Subsequent works will suggest that what

[6] For a defense of this interpretation, see Paul Guyer, "Kant's Morality of Law and Morality of Freedom," in *Kant and Critique*, pp. 43–89, and "The Possibility of the Categorical Imperative," *Philosophical Review* 104 (1995): 353–85, reprinted in Guyer, ed., *Kant's Groundwork of the Metaphysics of Morals: Critical Essays* (Lanham: Rowman & Littlefield, 1998), pp. 215–46, as well as Barbara Herman, *The Practice of Moral Judgment* (Cambridge, Mass.: Harvard University Press, 1993), esp. chap. 10.

[7] For an especially clear statement of this view, with its emphasis on collective rather than individual happiness and a clear distinction between happiness as the impermissible motive of virtue and happiness as the ideal object of virtue, see the essay "On the Old Saying: That May Be Right in Theory but does not Work in Practice," Section I, esp. 8:279–84 of vol. VIII of the Akademie edition of *Kants gesammelte Schriften*.

this means is that it would be irrational for us to act to bring about an end or object that we did not believe to be possible—or knew to be impossible—even if bringing about that end is not the *motivation* of our action. Thus it will be rational for us to act as morality requires only if the sphere within which we have to act can be conceived as one where it is possible to realize the outcomes of our action; it is in this way that nature and freedom must constitute a single system.

2. Such a necessary connection, Kant next claims, "can be hoped for only if it is at the same time grounded on a **highest reason**, which commands in accordance with moral laws, as at the same time a cause of nature" (*CPuR*, A 810/B 838).[8] If we have to think of the laws of nature as compatible with the realization of an end that is in fact commanded by the moral law, then we have to think of nature as being caused in a way that makes this true, and the most natural way for us to do this, given our own understanding of causation, is to think of nature as being caused by an intelligent author who in designing it takes the demands of morality into account as well, "a wise author and regent" (A 811/B 839). Kant then introduces an argument, prominent in both of the two subsequent critiques as well, that only morality can lead to a *determinate* conception of God as "single, most perfect and rational," a specification of His predicates to which "speculative theology" could never lead even if it could legitimately lead to the idea of a first cause at all (A 814/B 842).

At this point, Kant takes a next step that will not be repeated in his subsequent expositions of the doctrine of the highest good. He argues that although "we must assume the moral world to be a consequence of our conduct in the sensible world," the senses "do not offer such a connection to us," and the realization of the highest good that we must be able to suppose to be a consequence of our conduct must therefore be supposed to lie in "a world which is future for us" (*CPuR*, A 811/B 839), a "world which is not now visible to us but is hoped for" (A 813/B 841). Here Kant treats the postulates of both God and immortality as conditions necessary for the realization of the maximal happiness contained in the concept of the highest good. He postulates God as the cause of the connection between virtuous action and its appropriate outcome, but defers the realization of this happiness to a life beyond the sensible world, thereby

---

[8] In fact, Kant actually calls the "idea of such an intelligence" that would be "cause of all happiness in the world, insofar as it stands in exact relation with morality... [,] **the ideal of the highest good**," instead of reserving that title for the condition which such an intelligence would cause. See also *CPracR*, 5:125, where he describes the condition of maximal virtue conjoined with maximal happiness the "highest derived good" and God as the putative source of this condition the "highest original good."

having to postulate immortality as well. This partially undermines the unity of nature and freedom that has just been established, for now it seems as if nature must be conceived as necessarily compatible with the *intention* to do what morality requires of us, but not as necessarily compatible with the *realization* of the appropriate outcome of virtuous action, which apparently can be deferred beyond the realm of nature.

What would have to be a key premise for any such argument for an afterlife—namely, the assumption that happiness proportionate to virtue is not just *not evident* in the sensible world but actually *impossible* in the sensible world—goes undefended here, although without such a premise one could argue that the laws of nature merely need to make such happiness *possible* for action that would have it as its intended outcome to be rational.[9] Furthermore, Kant retreats from this position almost as soon as he states it, for he next argues that "this systematic unity of ends in this world of intelligences" must be conceivable as both a sensible and an intelligible world, and thus "leads inexorably to the purposive unity of all things that constitute this great whole, in accordance with laws of nature"; he goes on to say that "the world"—without qualification— "must be represented as having arisen out of an idea if it is to be in agreement with that use of reason without which we would hold ourselves unworthy of reason," and that for this reason "[A]ll research into nature is thereby directed toward the form of a system of ends, and becomes in its fullest development physico-theology" (*CPuR*, A 815–16/B 843–4). Here Kant again suggests that we can only make the actions required by the moral use of reason fully rational if we conceive of a single world—that in which we act—as being described by the laws of both nature and freedom, and of those laws as constituting a single system describing one and the same world.

3. No sooner has Kant argued that the postulation of a determinately conceived author of nature is the necessary condition of the highest good than he also insists that we must hold this concept of God to be correct "not because speculative reason has convinced us of its correctness but because it is in perfect agreement with the moral principles of reason":

Thus, in the end, only pure reason, although only in its practical use, always has the merit of connecting with our highest interest a cognition which mere speculation can only imagine but never make valid, and of thereby making it into not a demonstrated dogma but yet an absolutely necessary presupposition in reason's most essential ends. (*CPuR*, A 818/B 846)

[9] And in the *Critique of Practical Reason*, Kant will argue that the assumption that virtue cannot be followed with happiness in the sensible world is itself a merely subjective assumption (5:145).

Kant argues that we cannot infer a theoretical *is* from a moral *ought:* we can treat God and the unity of the natural and moral that he grounds as a presupposition of our conduct but not as an object of our knowledge.

Just what this means is a difficult issue, about which Kant will have something but perhaps not enough more to say. At this juncture, however, I only want to suggest that in the few pages of the "Canon of Pure Reason" Kant has already staked out three claims from which he will not depart in more than style and emphasis even in his last writings: (i) the appropriate outcome of virtuous action is the highest good, (ii) we must conceive of the world in which we act as described by a single set of both natural and moral laws with a single author for it to be rational for us to act as duty requires, but (iii) the postulation of this systematic unity of nature and freedom and its ground must always remain a presupposition of conduct and not a claim of speculative theology or dogmatic metaphysics.

## III

I now turn to Kant's treatment of the highest good in the *Critique of Practical Reason*.[10] The treatment of the highest good and of its implications for the systematic union of nature and freedom in the second *Critique* is largely continuous with that in the first. Thus, as before, the main points are first, that the collective maximization of happiness contained in the concept of the highest good is in fact an appropriate object of virtuous conduct, not its motive, but also not a merely natural end that is externally constrained by the requirement of virtue; second, although there is still some wavering on this issue, on the whole Kant treats the happiness-component of the highest good—indeed, even more than the virtue-component—as something that must be capable of being realized in nature or the sensible world, which requires that the laws of nature be compatible with the laws of morality and that nature have a moral author; but third, again Kant insists that the postulation of such a common author of the enabling legislation of both the natural and the moral world is valid only from a practical point of view, and now he spells out a little more clearly what that restriction means.

1. The *Critique of Practical Reason* initially appears to be the most formalistic of Kant's ethical writings: Its opening exposition of the

---

[10] For further exposition of my views on several of the issues taken up in this section, see my "In praktischer Absicht: Kants Begriff der Postulate der reinen Vernunft," *Philosophisches Jahrbuch* 104 (1997): 1–18.

fundamental principle of morality equates the categorical imperative
with the requirement of the universalizability of maxims[11] and omits
any mention of the requirement of respect for rational agency as the end
in itself that even in the *Groundwork* is adduced as the ground of the
possibility of the categorical imperative.[12] This makes Kant's introduction of the highest good opaque, and has led some[13] to suppose that the
concept of the highest good is a hybrid concept, which combines the
moral but purely formal requirement of virtue as a concern for universalizability without regard to ends with a merely natural concern for
happiness that may be subjected to a requirement of maximization by
reason as a general striving for the unconditioned but not by practical
reason in any specifically moral sense. On this account, the requirement
that virtue be perfected or maximized *constrains* the pursuit of happiness, or subjects it to a moral condition, but does not entail any properly
moral interest in the realization of happiness, let alone in the maximization or systematization of happiness. But it is clear that this is not Kant's
position, although he does not make his grounds for rejecting it very
clear. On the contrary, although he is again at pains, as he was in the
"Canon," to stress that an interest in happiness cannot be any part of the
*motive* for the pursuit of the highest good (*CPracR*, 5:109, 113), Kant is
again also at pains to stress that the happiness-component of the highest
good is a genuine *object* of morality. This is clear in the following *locus
classicus*:

That virtue (as the worthiness to be happy) is the **supreme condition** of all that
which may seem desirable to us, thus of all our striving for happiness, thus that it
is the **supreme good**, has been proven in the Analytic. But it is not on that
account the whole and complete good, as the object of the faculty of desire of
rational finite beings; for in order to be that, **happiness** is also required, and not
merely in the partial eyes of the person who makes himself into an end, but even
in the judgment of an impartial reason, who considers the former in general as an
end in himself in the world. (*CPracR*, 5:110)

Although highly compacted, this passage is significant both in what it
says and what it does not say. It does not say that the desire for happiness
is a merely natural desire, or a desire of a merely natural being; on the
contrary, it suggests that the desire for happiness is a *rational* desire of a
finite being, and one that is recognized by reason as such in regarding

[11] See particularly §4, Theorem III, 5:26–7.
[12] See *G*, 4:428; for discussion, see my article "The Possibility of the Categorical
Imperative" (see note 6).
[13] Notably Lewis White Beck; see *A Commentary on Kant's Critique of Practical
Reason* (Chicago: University of Chicago Press, 1960), esp. pp. 242–5.

a being who is both rational but also placed in a world as an end in himself. Thus, although talk of an end in itself has heretofore been excluded from the *Critique of Practical Reason*, at this crucial point it appears, suggesting that what underlies the concept of the highest good even here is the view that what morality requires, out of respect for reason rather than a mere desire for happiness, is respect for rational agency as such. But rational agents or ends in themselves are finite creatures who *have* ends, so that what respect for them *as* ends requires is respect for, or the preservation and promotion of, their capacity to *have* and *pursue* ends; and since what happiness consists in is the attainment of ends, virtue therefore actually requires and does not just constrain the impartial pursuit of happiness. It is in this way that the happiness-component of the highest good is part of the object of morality—the other part, of course, being the cultivation of the virtuous *motivation* of duty itself—and not just a merely natural end externally constrained by morality.

2. Second, although there is still one point of obscurity on this issue, for the most part the second *Critique* stresses more clearly than the first that the happiness that comprises part of the highest good is to be conceived of as realizable *in nature* and therefore requires the postulation of a morally motivated author *of nature*. Early in his discussion, Kant argues that the proposition that striving after happiness itself produces a virtuous disposition is "**absolutely false**," but that the proposition that striving after virtue produces happiness is not absolutely but only "**conditionally** false," for it is false if considered as a claim about a "form of causality in the sensible world" but might be true if "my existence is thought of as a noumenon in an intellectual world" (*CPracR*, 5:114). This might be taken to imply that the happiness that is to be connected with virtue in the highest good need not and perhaps cannot be thought of as a happiness that is to be realized within the sensible realm of nature, but somewhere else. Kant does not, however, draw this conclusion. Rather, he only denies that the connection between virtue and happiness in nature is *immediate*: He states that "it is not impossible that the morality of disposition have if not an immediate than a mediate and indeed necessary connection as cause (by means of an intelligible author of nature) with happiness as an effect in the sensible world" (5:115). Such a connection would be merely contingent in the case of a nature that contains merely our own powers as revealed by our own senses, but, Kant implies, if nature is regarded *both* as object of the senses and as the product of an intelligent author, then the connection would be necessary rather than contingent.

By bringing God into the argument from the highest good in the form of the intelligent author of nature, in other words, Kant implies that the happiness required by the highest good must be realizable within nature and not elsewhere. He continues to imply as much when he dramatically separates the postulation of immortality from the postulation of God in the ensuing discussion. Conceiving of the highest good as requiring the maximization of both virtue and happiness (not, as he is sometimes taken to suggest, mere proportionality between the two),[14] Kant argues that the maximization of virtue, or development of a holy will, cannot be expected to occur in a finite phenomenal lifetime, and that we must think of that as something that takes place in immortality (*CPracR*, 5:122–3). But he does not go on to say the same thing about happiness and God as its ground. Instead, he argues that the existence of God must be postulated as the "cause of the whole of nature" in order to explain "the possibility of the second element of the highest good." This only makes sense if the happiness that is required by the concept of the highest good is envisioned as occurring within nature.

Kant's argument for this point is tricky. He begins by stating that the "acting rational being in the world is not at the same time the cause of the world and of nature itself," and thus that there cannot be a ground of a "necessary connection between morality and the happiness proportionate to it" in the constitution of an ordinary agent considered by itself (*CPracR*, 5:124). The next claim Kant makes, however, is not what we might expect, namely that God must be postulated as the ground of such a necessary connection; rather, he argues that a supreme cause of nature must be postulated as "the ground of the agreement of nature not merely with a law of the will of rational beings but of the representation of this **law**, in so far as they make it into the **supreme determining ground of their will**, thus of agreement not merely with the form of morals, but with their morality as the determining ground of that, i.e., with their moral disposition"; thus the highest good is only possible "insofar as a supreme cause of nature is assumed which has a causality in accord with the moral disposition" (5:125). In other words, a moral cause of nature is

---

[14] In other words, the highest good is not any part of a doctrine of punishment or retribution: It does not imply that the virtuous should be rewarded with happiness and the vicious punished with unhappiness, but simply that the object of morality is to strive for the maximum of virtue and the maximum of happiness. In making this claim, I reject the supposition frequently made that Kant's doctrine of the highest good rests on a principle of proportionality that itself has no clear basis in his conception of principles of pure practical reason. For another critique of this supposition, see Andrews Reath, "Two Conceptions of the Highest Good in Kant," *Journal of the History of Philosophy* 26 (1988): 593–619.

postulated here in order to insure that human beings as natural creatures are capable of forming moral intentions, or being virtuous. Nevertheless, Kant goes on to claim that the God so introduced, as the "**highest original good**," is the ground of "a **highest derived good** (of the best world)," and then to argue that it is our duty "to endeavor to produce and advance the highest good in the world" (5:126). Since it is the complete highest good and not just virtue as one of its two components that is to be produced in the world, the implication is clear that not only virtuous intention but happiness as its intended outcome must be conceived by us as possible within the world, not somewhere else, and that God as a moral author is being postulated as the ground of the possibility of both virtue and happiness in the world, the same sensible world where we ourselves could connect these two components only contingently but where God can make their connection, or the systematic union of nature and freedom, necessary.

3. As in the first *Critique*, however, Kant also immediately restricts the force of this argument with the claim that it is valid "only from a practical point of view" (*CPracR*, 5:133). This is now presented as a complex restriction: the coherence of moral conduct requires (i) that we postulate the *possibility* of the realization of the happiness called for in the concept of the highest good in the sensible or natural world, which in turn requires (ii) that we postulate the *actual existence* of God, where, however, (iii) that postulation is not entailed by any theoretical considerations whatsoever but is only a practical presupposition of our conduct in accord with the demands of morality and where, moreover, (iv) the *predicates* for the *determination* of this concept of God cannot be furnished by any theoretical speculation but only by the demands of morality. In order to understand Kant's notion of a postulate of practical reason and thus the epistemic status of his conception of the systematic unity of nature and freedom, we need to touch on each of these points, even if only briefly.

(i) What we must postulate in order to make action rational is the *possibility* of realizing the end foreseen and intended by that action, not a guarantee of the actual realization of that end. Thus at the outset of the section from which we have been quoting Kant says that the moral law must "lead to the possibility of the second element of the highest good" (*CPracR*, 5:124), and at the end of its first long paragraph he writes that "the postulate of the possibility of the **highest derived good** (of the best world) is at the same time the postulate of the actuality of a **highest original good**, namely the existence of God" (5:125). This point is important, for it sometimes seems as if Kant thinks an endeavor is rational only if its success is in some sense guaranteed,[15] but here he clearly suggests that as long as an enterprise is *motivated* by sufficiently weighty grounds, as morality above all is, then its pursuit is rational as long as its successful outcome is *not impossible*.[16]

(ii) To explain how we can conceive of nature as a sphere in which the realization of the highest good is even guaranteed to be *possible*, however, we must think that the *actual* ground of its existence is the existence of God, not merely that God is a possible cause of it. Presumably the thought here is that if God is merely a possible cause of nature, but there are other possible causes of it as well, then if one of those other causes is the actual cause of nature, the realization of the highest good in nature may not even be possible; but if God is the actual cause of nature, then the realization of the highest good is assuredly possible. Thus the content of the postulation of God is an existence-statement, not a merely possibility-statement: "the possibility of this highest good . . . occurs only under the presupposition of the existence of God" (*CPracR*, 5:125).

(iii) At the same time, however, Kant hedges the semantically existential *content* of the practical postulate of God with restrictions on its epistemic *force*. Thus he immediately follows the last remark cited with the statement that "this moral necessity is **subjective**, i.e., a need, and not **objective**, i.e., itself a duty; for there cannot be any duty to assume the existence of a thing (since this pertains merely to the theoretical use of reason" (*CPracR*, 5:125). Alternatively, he goes on to say that from a theoretical point of view the assumption of the existence of God would be, as a ground of explanation, a mere "hypothesis," although with regard to "an object set for us by the moral law" it can be a "**belief and even a pure belief of reason**" (5:126). Kant clarifies this distinction by suggesting that there are two conditions for a practical postulate. First, the concept to be postulated must itself be *not impossible* or free from contradiction, even from a purely theoretical point of view. Second, the affirmation of the reality of the concept, even if itself unwarranted by any

---

[15] For instance, in the Introduction to the *Critique of Judgment*, he writes as if we must adopt the principle that nature *is* systematic if it is to be rational for us to strive to find systematic concepts of it (*CPJ*, Introduction IV, 5:183–4).

[16] The same point is also made in a striking comment in a note from the 1790s, which was incorporated into Jäsche's edition of Kant's *Logic*. Here Kant writes that belief in the practical postulate of the highest good "is the necessity of assuming the objective reality of the highest good, i.e., the possibility of its object as *a priori* necessary object of choice. If we look merely to actions, we do not need this belief. However, if we would go beyond actions to the possession of the end that is possible through them, then this must be thoroughly possible" (R 2793, 16:515; see *Logic*, 9:69 n.).

theoretical ground, must still not be arbitrary, for then it would be mere theoretical hypothesis; instead, it must be something that we must believe if it is to be rational and coherent for us to act in a certain way, where acting in that way is itself morally requisite. Kant suggests these two conditions when he writes, first, that the postulates of practical reason are "(transcendent) thoughts in which there is nothing impossible," which implies that they must have noncontradictory theoretical content, and then that what would otherwise be "**transcendent** and merely **regulative** principles of speculative reason" become "**immanent** and **constitutive** insofar as they are grounds for **making actual** the **necessary object** of pure practical reason (the highest good)" (5:135). This, perhaps especially the use of the phrase "making actual," suggests that a rational belief is something that must be believed in order to make a form of conduct coherent, but that it has no force outside of that context.

Thus far, then, we have the claims that the highest good must be considered to be *possible* in nature, and that its ground, a moral Author of nature, must be considered to be *actual* from a practical point of view, where that in turn means that it must be *theoretically* possible and a necessary presupposition of a mode of *conduct*, but not otherwise grounded. Finally, Kant adds the last element of his position, the claim that (iv) the concept of God can be given *determinate content* only from a practical point of view, that is, the only predicates that can be ascribed to him in order to amplify the vague conception of him as the author of nature are those that are necessary to conceive of him as the ground of the realizability of the highest good. This argument is expanded beyond the hint at it offered in the "Canon," but still not developed at the length it will be in the *Critique of Judgment*. The argument is essentially a tacit response to Hume's critique of the argument from design in his *Dialogues concerning Natural Religion*: Kant agrees with the Philo of Dialogue XII[17] that the most that we could infer from the amount of "order, design and magnitude" we observe in nature is that it has an author who is to *some* degree "wise, beneficent and powerful," but responds that we can only infer that this author is "all-knowing, all-good and all-powerful" (*CPracR*, 5:139) on the ground that these are the qualities necessary for him to ground the possible realization of the highest good. Thus, God must be conceived of as "**all-knowing** in order [for him] to know my conduct in its innermost disposition in all possible cases and throughout

---

[17] See David Hume, *The Natural History of Religion and the Dialogues concerning Natural Religion*, ed. A. Wayne Colver and John V. Price (Oxford: Clarendon Press, 1976), pp. 244–5.

the future," or in order to judge my virtue, and he must be "**all-powerful**" and "**all-present**" in order "to apportion to it the appropriate consequences" (5:140). Thus, Kant's moral theology consists not merely in the claim that only morality gives us a ground for *believing* in the *existence* of God; it also includes the claim that only morality gives us a *determinate conception* of God.

On the basis of this conception, however, we can then conceive of the systematic union of nature and freedom through their common author; the concept of this single system is thus reached through the concept of the highest good, which is itself a morally necessary concept, and is therefore valid though only from a practical point of view, as itself a postulate for which God is the ground. Let us now see whether Kant modifies that thought at all at the next stage of his thought.


## IV


The *Critique of Judgment* is a work of great complexity as well as obscurity. One measure of the complexity of the work is that although its division into the two main parts of a "Critique of Aesthetic Judgment" and a "Critique of Teleological Judgment" might be taken to suggest that there are two main objects for the single power of reflective judgment that is supposed to be under analysis in the work as a whole, namely objects of beauty on the one hand and natural organisms on the other, in fact at least *five* distinguishable objects of reflective judgment are actually discussed: two in the aesthetic sphere, namely (i) particular objects of *beauty*, the internal quasisystematicity of whose parts is recognized by aesthetic judgment rather than by conceptual judgment, but which may be either naturally occurring objects or products of human intentional artistic activity, and then (ii) boundless regions of nature, which are the causes[18] of the experience of the *sublime*; and three connected with the idea of teleology, namely: (iii) individual natural objects, the internal organization of whose parts can be judged under a concept of reciprocal causation rather than by merely aesthetic judgment, or *organisms*; (iv) the system of empirical scientific *concepts* standing under the purely

---

[18] It might seem natural to say that regions of nature (mountain ranges, seas, etc.) are the *objects* of our experience of the sublime, but Kant actually denies this because he wants to emphasize that what we ultimately admire and enjoy in the experience of the sublime is not nature as such but rather our own capacities of theoretical and practical reason to both form the idea of the magnitude of nature and also to resist its threats; see *CPJ*, §23, 5:245–6.

formal laws of nature furnished by the categories and manifesting further internal organization in the form of homogeneity, specificity and affinity; and finally, (v) the whole of *nature* itself as a system, including but by no means limited to those internally systematic parts of nature that are themselves systems, that is, organisms. Kant explores many relations and analogies among these various objects, making his argumentation in this work particularly dense.

But in fact the work begins and ends with a claim with which we are already familiar. This is the claim that even though—or precisely because—the great abyss between nature and freedom cannot be bridged by the *theoretical* use of reason, it can and must be bridged by the *practical* use of freedom, from whose point of view nature must be able to be seen as a realm within which morality's demands on both our actions and their outcomes can be satisfied. In Kant's words, the concept of freedom "**should** have influence" on the concept of nature, "namely the concept of freedom should make the end which is set forth through its laws actual in the sensible world; and nature must therefore be able to be so conceived that the lawfulness of its form is at least in agreement with the possibility of the end which is to be effected within it in accordance with the laws of freedom" (*CPJ*, Introduction II, 5:176). That is to say, in this work Kant reiterates two theses already made clear in the previous *Critiques*, that the fundamental principle of morality does not just constrain our natural ends but itself sets an overarching end for us, the highest good, and that this end must be capable of being realized in nature in order for our actions that have it as their end to be rational and coherent; and the reiteration of this theme within a general theory of reflective judgment and its regulative principles only clarifies the position, already suggested as "the practical point of view," that this conception of the unity of nature and freedom is to be treated, like a maxim for the conduct of inquiry, as a principle that may have the form of a proposition about objects but that is not asserted to have an ordinary objective truth-value.

The argument underlying Kant's *Critique of Teleological Judgment* can be outlined like this. Starting from the side of theoretical judgement,[19] we see that the peculiar complexity of individual organisms makes it necessary for us to conceive of them as if they were products of intelligent design, that the necessity of so conceiving of individual organisms also makes it inevitable for us to conceive of nature as a whole

---

[19] I have explored this argument further in "From Nature to Morality: Kant's New Argument in the 'Critique of Teleological Judgment' "; in this volume, Ch. 12.

as a systematic product of intelligent design, but that although there is thus a purely theoretical impetus for us so to conceive of nature as a whole, it is not in fact possible for us to form any *determinate* and *unique* conception of nature as a whole as a system except by treating some part of that system, namely humankind, as *its* end because it is an end *in itself*, a characterization that is possible only from a moral point of view. At the same time, morality itself requires that we conceive of humankind as an end in itself and also conceive of the moral perfection of humankind, in the form of the highest good, as something possible within nature and indeed as the end of nature as a whole. So the ultimate argument of Kant's teleology is that the scientific point of view contains an idea of systematicity that can only be satisfied by the moral point of view, and conversely that the moral point of view requires us to conceive of nature as a sphere within which humankind can successfully work out its moral vocation. Yet whether we start from the scientific or the moral end of this argument, in either case what we get is a regulative principle of conduct rather than a theoretical principle of cognition.

Kant's commitment to such an argument is confirmed by several striking outlines of it among his notes. The first such outline, which neatly shows the steps from individual organisms to a view of nature as a purposive system as a whole and then the need to bring in moral considerations in order to make that system determinate, apparently dates from the 1780s:

**Moral proof.** We find **ends** in the world; these give our insight an indication of a being which would be in accordance with **the analogy** of an **intelligent cause** of the world. But its **concept is not determined** through this [analogy] either for the theoretical or practical principles of our use of reason: Because it **explains nothing** in regard to the former and **determines nothing** in regard to the latter.

Only reason, through the **moral law**, gives us a **final end**. This cannot be attained through our powers, and yet we are to have it as our aim. It can be brought about **only in the world**, consequently so far as **nature agrees with it**. A nature, however, which agrees with a moral final end, would be a **morally effective** cause. Thus we must assume a being **outside** of nature as its author, which would be a **moral being**, a cause of the world equipped with understanding and will. (R 6173, 18:477–8)

The first paragraph shows that the idea of particular systems within nature introduces at best an indeterminate idea of nature as a whole as a system; the second paragraph shows that the final end of morality, the highest good, necessarily introduces a certain view of nature as compatible with that end and of its author as determined above all by the moral predicates necessary to explain that compatibility.

A second note from the next decade outlines the second stage of this argument particularly clearly:

First the representation of the world as a system of the *nexus finalis physici* (*causarum finalium physicarum* among which mankind must also be). Thus an intelligent primordial being, but not yet God, because the concept of the perfection of the world from experience is not adequate for that. Now the representation of the world as of a *systematis causarum finalium moralium* for the highest good. For humankind, which is a member of the *nexus finalis physici* but also touches on a principle of a higher *nexus finalis* in itself, also relates its existence in regard to the same intelligent author; but the concept of that is that of a being as the author of the highest good, because this alone is appropriate to the end-relation of the moral human. (R 6451, 18:723)

Here Kant skips the first step of the argument, but again spells out clearly that only a moral conception of God that is in fact based on the moral end of human beings can provide a determinate conception of the world as a whole as a system of causes.

Let us now look at the details of this argument in its fullest exposition in the *Critique of Judgment*.

1. First, the Introduction to the third *Critique* lays out the framework of Kant's argument: the critique of teleological judgment is to bridge the gap between the realms of nature and freedom precisely by showing us that it is *possible* to realize within nature the final end the pursuit of which is made *necessary* by practical reason. As Kant puts it,

The effect in accordance with the concept of freedom is the final end [*Endzweck*] which (or the appearance of which in the sensible world) should exist, for which the condition of its possibility in nature (in the nature of the subject as sensible being, namely as human being) is presupposed. What the power of judgment presupposes *a priori* and without regard to the practical yields the mediating concept between the concepts of nature and the concept of freedom, which makes possible the transition from the purely theoretical to the purely practical, from the lawfulness in accordance with the former to the final end in accordance with the latter, in the concept of a **purposiveness** of nature: for thereby is the possibility of the final end known, which can become actual only in nature and in harmony with its laws. (*CPJ*, Introduction IX, 5:195–6)

That is, a teleological view of nature that is not itself dictated by morality will nevertheless show nature, above all our own nature as creatures in the sensible world, to be suitable for the realization of the final end that is dictated by morality.

2. Next, the opening move of the *Critique of Teleological Judgment* in particular is to argue that the teleological viewpoint that is forced upon us by the attempt to comprehend individual organisms in nature also makes it natural for us to conceive of nature as a whole as a system that is designed by an intelligent author and must therefore have or be compatible with a final end. In my view, Kant's interest in making this point is what motivates him to discuss the problem of understanding organisms at all.[20] For present purposes, we will have to take for granted Kant's argument that organic processes such as growth, self-maintenance, and reproduction (*CPJ*, §64, 5:371–2) involve a kind of reciprocal causation that cannot be understood through our mechanical model of temporally unidirectional causal influence, but instead require, precisely in order to accommodate them to our ordinary conception of the temporal direction of causation, the postulation of an antecedent design of the organism and therefore an antecedent designer (§65, especially 5:373)—an argument that has, to say the least, been put into question by the modern synthesis of genetics and natural selection. The point to be emphasized here is Kant's next move, the argument that once we have conceived of particular organisms or "physical ends" as systematically organized products of design, it then becomes irresistible for us to conceive of nature as a whole as a systematic organization with an end. This is in fact the final move of the "Analytic of Teleological Judgment":

It is only matter, insofar as it is organized, which necessarily carries with it the idea of it as a natural end, since its specific form is at the same time a product of nature. But now this concept necessarily leads to the idea of the whole of nature as a system in accordance with the rule of ends, to which idea now all mechanism of nature in accordance with principles of reason must be subordinated (at least for the investigation of natural appearance thereby). The principle of reason is permissible only subjectively, i.e., the maxim that everything in the world is good for something, nothing in it is in vain; and through the example which nature gives in its organic products one is justified, indeed invoked to expect nothing in it and its laws except what is purposive in the whole. (*CPJ*, §67, 5:378–9)

... if we have once discovered in nature a capacity for bringing forth products which can only be conceived by us in accordance with the concept of final causes, then we go further and may also estimate those which do not (either in themselves or even in their purposive relation) make it necessary to seek out another principle for their possibility beyond the mechanism of blindly efficient causes as nevertheless belonging to a system of ends. (5:380–1)

---

[20] For further discussion of this point, see my "Organisms and the Unity of Science," in *Kant and the Sciences*, ed. Eric Watkins (New York: Oxford University Press, 2000); in this volume, Ch. 5.

Two points must be noted here. First, as Kant stresses in the first of these paragraphs, in the following §68, and then in the whole of the following "Dialectic of Teleological Judgment," from a purely theoretical point of view we are not justified in conceiving of a teleological view either of natural organisms or of the whole of nature as anything more than a heuristic, methodological or regulative principle intended to encourage and guide us in investigations ultimately aimed at discovering mechanical explanations of natural phenomena (of precisely the type that modern evolutionists have discovered): The term "purposiveness" "signifies only a principle of the reflective, not the determinant power of judgment and therefore should not introduce a special ground of causality, but only add to the use of reason another sort of research than that in accordance with mechanical laws in order to supplement the inadequacy of the latter itself for the empirical investigation of all the particular laws of nature" (*CPJ*, §68, 5:383). Even from the theoretical point of view then, let alone the practical point of view, the conception of systems within nature, and presumably the idea of nature as a whole as a system that is suggested by the first, remain subjective ideas rather than objective dogmas. Second, as Kant stresses at the outset of §67, the idea of nature as a system as a whole, room for which is created by the special condition necessary for us to conceive of organisms, does not itself yield any *unique* and *determinate* way of seeing nature as a whole as a system: we might think that grass is necessary to nourish cattle and cattle in turn to nourish humans, but from a purely scientific point of view we cannot see any reason why we should not instead think that the purpose of both cattle and humans is just to facilitate the growth of grass (5:378; §82, 5:427).

3. Kant's next move, then, will be to argue that in order to form a unique conception of nature as a determinate system aimed at the promotion of any particular end, we must introduce the idea of something that is intrinsically final or an end in itself, something that is not just chosen arbitrarily as the endpoint of a system of final causes but that must be conceived as an end and that imposes on us a view of the other elements of nature as organized in its service. Such a conception can only be provided by morality, which dictates that we conceive of mankind and its highest good as an end in itself; and morality in turn requires that we be able to conceive of nature as an arena within which the end it imposes can be achieved. Thus the teleological perspective that is necessitated by the intellectual puzzle of organisms opens up for us a possibility of seeing nature as a whole as a system, but this cannot be made determinate without appeal to morality, and in any case morality requires us to take a view of nature as well as reason as purposive, so the possibilities

of the scientific view of nature and the necessities of the moral view of nature ultimately coincide. This is the complex point for which Kant argues in the "Methodology of Teleological Judgment," precisely because this is nothing less than the investigation of the ultimate conditions for the *application* of teleological judgment.

Kant begins the "Methodology" by reiterating that teleology furnishes no constitutive principles for either natural science or theology, but only reflective principles, principles for the critique of the use of judgment that will show us how natural science and theology must ultimately, although only subjectively, be combined (*CPJ*, §79, 5:417). Next, going beyond his earlier suggestion that teleological principles have a purely heuristic function in encouraging and guiding us in the search for mechanical explanations, he argues that mechanical explanations, of the development of natural forms, even a completely worked out theory of evolution[21] (§80, 5:418–19), "only push the explanation further back" (420) and still require some explanation of why it is purposive for nature to be constituted with such mechanisms, which can only be provided by an appeal to an end and its intelligent author (421). We must thus conceive of the mechanisms of nature as "the instrument of an intentionally acting cause, to whose end nature in its mechanical laws as subordinated" (§81, 5:422). Kant then asserts that "the possibility of the union of two such different types of causality" must lie in the "supersensible substrate of nature," for there our ignorance prevents us from explaining but at the same time prevents us from precluding such a combination; but he then also insists that we can conceive of an intelligent and purposive creation of nature through mechanical means only if we can find something *in* nature that is itself intrinsically final and gives the rest of nature a point. Reiterating his claim that the means–end relation we introduce into the system of nature as a whole must not be arbitrary, Kant in effect lays down two conditions on the nonarbitrary end of nature.

First, he states that "the ultimate end of creation here on earth" must be one "which can form a concept of ends for itself and can through its reason make a system of ends out of an aggregate of purposively formed things" (*CPJ*, §82, 5:426–7). Kant does not state explicitly why the final end *in* nature must be capable of forming a conception of ends when that final end is also conceived of as the final end *of* a supersensible cause; but we

---

[21] I use this word here in its contemporary sense, not in Kant's own sense in which it refers to a theory of "individual preformation" according to which all natural forms in nature as originally created (*CPJ*, §81, 5:423), a sense diametrically opposed to the contemporary sense of "evolution."

can take this claim to be a reminder that we are after all within the realm of reflective judgment, and that this whole story of ends is an artifact of our own judgment that will be inconceivable unless we ourselves can conceive of ends and of nature as a system of and for this end. In any case, however, the requirement that the ultimate end of nature itself be able to form the conception of ends is only a necessary, not a sufficient condition for the view of nature as a system of ends. For Kant next argues that the end that this ultimate end of nature conceives must not itself be a merely natural end, such as mere happiness, but an unconditional end the value and the setting—if not the realization—of which is independent of nature. Kant stresses the most obvious reason why a merely natural condition such as happiness *per se* cannot be the ultimate end of nature, namely that nature does not seem particularly well adapted to produce this condition (§83, 5:430–1); but he leaves tacit the more important point that even if nature did produce happiness, then there would still be nothing to distinguish this natural condition as the putative end of nature from any other natural condition and thus give a unique end to the system of nature as a whole. So what is necessary is an end that makes its agent an end in itself from a rational and not merely natural point of view. This, like the first condition of being able to conceive of ends at all, is only satisfied in the case of a human being, and is satisfied in particular only by "the formal, subjective condition of setting ends for himself in general and (independent of nature in his determination of ends) of using nature as an appropriate means for the maxims of his free ends in general" (431). In other words, what makes man an end in himself in the moral point of view, namely the intrinsic value of free and rational agency, is the only unconditional end that can be conceived to be the end of the system of nature as a whole as well, and the final end that is sought by scientific judgment in its attempt to conceive of nature as a system can only be the one furnished by moral reason, which would in any case impose this idea upon nature.

The contrast that Kant draws in the present argument between "happiness on earth" (431) on the one hand and "the culture of discipline" on the other, that which consists in "the liberation of the will from the despotism of desires, through which, by our attachment to certain natural things, we are made incapable of choosing for ourselves" (432), might appear to undercut the claim I have been making that throughout the three *Critiques* Kant sees the unity of nature and freedom as the possibility of the realization of the highest good, which of course includes happiness, and indeed happiness that is to be possible "on earth." This appearance is misleading, however, for what Kant is excluding as the ultimate end of nature is only mere happiness, or happiness conceived of as being produced by merely natural means rather than by human choice governed by reason; if the highest good is conceived of as containing not merely happiness proportionate to virtue but happiness produced *through* the virtuous exercise of human freedom, then this remains the intended end of virtuous human action and thus the ultimate end of nature. This should already be clear from the characterization of that capacity that makes human beings the ultimate end of nature as the capacity to be rational *in setting ends*, for rational agents set ends in order to realize them, and in the realization of ends lies happiness. But the point is also clear in the language Kant uses in his own summaries of the argument we have just rehearsed. Thus, drawing its exposition to a close, he writes:

Now we have only a single sort of being in the world whose causality is teleological, i.e., directed to ends, and yet at the same time so constituted that the law in accordance with which it has to determine its ends is represented by it as unconditional and independent of natural conditions but necessary in itself. The being of this sort is mankind, but considered as noumenon; the only natural being in which we can yet cognize a supersensible capacity (**freedom**) and even the law of its causality together with its object, which it can set before itself as the highest end (the highest good in the world) on the part of its own constitution. (*CPJ*, §84, 5:435)

Even though man must be regarded as noumenal in order to be regarded as free, the sphere of his activity and thus where he has to realize his own highest good, which is as it were transitively the ultimate end of the whole of nature, the end to which so far as man can "he must subject the whole of nature," is "in the world." Likewise, summing up his whole critique of the eighteenth-century natural theology or argument from design and his alternative of a moral theology several sections later, Kant lays even more stress on the earthly arena within which the end of morality must be realizable. Using something very much like the dual formula I have used, that the highest good unifies nature and freedom because it must be seen as the ultimate end of both, Kant writes:

The moral law as formal rational condition of the use of our freedom obligates us for itself alone, without depending on any end as material condition, but it nevertheless also determines for us, indeed *a priori*, a final end, to strive after which it makes obligatory for us: and this is the **highest good in the world** possible through freedom. (*CPJ*, §87, 5:450)

Thus, the third *Critique* maintains the position that even though the highest good is nonnatural in the sense of being made an end by freedom rather than nature, it must be realizable in nature, and nature and freedom must be able to be conceived of as a single system with a common ground in order to satisfy that condition.

4. In the *Critique of Teleological Judgment,* Kant states the argument that it is only the necessity of postulating a condition for the realizability of the highest good that justifies us in postulating the existence of an intelligent author of nature and only these same conditions that allow us to ascribe determinate predicates to this God at even greater length than he did in the *Critique of Practical Judgment (CPJ,* §§85–7). Befitting his new presentation of his moral theology as part of a general theory of reflective and regulative judgment, he is also more explicit than before about the "Limitation of the validity of the moral proof" (§88, 5:453). His new discussion of this limitation is worth our attention because the light it sheds on Kant's conception of a practical postulate will be crucial in determining whether the *Opus postumum* represents any radical change in Kant's view of the unity of nature and freedom. The two key points that Kant here suggests are implied by the restriction that "the idea of a final end in the use of freedom" has "a subjectively-**practical** reality" (453) are, first, that from a theoretical point of view all that can be established is that the object of the postulate, the highest good or its ground, the existence of God, is not contradictory or impossible, and second, that the representation of this object from a practical point of view as not just possible but actual serves not to ground any cognitive claim but to direct our energies in moral conduct. Kant makes the first of these points when he writes:

The actuality of a highest morally-legislative Founder is therefore sufficiently demonstrated merely **for the practical use** of our reason, without determining anything theoretically in regard to its existence. For [reason] requires for the possibility of its end, which is set for us by its own legislation, an idea, through which the incapacity of prosecuting it in accordance with the merely natural concept of the world would be removed (adequately for the reflective judgment). (456)

Here, the point is that in order for our pursuit of the end of reason to be noncontradictory, we must be able to conceive of that object and its ground as free of contradiction. Second, Kant stresses that the point of the postulation of these ideas is not cognition but conduct:

The final end is merely a concept of our practical reason and cannot be deduced from any data of experience for theoretical judgment, nor be related to their cognition. No use of this concept is possible except solely for practical reason in accordance with moral laws; and the final end of creation is that constitution of the world which agrees with that which we can determinately produce only in

accordance with laws, namely the final end of our pure practical reason...
—Now through the practical reason which sets this end for us we have, in a
practical regard, a ground, namely the application of our powers for effecting it,
for assuming its realizability... (§88, 5:455)

The role of the idea of the realizability of the highest good is simply to
encourage us to use our own powers to bring it about, and Kant's claim is
that it has no validity outside of this use. Postulates of practical reason,
then, are "subjectively-practical" in the sense that they must be theoretically noncontradictory and practically necessary and efficacious in
directing our conduct toward purely moral goals, and have no other
force.

5. Before leaving the *Critique of Judgment*, I want to spend a moment
on the issue of Spinozism, which is a recurring although by no means
dominant theme in the work. Two key objections that he makes to this
doctrine, as he understands it, are, first, that Spinozism eliminates any
conception of intentionality, design and choice both within the world
and within the substance that is its ground; and, second, that Spinozism
eliminates any recognition of contingency in our objects of either knowledge or action. These are both grave objections from Kant's point of
view, and it would take strong evidence to prove that he ever gave up
these objections.

Both of these points are made in the "Dialectic of Teleological Judgment." Kant first objects that Spinozism is a system of *fatality*, and that
the "fatalism of purposiveness" is also an *idealism* thereof, that is, a view
on which there is the mere appearance but no reality of design and choice
both on the part of God and of any of his modes, such as ourselves.
Kant's reason for saying this is his view that, while according to Spinoza
the "conception of the original being is not to be understood," it is clear
that the connection of ends in the world "is derived from a primordial
being, but not from its understanding, hence not from any intention, but
from the necessity of its nature and the unity of the world that stems from
that" (*CPJ*, §72, 5:391–2). Now, it might not seem fair for Kant to charge
Spinoza with advocating a mere "idealism" with regard to ends, whether
in God or in his modes, since Kant himself, after all, insists that the
purposiveness of the world and its author and perhaps even ourselves is
demonstrable only from the practical point of view and not from a
theoretical point of view. But that is precisely Kant's point: In his view,
Spinoza's argument for a necessitarian God who has no freedom
and intention in himself and therefore eliminates all freedom and intentionality from the world is based on an illegitimate elevation of the

theoretical and mechanical worldview of empirical science into a meta-physical dogma and an elimination of any practical conception of God. This seems to be what Kant means when he asserts that Spinozism is based on "a mere misinterpretation of a universal ontological concept of a thing in general": Spinoza's theory is a version of "physicotheology," which excludes a teleological conception of nature simply by carrying "mere theoretical principles of the use of reason" beyond their legitimate empirical application into a theological application, with no appeal to the moral point of view (§85, 5:440). Indeed, this could even explain what Kant means by his otherwise remarkable assertion that Spinoza is convinced "that there is no God and (since it follows in the same way in regard to the object of morality) no future life" (§87, 5:452): Since on Kant's account there can be neither a determination of the predicates of God nor a proof of his existence except as presuppositions of the realizability of the highest good, Spinoza's purely theoretical meta-physics has eliminated any basis for a rational conception of and belief in God.

Second, Kant also objects that Spinoza's system eliminates all *contingency*. He states that "on account of the unconditional necessity of the [substrate of natural things] together with those natural things as accidents inhering in it," Spinoza leaves to natural forms "the unity of ground which is requisite for all purposiveness, but at the same time rips from them the contingency, without which no **unity of end** can be conceived, and with that takes away everything **intentional**, just as he takes all understanding away from the primordial ground of natural things" (*CPJ*, §73, 5:393). Here, the point seems to be that intentionality and choice must be conceived as being exercised on material that is to some extent independent of that choice, or contingent with respect to what the intention and choice try to make necessary. Whether this leads to a theology any more orthodox than Spinoza's may be questionable—it would seem to lead to the pagan conception of a demiurge rather than to the Judaeo-Christian conception of a creator *ab nihilo*—but it may well be argued that it leads to a more coherent conception of *human* action than Spinoza has to offer, one on which human action must take place in an arena that it does not literally create, in which therefore success in the pursuit of any end, *a fortiori* in the pursuit of the ultimate end, must be able to be seen as *possible* but not as *guaranteed*. This would certainly fit with the doctrine that we have now seen Kant advocate in both the second and third *Critiques*, namely that we must conceive of God as the ground of the laws of nature as well as of morality so that we may conceive of success in our moral action as *possible*. If we were to see such success as impossible, it would be patently incoherent for us to attempt to act as morality demands; but at the same time, if we were to see success in our actions as *guaranteed*, that, too, would undermine the seriousness of our efforts to concentrate our moral powers in our actions. The only coherent conception of nature for Kant the moralist to adopt is one in which success in our morally obligatory enterprises is possible in accordance with the laws of nature but guaranteed, if at all, only by the rigor and vigor of our own efforts in accordance with the laws of freedom. This is precisely the conception of nature as grounded in a morally intelligent author who yet has a healthy respect for contingency that Kant opposes to Spinozism.

As deeply seated as this conception of nature is in Kant's conception of morality, it would be striking indeed if he were to have given it up in his final years. Let us now conclude with a look at the *Opus postumum* to see if that text warrants the conclusion that Kant did radically revise the conception of the system of nature and freedom that he had evolved without fundamental change throughout his three *Critiques*.

## V

In his final years, Kant worked on a project he called the "Transition from the Metaphysical First Principles of Natural Science to Physics," in which he attempted to argue for the existence of an all-pervasive ether,[22] a detailed yet *a priori* system of forces, and so on, and also worked on a more general restatement of the principles of transcendental philosophy. Whether these efforts represent a refinement and extension or a radical revision of his earlier views continues to be debated. Here, I will join this debate only on a narrow front, and suggest that a view for which Kant argued prominently in the final stages of his work, the Seventh and then the First Fascicles, namely that both God and the world-whole are not ontological realities existing outside of human thought but are rather ideas imposed on and realized in human experience by human thought, does not represent a radical revision of Kant's earlier thought but only a restatement of it, and that Kant makes this continuity clear by a *contrast* between his own transcendental idealism and Spinozism, a contrast continuous with what he had already offered in the *Critique of Judgment*.

---

[22] See my "Kant's Ether Deduction and the Possibility of Experience," in *Akten des Siebenten Internationalen Kant-Kongresses*, vol. II/1, ed. G. Funke (Bonn: Bouvier, 1991), pp. 119–32; in this volume, Ch. 4.

Kant defines the conception of transcendental idealism that he held at the end of his life in passages like these:

There is a God, not as a world-soul in nature but as a personal principle of human reason (*ens summum, summa intelligentia, summum bonum*), which, as the idea of a holy being, combines complete freedom with the law of duty in the categorical imperative of duty; both **technical-practical** and **moral-practical** reason **coincide** in the idea of God and the world, as the **synthetic unity of transcendental philosophy.** (*OP*, I.II.1, 21:19; Förster, 225)[23]

and:

God and the world are ideas of moral-practical and technical-practical reason, founded on sensible representation; the former contains the predicate of personality, the latter that of [*gap*]. Both together in one system, however, and related to each other under one principle, not as substances outside my thought, but rather, the thought through which we ourselves make these objects (through synthetic *a priori* cognitions from concepts) and, subjectively, are self-creators of the objects thought. (*OP*, I.II.3, 21:21; Förster, 228)

Kant makes the following claims in such passages. Both God and the world are ideas originating in our own thought, but imposed upon sensible representation, as an irreducibly external element in experience, and producing objects, as combinations of both intuition and concept, through this imposition. The idea of God is generated in connection with our recognition of our duty, as an image of the source of unconditional legislation that actually lies within our own practical reason, and is thus the "moral-practical" idea. The idea of the world is the idea of the unitary and law-like spatiotemporal realm imposed on our sensible representation by sensibility and understanding, but also the idea of the natural sphere within which we can perform our duty and realize our ends, and is thus a "technical-practical" idea. As much the product of our own reason as the idea of God, the laws of nature must be compatible with the moral legislation summed up in our idea of God and indeed subordinated to it, in the sense that we must always conceive of nature as a sphere in which the performance of duty and the achievement of its intended ends are possible.[24] But in both cases God and the

---

[23] I depart from Förster's use of italics to indicate both emphasis and Latin in quotations from the *Opus postumum*.

[24] For example, "God and the world are not coordinated beings, but the latter is subordinated to the former" (*OP*, VII.X.1, 22:127; Förster, 201), and "The complex of all beings as substances is God and the world. The one is not coordinated as an aggregate with the other, but subordinated to it in its existence, and combined with it in one system;

world cannot be thought of as substances existing independently of our thought, and are instead constructions generated from our thought, the idea of God from our consciousness of our duty and our freedom to perform it and the idea of the world both from our theoretical forms of intuition and understanding but also from our idea of nature as a sphere within which we can successfully perform our duty. Thus Spinozism is right in its general form of seeing both nature or the order of causes and thought or the order of reasons as modes of an underlying substance, but wrong in identifying God as that substratum of which nature and ourselves are modes. We ourselves are the substratum from which both God and nature are projected unities. Kant may indeed mention Spinoza more often in the *Opus postumum* than ever before, but only to make even more pointedly the kind of contrast he had already suggested in the *Critique of Judgment*.

To sustain my view that these claims are continuous with Kant's previous conception of the unity of nature and freedom, there are three points we need to look at in some more detail: first, Kant's introduction of the idea of God as the image of our unconditional duty rather than the condition of the possibility of the highest good; second, Kant's claim that a moral-practical God and a technical-practical nature are mere ideas rather than propositions about external existences that are valid only from a practical point of view; and third, Kant's comments about Spinoza. On each of these issues I suggest that there is less change than may initially meet the eye.

1. There can be no doubt that in these last stages of the *Opus postumum* Kant links the idea of God to the idea of duty in a way that he had not previously emphasized. He repeatedly states that the idea of God is an image of our own capacity as legislators of unconditionally binding moral law; for example,

The categorical imperative is the expression of a **principle of reason** over oneself as a *dictamen rationis practicae* and thinks itself as law-giver and judge over one, according to the categorical imperative of duty (for thoughts accuse and exonerate one another), hence, in the quality of a person. Now **a being which has only rights and no duties is God**. Consequently, the moral being thinks all duties, formally, as divine commands; not as if he thereby wished to certify the existence of such a being: For the supersensible is not an object of possible experience (*non dabile sed cogitabile*) but merely a judgment by analogy—namely, to think all

not merely technically but morally-practically" (*OP*, I.I.1, 21:12; Förster, 220, translation modified).

human duties **as if** divine commands and in relation to a person. (*OP*, VII.X.2, 22:120; Förster, 202–3)

By conceiving of the commands of duty that in fact originate in our own reason *as if* they were commands of a divine person, we can make clear to ourselves several key points about duty, above all its unconditionally obligatory character and also the fact that it may be in conflict with our merely sensual inclinations, and thus can seem to us like the command of another person if we identify—as of course we should not—our own personality solely with our merely sensual side. The first of these points in particular might seem to be confused by Kant's suggestion that God is a being who has rights but no duties at all; he could hardly be an image of our own obligation under duties if he has none. Perhaps Kant puts the point he is driving at here better in other passages when he writes that "The concept of God is... the concept of a being that can **obligate all** *moral beings* without itself being obligated" (*OP*, VII.X.2, 22:121; Förster, 203; see also VII.X.3, 22:124, 127; Förster, 205, 207); this can be taken to express the primacy of obligation over duty in Kantian ethics, or the fact that our duties arise from obligations we place ourselves under because of the demands of our own practical reason rather than from rights as claims made upon us by others independently of our own legislation.[25]

A first point to note here is that Kant does not introduce the idea of God just as an image of our power to *legislate* moral laws, but also as an image of our power to *judge* ourselves morally, and, even more importantly, as an image of our power to *execute*, that is, act in accordance with, moral laws. Thus he writes: "The concept of God is the idea of a moral being, which, as such, is judging [and] universally commanding. The latter is not a hypothetical thing but pure practical reason itself in its personality, with reason's moving forces in respect to world-beings and their forces" (*OP*, VII.X.1, 22:118; Förster, 201–2); and he defines the idea of God as "the idea of an omnipotent moral being, whose willing is a categorical imperative for all rational beings, and is both all-powerful with regard to nature as well as unconditionally, universally commanding for freedom" (*OP*, VII.X.4, 22:127; Förster, 207). Likewise, in this context Kant explicitly asserts the principle that "If I **ought** to do something, then I must also be **able** to do it" (*OP*, I.II.1, 21:16; Förster, 223),

---

[25] For an account of the primacy of the concept of obligation over that of right in Kantian ethics, see Onora O'Neill, *Constructions of Reason: Explorations of Kant's Practical Philosophy* (Cambridge: Cambridge University Press, 1989), for example, pp. 187–93.

thereby suggesting that if our own capacity to command is reflected in our image of God then so is our capacity to perform. Throughout this discussion, then, Kant states that God, that is, our own reason, is efficacious not just in giving commands but in imposing its "moving forces" on nature, that is, "world-beings and their forces." So just as he here immediately interprets the categorical imperative as "the expression of a moral and holy, unconditionally commanding will" (*OP*, VII.X.3, 22:123; Förster, 205), which we imagine as in God but that is actually in ourselves, so he also equally immediately infers from the categorical imperative a capacity to act in nature but in accordance with that law, which we imagine as being in God but that is actually in ourselves. Through the image of God we therefore represent both the laws of freedom themselves and also the unity of nature and freedom that we must postulate in order to think of ourselves as capable of actually acting in accordance with these laws.

Now it might seem as if we have here come upon several fundamental differences between Kant's position in the *Opus postumum* and in his earlier works. First, while earlier Kant had postulated God in order to ground our conception of the realizability of the *ends* of duty in the form of the highest good, here he seems to bring God into the picture much earlier as an image of our capacity to recognize and act in accordance with duty regardless of any consideration of its ends. There are reasons, however, why we should not take this fact to indicate any fundamental change of view. (i) First, at least once in the *Critique of Practical Reason* Kant had already argued that the postulation of God was necessary for our recognition of the possibility of the virtue – as well as of the happiness-component of the highest good, that is, to explain our capacity to perform our duty as well as the likelihood of that performance having its intended outcome (*CPracR*, 5:125). (ii) Second, since there is a direct connection between the concept of duty and the concept of happiness in the highest good, namely that our duty is in fact to preserve and promote rational agency as the capacity to set and pursue ends and happiness just is the successful pursuit of ends, Kant does not need to make any special mention of happiness and the highest good; a genuine capacity to act in accordance with moral law will also bring happiness in its train, at least so far as the contribution of human agents is concerned. (iii) Finally, it should be noted that at least once in these late fascicles Kant does explicitly mention the highest good; thus he suggests that "[T]he intelligent subject which grounds the combination of God with the world under a principle" is the source of:

The highest nature
The highest freedom    (blessedness
The highest good       happiness)

(*OP*, I.II.3, 21:23; Förster, 229)

So in Kant's argument that the idea of God is the image of our capacity to recognize and perform our duty rather than the conception of our ground for expecting happiness seems to be a change more in emphasis than in doctrine.

2. One could well ask, however, if there is not an important change in Kant's conception of God from the object of a postulate of pure practical reason to a mere idea. Here, too, I would suggest that the change in Kant's form of expression is striking but not radical. It is true that in Kant's earlier work he tended to conceive of a practical postulate as something that had the logical *form* of an existential proposition, asserting that an entity or condition, in this case God, actually exists, but with only the *force* of a presupposition of action rather than any genuine cognition, whereas here Kant speaks of a mere idea of God without any logically propositional assertion of his existence at all. But in fact the sort of thing Kant says about the force of this idea is very similar to what he earlier said about the force of a practical postulate. On the one hand, Kant repeatedly insists that God cannot be proven to exist "as substance outside the subject," but is, rather, "thought" (*OP*, I.II.3, 21:23; Förster), and this seems an even more subjectivist claim than in the earlier writings, where God seems to be conceived of as existing outside us but cannot be theoretically proven so to exist. Indeed, often Kant even goes so far as to suggest that because God is so clearly an idea, the proposition that He exists outside of us, the thinkers, does not even make any sense:

The concept of such a being is not that of substance—that is, of a being which exists independent of my thought—but the idea (one's own creation, thought, object, *ens rationis*) of a reason which constitutes itself into a thought-object and establishes synthetic *a priori* propositions, according to principles of transcendental philosophy. It is an ideal: There is not and cannot be a question as to whether such an object exists, since the concept is transcendent. (*OP*, I.III.1, 23:27; Förster, 231)[26]

---

[26] Another relevant citation: "It is not a **substance** outside myself, whose existence I postulate as a hypothetical being for the explanation of certain phenomena in the world; but the concept of duty (of a universal practical principle) is contained identically in the concept of a divine being as an ideal of human reason for the sake of the latter's law-giving [*breaks off*]" (*OP*, VII.X.2, 22:123; Förster, 204). For further instances of the claim that God is not "outside" but "inside" the human thinker, see *OP*, VII.V.2, 22:51 and 53

And even when Kant continues to use the language of postulation, he qualifies the existence-claim in a way that he did not before:

The existence of such a being, however, can only be **postulated** in a practical respect: Namely the necessity of acting in such a way as if I stood under such a fearsome—but yet, at the same time, salutary—guidance and also guarantee, in the knowledge of all my duties as divine commands... hence the **existence** of such a being is not postulated in this formula, which would be self-contradictory. (*OP*, VII.X.1, 22:116; Förster, 200)

On the other hand, even as Kant modifies his language, he makes it perfectly clear that the force of entertaining the idea of God is precisely the same as the force that he previously assigned to the postulation of his existence, namely it is a representation without theoretical force but one which plays an essential role in making our conduct coherent. In the passage just cited, for example, Kant referred to a necessity of *acting* rather than *asserting*, and in this striking comment further down the same sheet he appropriates the Pauline language of the traditional theologian into his own framework of the presuppositions of conduct rather than cognition: "In... the idea of God as a moral being, we live, move, and have our being; motivated through the knowledge of our duties as divine commands" (22:118; Förster, 201). Here we have knowledge of the divinity of our own moral commands but not of the actual existence of any source for them but ourselves. The purely practical necessity of the idea of God is likewise stressed here:

It is not a **substance** outside myself, whose existence I postulate as a hypothetical being for the explanation of certain phenomena in the world; but the concept of duty (of a universal practical principle) is contained identically in the concept of a divine being as an ideal of human reason for the sake of the latter's law-giving. (*OP*, VII.X.2, 22:123; Förster, 204)

As in his earlier works, Kant's real concern is not with the issue of whether or not we assert an existential proposition about God with a theoretical truth-value, but rather with the point that whatever our representation of God, mere idea or more complex proposition, it plays no theoretical role in "the explanation of certain phenomena," but rather functions as an ideal in our self-legislation and its execution.

Above all, what Kant is concerned to stress is that the idea of God is an ideal for our own conduct and not a piece of theory; this passage, I suggest, reveals the role that the concept of a rational being in general

(Förster, 211, 212); VII.V.3, 22:56 (Förster, 214); VII.V.4, 22:60 (Förster, 217); and I.VII.2, 21:92 (Förster, 252).

should be recognized to have had through Kant's exposition of his ethics, an ideal to which we aspire rather than a theoretical concept for the explanation of anything:

There are two ways in which men postulate the existence of God: they say sometimes: There exists a divine **judge** and **avenger,** for wickedness and **crime** require the extinction of this loathsome race. On the other hand, reason thinks of an **achievement** of which man is capable—to be able to place himself in a higher **class,** namely that of autonomous (through moral-practical reason) beings, and to raise himself above all merely sensuous beings... he is such a being, not merely **hypothetically,** but has a destination to enter into that state, to be the originator of his own rank—that is, obligated and yet thereby self-obligating. (*OP*, VII.X.1, 22:117–18; Förster, 201)

This passage clearly expresses the view that what practical reason requires and provides is a coherent set of ideals within which to pursue our conduct, not a theoretically demonstrable set of cognitions; this was Kant's view during the critical period, and here we have evidence that it remained such until the end of his life. And the unity of nature and freedom under a God who is a projection of our own capacity to construct both moral and natural law remains firmly within this framework.

3. I will conclude with a comment on Kant's final attitude toward Spinoza. Kant mentions Spinoza far more frequently in the last two fascicles of the *Opus postumum* than in any earlier writing, but that fact itself only raises the question of whether he does this because his views have moved closer to some form of Spinozism or because he is more concerned than ever to clarify his difference with Spinoza (perhaps due to the increasing approval of Spinoza among his younger contemporaries). My view is that the latter is the case. We have just seen that throughout his final stage Kant remains committed to the view that metaphysics can only have a moral-practical rather than theoretical foundation, which was already the basis for his critique of Spinoza's theology in the *Critique of Judgment*. But we are not limited to indirect arguments like that; Kant also tells us quite explicitly what he thinks is wrong with Spinoza's whole approach. "Spinoza's concept of God and man, according to which the philosopher intuits all things in God, is enthusiastic," Kant tells us (*OP*, I.II.1, 21:19; Förster, 225), and "A concept is enthusiastic if that which is in man is represented as something which is outside him, and the product of his thought represented as thing in itself (substance). *Principia sunt dictamina rationis propriae*" (*OP*, I.II.4, 21:26; Förster, 231). Spinoza is right to conceive that there is a

common ground of the orders of nature and freedom, in other words, but wrong to think that this can be anything other than the principles of our own proper reason, above all our own practical reason. Thus, nearly as many times as Kant mentions Spinoza, he insists that Spinoza has "reversed" or "transformed" genuine idealism: "Not that we intuit in the deity, as Spinoza imagines, but the reverse: that we carry our concept of God into the objects of pure intuition in our concept of transcendental philosophy" (*OP*, VII.V.4, 22:59; Förster, 216).[27] And even when Kant seems to indicate acceptance rather than rejection of Spinoza, it is only a Spinoza whose view has already been transformed into Kant's own moral-practical transcendental idealism: "According to Spinoza, I see myself in God who is legislative within **me**" (*OP*, VII.V.3, 21:54; Förster, 213). Throughout these pages, Kant contrasts to anything resembling the views of the historical Spinoza a conception of our images of both God and the world as founded in the ideals of our own practical reason. It was precisely his failure to adopt such a viewpoint, Kant had already argued in the *Critique of Judgment*, that prevented Spinoza from producing a valid argument for God.

There seems to me ample evidence, then, to conclude that the conception of the unity of nature and freedom that Kant was striving to formulate for his final statement of transcendental philosophy is not merely compatible with but in all essentials identical with that which he had advocated throughout his critical years, and that for all the changes in detail in argumentation and application which he made during the two decades after 1781, Kant's grand vision of the foundation of the unity of nature and freedom in the power of human reason remained largely unchanged.

---

[27] See also *OP*, VII.V.3, 22:56 (Förster, 214); I.II.3, 21:22 (Förster, 228); and I.IV.4, 21:50 (Förster, 241).

# 12

# From Nature to Morality: Kant's New Argument in the 'Critique of Teleological Judgment'

I

As the conclusion of each of the three *Critiques*, Kant argues that the rationality of moral conduct requires a conception of the laws of nature as favorable for the realization of human objectives. His argument is that the possibility of the highest good as the complete good and ultimate object of morality requires that we conceive of the laws of nature as compatible with the realization of the form of happiness set as a goal by this concept, a possibility that we can conceive only by postulating an intelligent author of the laws of nature who also has an eye on the requirements of the moral law, 'a supreme cause of nature having a causality in keeping with the moral disposition.'[1] Kant's various accounts of the highest good are by no means unequivocal,[2] but for

This chapter was originally presented at a conference at the Austrian Academy of Sciences in Vienna, and was first published in Hans Friedrich Fulda and Jürgen Stolzenberg (eds.), *Architektonik und System in der Philosophie Kants* (Hamburg: Felix Meiner Verlag, 2001), pp. 375–404. It is reprinted here with permission of the publisher.

[1] *CPracR*, 5:125. The following conventions will be used to locate citations. Citations from the *Critique of Pure Reason* will be located by the pagination of the first (A) and second (B) editions, included in all modern editions and English translations. Other citations will be located by the pagination of *Kant's gesammelte Schriften*, edited by the Royal Prussian (later German) Academy of Sciences (Berlin: Georg Reimer, later Walter de Gruyter & Co., 1900 ff.). Citations from the *Critique of Judgment*, which appears in volume 5 of this, the so-called 'Akademie edition,' will be given by the volume and page number preceded by the section number, a roman or arabic numeral, depending on whether the section is from the introduction or the body of the text. All translations from the *Critique of Judgment* are my own. Citations to Kant's works other than these two will include the volume as well as page number from the Akademie edition. Translations will be as indicated. The translation of the passage cited from the *Critique of Practical Reason* is from Immanuel Kant, *Practical Philosophy*, translated and edited by Mary J. Gregor, with a General Introduction by Allen W. Wood (Cambridge: Cambridge University Press, 1996), p. 240.

[2] There is of course a large literature on the concept of the highest good. Useful recent discussions of some of it may be found in Andrews Reath, 'Two Conceptions of the

present purposes we may consider something like the following to be his basic argument from the necessity of the highest good to the possibility of its realization in accordance with the laws of nature: Virtuous action must, of course, be motivated by respect for the moral law rather than by any natural inclination toward happiness, whether the relevant agent's own happiness or the happiness of any others about whom an agent may happen to care. However, the universalizability of one's maxims that the moral law commands is itself grounded in the recognition of humanity, in the person of all including oneself, as the sole necessary and unconditional object of value and therefore end of human action. Respect for humanity as the necessary end of action in turn requires respect not for only the existence of all human beings as ends in themselves, but also for their capacity to set their own ends freely, and even requires the adoption of policies and performances of actions intended to advance the fulfillment of freely and permissibly chosen particular ends. But human happiness simply consists in the satisfaction of ends, so a complete object of morality that includes the satisfaction of a whole of all 'particular human ends in systematic connection'[3] in fact requires the adoption of policies and performance of actions that would produce a systematic form of human happiness, at least under ideal circumstances.[4] Further, it would be irrational for us to act as duty commands if we did not believe that the realization of the object it turns out to command is at least possible. This condition can be satisfied only if we conceive of the laws of nature as making possible the realization of the form of human happiness that is commanded by morality. Since we can conceive of laws only as the product of thought, this requires us to conceive of the laws of nature as the product of an intelligent author 'having a causality in keeping with the moral disposition.'[5] Of course, Kant stresses in all his presentations of this train of thought that it is not intended as an argument in speculative metaphysics, demonstrating the truth of the

---

Highest Good in Kant,' *Journal of the History of Philosophy* 26 (1988): 593–620; Stephen Engstrom, 'The Concept of the Highest Good in Kant's Moral Theory,' *Philosophy and Phenomenological Research* 52 (1992): 747–80; and Victoria S. Wike, *Kant on Happiness in Ethics* (Albany: State University of New York Press, 1994), chs. 5 and 6, pp. 115–63.

[3] See G, 4:433.

[4] See CPuR, A 809 f./B 837 f.

[5] For a more detailed account of this argument, see my article 'In praktischer Absicht: Kants Begriff der Postulate der reinen praktischer Vernunft,' *Philosophisches Jahrbuch der Görres-Gesellschaft* 104 (1997): 1–18. One of the clearest of all of Kant's accounts of the highest good is that found in Section I of the 1793 essay 'On the Common Saying: That May Be Correct in Theory, but it is of No Use in Practice,' where Kant rejects Christian Garve's interpretation that he has made the rationality of morality dependent upon the promise of *one's own* or "selfish" happiness; see especially 8:278–84.

theoretical propositions that it seems to yield, but is rather to be understood as a complex of ideas, valid only "from a practical point of view," which somehow is sufficient to keep our moral dedication intact in spite of the impossibility of our having adequate theoretical evidence of its truth.

Now in the Introduction to the *Critique of Judgment*,[6] Kant famously claims 'there is an incalculable gulf fixed between the domain of the concept of nature, as the sensible, and the domain of the concept of freedom, as the supersensible' (*CPJ*, Introduction II, 5:175 f.), which needs to be bridged. He then claims that although this gulf cannot be bridged 'by means of the theoretical use of reason' (5:176), it can be bridged, 'not with regard to the cognition of nature, but from the consequences' of 'the concept of freedom (and the practical rule that it contains)' for nature (*CPJ*, Introduction IX, 5:195). Even though we think of the domains of nature and freedom 'just as if each were different worlds, the first of which can have no influence on the second,' constructing the bridge between them becomes possible when we realize that 'the latter **ought** to have an influence on the former, namely the concept of freedom should make the ends set by its laws real in the world of sense, and nature must consequently also be able to be so conceived that the lawfulness of its form is at least harmonious with the possibility of the ends that are to be realized in it in accordance with the laws of freedom' (*CPJ*, Introduction II, 5:175 f.). But this suggests that the argument that will bridge the incalculable gulf is just the inference from the object set for us by morality to the possibility of realizing that object in nature that Kant had already expounded in the first two critiques. The fact that Kant rehearses the argument from the highest good as the object of morality to a conception of the laws of nature and their author as providing the condition of its possibility one more time in the late sections of the second half of the *Critique of Judgment*, the 'Critique of Teleological Judgment' (*CPJ*, §§ 87 f.), confirms this impression. These passages suggest that there is no novelty in the *Critique of Judgment's* bridging of the alleged gulf, although its restatement of the argument from the highest good as part of a theory of *reflective* judgment gives Kant a new way to emphasize that the postulates of practical reason are

---

[6] That is, the introduction published with the text, which was written only once the text was complete, not the earlier draft of an introduction now known as the 'First Introduction' (found in the Akademie edition in vol. 20 (1942), pp. 192–261). A convenient summary of what is known about the relation between the two versions of the introduction may be found in Immanuel Kant, *Schriften zur Ästhetik und Naturphilosophie*, edited by Manfred Frank and Véronique Zanetti (Frankfurt am Main: Deutscher Klassiker Verlag, 1996), pp. 1158–64.

*regulative* principles for the guidance of human conduct and not *constitutive* principles for the enrichment of human knowledge.

Although there is no novelty in Kant's repetition of the argument from the highest good to a certain conception of the laws of nature and their author,[7] the 'Critique of Teleological Judgment' does introduce a striking new argument into Kant's philosophy. This is an argument that the scientific study of *nature* also requires us to adopt the regulative principle that human morality is the final end (*Endzweck*) of nature. Thus Kant now argues that whether we start from the standpoint of scientific inquiry or that of moral conduct, we must ultimately reach the same conception of nature as a realm governed by laws that make possible the realization of the ultimate object of morality. In Kant's words: 'For theoretical reflective judgment, physical teleology was sufficient to prove an intelligent cause of the world from physical ends; for practical reflective judgment, moral teleology accomplishes this through the concept of a final end, which it is compelled to ascribe to the creation from a practical point of view. The objective reality of the idea of God, as the moral author of the world, cannot be displayed through physical ends **alone**; nevertheless, when the cognition of these is combined with that of the moral end, then the former, by means of the maxim of pure reason to seek unity of principles as far as is possible, become of great importance, supporting the practical reality of that idea through the reality for the power of judgment that it already has from a theoretical point of view' (*CPJ*, §88, 5:456).

In Kant's ultimate system of nature and freedom, theoretical and practical reason join forces to impose upon us a single conception of the world that is regulative for both inquiry and conduct.[8]

---

[7] Even this argument cannot be understood unless it is first recognized that the happiness comprised in the highest good is a happiness that must be realized *in nature*. Kant himself is sometimes confused about this point (e.g., *CPuR*, A 811/B 839), though usually not (see A 819/B 847; *CPracR*, 5:124 f.; *CPJ*, §87, 5:450; 'Theory and Practice,' 8:279).

[8] Those commentaries on the 'Critique of Teleological Judgment' that reach the issue of its connection to Kant's moral theory at all typically see it as presenting only the argument from the highest good to its realizability in nature that Kant had already suggested in the previous two critiques; see, for example, Klaus Düsing, *Die Teleologie in Kants Weltbegriff*, Kantstudien Ergänzungsheft 96 (Bonn: Bouvier, 1968), pp. 102–15. He argues that nothing in nature can itself lead us to a moral idea, although a teleological view of nature can explain how 'the final end and its effects are possible in our world' (115).

For an exception to this generalization, see the recent article by Jürg Freudiger, 'Kants Schlußstein: Wie die Teleologie die Einheit der Vernunft stiftet,' *Kant-Studien* 87 (1996): 423–35. He comes close to the interpretation to be presented here by arguing that the point of Kant's excursus into teleology—what he calls Kant's 'fourth critique'—is to show that the 'supersensible' which must underlie nature, according to Kant's theoretical philosophy, is identical with the 'supersensible' that is contained in the concept of freedom

Kant's new argument is certainly alien to the post-Darwinian frame of mind. It is also complicated, confusing and in one key step possibly confused as well. My aim here is simply to lay it out clearly enough to establish its position as the central argument of the 'Critique of Teleological Judgment' and to draw attention to one tension within it. The argument begins with the claim that understanding the character of one kind of object that we encounter in nature, namely what we now call *organisms*, requires us to conceive of them as the product of *intelligent design*, and follows this with the inference that once we are forced to look at organisms this way, it becomes inevitable for us at least to try to see the *whole of nature* as a systematic product of intelligent design as well. The argument then contends that once we have formed the idea of an intelligent design for nature, and hence an intelligent *designer* of nature, it will be inevitable for us to seek for an *intelligible purpose* for nature. This is because, working with the only example of intelligent activity known to us, namely our own, we cannot conceive of productive activity that is intelligent yet not also purposive. Next, Kant will argue that we have no way of forming a *determinate conception* of a unique purpose for nature except by conceiving of something that is a *necessary* because *unconditional* end *for us*. Finally, Kant argues that the only candidate for such an end is our own moral vocation and the end it imposes on us. The argument is thus meant to show that the only way we

(425). His interpretation, however, differs from mine on three key points. First, he does not state that Kant reaches his idea of the single author of the laws of both nature and freedom by *two* parallel arguments, the well-known one beginning from the moral imperative of the highest good and the less well-known, which I will expound here, beginning from questions arising in scientific inquiry. Second, since he does not discuss how Kant actually makes his move from the experience of organisms to the necessity of teleology (428), he does not show that Kant employs three different arguments here, the last of which puts the special role of organisms into question; nor does he ask how Kant makes the inference from the purposiveness of organisms to the purposiveness of nature as a whole. Third, in his discussion of the capstone (to use his term) of Kant's argument from teleology to morality (430), he does not make sufficiently clear that the concepts of the "ultimate end" (*letzter Zweck*) and "final end" (*Endzweck*) of nature are distinct concepts, thus that Kant actually supplies an *argument* that the only candidate that can satisfy the non-normative concept of the "ultimate end" of nature is what also satisfies the normative concept of the "final end" of nature, namely, humanity in its moral vocation.

A recent paper by Thomas Pogge, 'Kant on Ends and the Meaning of Life,' in Andrews Reath, Barbara Herman, and Christine M. Korsgaard, *Reclaiming the History of Ethics: Essays for John Rawls* (Cambridge: Cambridge University Press, 1997), pp. 361–87, recognizes that Kant separates the concepts of the ultimate and the final end before concluding that both are instantiated by a single thing, namely human morality and its object; but Pogge does not explore any of the details of the argument from organisms that will be examined here.

can conceive of both organisms in particular and nature as a whole as intelligently designed systems is by thinking of the laws of *nature* as aimed at the realization of the highest good set for us as the ultimate object of *morality*.

Kant stresses throughout his exposition of this argument that our difficulty in comprehending organisms is due to the character of our own cognitive constitution, and that we can only appeal to our own self-understanding to deal with this difficulty. The argument therefore yields regulative principles of reflective judgment rather than constitutive principles of theoretical understanding. Thus Kant claims that this vision of nature plays only a heuristic role, though an indispensable one, in the conduct of scientific inquiry. But he similarly denies that the conception of the laws of nature and their author to which we are driven by the concept of the highest good is a constitutive thesis of speculative metaphysics; 'it is far from sufficient to demonstrate the objective reality of this ideal from a theoretical point of view, but is fully satisfying from a moral-practical point of view.'[9] In both cases, the teleological conception of the world is an *a priori* conception that serves as a guide and possibly a spur to action, though one of those actions is the construction of empirical theories of the natural world in our capacity as scientific investigators and the other is our conduct as moral agents in the same natural world.

I will not debate the plausibility of this grand vision. However, I will draw attention to one problem in Kant's argument. This is that Kant actually raises *three* different problems about our comprehension of organisms that are supposed to require us to conceive of them as the products of intelligent design: he argues that organic processes do not fit our usual, mechanical model of *causation*, and that we can only conceive of these processes as the effects of antecedent design; that the centrality of the principle of *inertia* to our conception of *matter* precludes any reduction of organic *life* to the merely material; and that the always *general* or "discursive" nature of our concepts leaves too much about the *determinacy* or *particularity* of organisms *contingent* for us to tolerate, a problem that we try to remedy by conceiving of organisms as the product of a kind of intelligence more powerful than our own. This last consideration, however, applies to *all* fully determinate particular objects in nature, organic or not, and thus obviates the need for a separate inference from a teleological view of organisms to a teleological view

---

[9] From the draft of an essay on the 'Real Progress of Metaphysics,' 20:307.

of nature as a whole. Since Kant does not appear to acknowledge this problem[10] we will only be able to speculate on a solution to it.

2

1. The argument that dominates the 'Critique of Teleological Judgment' is that a special difficulty which we encounter in attempting to understand *organisms* as a distinctive kind of object among the others that we experience in nature leads us to a teleological conception of them which we then attempt to extend to *nature as a whole*. To adopt such a perspective on organisms and then on nature as a whole is to conceive of them *as if* they were the products of intelligent and purposive agency that we must conceive of in *analogy* with our own productive powers. Later Kant will add that just as we must conceive of our productive powers as put to the service of our moral end, so must we conceive of the productive power behind nature as put to the service of that same moral end.

The first step of this argument is the claim that we encounter a special difficulty in understanding organisms that first requires us to take a teleological perspective on nature at all: 'Organized beings are, therefore, the only beings in nature which, even when considered in themselves and without a relationship to other things, must still be able to be considered as ends of nature, and which therefore first provide objective reality for the concept of an **end** that is not a practical end, but an end **of nature**, and thereby provide for natural science the basis for a teleology ...' (*CPJ*, §65, 5:375 f.).

---

[10] None of the commentators on the 'Critique of Teleological Judgment' whom I have read distinguish these three different arguments; *a fortiori*, none askes what happens to the special place of organisms in Kant's argument once he introduces his argument from the contingency of particularity relative to our general concepts (§§76 f.). On the contrary, many German commentators especially proceed as if the latter problem is the only problem about our comprehension of organisms that Kant recognizes. See, for instance, Düsing, *Die Teleologie in Kants Weltbegriff*, pp. 89 f.; Joachim Peter, *Das transzendentale Prinzip der Urteilskraft*, Kant-Studien Ergänzungsheft 125 (Berlin: Walter de Gruyter, 1992), pp. 1, 188; and Véronique Zanetti, 'Kants Antinomie der teleologischen Urteilskraft,' *Kant-Studien* 84 (1993): 341–55, at pp. 350 f. Henry E. Allison, 'Kant's Antinomy of Teleological Judgment,' *Southern Journal of Philosophy* 30 Supplement (1991): 25–42, also suggests that it is 'the discursivity of our understanding' which 'underlies the necessity of estimating living organisms in light of the idea of an intelligent cause' (34). I will argue below that although Kant introduces his discussion of the "discursivity" of human understanding in the context of a discussion of organisms, the problems raised by this "discursivity" are neither specially suggested by organisms nor limited to organisms.

Kant reaches this conclusion by two steps. First, he observes that there is nothing in our experience of nature that initially forces a conception of its "**relative**" or *external purposiveness* upon us, that is, a conception of some things in nature as means to the existence of others as ends: of course we can view driftwood and reindeer as means to the existence of humans in inhospitable arctic climes, but since we may see no reason why human beings should live in such inhospitable places to begin with, there is apparently nothing that forces us to impose such a means–end relationship on our understanding of nature at all (*CPJ*, §63, 5:368 f.).[11] In organisms, however, we encounter natural objects that we can only understand through a conception of *internal* purposiveness, a reciprocal relation of the parts of the object to each other and to the object as a whole. We cannot understand this relation on the basis of our ordinary conception of causation, so we must instead conceive of organisms as if they were products of intelligent design. This conception of organisms, forced upon us by our actual experience, will in turn lead to the conception of nature as a whole as a system with an ultimate end, and will by this means require us to discover a plausible conception of the external purposiveness of nature after all.

The initial reason why we must see organisms as manifesting internal purposiveness and as driving us thereby to a conception of their intelligent design is that we must see an organism as "**both cause and effect of itself,**" which defies our ordinary understanding of causation. On our ordinary understanding, 'The causal connection is a nexus that constitutes a series (of causes and effects), which always goes forward' (*CPJ*, §65, 5:372); that is, we always conceive of a cause as preceding its effect in time (or at least not succeeding it).[12] Further, on our ordinary conception causation is "mechanical" or reductionist; we see the character of

---

[11] This exclusion must be understood as provisional; Kant's eventual argument will be that once the experience of organisms forces the conception of their *internal* purposiveness upon us, then we *will* be forced also to conceive of nature as purposive *relative* to our own final purpose, that is, our moral and not just our cognitive purpose. In his comment on this passage, J. D. McFarland does not make it clear that Kant's exclusion of relative purposiveness is only provisional (*Kant's Concept of Teleology* (Edinburgh: Edinburgh University Press, 1970), p. 100); and since he stops his commentary short of the Doctrine of Method of the 'Critique of Teleological Judgment,' which is where Kant overcomes this initial difficulty by introducing our own final moral end as the ultimate end of nature as well, it is not clear that McFarland does recognize the merely provisional nature of Kant's initial statement.

[12] Kant tries to maintain the premise that a cause always precedes its effect in the face of examples of simultaneous causation by appealing to the idea that the interval between cause and effect can be vanishingly small (see *CPuR*, A 203/B 248). Redescribing the temporal structure of causation by saying the cause can never succeed its effect is what he needs for the present argument.

a whole as being entirely determined by the antecedent and independent character, behavior and relation of its several parts, in particular, by the motions of these parts in accordance with the laws of mechanics. But, Kant claims, we cannot comprehend organisms solely in these terms. In an organism, we see the character of the parts as determining the character of the whole, but we also see the character of the whole as determining the existence and character of its parts. We also see the parts as both producing but yet depending upon each other. In our experience of organisms, therefore, we are forced to recognize causal connections which, 'if considered as a series, would thus introduce backwards as well as forwards dependency.' However, the only model that *we* have for understanding such forms of causal relation is that of our own technical or artistic production, in which our antecedent *representation* of a whole is the cause of the existence of parts which are in turn the cause of the subsequent actual existence of the whole, and which make sense only given their planned and intended relationships to each other and to the envisioned whole. Here Kant alludes to the Aristotelian example of building a house, where the antecedent representation of the house (and, for example, the income that renting it will bring) is the cause of the production or acquisition of a particular set of parts that can be constructed into the envisioned whole.[13] Thus, Kant supposes, we must understand organisms at least *as if* they were the product of an antecedent design in an intelligent author; the parts of which are made as they are because only thus can the whole function as intended.

Kant offers three examples of the kinds of organic processes that he thinks can only be conceived of in these teleological terms, namely reproduction, growth, and self-maintenance (*CPJ*, §64, 5:371 f.). These are all supposed to be examples of how in an organic 'product of nature every part is conceived of existing, only **through** all the others but also **for the sake of the others** and, the whole' (*CPJ*, §65, 5:373), and of why an organism is not only an '**organized**' but also a '**self-organized** being' (5:374). In such a being we conceive of the parts as if they 'produce one another reciprocally in their form as well as in their relation to each other and thus bring forth a whole out of their own causality, the concept of which is in turn the cause of them (in a being which possesses a causality from concepts appropriate to such a product)' (5:373). We may now doubt whether such organic processes defy our ordinary conception of causation; as we now understand them, processes such as evolution by natural selection and both growth and reproduction by the transmission

---

[13] See Aristotle, *Physics*, Book II, ch. 3, 194b–195b.

and subsequent expression of genetic material are paradigmatic examples of temporally unidirectional causal processes, and from a philosopher's point of view have been adopted by scientists precisely because they bring hitherto incomprehensible processes into our ordinary paradigm of scientific explanation. As if to anticipate this objection, however, Kant subsequently adduces a more general reason why organisms cannot be understood mechanically. This claim is that *life* itself cannot be understood as a product of mere matter because matter is governed by the law of *inertia*: 'The possibility of a living matter cannot even be thought (its concept contains a contradiction, since lifelessness, **inertia**, constitutes the essential characteristic of matter); the possibility of a living matter and of all of nature, as an animal, can only be used out of necessity (in behalf of a hypothesis of purposiveness at large in nature) insofar as it is revealed to us in the organization of nature in the small; its possibility can by no means be understood *a priori*' (*CPJ*, §73, 5:394).

Kant does not explain the premises of this argument in the *Critique of Judgment*. But it rests on two principles that he maintains elsewhere. First, the principle of inertia entails that all change in the condition of an object comes from the action of an external force upon it, not any force internal to it. As Kant puts the 'Second Law of Mechanics' in the *Metaphysical Foundations of Natural Science*: 'Every change of matter has an external cause.'[14] By contrast, *life* is the power to move or change in response to internal rather than external forces. As Kant put it in his lectures on metaphysics, 'All matter is lifeless and thus contains no ground of life in it. Life must depend upon an immaterial, thinking principle; this principle cannot be material, for by the principle of life we always imagine something which determines itself from inner grounds, which matter, which can always be moved only by outer causes, cannot.'[15] Thus Kant infers that since the internal forces we find in organisms cannot be understood to be in matter by its own nature, they must be conceived to arise from something immaterial, which we will in turn conceive as an intelligence.[16]

---

[14] *Metaphysical Foundations of Natural Science*, 5:543. For an explicit identification of this law with the principle of inertia, see Michael Friedman, 'Kant and the Twentieth Century,' in Paolo Parrini, ed., *Kant and Contemporary Epistemology* (Dordrecht: Kluwer, 1994), pp. 27–46, at p. 27.

[15] *Metaphysik* K2, 28:765; translation from Immanuel Kant, *Lectures on Metaphysics*, edited and translated by Karl Ameriks and Steve Naragon (Cambridge: Cambridge University Press, 1997), p. 405.

[16] This distinct ground for a teleological view of organisms is at work in a remarkable passage in which Kant almost—but not quite—anticipates Darwinism. Kant writes that 'the admirable simplicity of the basic design' of so many species of animals can be

In both his particular argument about organic processes and his general argument about life, however, Kant severely restricts the force of his claims from the outset. In arguing that we can only conceive of organic processes as products of design because we have to conceive of them as if the parts of a whole were produced by an antecedent design of the whole, he insists that this conception of an organism can only be an *analogy* with human artistic production (*CPJ*, §72, 5:390). There are also many *disanalogies* between organic processes and human artistic production: for example, even the best products of our art, such as a fine watch, do not have all the 'formative powers' such as reproduction and self-repair that organisms have (*CPJ*, §65, 5:374)—in Kant's terms, the products of human art are 'organized' but not 'self-organized.'[17] And even after his introduction of the argument that it is the law of inertia itself which precludes a purely mechanical explanation of life, Kant continues to insist that the validity of the teleological view of organisms is restricted to our own understanding of them precisely because it is forced upon us by the **'peculiar constitution of our own cognitive faculties'** (*CPJ*, §75, 5:397). These claims imply that the unidirectional conception of causation and the inertial interpretation of causation in matter are valid for the human point of view, but cannot be maintained to be valid for all possible views of nature, thus for nature in itself. Because of the supposed limits of our cognitive faculties, Kant maintains, we can be confident that 'no Newton could ever arise who could make the generation of even

explained by 'the shortening of this member and the lengthening of another, by the involution of this part and the evolution of that one,' which in turn 'strengthens the suspicion of an actual kinship [*Verwandtschaft*]' of all species 'in their generation from a common primordial mother [*Urmutter*] through the gradual approximation of one species of animal to another... from man to the polyp and from this even to mosses and lichens and finally to the lowest stage of nature observable to us' (*CPJ*, §80, 5:418 f.). He even goes so far as to suggest that this 'mechanism' of natural change, as he explicitly calls it, can be understood as a process of increasing adaptation to animals' 'native surroundings and relations to each other' (5:419), although he does not suggest that adaptation is achieved by the natural selection of random mutations. Nevertheless, Kant's view falls short of a contemporary understanding of evolution because he continues to insist that no matter how well the *changes* in forms and species of organisms can be explained by mechanical processes, the *origin* of life itself can never be explained mechanically: for all his success, the **'archaeologist'** of nature' must 'nevertheless in the end ascribe to this common mother and organization purposively aimed at all these creatures, without which the possibility of the purposive form of the products of the animal and plant kingdoms is not to be conceived at all' (419). Kant remains convinced that we cannot understand life as arising through merely mechanical causes, although once life is granted we can imagine it as evolving into its diverse forms through all sorts of mechanical processes.

[17] Perhaps computers that can diagnose their own malfunctions, or computers that can regulate the production-line for more computers, might shake Kant's faith in this point—but probably not very much.

a blade of grass comprehensible in accordance with natural laws that no intention had ordained'; but at the same time it would be entirely 'presumptuous' of us to judge that just because *we* cannot understand in mechanical terms alone how an organism is generated and maintained, 'if we could penetrate to the principle of nature in the specification of its universal and known laws, there **could** not lie hidden a sufficient ground of the possibility of organized beings without their generation from an intention (thus in a mere mechanism)' (*CPJ*, §75, 5:400; cf. *CPJ*, §67, 5:378). And because we cannot assert dogmatically the validity of the very conceptions of matter and causation which make understanding organic life difficult for us, we also cannot assert the objective validity of the teleological conception of an intelligent designer by means of which we overcome this difficulty. Thus, the conception of organisms as manifesting internal purposiveness as a product of intelligent design does not furnish us with any knowledge of the properties of such objects but only 'guides our research about objects of such a kind by means of a distant analogy with our own causality according to ends' (*CPJ*, §65, 5:375).

2. The next step in Kant's argument is the claim that even if it is only the special case of organisms that forces us to consider the idea of an intelligent designer, once we have introduced this idea we will inevitably consider such an agency as the intelligent source of *nature as a whole*, and thus consider nature as a whole as a system manifesting a purposive relation among all its parts analogous to that which holds among the parts of an organism. This extension of Kant's argument immediately follows his initial analysis of why we must conceive of organisms as products of design: 'It is thus only matter, insofar as it is organized, which necessarily introduced the concept of itself as an end of nature, but its specific form is at the same a product of nature. But now this concept necessarily leads to the idea of the whole of nature as a system in accordance with the rule of ends, to which idea all mechanism in nature must now be subordinated in accordance with principles of reason (at least for the investigation of the appearance of nature)' (*CPJ*, §67, 5:378 f.).

Kant repeats this move at least three times, testifying to its importance for him (e.g., *CPJ*, §67, 5:380 f.; §71, 5:391; §78, 5:414).[18] And again,

---

[18] In another passage that should be noted, Kant observes that once we have been forced to introduce the teleological perspective by our experience of organisms, it will also be natural for us to look at *natural beauty* as evidence of the design of nature, even though no such thought was needed as part of the original explanation of our experience of natural beauty: 'Even beauty in nature, i.e., its agreement with the free play of our cognitive faculties in the apprehension and adjudgment of its appearance, can be

Kant insists that this expansion of the teleological perspective is heuristic and even experimental, stimulating and guiding us in our attempt to discover ever more extensive laws of nature: 'Once such a guide for the study of nature has been assumed and been found to be confirmed, we must at least try this maxim of the power of judgment on the whole of nature, since many of nature's laws may be able to be discovered by means of this maxim which would otherwise remain hidden because of the limitation of our insight into the inside of the mechanism of nature' (*CPJ*, §75, 5:398).

However, Kant does not say *why* it is inevitable for us to extend the conception of intelligent design from organisms to the whole of nature, even if this extension is undertaken only in an experimental spirit.[19] But it seems likely that by his suggestion that this extension is "in accordance with principles of reason," Kant means to say that the extension is a product of human reason's attempt to subsume all of its objects under a single ultimate principle. Thus, we naturally suppose that all of the causal processes we need to conceive of nature, even organic ones, must fall under a single form of explanation that applies to nature as a whole. In other words, it is inevitable for human reason—although perhaps not for other forms of thought—to include a teleological component in its ideal ultimate explanatory principle if it is forced to do so by any of its objects of experience, thus to seek to apply that same principle to the rest of its objects even where the latter would not themselves force the adoption of that principle when considered in isolation.[20] In fact, on

considered in this way as objective purposiveness of nature in its whole, as a system of which mankind is a member: namely, once organized beings, given at hand, have justified us in the idea of a great system of the ends of nature' (*CPJ*, §67, 5:380).

Contrary to the view recently argued for by Georgie Dickie, who claims that Kant's explanation of our experience of natural beauty in the 'Critique of Aesthetic Judgment' presupposes a teleological approach to objects in nature, this passage makes it clear that a teleological perspective on natural beauty is an additional intepretation of what we have already experienced as beautiful, necessitated and justified only by the teleological perspective we are forced to adopt in order to understand organisms. See George Dickie, *The Century of Taste: The Philosophical Odyssey of Taste in the Eighteenth Century* (New York: Oxford University Press, 1996), pp. 99–103.

[19] One commentator has suggested that this extension is based on the factual consideration that an organism needs inorganic material to survive, thus that organisms and (at least some) inorganic material in their environment must constitute an ecological system (Düsing, *Die Teleologie*, pp. 121 f.). This proposal would make Kant's extension entirely empirical, and there is no evidence that this is what Kant intends.

[20] For at least a suggestion of such an interpretation, see Wolfgang Bartuschat, *Zum systematischen Ort von Kants Kritik der Urteilskraft* (Frankfurt am Main: Vittorio Klostermann, 1972), who writes that an *Idee* is 'eine absolute Einheit der Vorstellung,' thus that the purpose exhibited for the idea for the manifoldness of nature must extend to *everything* that lies in the product of nature (p. 186).

Kant's conception of reason, it will be inevitable for human reason to seek such a unification of principles *unless* it is stopped in its tracks either by some external counter-example or some internal self-contradiction. Indeed, only such an interpretation makes sense of the structure of the 'Critique of Teleological Judgment,' for Kant's extension of the teleological viewpoint from the special case of organisms to all of nature is immediately followed by the 'Dialectic of Teleological Judgment,' which considers nothing other than the question of whether there is an antinomy lurking in the application of both the mechanical and teleological principles of explanation to both organisms and all of nature. This is precisely what we should expect if the extension of the teleological principle is an expression of reason's fundamental and inescapable interest in unity.

Finding the ground for the extension of the teleological viewpoint to all of nature in the characteristic behavior of human reason would not make the teleological principle *constitutive*, of course. In the *Critique of Pure Reason*, Kant argued that reason cannot establish theoretical propositions by itself, but only with the assistance of sensibility and understanding; and since the limits of our sensibility itself preclude the confirmation of any claim about the content of all of nature,[21] any theoretical principle of reason can only be regulative. In the idiom of the third *Critique*, this means that the conception of nature as a single system can only be heuristic, encouraging and guiding us to seek out purposive relations among all parts and aspects of nature. In fact, what Kant initially stresses is that this principle encourages us to extend the scope of *mechanical* explanation in nature: under its aegis we seek to give explanations in the terms that we do understand to relations among natural objects that we might not have noticed without the idea of nature as a single system. Through this idea 'we get a clue to consider things in nature in relation to a ground of determination that is already given ... and to extend our knowledge of nature [*Naturkunde*] in accordance with another principle, namely that of final causes, yet without injury to the mechanism of its causality' (*CPJ*, §67, 5:379). In the first instance, then, the idea that nature as a whole is a single system only urges us to expand the scope of explanation in accordance with mechanical causation. Yet the *heuristic* status of the principle of universal teleology

---

[21] Sensibility allows for the confirmation of unconditional claims about the the the spatio-temporal *form* of all of nature, but since that very form implies the indefinite extent of nature, it also precludes unconditional claims about everything that can be found *in* space and time. This is the lesson of the 'Antinomy of Pure Reason,' of course.

should not be mistaken for an *optional* status.[22] Kant never allows that any principle that has its origin in reason is optional; even if such a principle is merely regulative, Kant always argues that it is also indispensable, indeed that principles of reason can be given their appropriate form of transcendental deduction only by being shown to be indispensable regulative principles.[23]

As I said, since the extension of the teleological point of view from organisms to nature as a whole is an expression of reason's fundamental interest in unity, it would be natural for Kant to interrupt his argument to see whether this extension is subject to any fatal antinomy. In his own exposition, this is exactly what he does next. However, I am going to postpone my discussion of Kant's 'Dialectic of Teleological Judgment' so that we will neither lose sight of his larger argument nor rush over the problem lurking in this 'Dialectic.'

3. The next premise in Kant's overall argument is that whatever we can consider to be the origin of *intelligent design* we must also conceive to act with a *purpose;* thus we must conceive there to be a purpose for existence of both organisms and, given the previous step, the system of nature as a whole. Kant connects the idea of 'a cause whose capacity to act is determined through concepts' with that of a 'capacity to act in accordance with ends (a will)' from the outset of his argument (*CPJ*, §64,

---

[22] This suggestion is made by McFarland, who writes 'But we do not *have* to view the world as a whole, as purposively organized... The principle of reason for judging all of nature teleologically is a way in which we *may* investigate nature; but it is not a way in which we *must* investigate it, as we *must* investigate organisms as if they are purposive' (*Kant's Concept of Teleology*, p. 114). In support of this, he quotes Kant's statement that the use of the (teleological) maxim for judgment in regard to "the whole of nature" 'is to be sure useful, but not indispensable, because nature as a whole is not given to us as organized (in the strictest sense of the word introduced above). But in regard to those products of nature which must only be judged as formed intentionally and not otherwise in order to acquire even an empirical cognition of their inner constitution, that maxim of reflective judgment is essentially necessary' (*CPJ*, §75, 5:398; McFarland, pp. 114 f. n.). But perhaps the emphasis in this passage should be on the word 'given': only organisms are *given* to us as organized, thus only in their case does *experience* force the teleological viewpoint on us; but once that experience has forced this standpoint upon us, then the unifying character of *our own reason* forces upon us at least the heuristic extension of this principle to the whole of nature. In any case, the passage cited by McFarland needs to be reconciled with Kant's previous claim that the concept of organized matter 'necessarily leads to the idea of all of nature [*der gesamten Natur*] as a system in accordance with the rule of ends, to which idea all mechanism of nature must be subordinated in accordance with principles of reason (at least to investigate the appearance of nature in accordance with it)' (*CPJ*, §67, 5:379). This seems to set forth the idea of a *necessary* even though merely *heuristic* principle.

[23] See the deduction of the ideas of reason as heuristic principles in the second part of the Appendix to the Transcendental Dialectic of the first *Critique* (A 671/B 699), and the similar deduction in the published Introduction to the *Critique of Judgment*, V, 183 f.

5:369 f.). But his clearest statement of this premise comes in the final summary of his argument: 'If we assume the final connection in the world to be real and a special kind of causality, namely that of an **intentionally acting** [*wirkenden*] cause, then we cannot stop at the question: why do things of the world (organized beings) have this or that form, why do they stand in this or that relationship to other things in nature; rather, as soon as an understanding is conceived that must be regarded as the cause of the possibility of such forms, because they are really found in things, then at the very same time we must ask about the objective ground that could have determined this productive understanding to an action [*Wirkung*] of this sort, which is then the final end [*Endzweck*] for which such things exist' (*CPJ*, §84, 5:434; see also §81, 5:422 and §82, 5:426).

An intelligent agent simply does not act without an end in mind. As before, Kant does not offer an explicit argument for this premise. But presumably what he is doing here is working out the implications of the analogy which he has all along been claiming governs our teleological thinking. We do not undertake planned and rule-governed activity without some particular purpose and goal in mind, and moreover, Kant assumes, insofar as we are fully rational we do not act without some unique and necessary end in mind,[24] the search for unconditional unity, again, being essential to reason. So insofar as we conceive of the rational ground of nature in analogy with ourselves as rational agents, we will conceive of any agency that acts in accordance with an antecedent representation of the object it is to produce as acting with an antecedent representation of the unique and necessary goal it thereby hopes to attain as well.[25]

Of course, Kant has also stressed from the outset that the analogy between the technical or artistic activity of human beings and a teleological conception of organisms is incomplete (*CPJ*, §65, 5:374); so naturally it can be questioned whether the connection between design and purpose that is self-evident in our own activity should be extended to the ground of nature as well. But, as in the extension of teleology from individual organisms to nature as a whole, Kant sidesteps this worry by suggesting that the present conclusion is also not just heuristic but also experimental: he is not claiming that there is an unimpeachable theoretical basis for the connection (*CPJ*, §68, 5:381), but rather proposing it to see whether it has valuable and indispensable consequences for the conduct of inquiry and ultimately for conduct in the more ordinary

[24] See *G*, 4:427, and *Rel.*, 6:4.
[25] See also Düsing, *Die Teleologie in Kants Weltbegriff*, p. 208.

sense as well, that is, for morality. The strength of the inference, in other words, may ultimately turn as much on what purpose we could conceive the design of nature as a whole to have, and what the implications of this conception for our own conduct are, as any argument that could be made for it independently of these conclusions.

4. The final step of Kant's argument then considers what we can conceive the purpose of an intelligent and purposive ground of nature to be. Kant tackles this question in the third section of the 'Critique of Teleological Judgment,' its 'Doctrine of Method.' The treatment of this question under that title can suggest that here is where the application of teleological judgment, or its pay-off, is to be found.[26]

The 'Doctrine of Method' begins with three sections (§§79–81) in which Kant partially anticipates the later idea of evolution but still insists that the origin of life itself requires an immaterial and therefore as far as we can conceive intelligent ground.[27] Kant then reminds us of his previous conclusion that we can conceive of an intentionally acting cause of nature only if we also ascribe some end to it (§81, 5:422), and finally raises the question of what this end might be. At this point, we might expect an argument that this end must be something we ourselves can conceive, because the entire theory of teleological judgment is supposed to be based on the limits of our own cognitive capacities, and hence something that we can conceive of as being realized in nature, where our own ends must be realized. Kant clearly assumes this, but he does not say so explicitly. He explicitly introduces a different constraint on anything that we can conceive of as the end of nature, namely, that whatever we might conceive as the purpose of nature must be something that we must be able to conceive of as an *unconditional* end or end in itself. Kant's argument is then that there is only one thing that we can conceive of that satisfies that constraint, namely the development of human morality with all that this entails, including the object it sets for all our efforts, the highest good. This end will bridge the gap between the sensible and the supersensible that Kant worried about at the outset of the whole book, and that he re-introduced as the condition of the compatibility of mechanical and teleological explanation, because the possibility of human freedom as the end of nature must be grounded in the supersensible side of our own constitution, but the object which human

---

[26] However, there is no justification for *translating* the title of the section 'Theory of the Method of Applying the Teleological Judgment,' as Meredith did (Immanuel Kant, *Critique of Teleological Judgment*, translated by J. C. Meredith (Oxford: Clarendon Press, 1928), p. 75).

[27] See note 16 above.

freedom itself sets for us, the realization of the highest good, must be realized within nature. Thus Kant argues that the only thing we can conceive of as an unconditional end for nature, though set as an end by reason rather than mere nature, is also something that must be realizable in nature.[28]

Kant accomplishes this last stage of his argument by distinguishing between an 'ultimate end' (*letzter Zweck*) of nature and a 'final end' (*Endzweck*) for it, and then arguing that the ultimate end and the final end must be the same, namely the realization of the highest good. The initial difference between the concepts of the ultimate and the final end, which once again Kant hardly makes explicit, seems to be a distinction between what might be thought as the value-neutral last stage of some causal process and a value-positive goal of such a process. It is presumably an objective of theoretical reason, transformed into a goal of reflective judgment, that we be able to conceive of an end-point for nature conceived of as a causally linked series of events, while it is a requirement of practical reason, also transformed into a regulative ideal of reflective judgment, that the ultimate end of nature also be a final end, something of unconditional and intrinsic value. Kant's argument then takes the form of showing that the expression of human freedom in the form of morality is in fact the only thing that can be thought of as both the ultimate end of nature, or its aim from an explanatory point of view (*CPJ*, §§82 f.), but also the final end for nature, or its only possible aim from an evaluative point of view (*CPJ*, §84).

In somewhat more detail, the argument proceeds as follows. Kant first reminds us of what he had observed at the very beginning of the 'Critique of Teleological Judgment,' namely that from an initial view of nature there can be no thought of any determinate end for it at all, ultimate or final: we might think that plant life exists in order to support animals that are in turn of use to us, but we could just as easily imagine that animals and even we ourselves exist merely to fertilize and care for the plants

---

[28] This point seems to have escaped numerous commentators. Düsing holds that the highest good as the 'proper object of practical reason' is an ' "objective final end of the human race" which must lie outside of nature,' and which can at best be prepared for rather than actually realized by any condition of culture that can be realized within nature, even the condition of perpetual peace (*Kants Begriff der Teleologie*, p. 222). Zanetti thinks that Kant's solution to the antinomy of teleological judgment collapses because of the contrast between the '*possibility* of a purposive-cause *in nature*' and the '*necessity* of a *supersensible* purposive-cause' ('Kants Antinomie der teleologischen Urteilskraft,' p. 354). But Kant's point is precisely that the end *for* nature that we can conceive a supersensible cause to set for it, which is nothing other than the end that we can set *for ourselves* in virtue of our supersensible capacity of freedom, is nothing other than the realization of the highest good *in* nature.

(*CPJ*, §82, 5:427). In order even to begin to think about an end for nature, we have to think of mankind as its end, because the human being 'is the only kind of being on earth that is capable of making a concept of ends for itself and, by means of its reason, making a system of ends out of an aggregate of purposively formed things' (5:426 f.). As the only sort of being that can form a conception of ends, Kant's argument seems to be, mankind must be the origin of all ends, and therefore the only candidate for the ultimate end in any explanatory account of nature.[29]

This argument takes the crucial step of implying that even if we must conceive of nature as the product of a supersensible agency in order to explain its apparent design, we can nevertheless conceive of the purpose that is the point of this agency's action only as something that is from at least one point of view within rather than outside of nature, namely humankind itself. But the mere thought that mankind must be the *ultimate* end of nature because it is the only being of which we have any experience that is capable of setting ends hardly suffices to determine a unique or even coherent end for nature as a system. This is because human beings set all sorts of ends for themselves, many if not most of which are utterly unsuitable for being considered as the *final* end of nature. From here we can see Kant's argument as proceeding in two further steps. First, he argues that any naturalistic conception of human happiness is both logically and empirically unsuitable as a candidate for the *ultimate* end of nature. The logic of human happiness unsuits it for such a role because individual conceptions of happiness are often internally incoherent and/or externally incompatible with each other, and thus

---

[29] This conception of humans as the originators of all value has been presented as the basis of Kant's ethical theory by Christine Korsgaard; see her *Creating the Kingdom of Ends* (Cambridge: Cambridge University Press, 1996), chs. 4 and 6. I think it is clear at least in the present context that this is only one premise in Kant's value theory, and that he will go on to argue that human beings must recognize their own freedom as an end in itself in order properly to employ their capacity to give value to everything else in nature by setting ends. Without something that functions as an objective constraint on their unique capacity to set ends, humans could also disvalue everything in nature.

Jürg Freudiger comes closer to the argument made here when he suggests that what makes mankind into the 'ultimate end' of nature, namely his own capacity to set and thus be the source of ends, does not itself automatically make man into a final end, something that is not a mere means to something else ('Kants Schlußstein', p. 430). He then claims that Kant's 'second step is not entirely developed,' but consists merely in a vague allusion to the fact that 'man is a citizen of two spheres' and only thereby 'comes into question as a final end' (p. 431). I think that Kant can be given credit for clearly recognizing that establishing that mankind is suitable for the role of an ultimate end in virtue of his capacity to set ends does not suffice to establish that mankind is the final end of nature, and then explicitly maintaining that this second claim can be sustained only by introducing the premise that mankind's capacity to set ends freely is itself of unconditional value.

offer no possible determinate end for nature; and even an individually coherent and interpersonally consistent conception of human happiness would seem empirically unsuitable for this role because nature seems to pay no regard to human happiness: 'in its destructive actions, in pestilence, famine, flood, frost, attacks from animals great and small, etc., nature spares mankind just as little as any other animal' (*CPJ*, §83, 5:430). Only a human end that can be both coherently conceived and plausibly seen as an actual end of nature can be a candidate for the ultimate end of nature. Kant then argues that from 'among all mankind's ends in nature' the only candidate for an ultimate end that is left is 'the formal, subjective condition, namely the capacity for setting ends for itself and using nature as means suitable to the maxims of its free ends (independent from nature in the determination of these ends)' (*CPJ*, §83, 5:431). This is what Kant calls human 'culture,' not in the sense of the mere development of skills and talents that might be useful for the achievement of any human ends regardless of their moral value but rather in the sense of 'the liberation of the will from the despotism of desires which, by their attachment to certain things in nature, would make us incapable of choosing for ourselves' (5:432). In other words, the only candidate for the *ultimate end* of nature is the self-disciplined expression of human freedom that is the essence of human morality.

The final stage of this argument is then Kant's claim that the very same thing, the expression of human freedom through the development of morality, is the only thing that is fitted to be the *final end* of nature because it is the only thing that is of unconditional value. Kant's exposition of this claim is, to say the least, compressed. He begins §84 with a definition of a final end as 'that end, that requires no other as the condition of its possibility' (5:435). This might make it sound as if the concept of a final end is an explanatory concept after all, and a hopeless one at that, like an uncaused cause. And perhaps Kant even has something like that in mind, for he subsequently argues that 'the final end is not an end which nature would be sufficient to bring about and produce in accordance with its idea, because it is unconditioned' and nothing in nature is unconditioned, precisely because all 'grounds of determination to be found in nature itself are themselves always in turn conditioned,' i.e., there is nothing in the causal order of nature that is not determined by a prior cause (5:435). But it seems clear that what Kant is really looking for is something that is of unconditional value, something the mere idea of which is a sufficient *reason* for its existence rather than a sufficient cause, something which blocks any further question 'why (*quem in finem*) it exists?' In any case, Kant's key claim is the expression of human freedom in the form of morality is the only thing that is of unconditional *value*. It is thus the only candidate for the *final* end of nature, so the only candidates for the ultimate end of nature and for the final end of nature turn out to be the same: 'Now we have only one sort of being in the world whose causality is teleological, i.e., directed at ends, and yet is at the same time so constituted that the law in accordance with which it has to determine ends is represented by itself as unconditional and independent from natural conditions but yet as necessary. The being of this sort is the human being, but considered as noumenon: the only natural being in which we can cognize a supersensible faculty (*freedom*)... together with the object which it can set before itself as the highest end (the highest good in the world) from the side of its own constitution' (*CPJ*, §84, 5:435).

This extraordinary paragraph packs in an awful lot. First, it draws the conclusion that the only thing that is a viable candidate for being the ultimate end of nature because it explains the setting of ends—namely human freedom—is also the only thing that is a candidate for being the final end of nature because it is of unconditional value. Second, it says that this end, or mankind as the bearer of this end, is something that must be conceived of as outside of nature, because its possibility requires the conception of the supersensible as the ground for the sensible world, but at the same time must be regarded as something that is also manifest in the natural world, in human beings as creatures in nature. Third, it makes into the final end of nature not only human freedom as the capacity that is the basis of morality, but also the highest good, which is the object set for us by morality. This is clearly represented through the remainder of the 'Critique of Teleological Judgment' as a condition which is to be realized *within* nature (*CPJ*, §87, 5:450). Thus to conceive of nature as an intentional product of design also requires us to conceive of it as a system aimed at the highest good, and we can only do this by conceiving of the laws of nature as laws consistent with the human realization of the highest good—the very same conception of nature that we reach, according to Kant's first two critiques as well as to the remainder of the third, by starting out from purely moral reflection on the highest good and the conditions of the rationality of our efforts to realize it.

This conclusion might appear to conflict with Kant's observation that nature seems to show no special favor toward human happiness; in the claim that human morality is the only thing we can conceive of as the final end of nature, but that through this status for morality the highest good as the object of morality in turn becomes the final end of nature,

Kant seems to claim that happiness must be the end of nature after all. How are these two claims to be reconciled? In part, the answer must be that happiness as Kant first talked about it was happiness conceived as a *merely* natural object of inclination, the happiness of oneself and perhaps of some others contingently near and dear to one, conceived of over the short rather than the long range; the happiness conceived in the concept of the highest good, however, that is, the happiness of humankind as a whole as a product of human virtue, is not a natural object of inclination at all, but rather a conception imposed upon natural inclination by the free exercise of human reason.[30] Second, we may also have to take Kant's observation about nature's indifference to our happiness to have been meant in an at least partially provisional way. Nature certainly seems indifferent to human happiness on first glance, and perhaps it really is indifferent to merely natural or selfish conceptions of human happiness; but it may still be possible to see it as well-disposed to human happiness in the long run, to human happiness as the long-run product of human virtue—and virtue itself is not something that we have any expectation will be fully achieved in any short run. In any case, Kant seems to hold that we have to be able to conceive of nature as having this special form of human happiness in the long run as its goal in order to be able to conceive of it as having any intelligent and therefore purposive design at all.

3

This concludes my account of the main and novel argument of the 'Critique of Teleological Judgment.' Earlier, however, I noted that if the crucial step of this argument in which the teleological principle is extended from organisms to all of nature is to be seen an expression of reason's demand for unity, then we should expect Kant to argue that this extension is not undermined by an antinomy. This is just what he does in the 'Dialectic of Teleological Judgment.'[31] But Kant's exposition of the

---

[30] See my article 'Freiheit als "der Innere Werth der Welt",' in Christel Fricke, Peter König, and Thomas Petersen, eds., *Das Recht der Vernunft: Kant und Hegel über Denken, Erkennen und Handeln* (Stuttgart: Fromann-Holzboog, 1995), pp. 231–62; trans. as 'Freedom as the Inner Value of the World,' in my *Kant on Freedom, Law, and Happiness* (Cambridge: Cambridge University Press, 2000), pp. 96–125.

[31] In the opening of her article 'Kants Antinomie der teleologischen Urteilskraft,' Zanetti suggests that the point of the antinomy is to establish that human freedom can be effective in a world apparently governed by mechanical causal laws (pp. 341 f.). This needs to be refined, for presumably Kant has already established that human beings are

'Dialectic' also raises a problem about the starting-point of the entire argument we have just considered. For the most general point of the 'Dialectic' is that the mechanical and teleological principles of explanation can be reconciled, not just by regarding both principles as merely regulative rather than constitutive, but ultimately by regarding mechanical causation as itself the sensible expression of the purposiveness of the supersensible ground of nature, thus as the means through which the end of nature is achieved. This implies, however, not only that all of nature can be seen as purposive, but equally that all of nature can at least in principle be seen as mechanically explicable; and this may seem to undermine Kant's opening claim that it is the mechanical inexplicability of organisms that leads us to a teleological view of nature in the first place.

This problem is not apparent in Kant's initial formulation of the antinomy of teleological judgment. Kant begins by arguing that there cannot be an antinomy of reason between the two purportedly constitutive principles that 'All generation of material things is possible in accordance with merely mechanical laws' and 'Some generation of such things is not possible in accordance with material laws' because neither of these principles can be proved by reason at all (*CPJ*, §71, 5:387).[32] Instead, he says, the question can only be whether there is a conflict between what he calls two 'maxims' of reflection or 'regulative principles for research,' the first maxim that 'All generation of material nature cannot be judged as possible except in accordance with merely mechanical laws' and the second maxim that 'Some products of nature cannot be judged as possible in accordance with merely mechanical laws' (5:387).

It is often thought that pointing out the regulative character of these principles is itself Kant's resolution of the question of an antinomy. But it should be noted that Kant says that this is only the 'preparation' for a solution to the antinomy (*CPJ*, §71, 5:388),[33] and this is a good thing, because it seems as if there is still a conflict even between the two mere

free to form whatever *intentions* morality might require in the third Antinomy of the first *Critique* and the treatment of freedom in the second; what remains to be shown by the arguments of the 'Critique of Teleological Judgment' is that the laws of nature are compatible with or even conducive to the successful *realization* of freely formed human intentions.

[32] Kant apparently intends to make a contrast with the 'Antinomy of Pure Reason' in the first *Critique*, where his argument is that each of the opposed theses and antitheses appears to be required by pure reason.

[33] This point has been noticed by a number of commentators, including McFarland, *Kant's Concept of Teleology*, p. 121; Peter McLaughlin, *Kant's Critique of Teleology in Biological Explanation* (Lewiston: Edwin Mellen Press, 1990), p. 131; and Zanetti, 'Kants Antinomie der teleologischen Urteilskraft,' p. 345.

maxims of reflection.[34] If there really are some objects that cannot be judged to be possible on a purely mechanical conception of causation, then, assuming the principle that 'ought implies can,'[35] we could not reasonably be enjoined even to try to judge all objects as *possible* solely on mechanical principles. Kant obscures this point when he claims that in his contrast between the two maxims of reflection 'it has not been said that those forms [of organisms] were not possible in accordance with the mechanism of nature' (*CPJ*, §70, 5:388). That may be true, but we are still being told by the first maxim to 'judge as possible in accordance with merely mechanical laws' some products of nature which the second maxim tells us 'cannot possibly be judged in accordance with merely mechanical laws' (*CPJ*, §70, 5:387), and thus the first maxim enjoins an impossible task on us.[36]

What would not be contradictory, however, would be the principles that 'Everything in nature can be judged as possible in accordance with merely mechanical laws' and 'Some (or all) things in nature can **also** be judged as possible in accordance with non-mechanical (or teleological) laws.' In other words, the only way to reconcile the conflict between the first maxim for the judgment of nature that Kant formulates and any teleological conception of it would be to argue that at least some objects can be judged in accordance with *both* mechanical and teleological principles.[37] And in proceeding beyond the mere 'preparation' for a solution to the antinomy, this is exactly what Kant goes on to defend. He argues first that even though we can have no expectation of explaining organisms purely mechanically it would still be presumptuous for us to insist that there *is* no mechanical explanation of the organic (*CPJ*, §75, 5:400). And then he argues that the way to reconcile the two maxims is to realize that they work at different levels: we can conceive of explaining

---

[34] See McLaughlin, *Kant's Critique of Teleology*, pp. 134, 139 (at p. 138 n. 5 McLauglin cites older commentators who failed to see this point); Allison, 'Kant's Antinomy of Teleological Judgment,' p. 29; and Zanetti, 'Kants Antinomie der teleologischen Urteilskraft,' pp. 344 f.

[35] It is sometimes noted that Kant does not explicitly formulate this principle in his famous argument from consciousness of the moral law to the recognition of freedom in the *Critique of Practical Reason* (5:29 f.). But he does formulate it explicitly and repeatedly in the *Religion* (e.g., 6:47, 62 f.).

[36] Perhaps it is thus an example of what Allen Wood has called an *absurdum practicum*; see his *Kant's Moral Religion* (Ithaca: Cornell University Press, 1970), pp. 25–34. In his treatment, Allison stresses that even regulative principles entail ontological commitments, so the antinomy between mechanism and teleology cannot be resolved merely by asserting that the maxims to seek mechanical explanations for all objects but teleological ones for some are regulative ('Kant's Antinomy of Teleological Judgment,' pp. 31 f.).

[37] This point is also made by McLaughlin, *Kant's Critique of Teleology*, p. 130, and Zanetti, 'Kants Antinomie der teleologischen Urteilskraft,' p. 345.

anything in nature *both* mechanically and teleologically because we can conceive of the supersensible ground of nature as expressing its purposiveness *through* its legislation of the mechanical laws of nature:[38] 'The principle that is to make possible the unifiability of both of them in the judgment of nature in accordance with them must be posited in what lies outside of both of them (thus as outside the possible empirical representation of nature), but in what contains the ground of them both, i.e., in the supersensible, and each of the two sorts of explanation must be related to that' (*CPJ*, §78, 5:411 f.)

Once we adopt this point of view, two maxims of judgment can be held simultaneously, although not the two that Kant originally formulated but rather the two maxims 'Everything in nature must be able to be judged in accordance with mechanical laws' and 'Some (or even all things) must also be able to be judged in accordance with a teleological conception.' It may be noted that affirming the first of these maxims in this way obviates any need to see Kant as giving up the first *Critique*'s claim for the universal validity of a principle of causation immanent within nature.[39]

---

[38] Henry Allison suggests that by connecting the concept of a purposive cause solely to the constitution of our cognitive faculties, Kant resolves the antinomy by separating the maxims of reflective judgment from any ontological commitments at all ('Kant's Antinomy of Teleological Judgment,' p. 34). I would instead suggest that Kant's solution takes the form of solving the antinomy by means of an ontological conception, namely the conception of a supersensible ground of the sensible world which achieves its purposes through mechanical laws, where however the *objective validity* or epistemic status of this conception is not asserted dogmatically but is restricted to our own subjective point of view.

Peter McLaughlin also tries to eliminate any ontological element from Kant's solution to the antinomy, holding that its solution consists simply in recognizing that although *we* must always explain things mechanically (or, as he also calls it, reductionalistically), nature simply does not allow all of its products to be explained this way; the solution to the antinomy is just to accept this fact (*Kant's Critique of Teleology*, p. 162). This interpretation has the virtue of maintaining the special status of organisms in Kant's conception of natural science, unlike the solution by appeal to the supersensible, which could survive even a complete mechanical explanation of organisms; but it fails to show how the solution to the antinomy contributes to Kant's larger objective in the *Critique of Judgment*, that of unifying the theoretical and practical points of view.

[39] See McFarland, *Kant's Concept of Teleology*, pp. 119–22. Zanetti also raises the problem of whether the antinomy of teleological judgment requires any revision of Kant's view of the universal validity of causation in the first *Critique*. She argues that what Kant should have concluded from the antinomy is that a mechanical conception of causation (in which only the character of the parts of an object determine the behavior of the whole; see Allison, 'Kant's Antinomy of Teleological Judgment,' p. 27) is a necessary but not a sufficient condition for the complete causal explanation of the behavior of some objects (pp. 350–2); indeed, her identification of the problem about comprehending organisms with the problem about the incomplete determination of particulars by discursive general concepts that Kant discusses in *CPJ*, §§76 f. is clearly intended to make room for this proposal. She laments that Kant solves the antinomy instead by arguing that the distinc-

At the same time, this solution throws Kant's original claim about the mechanical inexplicability of specific organic functions into doubt.

This problem may not be apparent in the first part of Kant's resolution of the antinomy. Here (*CPJ*, §§72–4) Kant considers four systems for dealing with life and its appearance of purposive design in nature.[40] Two of these are what he calls 'idealist' systems, by which he means that they actually *explain away* any appearance of purposiveness in nature. The other two are 'realist' accounts, that is, they purport to give adequate explanations of something that is not to be explained away (*CPJ*, §72, 5:391). The two "idealist" accounts are the system of 'accidentality,' i.e., Epicureanism, according to which any appearance of design in nature is the product of utterly accidental collisions among bits of matter, and the system of 'fatality,' ascribed to Spinoza, on which everything in nature is the product of an original being as the underlying ground of nature, but is not to be attributed to any 'understanding' or intelligence in such a ground, and is not designed (5:391 f.). The two systems of 'realism' are, first, the 'physical' or 'hylozoistic' system, in which real design in nature is a product of 'the **life of matter**' itself, and, second, the 'hyperphysical' or 'theistic' system, according to which design in nature is a genuine product of the 'primordial source of the universe' conceived as an 'intentionally acting (originally living) intelligent being' (5:392). Kant then argues that the first three of these systems implode before they even get off the ground, but that the fourth, theism, while it cannot be dogmatically demonstrated, is at least not internally incoherent, and can therefore be adopted as a principle of reflective if not determinant judgment. Both the system of accidentality and the system of fatalism eliminate all '**unity of purpose**' and any appearance of '**intentionality**' (*das Absichtliche*) (*CPJ*, §73, 5:393); moreover, while Epicureanism makes everything in nature contingent, which undermines our conception of experience, Spinozism removes all contingency from nature, which equally belies our own experience (*CPJ*, §80, 5:421). Hylozoism, in turn, is impossible because the idea of 'a living matter' is self-contradictory: here is where Kant insists that 'lifelessness, **inertia**,

tion between the supersensible and the sensible allows objects to be seen as both sufficiently determined by mechanical laws and by a teleological purpose at the same time (pp. 352, 354 f.). But if she rejects that point of view completely, then one is left wondering what has become of her original characterization of the point of the antinomy as being that of showing the effectiveness of (a supersensible) freedom in the (sensible) world of nature.

[40] A useful discussion of these four systems may be found in Bartuschat, *Zum systematischen Ort von Kants Kritik der Urteilskraft*, pp. 199–205.

constitutes the essential character of matter' (5:394). Thus, only the idea that the appearance of design in living matter is imparted to it from an outside intelligent source is even coherent. Such theism cannot 'dogmatically establish' the 'possibility of natural ends' any more than the other theories can, but we can at least coherently conceive of an 'intentional causality for the generation of nature' in 'an understanding ascribed to a primordial being' (5:395). In this argument, it still appears to be the peculiar nature of organisms as living matter that requires us to conceive of an intelligent and purposive supersensible ground of sensible nature and then to extend that thought to the whole of nature.

In Kant's next argument, however, the teleological perspective on the whole of nature is not suggested by the special case of the experience of organisms, but is immediately reached by a general consideration about the knowledge of nature, organic or not. This argument appears in §§76 f. of the 'Dialectic' of the 'Critique of Teleological Judgment.'[41] Kant makes it sound as if this argument has a special connection with 'physical ends' or organisms, saying that the conception of such an object as a **product of nature** involves 'natural necessity and yet at the same time a contingency of the form of the object in relation to mere laws of nature' (*CPJ*, §74, 5:396). That is, although we try to think of everything about an object in nature as being determined, the kind of causal laws we are able to apply to organisms—mechanical laws—are not in fact adequate to explain everything determinate about them. But Kant then goes on to make an entirely general point about the relation between laws and particulars that does not turn on the specific kind of objects or laws concerned. He argues that the distinctions between the possible and the

[41] A related argument appears in the introduction to the *Critique of Judgment*. There Kant argues that although we can explain the necessity of such high-level or entirely abstract laws of nature as the principle of universal causation as being due to 'the laws given by our understanding *a priori*,' these laws only establish 'the possibility of a nature (as object of the senses) in general,' and are not sufficient to furnish the laws for the particular 'manifold forms of nature as, as it were, so many modifications of the general concepts of nature.' Yet such particular laws, 'even though as empirical laws they may be contingent with regard to the insight of our understanding must still, if they are to be laws (as the concept of a nature requires) be able to be regarded as necessary on the basis of some principle of the unity of the manifold, even if it is unknown to us' (*CPJ*, Introduction IV, 5:179 f.). He then claims that: 'This principle can be nothing other than that, since general laws of nature have their basis in our understanding, which prescribes them to nature (although only in accordance with the general concept of it as nature), the particular empirical laws, in regard to that which is left undetermined in them by the general laws, must be regarded as if in accordance with such a unity that an understanding (although not ours) would have given them in order to make possible a system of experience in accordance with particular laws of nature for the sake of our own cognitive capacity' (*CPJ*, Introduction IV, 5:180; see also V, 5:183 f.).

actual as well as the necessary and contingent are inherent and entirely general limitations of human thought, deriving from the even more fundamental distinction between concepts and intuitions. General concepts and laws, whatever their specific character, can only represent an object as possible, and intuition is always needed to represent it as actual (*CPJ*, §76, 401 f.); and only those features of an object dictated by a concept of it seem necessary, while those further features presented only by (empirical) intuition always seem contingent (*CPJ*, §77, 406 f.). Thus, what makes a particular object fully determinate always seems contingent relative to any general concept we have for it. Yet we cannot tolerate this ineliminable residue of contingency, so we conceive of particular objects, like general laws, as if they were products of an intelligence greater than our own, whose concepts are sufficient to determine individual objects in every respect (*CPJ*, §77, 404 f.)—even though the very distinction between possible concept and actual existence that is the inherent limitation of our thought that starts us down this path also means that we know we can never have knowledge of the actual existence of such an intelligence (*CPJ*, §76, 5:402). Though Kant emphasizes this gap between general concept and fully particularized form in our knowledge of organisms (5:407 f.), this argument actually applies to all particular objects in nature. And for precisely that reason it is consistent with the resolution of the antinomy of teleological judgment that, as we saw, Kant needs in order to avoid contradiction even between two maxims of reflective judgment, namely one that argues that the mechanical and teleological perspectives on nature as a whole are compatible because we can think of the mechanical perspective as applying to all of the sensible and the teleological perspective to the supersensible, which achieves its purposes in the sensible realm *through* the mechanical laws of nature. In Kant's words, matter, even though 'its nature is in accordance with mechanical principles, can be subordinated to the represented end as means' (*CPJ*, §78, 5:414).

If this argument about the contingent and the necessary suffices to introduce a teleological perspective into natural science, then it does so even if, contrary to Kant's previous claims, specific organic functions and even the emergence of life itself could be explained in purely mechanical terms. Kant never acknowledges this, even though after his initial discussion of organic functions (*CPJ*, §§64–6) he does most often write as if we *cannot* set any specific limit to the possibility of mechanical explanations, even of organic functions, and know only in some unspecified general way that they will never be complete (e.g., *CPJ*, §68, 5:383). Yet both before and after the argument of §§76 and 77, Kant continues

to write as if the experience of organisms is indispensable for the introduction of the teleological point of view. Why? Why doesn't he treat the
special experience of organisms as a ladder that can be tossed aside once
we have climbed up to this more general argument? Here I can only
conjecture that Kant's focus on organisms is related to his claim that
among proofs of the existence of God the argument from design must
always be treated with a kind of respect that is not due to the more
abstract ontological and cosmological arguments because it is the 'clearest and the most appropriate to common human reason' (A 623/B 651).
That is, his assumption may be that the common and inescapable experience of organisms—the plants and animals on which we all depend
every day of our lives—makes the teleological perspective natural and
plausible to all normal human beings in a way that abstract philosophical
considerations like those concerning the contingency of the particular
relative to general concepts never could. In this way, the experience of
organisms would play an indispensable role in introducing the teleological perspective to normal human agents, the ultimate subjects of
Kant's moral anthropology, even though it is not necessary for a purely
philosophical deduction of this perspective. Privileging the experience of
organisms in this way would be entirely consistent with Kant's approach
to morality throughout the *Critique of Judgment*, which is meant
throughout to bridge the gulf between nature and freedom not for
rational beings in general but for real human beings, who find themselves
embodied in nature as we are.[42]

[42] For my argument that precisely such approach explains Kant's connection of aesthetics to morality in the first half of the *Critique of Judgment*, see 'Feeling and Freedom:
Kant on Aesthetics and Morality,' Chapter 1 of my *Kant and the Experience of Freedom:
Essays on Aesthetics and Morality* (Cambridge: Cambridge University Press, 1993), pp.
27–47.

# 13

# Purpose in Nature: What is Living and What is Dead in Kant's Teleology?

What is living and what is dead in Kant's teleology? To answer this question we must first have an account of Kant's teleology. This is no mean feat, since Kant was concerned with the issue of teleology for many decades, from his 1763 book *The Only Possible Basis for a Demonstration of the Existence of God* through the 1781 *Critique of Pure Reason* and then at length in the 1790 *Critique of the Power of Judgment*, the second half of which is a 'Critique of the Teleological Power of Judgment'. Even if we confine ourselves to the third *Critique*, the task of interpreting Kant's concept of teleology is still daunting, not only because his argumentation in this work is compact yet complex, and his prose and terminology involuted even by his own standards, but also because he offers numerous arguments for conceiving of nature in terms of design and purpose in the Introduction(s) to the work,[1] in its first half, the

An abbreviated German translation of this chapter appeared in Dietmar H. Heidemann and Kristina Engelhard (eds.), *Warum Kant Heute? Systematische Bedeutung und Rezeption seiner Philosophie in der Gegenwart* (Berlin: Walter de Gruyter, 2004), pp. 383–413.

[1] To make matters even more complicated, there are two extant versions of the Introduction to the *Critique of the Power of Judgment*, the so-called 'First Introduction' (FI), a draft that Kant wrote in early 1789, and the published version of the Introduction, written only after Kant had already delivered the body of the text to the publisher in the winter of 1790. Kant claimed that he revised the Introduction only because the first version was too long, but in fact the second and final version gave a much clearer account of the systematic significance of teleology for Kant, something that we can therefore assume only became fully clear to him as his composition of the text approached completion. For an account of the relation between the two versions, see my Editor's Introduction in Immanuel Kant, *Critique of the Power of Judgment*, ed. Paul Guyer, trans. Paul Guyer and Eric Matthews (Cambridge: Cambridge University Press, 2000), pp. xxxix–xliii. That translation will be cited throughout this essay, although citations will be located only by Kant's own section numbers and the volume and page number of the Akademie edition, that is, *Kant's gesammelte Schriften*, ed. the Royal Prussian (later German and then Berlin–Brandenburg) Academy of Sciences (Berlin: Georg Reimer, later Walter de Gruyter, 1900– ). The *Kritik der Urtheilskraft* appears in volume 5 of this edition (1913) and was edited by Wilhelm Windelband. Other works of Kant cited here are the *Critique of Pure Reason*, ed. and trans. Paul Guyer and Allen Wood (Cambridge: Cambridge University Press, 1998); the *Critique of Practical Reason*, the *Groundwork for the Metaphysics*

'Critique of the Aesthetic Power of Judgment', and within the 'Critique of the Teleological Power of Judgment' itself. The details of these arguments and the relations among them are not always clear, but what is clear is that Kant's interest in teleology in the third *Critique* was not confined to puzzles in the emerging science of biology, but was driven by his interest in clarifying the connection between theoretical and practical reason. Kant begins the work with the statement that although the laws of nature and the laws of freedom seem to be the laws of two distinct and incommensurable realms, nevertheless the ends of freedom, that is, the ends imposed upon us by the moral law, must be realizable in nature, that is, the realm governed by natural laws, and thus we must be able to conceive of nature as a realm within which the ends of morality can be achieved:

Now although there is an incalculable gulf fixed between the domain of the concept of nature, as the sensible, and the domain of the concept of freedom, as the supersensible, so that from the former to the latter (thus by means of the theoretical use of reason) no transition is possible, just as if there were so many different worlds, the first of which can have no influence on the second: yet the latter **should** have an influence on the former, namely the concept of freedom should make the end that is imposed by its laws real in the sensible world; and nature must consequently also be able to be conceived in such a way that the lawfulness of its form is at least in agreement with the possibility of the ends that are to be realized in it in accordance with the laws of freedom. (*CPJ*, Introduction II, 5:175–6)

The point of Kant's teleology is then to argue that there are aspects of our experience of nature that make it necessary for us to conceive of nature as purposive in a way that is also sufficient for the satisfaction of morality's requirement that its own ends be realizable in that nature. And this is what remains alive in Kant's teleology: while in the light of contemporary science it is hard to maintain Kant's view that there is anything about our experience of nature that forces us to conceive of it as the product of intelligent and rational design, Kant's view that the ends imposed upon us by morality must be realized within nature and thus that our moral reasoning must take account of the character and limits of our knowledge of nature remains of enduring significance.

of Morals, and the *Metaphysics of Morals*. Translations of the latter works, as well as Kant's 1793 essay *Theory and Practice*, are all drawn from Immanuel Kant, *Practical Philosophy*, ed. and trans. Mary J. Gregor (Cambridge: Cambridge University Press, 1996). Passages from the *Critique of Pure Reason* are located by the pagination of its first (A) and second (B) editions; all other passages are located by volume and page number in the Akademie edition.

Kant's critical reconstruction of traditional teleology consists of the following extended argument. In the Introduction to the third *Critique*, Kant argues that we can only conceive of particular laws of nature—presumably, laws of inorganic as well as of organic nature—as members of a system of such laws, and that we must conceive of such a system as the product of an intelligence similar to but more powerful than our own, although of course we can have no knowledge of the existence of any such thing. In the 'Critique of Teleological Judgment', he argues that our experience of organisms in particular requires us to conceive of them as if they were organized systems that are products of intelligent design, and further that once we have conceived of organisms in this way, we must also conceive of nature as whole—that is, the entities that comprise nature, not just the laws that describe it—as if were also the systematic product of intelligent design. Kant then argues in the 'Methodology of the Teleological Power of Judgment' that we cannot conceive of nature as the product of intelligent design without also conceiving of it as the product of purposive design, so we must be able to conceive of a purpose for the system of nature as a whole. Nothing less than an end of unconditional value can play this role, however, and the only thing that we can conceive of as unconditionally valuable is the development and exercise of our own freedom under the guidance of the moral law. We must then conceive of the moral use of our own freedom as the end of the system of nature. And this means not only that we must conceive of the laws of nature as compatible with the realization of the ends imposed upon us by morality, but also that we must conceive of our morality as something that can be realized in nature. What I argue here is that although there are obvious and perhaps fatal problems in Kant's argument that we must conceive of the realization of our own morality as the end of nature, there are enduring lessons in his view that we must conceive of our own morality as something that can be realized within nature.

## I. ENDS IN NATURE

Near the end of the Introduction to the third *Critique*, Kant repeats that a bridge must be constructed across the chasm between nature and freedom in order to assure us that the '**effect**' of freedom 'in accordance with its formal laws is to take place in the world' (*CPJ*, Introduction IX, 5:195). But now he adds that the 'power of judgment' is to provide 'the mediating concept between the concepts of nature and the concept of freedom' and thereby make 'possible the transition from the purely theoretical to the purely practical . . . in the concept of a **purposiveness** of nature', through which 'the possibility of the final end, which can become actual only in nature and in accord with its laws', can be known (5:196). What is the concept of the purposiveness of nature by means of which the power of judgment allows us to see the possibility of realizing the highest end of freedom as well?

Even if we leave aside any evidence of the realizability of the ends of morality in nature that may be afforded to us by the aesthetic judgment on the beautiful and the sublime, the power of judgment still leads us to conceive of two different forms of purposiveness in nature. In the Introduction to the third *Critique*, Kant argues that we can conceive of particular *laws* of nature only as members of a system of such laws, and that we can only conceive of such a system of laws as the product of an intelligence similar to but greater than our own, and thus as purposive. In the 'Analytic of the Teleological Power of Judgment', Kant argues that we can conceive of certain *entities* in nature, namely organisms, only as systems rather than as aggregates of parts, and that we can only conceive of such systems as products of design by an intelligence greater than our own. Moreover, the thought of individual organisms in nature as systems leads us to the conception of nature as a whole as a system, and thus also as the product of intelligent design. We may think of the systematicity of the laws of nature as a formal purposiveness, and the systematicity of individual organisms in nature and of nature as a system of both the organic and the inorganic as a material purposiveness. In either case, the next step of the argument will be the same: if we conceive of the source of either the formal or the material purposiveness of nature as intelligent design, we must also conceive of a purpose for that design. The final stage of Kant's argument will then be that only something of unconditional value can satisfy our conception of the purpose of nature, and that the only candidate for that is the development and exercise of our own freedom. The present section expounds and evaluates Kant's arguments for our ascription of both formal and material purposiveness to nature.

## 1. The Laws of Nature

Kant's argument that we must conceive of the laws of nature as comprising a systematic and purposive whole occurs only in the Introduction to the third *Critique*. The argument is based on the premiss that the 'universal' and 'transcendental laws' of nature that are given by the understanding (*CPJ*, Introduction IV, 5:179), that is, the 'synthetic principles of pure understanding' (*CPuR*, A 158/B 197), such as the principles that 'In all change of appearances substance persists, and its quantum is neither increased nor diminished in nature' (*CPuR*, B 224) and that 'All alterations occur in accordance with the law of the connection of cause and effect' (B 232) which are derived from the schematism of the pure concepts of the understanding or the categories, are not sufficient to determine the content of the particular laws of nature, such as, to use modern examples, the particular causal laws that govern such processes as nuclear fission, photosynthesis, the transcription of DNA sequences, and the like. Kant had already made this point in the first *Critique* when he wrote that 'Particular laws, because they concern empirically determined appearances, **cannot** be **completely derived** from the categories, although they all stand under them' (*CPuR*, B 165). But while there he might have given the impression that the categories need to be supplemented only by empirical intuition in order to yield particular laws of nature—'Experience must be added in order to come to know particular laws **at all**'—in the third *Critique* he argues that we must also conceive of the particular laws of nature that are not given to us by the categories but that we aim to discover—and which are therefore products not of the determining but of the reflecting use of the power of judgment, which seeks to find universals when only particulars are given (*CPJ*, Introduction IV, 5:179)—as members of a system of such laws. Why does he hold this?

(i) Kant suggests two different answers to this question. In the first draft of the Introduction, he stresses that it would not be rational for us to seek particular laws of nature not given by the transcendental principles of understanding unless we assumed that in the 'immeasurable multiplicity of things in accordance with possible empirical laws' there is in fact 'sufficient kinship among them to enable them to be brought under empirical concepts (classes) and these in turn under more general laws (higher genera) and thus for an empirical system of nature to be reached' (FI, V, 20:215); we must thus presuppose, as the 'special principle of the power of judgment', that '**Nature specifies its general laws into empirical ones, in accordance with the form of a logical system, in behalf of the power of judgment**' (20:216). Kant seems to be making two key assumptions here: first, that any law that we are to discover with our finite resources must be part of a body of laws that is not just relatively small but also systematically organized, and second, that it would not be rational for us to attempt to discover any particular laws of nature unless we have some sort of antecedent guarantee that the body of them is so organized. Kant then goes on to add that we can only conceive of the existence of the sort of systematicity among particular laws of nature that makes it possible for us to discover them as if it were a product of purposive design:

> For we call purposive that the existence of which seems to presuppose a representation of the same thing; natural laws, however, which are so constituted and related to each other as if they had been designed by the power of judgment for its own need, have a similarity with the possibility of things that presuppose a representation of themselves as their ground. Thus through its principle the power of judgment thinks of a purposiveness of nature in the specification of its forms through empirical laws. (20:216)

The existence of a systematic set of particular laws of nature in fact satisfies a purpose of our own, the goal of discovering such laws even though they are not directly entailed by the transcendental laws of nature; but we can only conceive of the existence of such a system of laws as if it were the product of an intelligent design of nature itself.

Whatever we might think of the final stage of this argument (which in any case does not yet ask what goal of unconditional value might have motivated the intelligent design of nature), at least one criticism of its initial step is obvious. Kant seems to presuppose that it is rational for us to attempt to realize a goal only if we have a guarantee that the achievement of that goal is at least possible, thus that it is rational for us to seek particular laws of nature only if we presuppose that the laws of nature really do constitute a manageable system. But we can object that if a goal is sufficiently important to us (as the discovery of particular laws of nature surely is) then it is rational for us to seek to attain that goal as long as we do *not* have any conclusive evidence that its realization is *im*possible. As one commentator has written, 'someone could say, "I am going to see whether I can systematize this body of data", without positively assuming that it can be systematized, although he could not sensibly make the attempt while *denying* the truth of the statement'. The presupposition of systematicity 'is related to the activity, not in a way that demands its conscious adoption, but simply its non-rejection'.[2] Of course, our 'non-rejection' of the impossibility of reaching our goal must be responsible rather than arbitrary if our conduct is to be rational: we must have some good reason to think that there is no necessary obstacle to our success, and cannot, for example, simply have failed to look for such an obstacle out of laziness or indifference. But if this condition is

---

[2] J. D. McFarland, *Kant's Concept of Teleology* (Edinburgh: University of Edinburgh Press, 1970), 86.

met, then rationality in the pursuit of a goal seems to require only the absence of proof of the impossibility of attaining it rather than a proof of the possibility of so doing. If this is right, then the rationality of searching for particular laws of nature does not depend upon a presupposition that there is a manageable system of them, *a fortiori* on the acceptance of any sort of explanation for the existence of such a system, but only on the absence of evidence that such a system does not exist.

(ii) This is a general problem for Kant's conception of rationality, which may undermine his argument for the postulates of pure practical reason as well.[3] But it does not obviously infect the other argument for the intelligent origin of the systematicity of the laws of nature that Kant offers in the Introduction to the third *Critique*.[4] What Kant argues here is that we must conceive of particular laws of nature as members of a system of such laws in order to lend them the appearance of *necessity* that their status as laws requires:

There is such a manifold of forms in nature, as it were so many modifications of the universal transcendental concepts of nature that are left undetermined by those laws that the pure understanding gives *a priori*, since these pertain only to the possibility of a nature (as object of the senses) in general, that there must nevertheless also be laws for it which, as empirical, may indeed be contingent in accordance with the insight of **our** understanding, but which, if they are to be called laws (as is also required by the concept of a nature), must be regarded as necessary on a principle of the unity of the manifold, even if that principle is unknown to us.

Kant then suggests that we can ascribe necessity to particular laws of nature only by seeing them as embedded in a system of laws, in which they can be seen as entailed by higher-order laws as well as entailing and thus making necessary even more particular laws subordinate to them:

The reflecting power of judgment, which is under the obligation of ascending from the particular in nature to the universal, therefore requires a principle that it cannot borrow from experience, precisely because it is supposed to ground the unity of all empirical principles under equally empirical but higher principles, and is thus the ground of the possibility of the systematic subordination of empirical principles under one another.

Here Kant is not arguing that we must presuppose that a system of laws of nature must exist in order for it to be rational for us to seek to discover

---

[3] See my article 'From a Practical Point of View: Kant's Conception of a Postulate of Pure Practical Reason', in my *Kant on Freedom, Law, and Happiness* (Cambridge: Cambridge University Press, 2000), 333–71.
[4] Kant makes this argument only in the published version of the Introduction.

any such law, which we have seen is dubious; rather, he is arguing that such a system must exist, whether or not we know very much about it, in order for particular laws within it to be necessary. From this point Kant then again argues that because (as the first *Critique* has shown) the only way in which we can comprehend the necessity of the universal and transcendental laws of nature is by seeing them as the products of our own forms of intuition and understanding, the only way in which we can conceive of the necessity of the particular laws of nature is by analogously regarding the systematic connection of them that lends each of them its semblance of necessity as the product of an intelligence which is similar to but more wide-ranging than our own, capable of prescribing particular as well as general laws to nature:

Since the universal laws of nature have their ground in our understanding, which prescribes them to nature (although only in accordance with the universal concept of it as nature), the particular empirical laws, in regard to that which is left undetermined in them by the former, must be considered in terms of the sort of unity they would have if an understanding (even if not ours) had likewise given them for the sake of our faculty of cognition, in order to make possible a system of experience in accordance with particular laws of nature. (*CPJ*, Introduction IV, 5:179–80)

Kant is careful to make it clear that in the final stage of this argument he is not offering the traditional argument in theoretical theology from the apparent design of the universe to the actual existence of its creator, the argument that Hume had so roundly criticized in his *Dialogues concerning Natural Religion* of 1779 and that Kant himself had rejected, under the name of the 'physico-theological proof', in the first *Critique* (*CPuR*, A 620–30/B 648–58); as he says, 'Not as if in this way such an understanding must really be assumed (for it is only the reflecting power of judgment for which this idea serves as a principle, for reflecting, not for determining); rather this faculty thereby gives a law only to itself, and not to nature' (*CPJ*, Introduction IV, 5:180).

But this caveat will not address our qualms about both the premiss and the conclusion of Kant's argument. Two objections about its starting point come to mind. First, although there are certainly some contemporary philosophers who have accepted the idea that particular laws of nature must be able to be seen as necessary truths and have attempted to make sense of this assumption,[5] by no means all contemporary philo-

---

[5] Here I am thinking of such philosophers as David Armstrong in *What is a Law of Nature?* (Cambridge: Cambridge University Press, 1983) and David Lewis in, for example, *Counterfactuals* (Cambridge, Mass.: Harvard University Press, 1973).

sophers are prepared to accept that even well-founded generalizations about the behaviour of particular sorts of objects in nature can plausibly be seen as necessary truths. Second, it is by no means clear that embedding particular generalizations in a hierarchically organized system of generalizations will lend much appearance of necessity to the individual members of such a system as long as we can imagine alternatives to the system as a whole. That is, unless a whole system of laws can be regarded as necessary, it is not clear in what sense its individual members can be considered necessary. Perhaps Kant intended to address this worry at the final stage of his argument by having us conceive the system of empirical laws that we strive to discover as if it were the product of an intelligence like our own—after all, such an intelligence would presumably not impose more than one possible system of laws on nature, just as we do not impose more than one pair of forms of intuition or set of categories on nature. But this raises a problem for Kant's whole model of explaining necessity by appeal to the structure of the mind that recognizes it: in what sense is the structure of that mind itself necessary? This is a question that Kant himself raises, though only once, as if in a fit of conscience, in a notorious passage of the first *Critique*'s transcendental deduction where he acknowledges that he can offer no ground 'for why we have precisely these and no other functions of judgment or for why space and time are the sole forms of our possible intuition' (*CPuR*, B 146).

So Kant's arguments that the existence of systematicity presuppose the existence of an intelligent source for it does not seem to have continuing vitality. This is not to say that in describing the details of his conception of the systematicity of the particular laws of nature Kant has failed to describe a continuing objective of scientific practice. On the contrary, two features of Kant's conception of such systematicity—which is actually more fully described in the Appendix to the 'Transcendental Dialectic' in the first *Critique* than in the Introduction to the third—remain of enduring value, and one of them will also be of great significance when we turn to Kant's attempt to link the systematicity of nature to the final end of morality. First, Kant characterizes systematicity by the criteria of homogeneity, specificity, and affinity, that is, by the goals of subsuming particular causal laws under maximally general laws, ideally even a single general law (homogeneity), of specifying more general laws to the maximal variety of particular objects (affinity), and of eliminating all gaps in the transition from more general to more particular laws or vice versa (affinity) (see *CPuR*, A 645–8/B 673–96). Surely these do characterize the continuing goals of science: Newton's unification of the laws of celestial and terrestrial mechanics under a single law of gravitational attraction, the explanation of both Mendelian patterns of inheritance and Darwinian mutation-and-selection by the biochemistry of DNA, and the search for a unifying principle for the four elementary forces of physics all represent either successful or continuing attempts to satisfy the demand for homogeneity, while something like the Darwinian explanation of speciation is obviously an attempt to satisfy the requirement of specificity. But, second, Kant also emphasizes that the goal of a *complete* system of natural laws is only a regulative ideal, and thus that our knowledge of nature is always incomplete. It is not in fact clear why he thinks that the goal of homogeneity can never be fully attained, that is, why we cannot successfully reduce scientific explanation to a single underlying principle—if the difference between the organic and the inorganic that he introduces in the third *Critique* is the reason for this assumption, Kant does not mention it in the first *Critique*. But it is obvious why the goal of specificity must remain a regulative ideal: if the task is to subsume all the variety of natural objects and processes under a single set of more general laws, that must remain a regulative ideal for the simple reason that no finite amount of scientific research will ever survey the infinitude of nature. 'The absolute totality of the series of these conditions in the derivation of their members is an idea which of course can never come about fully in the empirical use of reason' (*CPuR*, A 685/B 713). That science always seeks to systematize its results but that the infinitude of its objects entails that the laws that it has discovered and therefore the systematization of them can never be complete are surely results as valid for us as for Kant.

## 2. *Natural Ends*

We can now turn from Kant's account of formal purposiveness to his account of material purposiveness in nature, the subject matter of the 'Critique of the Teleological Power of Judgment' proper. At a superficial level, Kant's argument is simple. Our conception of nature as a whole as a material system of interrelated entities, like our conceptions of the formal system of laws of nature, of the systematic implementation of the ends of reason, and of the realization of the system of the ends of reason in the system of nature, are all ideas of reason, but to apply them to our actual experience of nature we need to find—by use of the reflecting power of judgment—something that counts as a concrete experience of systematic purposiveness *within* nature. This is the role played by our experience of organisms, which Kant calls both 'organized beings' and 'natural ends'. His claim about organisms is that we cannot comprehend them by our ordinary mechanical model of causality, where the existence and properties of a whole are always explained simply by the aggregation of previously existing parts, but can instead comprehend them only as systems where whole and parts are each cause and effect of the other; and then he claims that we can only conceive of such systems as the products of intelligent design, although precisely since our theoretical cognition is limited to mechanical causality, we can have no theoretically adequate grounds for asserting the existence of the necessary designer. Nevertheless, once we have introduced the idea of an intelligent design and hence a designer for organisms within nature, two further steps are inevitable for us: first, we will think of such a design and designer as manifest not only in parts of nature, namely organisms, but in the whole of nature as a single system; second, we will also think of such a design and designer not only as intelligent but purposive, and thus seek a purpose for the system of nature as a whole. Here is where Kant then assumes that only something of unconditional value could count as the purpose of such a system, that only the realization of our own freedom in the form of the highest good is of unconditional value, and thus that we can conceive of nature as a system only if we conceive of it as a system compatible with and indeed intended for the realization of the highest good as the final end of morality. The conception of nature that begins with our experience of organisms is thus supposed to lead to the same conclusion to which we are also led by the postulates of pure practical reason, namely that nature must be conceived of as an arena for the realization of our moral ends.

At this level, Kant's argument is straightforward. But its details are complex and sometimes confusing, and while we could evaluate the moral implications of Kant's view that the systematic ends of morality must be realized within the system of nature on the basis of this general sketch, there are other issues about the continuing interest of Kant's teleology that depend on a closer consideration of his argument. One issue for closer discussion is Kant's account of how the experience of organisms is supposed to lead to a conception of an intelligent source for their design, for Kant suggests several different reasons why we cannot comprehend organisms on the model that is otherwise adequate for our conduct of scientific inquiry. The other issue that needs discussion is Kant's attempt to reconcile our ordinary mechanical model of causation with our conception of both organisms and nature as a whole as purposive systems in the 'Dialectic of the Teleological Power of Judgment'.

(i) Kant begins his discussion of teleology with a critical argument that we have no apparent justification for seeing some things in nature as mere means to others as ends—for example, for seeing the sandy plains of northern Europe, left behind by ancient seas, as means to extensive pine forests as ends—or, in his terms, for introducing the concept of 'relative purposiveness' into our conception of nature (*CPJ*, §63, 5:366–9). Instead, any application of the idea of purposiveness to nature can begin only with the 'internal purposiveness' of organisms as 'natural ends' (*CPJ*, §64, 5:369). Kant 'provisionally' defines a natural end as a thing that '**is cause and effect of itself**' (5:370), and then gives three examples of what he has in mind: in the case of reproduction, one organism is the cause of another as an individual, but 'generates itself as far as the **species** is concerned', and from this point of view the organism as a whole is the cause of itself; in the case of growth, an organism 'generates itself as an **individual**' by transforming bits of external matter into parts of itself, thus by the whole being the cause of its own parts and through them of its own subsequent existence; and in the case of ordinary self-maintenance, the parts of an organism are the cause of the whole, as when the leaves of a tree keep it nourished, but the whole is also the cause of the parts, since the leaves cannot function without the rest of the tree (5:371–2). Kant's claim is that we cannot understand such organic processes on our ordinary, mechanical model of causation, where the character of a whole is determined entirely and only by the character of its parts, and that in these cases we must also see the character of the parts as dependent on the character of the whole.[6] He then argues that we can partially model such an alternative conception of causation by analogy with our own intentional production, where the whole determines the parts in the sense that our antecedent conception and plan of a whole lead to the production of the parts that are then assembled into the actual whole. But this analogy is not really adequate for comprehending organisms, because in organisms 'each part is conceived as if exists only **through** all the others, thus as if existing **for the sake of the others** and **on account of** the whole', but also 'as an organ that **produces** the other parts', and 'only then and on that account can'

---

[6] Peter McLaughlin in particular has argued that the aspect of our ordinary conception of causation that makes it unsuitable for the explanation of characteristic organic processes is not that we ordinarily assume that a cause must be temporally antecedent or at least not successive to its effect, but rather that the character of a whole is always the effect of the character of its parts and not vice versa; see his *Kant's Critique of Teleology in Biological Explanation: Antinomy and Teleology* (Lewiston, NY: Edwin Mellen Press, 1990), 152–6.

something, 'as an **organized** and **self-organizing** being, be called a natural end' (*CPJ*, §65, 5:373–4). Our own works of art are organized but not self-organizing; for example, in a watch, 'one part is the instrument for the motion of another, but one wheel is not the efficient cause for the production of the other: one part is certainly present for the sake of the other but not because of it' (5:374). So we can only conceive of organisms by means of 'a remote analogy with our own causality in accordance with ends' (5:375); we have to think of organisms as if they were the product of a designer more intelligent than ourselves, whose conception of the whole of such organisms can produce parts capable of producing each other as well as the whole, and of yielding a whole that can then maintain, produce, and reproduce its own parts.

Kant criticizes traditional teleology by adding that

The concept of a thing as in itself a natural end is ... not a constitutive concept of the understanding or of reason, but it can still be a regulative concept for the reflecting power of judgment, for guiding research into objects of this kind and thinking over their highest ground ... not, of course, for the sake of knowledge of nature or its original ground, but rather for the sake of the very same practical faculty of reason in us in analogy with which we consider the cause of that purposiveness. (*CPJ*, §65, 5:375)

This dense statement makes three important points. First, the concept of organisms as natural ends with the special kind of internal systematicity that Kant has attempted to characterize, as well as the concept of the ground or cause of such natural ends and their internal systematicity, is regulative rather than constitutive. Second, the concept of the organism as a natural end can guide research into it, which in the next section Kant will in fact suggest to be research into the *mechanical* causality by means of which an organism effects the various purposes that can be ascribed to it as a system and to its organs as subsystems. And third, the further point of such a conception of organisms will be for the sake of our 'practical faculty of reason'. That is the point that Kant will develop in the 'Methodology of the Teleological Power of Judgment', but only after the intervening claim that the concept of matter as a natural end 'necessarily leads to the idea of the whole of nature as a system in accordance with the rule of ends' (*CPJ*, §67, 5:378–9).

At this point, however, the contemporary scientist will certainly object that the latter stages of Kant's argument stand on a rotten foundation, because he has failed to adduce any organic process that cannot in fact be understood by means of our ordinary mechanical model of causation. The ability of organisms to reproduce themselves is now well understood as a process in which parts of one or two organisms, namely their genetic material, produce parts of the next generation of such organisms, e.g. stem cells, which can in turn explain the character of those next organisms as wholes. The ability of organisms to grow is now well explained by the function of specific parts, such as enzymes, to extract nutrients from their intake that can be transformed by ordinary chemical processes into fuel and materials for other parts of the organism, such as voluntary and involuntary muscles. The ability of organisms to maintain their existence is also explained by the powers of their parts, such as the ability of immune system cells to destroy foreign pathogens. Of course, not every element of mechanical explanations of reproduction, growth, and self-maintenance is available yet: for example, it remains to be discovered how the approximately 30,000 genes in the human genome express themselves in the 120,000 different proteins of the human proteome, or how infant stem cells differentiate themselves at the right times into a variety of different adult tissues. But contemporary scientists proceed in the confidence that 'mechanical' answers to these questions will be found. Moreover, contemporary scientists also proceed in the confidence that further mechanical, in this case evolutionary, explanations for the existence of the mechanical bases of organic processes will likewise be found. Further, although one might be tempted to say that contemporary scientists surely accept Kant's view that every part of an organism serves some function in the systematic life of the whole, although unlike Kant they are confident that a mechanical explanation of both the origination and the activity of every part of an organism can at least in principle be found, even that assumption may be indefensible: Stephen Jay Gould long argued that the mechanism of natural selection can carry along all sorts of non-functional by-products or 'spandrels' that are mechanically connected with functional and selected traits, as long as those spandrels are not *dys*functional, that is, as long as they do not compromise the reproductive success of the organism; and contemporary genomics at least currently tolerates the idea of long stretches of 'junk DNA' in chromosomes, by-products of past evolution, that can be carried along with the currently vital stretches of DNA as long as they do not harm the organism (that is, reduce the probability of its reproductive success). So even as a regulative principle the idea that every part of an organism is a vital and valuable part of it as an internally purposive system seems doubtful.

(ii) Thus Kant's argument that the experience of organisms necessarily introduces a conception of purposiveness that we must extend to nature as a whole and then connect to our moral objectives seems dubious from the start. But before we can conclude that, we must observe that Kant may suggest one or two alternative accounts of how this experience leads us to a reflective judgment that applies the idea of purposiveness to nature. The argument considered thus far turns on the claim that paradigmatic sorts of organic processes cannot be explained mechanically, and thereby lead us to the idea, although not any knowledge, of an alternative sort of causation through intelligent and purposive design. But at a later point in his exposition—in the 'Dialectic of the Teleological Power of Judgment', to which we shall subsequently return—Kant suggest that it is not specific organic processes but the general 'possibility of a living matter' that 'cannot even be conceived' on the basis of our ordinary conception of matter, because while 'lifelessness, **inertia**, constitutes [the] essential characteristic' of matter, living organisms apparently violate the law of inertia (*CPJ*, §73, 5:394). Kant does not actually explain the 'contradiction' in the concept of a 'living matter', but presumably his thought is that living organisms violate the law of inertia whenever they initiate a change in their own condition without having been acted upon by an external agent. If this is what he means, then his argument would be that the mere possibility of self-generated change or motion, surely the most elementary characteristic of any organism, defies comprehension by our ordinary model of causation and requires at least the conception of an alternative model of causation for organisms.

However, the contemporary scientist is hardly more likely to be moved by this argument than by Kant's first. Indeed, one would presumably appeal precisely to a mechanical model of organisms to refute this argument: that is, one would appeal to the motions of specific parts of an organism to explain any changes in the rest or motion of the whole, and then explain the motions of those specific parts as the effects either of other specific parts of the organism or of the influence of external objects on the motion of the internal parts. Kant would have to do a lot more than to appeal to a 'contradiction' between life and inertia to find a starting point for his teleology here.

(iii) Kant returns to the 'special character of the human understanding, by means of which the concept of a natural end is possible'—indeed, necessary—'for us' in three sections of the 'Dialectic of the Teleological Power of Judgment', culminating in §77, the title of which has just been quoted (5:405). The general thesis of these sections is that the 'discursive' nature of the human intellect is what stands in the way of our complete understanding of organisms and requires us to 'base the possibility of those natural ends on...an intelligent being...in accord with the maxims of our reflecting power of judgment' (*CPJ*, §75, 5:400).

However, Kant suggests two different accounts of what he means by the discursive character of the human intellect. In §76, he suggests that the human intellect is discursive because it can form only general concepts, which can never fully determine all the properties of a particular object, and which therefore can never fully explain the necessity of all those properties; but since reason requires us to think of those properties as necessary, we must at least form the idea of an intelligent design for nature that would fully determine 'the purposiveness of nature in its products', although to be sure as a 'regulative (not constitutive)' principle of reason (5:404). In §77, however, although he again says that it is characteristic of our understanding 'that in its cognition, e.g., of the cause of a product, it must go from the **analytical universal** (of concepts) to the particular (of the given empirical intuition)', so that there is much that always remains contingent in the particular relative to the general concept under which we subsume it, he contrasts our understanding with one that would be 'intuitive' and therefore go 'from the **synthetically universal** (of the intuition of a whole as such) to the particular, i.e., from the whole to the parts, in which, therefore, and in whose representation of the whole, there is no **contingency** in the combination of the parts' (5:407). Here Kant suggests that the discursivity of our intellect is what limits us to inferring the properties of wholes from the properties of their parts and prevents us from seeing the necessity with which the whole also determines the parts. In order to accommodate our experience of organisms as wholes which do determine the character of their own parts, we then 'represent products of nature as possible only in accordance with another kind of causality than that of the natural laws of matter, namely only in accordance with that of ends and final causes', where 'the **representation** of a whole containing the ground of the possibility of its form and of the connection of parts that belongs to that' is considered as the cause of the object, although once again 'this principle does not pertain to the possibility of such things themselves (even considered as phenomena) ... but pertains only to the judging of them that is possible for our understanding' (5:408).[7]

---

[7] In his article 'Kant's Antinomy of Teleological Judgment' (*Southern Journal of Philosophy*, 30, suppl. (1991), 25–42), Henry Allison bases his account of the antinomy of teleological judgment on the account of discursivity suggested in Section 76, while Peter McLaughlin bases his interpretation of the antinomy on the account suggested in Section 77 (McLaughlin, *Kant's Critique of Teleology*, 169–76. As I have just suggested, each of these interpretations has a basis in Kant's text. As I will now suggest, each faces a philosophical problem of its own.

Kant's appeal to the discursivity of our understanding in §77 seems then just to provide a new name for the argument already made in §§64–5, the argument that since in our experience of organisms the whole seems to determine the character of the parts in a way that we cannot explain by the power of our own intellect, we conceive of organisms as if they were products of an intellect more powerful than our own. The argument then seems open to the criticism of that argument that has been afforded by the progress of modern biology, namely that such progress consists precisely in the increasing ability to explain how organisms function to preserve and reproduce themselves by means of the specific actions of their parts, and that there is no obvious end in sight for such explanatory progress. If, however, Kant's argument is rather that our general concepts of organisms necessarily leave some of their particular properties unexplained and therefore at least apparently contingent, as §76 seems to suggest, then Kant's present argument seems to collapse into the argument of the Introduction to the third *Critique*: while the inability of our general concepts to explain every property of a particular may be especially salient in our experience of organisms, surely this general principle is true for every phenomenon in nature. Indeed, at the end of §76, Kant explicitly returns to the language of the Introduction, suggesting that we need the concept of the purposiveness of nature to compensate for 'what is contingent' in 'the derivation of the particular laws of nature from the general' (4:404). And in that case not only does our experience of organisms seem to lose its special place in Kant's teleology, but the argument is also again opened up to the objection that we may not need to be able to see the particular laws of nature as necessary truths in any strong sense anyway.

## 3. The Antinomy of Teleological Judgment

So it is by no means clear that Kant has a sound argument that the experience in nature requires us to introduce even a regulative idea of the purposive design of nature. Thus his claim that 'It is in fact indispensable for us to subject nature to the concept of an intention if we would even merely conduct research among its organized products by means of continued observation' and his key inference that 'once we have adopted such a guideline for studying nature and found it to be reliable we must also at least attempt to apply this maxim of the power of judgment to the whole of nature' (*CPJ*, §75, 5:398) both seem to be ill-founded. It is nevertheless possible that there may be an important lesson in Kant's attempt to connect the view of nature as a purposive systematic whole with the demands of morality. I will shortly argue that this is indeed the case, but before doing so I want to discuss briefly another issue about the 'Dialectic of the Teleological Power of Judgment'.

Kant begins the Dialectic by contrasting two 'maxims' of the power of judgment, the maxim that 'All generation of material things and their forms must be judged as possible in accordance with merely mechanical laws' and the maxim that 'Some products of material nature cannot be judged as possible according to merely mechanical laws (judging them requires an entirely different law of causality, namely that of final causes)'. He contrasts this pair of maxims to a pair of 'constitutive principles of the possibility of the objects themselves', namely the 'Thesis' that 'All generation of material things is possible in accordance with merely mechanical laws' and the 'Antithesis' that 'Some generation of such things is not possible in accordance with merely mechanical laws' (*CPJ*, §70, 5:387). Many commentators have assumed that the resolution to the antinomy of the teleological power of judgment is simply to note this contrast, that is, to note that the first pair of maxims are just regulative principles of judgment and not constitutive claims about the nature of reality itself.[8] Indeed, Kant himself insists in the next section that 'All appearance of an antinomy between the maxims of that kind of explanation which is genuinely physical (mechanical) and that which is teleological (technical) therefore rests on confusing a fundamental principle of the reflecting with that of the determining power of judgment' (*CPJ*, §71, 5:389). However, Kant also entitles this section merely a 'preparation' for the solution of the antinomy, and as others have noted, talking about judgments rather than objects does not avoid an antinomy: that some objects in nature can only be judged teleologically is still inconsistent with the claim that all objects in nature can be judged mechanically.[9] So Kant's resolution of the antinomy of teleological judgment must be more complex than it initially appears.

The key to Kant's real solution to the antinomy emerges in the next two sections. In §72, Kant canvasses 'various systems concerning the systematicity of nature' (5:389). There are two main possibilities, he says, namely the '**idealism** or…the **realism** of natural ends' (5:391),

---

[8] For examples, see McLaughlin, *Kant's Critique of Teleology*, 138 n. 5, and Allison, 'Kant's Antinomy', 29 n. 1.

[9] See McFarland, *Kant's Concept of Teleology*, 121; Allison, 'Kant's Antinomy', 29–30; and McLaughlin, *Kant's Critique of Teleology*, 134. Indeed, McLaughlin argues that if Kant is to present a distinctive antinomy of *judgment* rather than *reason*, he must intend that the two maxims about judging and not merely the thesis and antithesis about the things themselves conflict (p. 135).

the former of which basically attempts to explain away the appearance of purposiveness or design in nature, while the latter accepts it and attempts to account for it. Kant further distinguishes two forms of each of these main possibilities. The idealism of purposiveness can take the form of 'casuality', as in ancient atomism, according to which the appearance of any design is a product of pure chance in the collision of atoms, or of 'fatality', the view that Kant ascribes to Spinoza, according to which the appearance of design is a necessary product of an original being, but not of the intellect and therefore not of any intention of this being, thus not a form of purposiveness (5:391–2). The two forms of realism of purposiveness are then 'hylozoism', according to which there is life in matter, in the form of 'an animating inner principle, a world-soul' that accounts for its design and purposiveness, and 'theism', which posits an 'intentionally productive' 'original ground of the world-whole' which is not, however, itself a part of the world-whole (5:392). In the next section, Kant then argues that 'None of the above systems accomplishes what it pretends to' (*CPJ*, §73, 5:392). The two forms of idealism do not explain how we even form the idea of the purposiveness of nature (5:393–4); hylozoism falls victim to the contradiction between something essential to life and the principle of inertia that is essential to matter (5:394); and finally theism is 'incapable of dogmatically establishing the possibility of natural ends as a key to teleology' (5:395), for reasons that Kant does not pause to explain but that presumably lie in the demonstration of the impossibility of any theoretical proof for the existence of God provided in the first *Critique*.

However, Kant also says that theism 'has the advantage that by means of the understanding that it ascribes to the original being it can best rid the purposiveness of nature of idealism and introduce an intentional causality for its generation', and concludes that 'for us there remains no other way of judging the generation of [nature's] products as natural ends than through a supreme understanding as the cause of the world' (although, as usual, 'that is only a ground for the reflecting, not for the determining power of judgment, and absolutely cannot justify any objective assertion') (*CPJ*, §73, 5:395). Even after the complexities of §§75–7, it becomes clear that this is the basis for Kant's solution to the antinomy of judgment: 'the principle which is to make possible the unifiability of both' the maxim of mechanical explanation and the maxim of teleological judgment 'must be placed in what lies outside of both (hence outside of the possible empirical representation of nature) but which still contains the ground of both, i.e., in the supersensible...on which we must base nature as phenomenon' (although of course 'from a theoretical point of view, we cannot form the least affirmative determinate concept of this') (*CPJ*, §78, 5:412). In other words, the only way we reconcile mechanical and teleological explanation is by a conception of the world as a whole as a product of its intelligent and purposive cause. Mechanical explanation can then be allowed full rein in phenomenal nature—even if we cannot always see how it is to work, and even if we have some reason to think we will never be able to see completely how it works—while purposiveness can be attributed to the extramundane ground of the world, which can be thought of as achieving its ends *through* the mechanical laws of phenomenal nature for which it is responsible. Only through the idea of such a ground, Kant argues, can we even conceive how 'the principle of the mechanism of nature and that of its causality according to ends in one and the same product of nature [can] cohere in a single higher principle and flow from it in common' (5:412). Only by means of such a model can we maintain both that 'It is of infinite importance to reason that it not allow the mechanism of nature in its productions to drop out of sight and be bypassed in its explanations; for without this no insight into nature can be attained' (5:410) and yet that 'it is an equally necessary maxim of reason not to bypass the principle of ends in the products of nature' (5:411). The two maxims of judgment originally contrasted do conflict if we attempt to apply them to the same objects without the benefit of any metaphysics, but if we conceive of nature as a whole governed by mechanical laws through which the ground of nature can nevertheless effect its purposes, then we do have a way of applying the concepts of both mechanism and purpose to objects without contradiction.[10]

I will close this section with two comments on this solution to Kant's antinomy. First, Kant now assumes that we should always at least strive for a mechanical explanation of everything in nature, and his continuing insistence that there is a special limit on our ability to provide mechanical explanations of organic processes beyond the general limit of incompleteness in all of our knowledge of nature seems arbitrary. Once we have recognized that we can only conceive of an intelligent ground of nature as standing outside of it and as responsible for its laws, then we can

---

[10] My suggestion that Kant's ultimate solution to the antinomy of teleological judgment depends upon the ascribing purposiveness to the supersensible ground of nature is hardly new; see McFarland, *Kant's Concept of Teleology*, 121–2. However, McFarland does not emphasize Kant's view that to see nature in this way inevitably leads us to see its mechanical laws as themselves instruments for the realization of a final end, as I am about to do.

conceive of the purposes of this ground as being effected through any and all of the laws it has prescribed to nature. We could thus think of the inorganic as well as of the organic as expressive of purposiveness, and have no reason to insist upon any special limits to our comprehension of organisms. We might still want to hold that there is something psychologically or phenomenologically striking about our *experience* of organisms, some way in which they make the idea of purposiveness especially salient for us that can then turn our thoughts to the idea of a purpose for nature, but we would not have to argue that there is some *a priori* limit to our ability to understand and explain them. Kant himself does not concede this point: he claims that although 'we do not know how far the mechanical mode of explanation that is possible for us will extend', we are 'certain of this much, namely, that no matter how far we ever get with that, it will still always be inadequate for things that we once acknowledge as natural ends' (*CPJ*, §78, 5:415)—but it is not clear why. Second, we may also note that Kant's resolution of the antinomy of judgment suggests the only possible model for a reconciliation of science and religious belief: if science is to permit a rational belief in the existence of a purposive creator of the cosmos, it can only conceive of such a creator as creating the natural laws of the world and of achieving his purposes through those laws rather than through any other interventions or miracles. In other words, Kant has firmly placed himself in the camp of both empiricists and rationalists who would accept only a watchmaker God, although he has added his critical insistence that the concept of such a God yields only a regulative principle for judgment and not a constitutive principle of knowledge. Presumably this lesson remains of enduring significance.

## II. THE END OF NATURE

The culmination of the 'Critique of the Teleological Power of Judgment' and indeed of the whole third *Critique* is the 'Methodology' of teleological judgment. Here Kant argues that if we are to view nature as a whole as a system, then we must find a point—a 'final end' (*Endzweck*)— for that system, but that the only thing that could possibly play that role is the one thing of unconditional value, namely human freedom, and its realization in the highest good. Thus we must see nature as a system that is not merely compatible with the achievement of the object of human morality but that even leads up to it, although of course in a way that does not undermine the fact that the object of morality, comprising virtue as well as happiness, can only be the product of human autonomy.

The key steps in the argument are these. First, as we have already noted, Kant regards it as necessary and inevitable that once we have been compelled to see individual organisms in nature as internally purposive systems that are the apparent products of intelligent design, we will also see nature as a whole as a purposive system (*CPJ*, §67, 5:379; §75, 5:398). This is to say that although there initially seemed to be no justification for ascribing 'relative purposiveness' to relations among creatures and environments in nature (*CPJ*, §63), once we have experienced 'internal purposiveness' in nature then we will also seek to find relative purposiveness in it. Kant never really explains what makes this transition inevitable, but at least suggests a premiss for it when he says that 'all of the mechanism of nature' must 'be subordinated' to the idea of 'a system in accordance with the rule of ends' 'in accordance with principles of reason' (*CPJ*, §67, 5:379). His thought is presumably that since the concepts of a system and of an intelligent designer of organisms are ideas of reason—although of course ones that can be employed only in the reflecting use of judgment—and reason always seeks unity, it will be inevitable for reason to seek to use judgment to apply these ideas in a unified way to the whole of nature. As he concludes in §67, 'the unity of the supersensible principle must then be considered as valid in the same way not merely for certain species of natural beings but for the whole of nature as a system' (5:381). Once again, we may note, this suggests that although Kant may suppose that there is something distinctive in our experience of organisms that leads us to the thought of purposive systematicity, once he has argued that this idea can be reconciled with mechanism only by applying it to a supersensible ground of nature that effects its purposes through mechanical laws, he really has no need to insist that organisms must forever remain beyond the explanatory scope of mechanism at the phenomenal level.

Assuming thus that reason requires us to look at all of nature as a system if we must look at anything within it as a system, Kant then infers that we must conceive of the system of nature as a whole as a product of intelligent design just as we conceive of any particular organisms within it. The next step in the argument is then Kant's assumption that once we conceive of the ground of nature as intelligent we will also conceive of it as purposive, that is, as having a goal in its creation of nature. He does not argue extensively for this premiss either, but at least suggests it when he equates the (reflective idea of the) *intelligent* production of individual systems in nature or of nature as a system with the *intentional* production of such systems (*CPJ*, §75, 5:399, and §78, 5:414), and holds that to think of the mechanism of nature itself as a product of intentional design is to think of it 'as if it were the tool of an intentionally acting cause to whose ends nature is subordinated, even in its mechanical laws' (*CPJ*, §81, 5:422). Then he assumes that if we must conceive of the ground of nature as an intelligent and intentional agent similar to but even more powerful than ourselves, surely we cannot conceive of it as acting without an adequate reason for its action, indeed an ultimately satisfying or 'final' end. This seems to be Kant's point in the following:

> Once we have had to base [the] internal possibility [of an organized being] in a causality of final causes and an idea that underlies this, we also cannot conceive of the existence of this product otherwise than as an end. For the represented effect, the representation of which is at the same time the determining ground of its production in an intelligently acting cause, is called an **end**. In this case, therefore, one can either say that the end of the existence of such a natural being is in itself, i.e., it is not merely an end, but also a **final end**; or it is outside of it in another natural being, i.e., it exists purposively not as a final end, but necessarily at the same time as a means. (*CPR*, §82, 5:426)

Kant also clearly assumes that we cannot think that the end of the creation of everything in the system of nature cannot always lie in something other than itself, for then there would be an unsatisfyingly infinite regress of reasons; we can conceive of a reason for the creation of nature only if we can conceive of something that is an end in itself or a final rather than merely relative end. Thus Kant argues that our mind naturally moves from the systematicity of particular organisms to the systematicity of nature as a whole, from there to the idea of an intelligent cause of nature as a whole, and from there to the idea of a purposive cause of nature that must act in accordance with a final end.

The next stage of Kant's argument begins with another version of what he told us in §63, namely that nothing in nature as such is evidently a final end of unconditional value for which anything or everything else in nature is merely a means (*CPJ*, §82, 426–8). He now explicitly applies this stricture to human beings as well, at least as far as humans aim directly at happiness and at the 'culture of **skill**,' that is, at the development of talents or aptitudes for the achievement of happiness as such (*CPJ*, §83, 5:430–1). Instead, the only candidate for a final end for nature even in human beings is 'the formal, subjective condition, namely the aptitude for setting [ourselves] ends at all (independent from nature in [our] determination of ends) using nature as a means appropriate to the maxims of [our] free ends in general' (5:431). As Kant argues in the next section,

Now we have in the world only a single sort of beings whose causality is teleological, i.e., aimed at ends and yet at the same time so constituted that the law in accordance with which they have to determine ends is represented by themselves as unconditioned and independent of natural conditions but yet as necessary in itself. The being of this sort is the human being, though considered as noumenon: the only natural being in which we can nevertheless cognize, on the basis of its own constitution, a supersensible faculty (**freedom**) and even the law of the causality together with the object that it can set for itself as the highest end (the highest good in the world). (*CPJ*, §84, 5:435)

Thus Kant concludes that if we are to see nature as a whole as a systematic product of purposive design, as our experience of organisms makes inevitable, and if we are to see such a purposive design as having a final end, as our own conception of rational agency requires, then the only thing we can possibly conceive of as the final end for nature is our own freedom and the object that it sets for us, the highest good.

The two key questions now to be considered are (1) why Kant thinks that the unconditional value of our own freedom makes the highest good our ultimate object, and (2) what follows from the fact that we must conceive of the highest good as something that is to be realized in nature, or as Kant says 'in the world'. But a preliminary point that should also be noted is that Kant is careful about just how much of this we can coherently see as the end *of* nature. Thus far I have ignored the distinction that Kant draws between the final end of nature and its *ultimate* end, as well as the contrast that he makes between the 'culture of skill' and the 'culture of training' or 'discipline' (*CPJ*, §83, 5:432). The distinction between the 'ultimate' and the 'final' end of nature is the distinction between that *within* nature to which we can take everything else to be a means and that *outside* of nature or that which is not merely natural which we can take to give a point to the creation of the whole system of nature. As the quotation from §84 makes clear, Kant understands human freedom as something non-natural or beyond nature that is of unconditional value and can thus give its point to the creation of nature. But precisely because it is non-natural, we cannot conceive it to be realized by natural processes alone, if at all. Rather, there must be an *ultimate* end *within* nature that is connected with but not identical to human freedom as the *final* end of nature, and which we can conceive of as being brought about by natural processes but also as providing the point of connection between nature and the unconditional value of freedom. This, I take it, is the role that the culture of discipline rather than skill is supposed to play: the culture of discipline must be an ability to control our own inclinations that we can see as developing within nature and by natural means but as allowing us to make our noumenal freedom of choice effective in the natural world. Kant's idea must be that the choice to use our freedom in the name of the moral law rather than self-love is a noumenal choice, but that to make it effective in nature we need to gain discipline and control over our inclinations by natural processes of education and maturation. We can see these processes as the ultimate end of nature, achievable within nature, because they are necessary conditions within nature for the realization of the unconditional value that can lie in freedom as a non-natural property of human beings.

1. So much for why the ultimate end of nature can only be the culture of discipline, not freedom itself. But when he comes to the final end of nature, why does Kant make this not just human freedom but also the highest good in the world? That is, why does Kant so directly connect the value of freedom to the highest good? It is by no means always clear in Kant's writings that the highest good should be considered the necessary object *of morality*. In the *Critique of Practical Reason*, for example, Kant characterizes 'virtue and happiness together' as the 'whole and complete good as the object of the faculty of desire' (*CPracR*, 5:110), but also seems to suggest that virtue is the sole object of morality proper, which then, through the moral law, both constrains what ends we may pursue in the name of happiness and also, as the 'worthiness to be happy', adds a condition of desert to the pursuit of happiness. In other words, the highest good seems to be a conjunction of virtue as the object of morality and happiness as the object of the sum of our merely natural desires. However, the most fundamental premisses of Kant's moral philosophy imply a more intimate connection between virtue and happiness, which is what Kant presupposes in the third *Critique*. If the moral law's requirement to act only on universalizable maxims is equivalent to the requirement to make 'humanity, whether in your own person or that of another', the necessary 'end in itself' in all our willing (*G*, 4:428–9), and if humanity is in turn conceived of as the 'ability to set oneself an end—any end whatsoever' (*MM*, DV, VIII, 6:392), then the requirement always to treat humanity as an end implies not merely the negative duty to refrain from destroying or unnecessarily restricting the ability to set ends in ourselves and others, but also the positive duty to promote the realization of the particular, freely chosen ends of others and even ourselves, as long, of course, as so doing is consistent with satisfying the negative part of duty. Kant makes this clear in the *Groundwork* when he argues for the duty of beneficence by means of the premise that 'there is still only a negative and not a positive

agreement with **humanity as an end in itself** unless everyone also tries, as far as he can, to further the ends of others' (*G*, 4:430). This requirement to promote the particular ends of others—as far as we can do so consistently with our resources, with our own legitimate ends, and with our other duties—is then incorporated into Kant's characterization of the 'empire of ends' (*Reich der Zwecke*) as the ultimate object of morality. The 'empire of ends' is defined as 'a whole of all ends in systematic connection (a whole both of rational beings as ends in themselves and of the ends of his own that each may set himself)' (*G*, 4:433). This formula makes it clear that morality requires us not just to allow others to set their own ends but also to work towards the systematic satisfaction of the ends that they set, that is, towards the satisfaction of a system of particular ends that is consistent with the free choice of each agent as an end in itself and, presumably, with the laws of nature that constrain the realization of particular ends and combinations thereof. But if happiness just consists in the satisfaction of ends, then a systematic promotion of ends as is required by the idea of an empire of ends would under ideal circumstances yield systematic happiness. To be sure, Kant insists, the desire for happiness, whether selfish or systematic, can never be part of the motivation or 'incentive' for the pursuit of virtue, but it is nevertheless the necessary 'object' of the 'purest morality'.[11] Thus, the concept of the highest good is not a mere conjunction of the aim of morality with our merely natural desires; rather, through the recognition that the freely chosen particular ends of ends in themselves are also necessary ends for us, it incorporates unselfish happiness into morality as the necessary object of virtue.[12]

2. Thus if we can conceive only of the moral use of human freedom as the final end of the system of nature, we must also conceive of the highest good possible in the world as the final end of nature, as Kant assumes not only in the passage from §84 (5:435) already cited but also in his recapitulation of his 'moral proof of the existence of God' in §87 (4:450) of the 'Methodology of the Teleological Power of Judgment'. From this result, two points of enduring importance follow. First, we cannot satisfy the demands of morality by simply considering what some specific maxim of duty requires of us on some isolated occasion, as

---

[11] See especially the 1793 essay 'On the Common Saying: That May Be Correct in Theory, but it is of No Use in Practice', 8:279–80. This essay provides what may be the clearest account of Kant's conception of the highest good.

[12] I have defended this interpretation of the highest good in a number of publications, most recently 'Ends of Reason and Ends of Nature: The Place of Teleology in Kant's Ethics', *Journal of Value Inquiry*, 36 (2002), 161–86; Ch. 8 in this volume.

philosophical examples, including Kant's own,[13] may so easily suggest; rather, we must always think about our duties systematically, and thus attempt to determine what the idea of a systematic whole of persons as ends in themselves and of their particular ends requires of us on any particular occasion of action. Kant himself does not say explicitly what this would actually require of us, but two thoughts seem obvious.

(i) First, we must seek a systematic organization among the *kinds* of duty that flow from the general requirement to seek an empire of ends, for example, a lexical ordering of the classes of our duties.[14] We might think that the examples of types of duties that Kant enumerates in the *Groundwork* (4:422–3 and 429–30) actually imply such a lexical ordering: our most fundamental obligation would be that not to destroy rational agents (e.g. by suicide); our next obligation, that not to destroy the conditions for the free exercise of rational agency (e.g. by lying or making deceitful promises), would be binding only when we can satisfy this duty without violating the first;[15] our further duty to cultivate our talents for all sorts of possible ends would be restricted by the condition that in so doing we do not violate either of the first two classes of duty; and finally we could only satisfy our duty to further the particular ends of others through beneficence in ways compatible with the satisfaction of the three prior sorts of duties. In addition, in attempting to satisfy the requirements of duty, perhaps especially although not exclusively the positive and 'imperfect' duties of self-development and beneficence, we must think systematically about the *domain* of our duties, that is, the effects of our maxims and actions on *all* of those persons who might be affected by them, not just on the immediate and most obvious victims or beneficiaries of our actions. And of course that group of persons will always be open-ended and indeterminate: it will certainly include more living persons than one to whom we are considering making a deceitful promise, for example, but it may not reasonably include all of living mankind, some of whom we cannot possibly affect in either a positive or negative way by our present action or by any of our

---

[13] I have in mind especially Kant's notorious 1797 essay 'On a Supposed Right to Lie from Philanthropy' (8:425–30).

[14] I borrow the phrase 'lexical ordering', of course, from John Rawls's lexical ordering of the principles of justice; see *A Theory of Justice*, rev. edn. (Cambridge, Mass.: Harvard University Press, 1999), 37–8, 53–4, 130–1. For more on this point, see ch. 10 above.

[15] Such a lexical ordering of the duty not to destroy rational agents as more fundamental than the duty not to restrict the free exercise of their agency is what would undermine Kant's argument in the essay on the right to lie that the duty not to lie is an absolute duty that must be satisfied even at the risk of costing the life of an innocent person. Again, see ch. 10 above.

actions; it will certainly include some members of future generations of mankind, for example the next few generations of people who will live near a factory we are considering building, but cannot possibly include all future human beings, and so on. In other words, if the final end of nature must be an empire of ends to be realized among real human beings really living in the natural world, then the system of our duties will be open-ended and indeterminate in a variety of ways, and responsible moral reasoning will always have to take this fact into account, although we will never be able to formulate any simple rules by means of which to do so.

(ii) The second result that follows from Kant's idea that we must think of the highest good of humankind as the final end of the system of nature is that we must always think of the system of humans as ends and of their particular ends as being realized *in a nature that is itself a system*, where our knowledge of *that* system is also always incomplete and open-ended. We must thus try to think systematically about the natural conditions for our actions and their effects on the system of nature as well as about the system of human beings, while at the same time realizing that our knowledge of nature and thus of the conditions for and consequences of our actions will always be indeterminate and incomplete, just as is our knowledge of the system of persons as ends who will be affected by our choices and actions. Kant makes clear in the Introduction to the third *Critique* that the idea of a system of the particular laws of nature is always only a regulative ideal for us (see especially Introduction V, 5:185–6), and in the 'Critique of the Teleological Power of Judgment' he makes it equally clear that the idea of a system of the organisms and other entities comprising nature materially rather than formally is also only a regulative ideal for us: the 'idea of the whole of nature as a system', the principle that 'everything in the world is good for something, that nothing in it is in vain', is 'not a principle for the determining but only for the reflecting power of judgment, that . . . is regulative and not constitutive' (*CPJ*, §67, 5:379). But if we must think of the systematic realization of our duties as taking place within nature, and the ideal of systematic knowledge of nature is itself only a regulative principle, then our reasoning about our duties will always be subject to the inescapable limitations of our knowledge of nature as well as to the indeterminacies inherent in the ideal of a systematic whole of human beings as ends in themselves and of their particular ends.

There is no way to spell out the consequences of these points in a short paper; indeed, what follows from them is that there can be no determinate way to spell out the conditions for fulfilling our obligations within actual nature at all. What we can say is only that we stand under an obligation always to reflect systematically upon the consequences of our choices for humankind and for nature as a whole, because we cannot specify more determinately than that where our obligations to humankind must be fulfilled. Sometimes it will be clear that our obligations to current and future generations combined with the laws of nature must prohibit certain courses of action, such as casual disposal of nuclear waste. Sometimes it may be clear that our obligations to current and future generations of our fellow humans require a destructive intervention in nature, as when securing water supplies for a large metropolitan area requires the destruction of the habitat for some population of organisms that is zoologically unique but in our best judgment not indispensable to any larger ecology. The idea that the systematic union of human ends must be achieved within the system of nature no more implies that we must treat the system of nature as inviolable than it can require that every single human desire or even every single human life be treated as inviolable. All we can say, I think, is that sometimes it may seem obvious what our duty to realize the highest good for mankind within the world of nature requires, and sometimes it may not seem obvious, but in neither case will we be able to find determinate rules that can make such decisions mechanical. That is what follows from the premises that our duties must comprise a system, that they must be fulfilled in a nature that we must conceive of as a system, but that our knowledge of a system is always incomplete and always a problem of the reflecting rather than determining use of judgment. Surely one of the deepest lessons of Kant's connection between teleology and morality is that the latter as well as the former requires not just a parallel but a conjoint use of reflecting judgment.

So what is living and what is dead in Kant's teleology? The idea that the laws of nature should constitute a system certainly motivates every scientist, and the idea that both particular organisms and larger ecologies are systems in which every part has a particular role to play is also a natural presumption of scientific research, although one that is always subject to limitations by what is actually discovered, as in the case of evolutionary spandrels and junk DNA. To this extent Kant has no doubt correctly described the maxims of practising scientists. It is far less clear that he has succeeded in showing that we can rationally seek to satisfy such maxims only if we think of nature as the product of some sort of intelligent design. Such an assumption might be necessary if rationality required us to have some sort of guarantee of the possibility of reaching our goals, whether cognitive or practical; but if the rationality of a line of inquiry or conduct requires only the absence of evidence for the impossibility of success, then the rationality of our inquiry into nature guided by such maxims does not require any speculation about the source of whatever order we might find in nature at all. It is also by no means clear that Kant has successfully argued that there is anything in our experience of organisms in particular that requires us to posit an intelligent design for nature; indeed, it is not even obvious that he has come up with a coherent argument for the inexplicability of organisms on a mechanical model of causation, for once he has argued that the only solution to the antinomy of teleological judgment is the idea of an intelligent ground of nature that lies outside of nature and achieves its purposes through the mechanical laws of nature, he has no reason for holding that our comprehension of organisms must forever remain separated from our comprehension of the rest of nature. The most he might argue, it seems, is that there is something about our experience of organisms that psychologically leads us to thoughts of intelligence and purposiveness in nature, and that we should treasure and cultivate such thoughts for their moral value as we treasure other forms of experience, such as the experience of the beauty of nature, that are not logically necessary but are nevertheless psychologically favourable for the promotion of morality (see *MM*, DV, §17, 6:443).

If Kant has not successfully argued that we must conceive of nature as the product of purposive intelligence, then he has also not successfully argued *on this ground* that we must conceive of a final end for nature. However, he has given us important hints about the implications of the fact that the final end of morality must be a systematic union of humans and their purposes that can only be realized *within* nature. By linking the system of nature and the highest good, he teaches us that we must think about our duties systematically and that we must think about their realization in nature systematically. That insight, combined with the recognition that completeness in our knowledge of both the system of duties and the system of nature can never be more than a regulative ideal, means that our conclusions about our duties and their effects on nature will always be, literally, a matter of judgment. That in turn means that among our duties will be the duty of recognizing and cultivating our power of judgment itself. In this regard Kant's critique of teleology offers a lesson of continuing and vital importance.

# BIBLIOGRAPHY

## PRIMARY SOURCES

ACHENWALL, GOTTFRIED, and JOHANN STEPHAN PUTTER, *Anfangsgründe des Naturrechts (Elementa Iuris Naturae)*, ed. and trans. Jan Schröder (Frankfurt am Main: Insel Verlag, 1995).

BECK, JAKOB SIGISMUND, *Erläuternder Auszug aus den kritischen Schriften des Herrn Prof. Kant*, 3 vols. (Riga: Hartknoch, 1793).

HUME, DAVID, *The Natural History of Religion and the Dialogues concerning Natural Religion*, ed. A. Wayne Colver and John Valdimir Price (Oxford: Clarendon Press, 1976).

—— *A Treatise of Human Nature*, ed. David Fate Norton and Mary Norton (Oxford: Oxford University Press, 2000).

KANT, IMMANUEL, *Kant's gesammelte Schriften*, ed. the Royal Prussian (later German and Berlin-Brandenburg) Academy of Sciences, 29 vols. (Berlin: Georg Reimer (later Walter de Gruyter, 1900– )).

—— *Anthropology from a Pragmatic Point of View*, trans. Mary J. Gregor (The Hague: Martinus Nijhoff, 1974).

—— *Bemerkungen in den 'Beobachtungen über das Gefühl des Schönen und Erhabenen'*, ed. Marie Rischmüller, *Kant-Forschungen*, vol. 3 (Hamburg: Felix Meiner Verlag, 1991).

—— *Critique of the Power of Judgment*, ed. Paul Guyer, trans. Paul Guyer and Eric Matthews (Cambridge: Cambridge University Press, 2000).

—— *Critique of Pure Reason*, ed. and trans. Paul Guyer and Allen W. Wood (Cambridge: Cambridge University Press, 1998).

—— *Critique of Teleological Judgment*, trans. J[ames] C[reed] Meredith (Oxford: Clarendon Press, 1928).

—— *Kritik der reinen Vernunft*, ed. Raymund Schmidt, 3rd ed., with bibliography by Heiner Klemme (Hamburg: Felix Meiner Verlag, 1990).

—— *Lectures on Ethics*, ed. Peter Heath and J. B. Schneewind, trans. Peter Heath (Cambridge: Cambridge University Press, 1997).

—— *Lectures on Metaphysics*, ed. and trans. Karl Ameriks and Steve Naragon (Cambridge: Cambridge University Press, 1997).

—— *Metaphysische Anfangsgründe der Rechtslehre*, ed. Bernd Ludwig (Hamburg: Felix Meiner Verlag, 1986).

—— *Opus postumum*, ed. Eckart Förster, trans. Eckart Förster and Michael Rosen (Cambridge: Cambridge University Press, 1993).

KANT, IMMANUEL, *Practical Philosophy*, ed. and trans. Mary J. Gregor (Cambridge: Cambridge University Press, 1996).

—— *Religion and Rational Theology*, ed. and trans. Allen W. Wood and George di Giovanni (Cambridge: Cambridge University Press, 1996).

—— *Schriften zur Ästhetik und Naturphilosophie*, ed. Manfred Frank and Véronique Zanetti (Frankfurt am Main: Deutscher Klassiker Verlag, 1996).

—— *Theoretical Philosophy, 1755–1770*, ed. and trans. David E. Walford (Cambridge: Cambridge University Press, 1992).

LOCKE, JOHN, *An Essay concerning Human Understanding*, ed. P. H. Nidditch (Oxford: Clarendon Press, 1973).

MOORE, G[EORGE] E[DWARD], *Ethics* (1912; Oxford: Oxford University Press, 1965).

## SECONDARY SOURCES

ALLISON, HENRY E., 'Kant's Antinomy of Teleological Judgment', *Southern Journal of Philosophy*, 30, suppl. (1991), 25–42.

—— *Kant's Theory of Taste: A Reading of the Critique of Aesthetic Judgment* (Cambridge: Cambridge University Press, 2001).

—— *The Kant–Eberhard Controversy* (Baltimore: Johns Hopkins University Press, 1973).

ARMSTRONG, DAVID, *What is a Law of Nature?* (Cambridge: Cambridge University Press, 1983).

BARTUSCHAT, WOLFGANG, *Zum systematischen Ort von Kants Kritik der Urteilskraft* (Frankfurt am Main: Vittorio Klostermann, 1972).

BECK, LEWIS WHITE, *A Commentary on Kant's Critique of Practical Reason* (Chicago: University of Chicago Press, 1960).

—— 'Can Kant's Synthetic Judgments be Made Analytic?', *Kant-Studien*, 67 (1955), 168–81; repr. in Beck, *Studies in the Philosophy of Kant* (Indianapolis: Bobbs-Merrill, 1965), pp. 74–91.

BERNSTEIN, JAY M., *The Fate of Art: Aesthetic Alienation from Kant to Derrida and Adorno* (University Park: Pennsylvania State University Press, 1990).

BUCHDAHL, GERD, 'The Conception of Lawlikeness in Kant's Philosophy of Science', *Synthese*, 23 (1971), 24–46.

—— 'The Relation between "Understanding" and "Reason" in the Architectonic of Kant's Philosophy', *Proceedings of the Aristotelian Society*, 67 (1966–7), 209–26.

BUDD, MALCOLM, 'The Pure Judgment of Taste as an Aesthetic Reflective Judgment', *British Journal of Aesthetics*, 41 (2001), 247–60.

CRAMER, KONRAD, *Nicht-reine synthetischer Urteile a priori. Ein Problem der Transzendentalphilosophie Immanuel Kants* (Heidelberg: Carl Winter Universitätsverlag, 1985).

CUMMISKEY, DAVID, *Kantian Consequentialism* (New York: Oxford University Press, 1996).

DENIS, LARA, 'Kant on the Wrongness of "Unnatural sex" ', *History of Philosophy Quarterly*, 16 (1999), 225–48.

DICKIE, GEORGE, *The Century of Taste: The Philosophical Odyssey of Taste in the Eighteenth Century* (New York: Oxford University Press, 1996).

DÜSING, KLAUS, *Die Teleologie in Kants Weltbegriff*, Kant-Studien Ergänzungsheft 96 (Bonn: Bouvier Verlag, 1968).

EDWARDS, JEFFREY, 'Spinozism, Freedom and Transcendental Dynamics in Kant's Final System of Transcendental Idealism', in Sally S. Sedgwick (ed.), *The Reception of Kant's Critical Philosophy* (Cambridge: Cambridge University Press, 2000), pp. 54–77.

ENGSTROM, STEPHEN, 'The Concept of the Highest Good in Kant's Moral Theory', *Philosophy and Phenomenological Research*, 52 (1992), 747–80.

FLOYD, JULIET, 'Heautonomy: Kant on Reflective Judgment and Systematicity', in Herman Parret (ed.), *Kants Ästhetik—Kant's Aesthetics—L'Esthétique de Kant* (Berlin: Walter de Gruyter, 1998), pp. 192–218.

FÖRSTER, ECKART, 'Kant's Notion of Philosophy', *Monist*, 72 (1989), 285–304.

—— 'Kant's *Selbstsetzungslehre*', in Eckart Förster (ed.), *Kant's Transcendental Deductions: The Three Critiques and the Opus postumum* (Stanford, Calif.: Stanford University Press, 1989), pp. 217–38.

FREUDIGER, JÜRG, 'Kants Schlußstein. Wie die Teleologie die Einheit der Vernunft stiftet', *Kant-Studien*, 87 (1996), 102–15.

FRIEDMAN, MICHAEL, 'Kant and the Twentieth Century', in Paolo Perrini (ed.), *Kant and Contemporary Epistemology* (Dordrecht: Kluwer, 1994).

GINSBORG, HANNAH, 'Korsgaard on Choosing Nonmoral Ends', *Ethics*, 109 (1998), 5–21.

GREGOR, MARY J., *The Laws of Freedom: A Study of Kant's Method Applying the Categorical Imperative* (Oxford: Basil Blackwell, 1963).

GUYER, PAUL, 'The Derivation of the Categorical Imperative: Kant's Correction for a Fatal Flaw', *Harvard Review of Philosophy*, 10 (2002), 64–80.

—— *Kant and the Claims of Knowledge* (Cambridge: Cambridge University Press, 1987).

—— *Kant and the Experience of Freedom* (Cambridge: Cambridge University Press, 1993).

—— 'Kant on Apperception and *a priori* Synthesis', *American Philosophical Quarterly*, 17 (1980), 205–12.

—— *Kant on Freedom, Law, and Happiness* (Cambridge: Cambridge University Press, 2000).

—— 'Kant's Intentions in the Refutation of Idealism', *Philosophical Review*, 92 (1983), 329–83.

—— 'Kant's Second Analogy: Objects, Events, and Causal Laws', in Patricia Kitcher (ed.), *Kant's Critique of Pure Reason: Critical Essays* (Lanham, Md.: Rowman & Littlefield, 1998), pp. 117–43.

GUYER, PAUL, 'The Postulates of Empirical Thinking in General and the Refutation of Idealism', in Georg Mohr and Marcus Willaschek (eds.), *Immanuel Kant. Kritik der reinen Vernunft* (Berlin: Akademie Verlag, 1998), pp. 297–324.

—— 'The Value of Reason and the Value of Freedom', *Ethics*, 209 (1998), 22–35.

—— (ed.), *Kant's Groundwork of the Metaphysics of Morals: Critical Essays* (Lanham, Md.: Rowman & Littlefield, 1998).

HENRICH, DIETER, 'Kant's Notion of a Deduction and the Methodological Background of the First *Critique*', in Eckart Förster (ed.), *Kant's Transcendental Deductions: The Three Critiques and the Opus postumum* (Stanford, Calif.: Stanford University Press, 1989), pp. 29–46.

HERMAN, BARBARA, *The Practice of Moral Judgment* (Cambridge, Mass.: Harvard University Press, 1993).

HÖFFE, OTTFRIED, *Categorical Principles of Law: A Counterpoint to Modernity*, trans. Mark Migotti (University Park: Pennsylvania State University Press, 2002).

—— *'Königliche Völker'. Zu Kants kosmopolitischer Rechts- und Friedenstheorie* (Frankfurt am Main: Suhrkamp Verlag, 2001).

KITCHER, PHILIP, 'Projecting the Order of Nature', in Robert E. Butts (ed.), *Kant's Philosophy of Science* (Dordrecht: D. Reidel, 1986), pp. 201–35; repr. in Patricia Kitcher (ed.), *Kant's Critique of Pure Reason: Critical Essays* (Lanham, Md.: Rowman & Littlefield, 1998), pp. 219–38.

KLEINGELD, PAULINE, 'Kants Argumente für den Völkerbund', in Herta Nagl-Docekal and Rudolph Langthaler (eds.), *Zum 200. Todestag Kants. Recht— Religion—Geschichte* (Berlin: Akademie-Verlag, 2004), pp. 99–111.

KORSGAARD, CHRISTINE M., *Creating the Kingdom of Ends* (Cambridge: Cambridge University Press, 1996).

—— 'Motivation, Metaphysics, and the Self: A Reply to Ginsborg, Guyer, and Schneewind', *Ethics*, 109 (1998), 49–66.

KUMAR, RAHUL, 'Contractualism on Saving the Many', *Analysis*, 61 (2001), 165–70.

LEWIS, DAVID K., *Counterfactuals* (Cambridge, Mass.: Harvard University Press, 1973).

LUDWIG, BERND, *Kant's Rechtslehre. Kant-Forschungen*, vol. 2 (Hamburg: Felix Meiner Verlag, 1988).

McFARLAND, J[OHN] D., *Kant's Concept of Teleology* (Edinburgh: Edinburgh University Press, 1970).

McLAUGHLIN, PETER, *Kant's Critique of Teleology in Biological Explanation: Antinomy and Teleology* (Lewiston, NY: Edwin Mellen Press, 1990).

MORRISON, MARGARET, 'Methodological Rules in Kant's Philosophy of Science', *Kant-Studien*, 80 (1989), 155–72.

—— *Unifying Scientific Theories: Physical Concepts and Mathematical Structures* (Cambridge: Cambridge University Press, 2000).

MULHOLLAND, LESLIE A., *Kant's System of Rights* (New York: Columbia University Press, 1990).

NELL, ONORA (O'NEILL), *Acting on Principle: An Essay on Kantian Ethics* (New York: Columbia University Press, 1975).

O'NEILL, ONORA, *Constructions of Reason: Explorations of Kant's Practical Philosophy* (Cambridge: Cambridge University Press, 1989).

PATON, H[ERBERT] J[AMES], *The Categorical Imperative: A Study in Kant's Moral Philosophy* (London: Hutchinson, 1947).

—— *Kant's Metaphysic of Experience*, 2 vols. (London: George Allen & Unwin, 1936).

PETER, JOACHIM, *Das transzendentale Prinzip der Urteilskraft*, Kant-Studien Ergänzungsheft 126 (Berlin: Walter de Gruyter, 1992).

POGGE, THOMAS W., 'Is Kant's *Rechtslehre* a "Comprehensive Liberalism"?', in Mark Timmons (ed.), *Kant's Metaphysics of Morals: Interpretative Essays* (Oxford: Oxford University Press, 2002), pp. 133–58.

—— 'Kant on Ends and the Meaning of Life', in Andrews Reath, Barbara Herman, and Christine M. Korsgaard (eds.), *Reclaiming the History of Ethics: Essays for John Rawls* (Cambridge: Cambridge University Press, 1997), pp. 361–87.

RAWLS, JOHN, *A Theory of Justice*, rev. edn. (Cambridge, Mass.: Harvard University Press, 1999).

REATH, ANDREWS, 'Two Conceptions of the Highest Good in Kant', *Journal of the History of Philosophy*, 26 (1988), 593–619.

ROSEN, ALLEN D., *Kant's Theory of Justice* (Ithaca, NY: Cornell University Press, 1993).

RUSH, FRED L., Jr., 'Reason and Regulation in Kant', *Review of Metaphysics*, 53 (2000), 837–62.

SAVILE, ANTHONY, *Kantian Aesthetics Pursued* (Edinburgh: Edinburgh University Press, 1993).

SIDGWICK, HENRY, 'The Kantian Conception of Free Will', *Mind*, 13 (1888); repr. in Sidgwick, *Methods of Ethics*, 7th edn. (London: Macmillan, 1907), pp. 511–16.

SILBER, JOHN, 'The Importance of the Highest Good in Kant's Ethics', *Ethics*, 73 (1962–3), 179–97.

TONELLI, GIORGIO, *Kant's Critique of Pure Reason within the Tradition of Modern Logic*, ed. David H. Chandler (Hildesheim: Georg Olms Verlag, 1994).

TUSCHLING, BURKHARD, 'The Concept of Transcendental Idealism in Kant's *Opus postumum*', in R[ussell] M. Dancy (ed.), *Kant and Critique: New Essays in Honor of W. H. Werkmeister* (Dordrecht: Kluwer, 1993), pp. 151–67.

—— 'Die Idee des transzendentalen Idealismus im späten *Opus postumum*', in Forum für Philosophie Bad Hamburg (ed.), *Übergang. Untersuchungen zum Spätwerk Immanuel Kants* (Frankfurt am Main: Vittorio Klostermann, 1991), pp. 105–45.

TUSCHLING, BURKHARD, 'System des transzendentalen Idealismus bei Kant? Offene Frage der—und an die—*Kritik der Urteilskraft*', *Kant-Studien*, 86 (1995), 196–210.

WIKE, VICTORIA S., *Kant on Happiness in Ethics* (New York: SUNY Press, 1994).

WILLASCHEK, MARCUS, 'Which Imperatives for Right? On the Non-Prescriptive Character of Juridical Laws in Kant's *Metaphysics of Morals*', in Mark Timmons (ed.), *Kant's Metaphysics of Morals: Interpretative Essays* (Oxford: Oxford University Press, 2002), pp. 65–88.

—— 'Why the "Doctrine of Right" does not belong in the *Metaphysics of Morals*', *Jahrbuch für Recht und Ethik*, 5 (1997), 205–27.

WOOD, ALLEN W., 'The Final Form of Kant's Practical Philosophy', in Mark Timmons (ed.), *Kant's Metaphysics of Morals: Interpretative Essays* (Oxford: Oxford University Press, 2002), pp. 1–22.

—— 'Humanity as an End in Itself', in Hoke Robinson (ed.), *Proceedings of the Eighth International Kant Congress*, vol. 1, pt. 1 (Milwaukee: Marquette University Press, 1995), pp. 301–19; repr. in Paul Guyer (ed.), *Kant's Groundwork of the Metaphysics of Morals: Critical Essays* (Lanham, Md.: Rowman & Littlefield, 1998), pp. 165–87.

—— 'Kant's Compatibilism', in Wood (ed.), *Self and Nature in Kant's Philosophy* (Ithaca, NY: Cornell University Press, 1984).

—— *Kant's Ethical Thought* (Cambridge: Cambridge University Press, 1999).

—— *Kant's Moral Religion* (Ithaca, NY: Cornell University Press, 1970).

—— 'The Moral Law as a System of Imperatives', in Hans Friedrich Fulda and Jürgen Stolzenberg (eds.), *Architektonik und System in der Philosophie Kants* (Hamburg: Felix Meiner Verlag, 2001), pp. 287–306.

ZANETTI, VÉRONIQUE, 'Kants Antinomie der teleologischen Urteilskraft', *Kant-Studien*, 84 (1993), 341–55.

# INDEX

Achenwall, Gottfried, 253 n. 12,
    260–1
action at a distance, 80
actuality, 47
aesthetic judgment, 45
affinity:
    of appearances, 23–5, 29
    of concepts in system, 18–20, 247
agency, 157–8, 173–4, 176–9
Allison, Henry E., 56 n. 3, 62 n. 8,
    320 n. 10, 337 n. 34, 338 n. 38,
    358 n. 7, 360 n. 8, 9
analogies of experience:
    second, 56, 66
    third, 79–80
analytic judgments, 203–8, 217–24
antinomy:
    between mechanical and final
        explanation, 96–8, 105–8
    of pure reason 14–15, 327 n. 21
    and systematicity, 26–8
    of teleological judgment, 335–42,
        359–63
apperception, transcendental unity of,
    33–4
appropriation, 237–9
Armstrong, David, 350 n. 5
autarky, 136–7
autocracy, 136–41
autonomy:
    and autocracy, 136–41
    formula of, 147–8, 156
    and freedom of will, 117–26
    value of, 126–36
avarice, 259

Bartuschat, Wolfgang, 326 n. 20,
    339 n. 40
beauty, 69–70;
    of art, 28 n. 8, 72 n. 18, 293
    and morality, 141–2
    of nature, 28, 88–9, 293, 325–6 n. 18
Beck, Jakob Sigismund, 46 n. 6

Beck, Lewis White, 184 n. 45, 203 n. 8,
    207 n. 13, 14, 287 n. 13
belief, 291–2
beneficence, duty of, 159, 161, 179–80,
    181, 255–7, 259, 273–4
Bernstein, Jay M., 73 n. 19
Buchdahl, Gerd, 11 n. 2
Budd, Malcolm, 69 n. 16

casuality, system of, 96, 339, 361
categorical imperative:
    definition of, 150–1
    formulations of, 146–50
    and idea of God, 307–9
    and principle of right, 198, 201, 208
    provability of, 208–9
    *See also* humanity, kingdom of ends,
        morality, universal law
categories:
    application of, 29–32
    as formal laws of nature, 30, 46
causation:
    reciprocal, in organisms, 93–6, 104
    *See also* empirical laws
charity, 266
coercion, 199–202, 223–30, 253–4,
    260–2
conflicts of duty, 267–74
conscience, 159 n. 16
contingency:
    and organisms, 98–101, 304–5,
        319–20, 340–1, 358–9
    and pleasure, 59–60, 68–73
Cummiskey, David, 273 n. 28

Darwin, Charles, 352
deduction:
    concept of, 205–6
    of ether, 74–85
    of principles of right, 202–3, 221–2
    of right to property, 230–42
    of systematicity, 27–8
Democritus, 96